INTEGRAL PSYCHOLOGY

INTEGRAL PSYCHOLOGY

Consciousness, Spirit, Psychology, Therapy

Ken Wilber

SHAMBHALA
Boston & London
2000

Shambhala Publications, Inc.
Horticultural Hall
300 Massachusetts Avenue
Boston, Massachusetts 02115
www.shambhala.com

©2000 by Ken Wilber

14 13 12 11 10 9 8 7

Printed in the United States of America
♾ This edition is printed on acid-free paper that meets the
American National Standards Institute z39.48 Standard.
Distributed in the United States by Random House, Inc.,
and in Canada by Random House of Canada Ltd

Library of Congress Cataloging-in-Publication Data
Wilber, Ken.
Integral psychology: consciousness, spirit, psychology,
therapy/Ken Wilber.—1st pbk. ed.
p. cm.
Condensed version of Ken Wilber's System, self, and
structure, which has previously only been available in
volume four of The collected works of Ken Wilber.
Includes index.
ISBN-13 978-1-57062-554-1 (pbk.: alk. paper)
ISBN-10 1-57062-554-9
1. Consciousness. 2. Psychology—Philosophy.
I. Wilber, Ken. Works. 1998. II. Title.
BF311.W5765 2000 99-053186
150—dc21

Contents

Note to the Reader

A DAYLIGHT VIEW

THE WORD *psychology* means the study of the psyche, and the word *psyche* means mind or soul. In the *Microsoft Thesaurus*, for *psyche* we find: "self: atman, soul, spirit; subjectivity: higher self, spiritual self, spirit." One is reminded, yet again, that the roots of psychology lie deep within the human soul and spirit.

The word *psyche* or its equivalent has ancient sources, going back at least several millennia BCE, where it almost always meant the animating force or spirit in the body or material vehicle. Sometime in sixteenth-century Germany, *psyche* was coupled with *logos*—word or study—to form *psychology*, the study of the soul or spirit as it appears in humans. Who actually first used the word *psychology* is still debated; some say Melanchthon, some say Freigius, some say Goclenius of Marburg. But by 1730 it was being used in a more modern sense by Wolff in Germany, Hartley in England, Bonnet in France—and yet even then psychology still meant, as the *New Princeton Review* of 1888 defined it, "the science of the psyche or soul."

I once started taking notes for a history of psychology and philosophy that I was planning on writing. I had decided to do so because, in looking at most of the available history of psychology textbooks, I was struck by a strange and curious fact, that they all told the story of psychology—and the psyche—as if it abruptly came into being around 1879 in a laboratory in the University of Leipzig, headed by Wilhelm Wundt, who indeed was the father of a certain type of psychology anchored in introspection and structuralism. Still, did the psyche itself just jump into existence in 1879?

A few textbooks pushed back a little further, to the forerunners of Wundt's scientific psychology, including Sir Francis Galton, Hermann von Helmholtz, and particularly the commanding figure of Gustav Fechner. As one textbook breathlessly put it, "On the morning of October 22, 1850—an important date in the history of psychology—Fechner had an insight that the law of the connection between mind and body can be found in a statement of quantitative relation between mental sensation and material stimulus." Fechner's law, as it was soon known, is stated as $S = K \log I$ (the mental sensation varies as the logarithm of the material stimulus). Another text explained its importance: "In the early part of the century, Immanuel Kant had predicted that psychology could never become a science, because it would be impossible to experimentally measure psychological processes. Because of Fechner's work, for the first time scientists could measure the mind; by the mid-nineteenth century the methods of science were being applied to mental phenomena. Wilhelm Wundt would take these original and creative achievements and organize and integrate them into a 'founding' of psychology."

Every textbook seemed to agree that Gustav Fechner was one of the major breakthrough figures in the founding of modern psychology, and text after text sang the praises of the man who figured out a way to apply quantitative measurement to the mind, thus finally rendering psychology "scientific." Even Wilhelm Wundt was emphatic: "It will never be forgotten," he announced, "that Fechner was the first to introduce exact methods, exact principles of measurement and experimental observation for the investigation of psychic phenomena, and thereby to open the prospect of a psychological science, in the strict sense of the word. The chief merit of Fechner's method is this: that it has nothing to apprehend from the vicissitudes of philosophical systems. Modern psychology has indeed assumed a really scientific character, and may keep aloof from all metaphysical controversy."[1] This Dr. Fechner, I presumed, had saved psychology from contamination by soul or spirit, and had happily reduced the mind to measurable empirical doodads, thus ushering in the era of truly scientific psychology.

That is all I heard of Gustav Fechner, until several years later, when I was rummaging through a store filled with wonderfully old philosophy books, and there, rather shockingly, was a book with a striking title—*Life after Death*—written in 1835, and by none other than Gustav Fechner. It had the most arresting opening lines: "Man lives on earth not once, but three times: the first stage of his life is continual sleep; the second, sleeping and waking by turns; the third, waking forever."

And so proceeded this treatise on waking forever. "In the first stage man lives in the dark, alone; in the second, he lives associated with, yet separated from, his fellow-men, in a light reflected from the surface of things; in the third, his life, interwoven with . . . universal spirit . . . is a higher life.

"In the first stage his *body* develops itself from its germ, working out organs for the second; in the second stage his *mind* develops itself from its germ, working out organs for the third; in the third the *divine* germ develops itself, which lies hidden in every human mind.

"The act of leaving the first stage for the second we call Birth; that of leaving the second for the third, Death. Our way from the second to the third is not darker than our way from the first to the second: one way leads us forth to see the world outwardly; the other, to see it inwardly."

From body to mind to spirit, the three stages of the growth of consciousness; and it is only as men and women die to the separate self that they awaken to the expansiveness of universal Spirit. There was Fechner's real philosophy of life, mind, soul, and consciousness; and why did the textbooks not bother to tell us *that*? That's when I decided I wanted to write a history of psychology, simply because "Somebody has *got* to tell."

(Tell that the notion of the unconscious was made popular by von Hartmann's *Philosophy of the Unconscious*, which was published in 1869—thirty years before Freud—and went into an unprecedented eight editions in ten years, and von Hartmann was expressing Schopenhauer's philosophy, which Schopenhauer himself explicitly stated he derived mostly from Eastern mysticism, Buddhism and the Upanishads in particular: under the individual consciousness lies a cosmic consciousness, which for most people is "unconscious," but which can be awakened and fully realized, and this making conscious of the unconscious was men and women's greatest good. That Freud directly took the concept of the id from Georg Groddeck's *The Book of the It*, which was based on the existence of a cosmic Tao or organic universal spirit. That . . . well, it is a long story, all of which powerfully reminds us that the roots of modern psychology lie in spiritual traditions, precisely because the psyche itself is plugged into spiritual sources. In the deepest recesses of the psyche, one finds not instincts, but Spirit—and the study of psychology ought ideally to be the study of *all* of that, body to mind to soul, subconscious to self-conscious to superconscious, sleeping to half-awake to fully awake.)

Fechner did indeed make extraordinary contributions to empirical and measurable psychology; his *Elements of Psychophysics* is justly regarded as the first great text of psychometrics, and it fully deserves all the accolades psychologists from Wundt onward gave it. Still, the whole point of Fechner's psychophysics was that spirit and matter were inseparable, two sides of one great reality, and his attempts to measure aspects of the mind were meant to point out this inseparability, not reduce spirit or soul to material objects, and certainly not to deny spirit and soul altogether, which seems to have nonetheless been its fate in the hands of less sensitive researchers.

Fechner maintained, as one scholar summarized it, "that the whole universe is spiritual in character, the phenomenal world of physics being merely the external manifestation of this spiritual reality. Atoms are only the simplest elements in a spiritual hierarchy leading up to God. Each level of this hierarchy includes all those levels beneath it, so that God contains the totality of spirits. Consciousness is an essential feature of all that exists. . . . The evidences of soul are the systematic coherence and conformity to law exhibited in the behavior of organic wholes. Fechner regarded the earth, 'our mother,' as such an organic besouled whole."[2]

Fechner himself explained that "as our bodies belong to the greater and higher individual body of the earth, so our spirits belong to the greater and higher individual spirit of the earth, which comprises all the spirits of earthly creatures, very much as the earth-body comprises their bodies. At the same time the earth-spirit is not a mere assembly of all the spirits of the earth, but a higher, individually conscious union of them." And the earth-spirit—Fechner was giving a precise outline of Gaia—is itself simply part of the divine-spirit, and "the divine-spirit is one, omniscient and truly all-conscious, i.e., holding all the consciousness of the universe and thus comprising each individual consciousness . . . in a higher and the highest connection."[3]

But this does not mean the obliteration of individuality, only its completion and inclusion in something even larger. "Our own individuality and independence, which are naturally but of a relative character, are not impaired but conditioned by this union." And so it continues up the nested hierarchy of increasing inclusiveness: "As the earth, far from separating our bodies from the universe, connects and incorporates us with the universe, so the spirit of the earth, far from separating our spirits from the divine spirit, forms a higher individual connection of every earthly spirit with the spirit of the universe."[4]

Fechner's approach to psychology was thus a type of *integral approach*: he wished to use empirical and scientific measurement, not to deny soul and spirit, but to help elucidate them. "To regard the whole material universe as inwardly alive and conscious is to take what Fechner called the *daylight view.* To regard it as inert matter, lacking in any teleological significance, is to take what he called the *night view.* Fechner ardently advocated the daylight view and hoped that it could be supported inductively by means of his psychophysical experiments."[5]

Well, it appears that the night view has since prevailed, yes? But there was a period, roughly during the time of Fechner (1801–1887) to William James (1842–1910) to James Mark Baldwin (1861–1934), when the newly emerging science of psychology was still on speaking terms with the ancient wisdom of the ages—with the perennial philosophy, with the Great Nest of Being, with the Idealist systems, and with the simple facts of consciousness as almost every person knows them: consciousness is real, the inward observing self is real, the soul is real, however much we might debate the details; and thus these truly great founding psychologists—when their real stories are told—have much to teach us about an integral view, a view that attempts to include the truths of body, mind, soul, and spirit, and not reduce them to material displays, digital bits, empirical processes, or objective systems (as important as all of those most certainly are). These pioneering modern psychologists managed to be both fully scientific and fully spiritual, and they found not the slightest contradiction or difficulty in that generous embrace.

This is a book about just such an integral psychology. While attempting to include the best of modern scientific research on psychology, consciousness, and therapy, it also takes its inspiration from that integral period of psychology's own genesis (marked by such as Fechner, James, and Baldwin, along with many others we will soon meet). This volume began that day in the wonderful old-book store, and the shocked recognition that Fechner's true story had rarely been told, and my subsequent historical research. The result was a very long textbook in two volumes, which includes a discussion of around two hundred theorists, East and West, ancient and modern, all working, in their own way, toward a more integral view; and it contains charts summarizing around one hundred of these systems.[6] For various reasons I have decided to publish it first in a very condensed and edited form—this present book—along with most of the charts (see charts 1 through 11, beginning on page 195).

As such, what follows is merely the briefest outline of what one type of integral psychology might look like. It attempts to include and integrate some of the more enduring insights from premodern, modern, and postmodern sources, under the assumption that all of them have something incredibly important to teach us. And it attempts to do so, not as a mere eclecticism, but in a systematic embrace, with method to the madness.

But the major aim of this book is to help start a discussion, not finish it; to act as a beginning, not an end. The reason I decided to publish this book in outline form first was to share an overview without crowding it with too many of my own particular details, and thus spur others to jump into the adventure: agreeing with me, disagreeing with me; correcting any mistakes that I might make, filling in the many gaps, straightening out any inadequacies, and otherwise carrying the enterprise forward by their own good lights.

For teachers using this as a text, and for the serious student, I have included extensive endnotes. In fact, this is really two books: a fairly short, accessible text, and endnotes for the dedicated. As usual, I recommend skipping the notes until a second reading (or reading them by themselves after the first). The notes do two things in particular: flesh out the outline with some of my own details (especially for students of my work), and make a series of specific recommendations for further readings, by other scholars, on each of the major topics. Thus teachers, for example, might consult some of these other texts (as well as their own favorites), make photocopies and hand-outs for the class, and thus supplement the main outline with any number of more specific readings. Interested laypersons can follow the notes to further reading in any of the areas. These recommendations are not exhaustive, only representative. For the recommended books on transpersonal psychology and therapy, I took a poll of many colleagues and reported the results.

I have not included a separate bibliography; the references on the charts alone are over a hundred pages. But today it is easy enough to get on the Internet and search any of the large booksellers for the various publications (which is why I have not included publisher information either). Likewise, I have often simply listed the names of some of the more important authors, and readers can do a book search to see which of their books are available.

I personally believe that integral psychology (and integral studies in general) will become increasingly prevalent in the coming decades, as the academic world gropes its way out of its doggedly night view of the Kosmos.

What follows, then, is one version of a daylight view. And, dear Gustav, this one is for you.

K.W.
Boulder, Colorado
Spring 1999

PART ONE

GROUND

The Foundation

Psychology is the study of human consciousness and its manifestations in behavior. The *functions* of consciousness include perceiving, desiring, willing, and acting. The *structures* of consciousness, some facets of which can be unconscious, include body, mind, soul, and spirit. The *states* of consciousness include normal (e.g., waking, dreaming, sleeping) and altered (e.g., nonordinary, meditative). The *modes* of consciousness include aesthetic, moral, and scientific. The *development* of consciousness spans an entire spectrum from prepersonal to personal to transpersonal, subconscious to self-conscious to superconscious, id to ego to Spirit. The *relational* and *behavioral* aspects of consciousness refer to its mutual interaction with the objective, exterior world and the sociocultural world of shared values and perceptions.

The great problem with psychology as it has historically unfolded is that, for the most part, different schools of psychology have often taken one of those aspects of the extraordinarily rich and multifaceted phenomenon of consciousness and announced that it is the only aspect worth studying (or even that it is the only aspect that actually exists). Behaviorism notoriously reduced consciousness to its observable, behavioral manifestations. Psychoanalysis reduced consciousness to structures of the ego and their impact by the id. Existentialism reduced consciousness to its personal structures and modes of intentionality. Many schools of transpersonal psychology focus merely on altered states of consciousness, with no coherent theory of the development of structures of consciousness. Asian psychologies typically excel in their account of consciousness development from the personal to the transpersonal domains, but have a very poor understanding of the earlier development from prepersonal to personal. Cognitive science admirably brings a scientific empiricism to bear on the problem, but often ends up simply reducing consciousness to its objective dimensions, neuronal mechanisms, and biocomputer-like functions, thus devastating the lifeworld of consciousness itself.

What if, on the other hand, *all* of the above accounts were an important part of the story? What if they all possessed true, but partial, insights into the vast field of consciousness? At the very least, assembling their conclusions under one roof would vastly expand our ideas of what consciousness is and, more important, what it might become. The endeavor to honor and embrace every legitimate aspect of human consciousness is the goal of an *integral psychology.*

Obviously, such an endeavor, at least at the beginning, has to be carried out at a very high level of abstraction. In coordinating these numerous approaches, we are working with systems of systems of systems, and such a coordination can only proceed with "orienting generalizations."[1] These cross-paradigmatic generalizations are meant, first and foremost, to simply get us in the right ballpark, by throwing our conceptual net as wide as possible. A logic of inclusion, networking, and wide-net casting is called for; a logic of nests within nests within nests, each attempting to legitimately include all that can be included. It is a vision-logic, a logic not merely of trees but also of forests.

Not that the trees can be ignored. Network-logic is a dialectic of whole and part. As many details as possible are checked; then a tentative big picture is assembled; it is checked against further details, and the big picture readjusted. And so on indefinitely, with ever more details constantly altering the big picture—and vice versa. For the secret of contextual thinking is that the whole discloses new meanings not available to the parts, and thus the big pictures we build will give new meaning to the details that compose it. Because human beings are condemned to meaning, they are condemned to creating big pictures. Even the "anti-big picture" postmodernists have given us a very big picture about why they don't like big pictures, an internal contradiction that has landed them in various sorts of unpleasantness, but has simply proven, once again, that human beings are condemned to creating big pictures.

Therefore, choose your big pictures with care.

When it comes to an integral psychology—a subset of integral studies in general—we have an enormous wealth of theories, research, and practices, all of which are important trees in the integral forest. In the following pages, we will be reviewing many of them, always with an eye to an integral embrace.

Elements of my own system, developed in a dozen books, are summarized in charts 1a and 1b. These include the structures, states, functions, modes, development, and behavioral aspects of consciousness. We will discuss each of those in turn. We will be drawing also on premodern, modern, and postmodern sources, with a view to a reconciliation. And we will start with the backbone of the system, the basic levels of consciousness.

1

The Basic Levels or Waves

THE GREAT NEST OF BEING

A TRULY INTEGRAL PSYCHOLOGY would embrace the enduring insights of premodern, modern, and postmodern sources.

To begin with the premodern or traditional sources, the easiest access to their wisdom is through what has been called the perennial philosophy, or the common core of the world's great spiritual traditions. As Huston Smith, Arthur Lovejoy, Ananda Coomaraswamy, and other scholars of these traditions have pointed out, the core of the perennial philosophy is the view that reality is composed of various *levels of existence*—levels of being and of knowing—ranging from matter to body to mind to soul to spirit. Each senior dimension transcends but includes its juniors, so that this is a conception of wholes within wholes within wholes indefinitely, reaching from dirt to Divinity.

In other words, this "Great Chain of Being" is actually a "Great Nest of Being," with each senior dimension enveloping and embracing its juniors, much like a series of concentric circles or spheres, as indicated in figure 1. (For those unfamiliar with the Great Nest, the best short introduction is still E. F. Schumacher's *A Guide for the Perplexed*. Other excellent introductions include *Forgotten Truth* by Huston Smith and *Shambhala: The Sacred Path of the Warrior* by Chögyam Trungpa, who demonstrates that the Great Nest was present even in the earliest shamanic cultures).[1] The Great Nest of Being is the backbone of the peren-

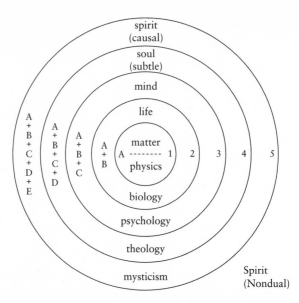

FIGURE 1. *The Great Nest of Being.* Spirit is both the highest level (causal) and the nondual Ground of all levels.

nial philosophy, and it would therefore be a crucial ingredient of any truly integral psychology.

For the last three thousand years or so, perennial philosophers have been in nearly unanimous and cross-cultural agreement as to the general levels of the Great Nest, although the number of divisions of those levels has varied considerably. Some traditions have presented only three major levels or realms (body, mind, and spirit—or gross, subtle, and causal). Others give five (matter, body, mind, soul, and spirit). Still others give seven (e.g., the seven kundalini chakras). And most of the traditions also have very sophisticated breakdowns of these levels, often giving 12, 30, even 108 subdivisions of the levels of being and knowing that can be found in this extraordinarily rich Kosmos.

But many of the perennial philosophers—Plotinus and Aurobindo, for example—have found around *a dozen levels of consciousness* to be the most useful, and that is roughly what I have presented in the charts (pp. 195–217).[2] My basic levels or basic structures are listed in the left column in all the charts. These are simply the basic levels in the Great Nest of Being, each transcending and including its predecessors—whether we use a simple five-level scheme (matter, body, mind, soul, spirit) or a slightly more sophisticated version (such as the one I have presented in the charts, and which I will explain as we proceed: matter, sensation, perception, exocept, impulse, image, symbol, endocept, concept, rule, formal, vision-logic, vision, archetype, formless, nondual).

To introduce a useful term: these basic levels are *holons* of consciousness. A holon is a whole that is part of other wholes. For example, a whole atom is part of a whole molecule, a whole molecule is part of a whole cell, a whole cell is part of a whole organism, and so on. As we will see throughout this volume, the universe is fundamentally composed of holons, wholes that are parts of other wholes. Letters are parts of words which are parts of sentences which are parts of entire languages. A person is part of a family which is part of a community which is part of a nation which is part of the globe, and so on.

Since each holon is embraced in a larger holon, holons themselves exist in nested hierarchies—or *holarchies*—such as atoms to molecules to cells to organisms to ecosystems. The Great Nest is simply a big picture of those levels of increasing wholeness, exactly as indicated in figure 1.[3] In short, the *basic levels* are the basic holons (stages, waves, spheres, nests) in the Great Nest of Being.

I use all three terms—basic *levels*, basic *structures*, and basic *waves*—interchangeably, as referring to essentially the same phenomenon; but each has a slightly different connotation that conveys important information. "Level" emphasizes the fact that these are *qualitatively* distinct levels of organization, arranged in a nested hierarchy (or holarchy) of increasing holistic embrace (each level transcending but including its predecessors, as shown in fig. 1). "Structure" emphasizes the fact that these are enduring *holistic patterns* of being and consciousness (each is a holon, a whole that is part of other wholes). And "wave" emphasizes the fact that these levels are not rigidly separate and isolated, but, like the colors of a rainbow, infinitely shade and grade into each other. The basic structures are simply the basic colors in that rainbow. To switch metaphors, they are the waves in the great River of Life, through which its many streams run.

There is nothing linear or rigid about these various waves. As we will abundantly see, individual development through the various waves of consciousness is a very fluid and flowing affair. Individuals can be at various waves in different circumstances; aspects of their own consciousness can be at many different waves; even subpersonalities in an individual's own being can be at different waves. Overall development is a very messy affair! The basic levels or basic waves simply represent some of the more noticeable bends in the great River of Life, nothing more, nothing less.

Charts 2a and 2b (pages 199–200) outline the basic levels or basic waves as conceived in a dozen different systems East and West. We will be discussing many others as we proceed. But it should be realized from the start that these levels and sublevels presented by the perennial sages are *not* the product of metaphysical speculation or abstract hairsplitting philosophy. In fact, they are in almost every way the codifications of *direct experiential realities*, reaching from sensory experience to mental experience to spiritual experience. The "levels" in the Great Nest simply reflect the full spectrum of being and consciousness available for direct experiential disclosure, ranging from subconscious to self-conscious to superconscious. Moreover, the discovery of these waves, over the years, has been communally generated and consensually validated. The fact that wherever they appear, they are often quite similar, sometimes almost identical, simply tells us that we live in a patterned Kosmos, and these richly textured patterns can be—and were—spotted by intelligent men and women in almost every culture.

Each senior dimension in the Great Nest—from matter to body to mind to soul to spirit—transcends and includes its juniors, so that living bodies transcend but include minerals, minds transcend but include vital bodies, luminous souls transcend but include conceptual minds, and radiant spirit transcends and includes absolutely everything. Spirit is thus both the very highest wave (purely transcendental) and the ever-present ground of all the waves (purely immanent), going beyond All, embracing All. The Great Nest is a multidimensional latticework of love—eros, agape, karuna, maitri—call it what you will, it leaves no corner of the Kosmos untouched by care nor alien to the mysteries of grace.

That point is as important as it is often forgotten—Spirit is fully transcendent and fully immanent. If we are to try to conceptualize Spirit at all, we should at least try to respect both points. These are shown in figure 1, where the highest sphere represents transcendental spirit (which is written with a small *s* to indicate that it is one level among other levels, albeit the highest), and the paper itself represents immanent Spirit as the equally present Ground of all the levels (with a capital *S* to indicate that it has no other). The patriarchal religions tend to emphasize the transcendental "otherworldly" aspect of spirit; and the matriarchal, neopagan religions tend to emphasize the fully immanent or "this-worldly" aspect of Spirit. Each of them is important, and a truly integral view would find ample room for both. (The context will determine which aspect of spirit/Spirit I mean, but both are always implied.)

The Great Holarchy of Being and Knowing: such is the priceless gift of the ages. This is the core of the perennial philosophy, and, we might say, it is the part of the perennial philosophy that has empirically been found most enduring. The evidence continues overwhelmingly to mount in its favor: human beings have available to them an extraordinary spectrum of consciousness, reaching from prepersonal to personal to transpersonal states. The critics who attempt to deny this overall spectrum do so not by presenting counterevidence—but simply by refusing to acknowledge the substantial evidence that has already been amassed; the evidence, nonetheless, remains. And the evidence says, in short, that there exists a richly textured rainbow of consciousness, spanning subconscious to self-conscious to superconscious.

At the same time, the fact that the perennial philosophers were the first to spot many of the colors in this extraordinary rainbow doesn't mean that modernity and postmodernity must come mute to the meeting. Nobody elucidated the nature of concrete and formal operational thinking like Piaget. And the ways in which some aspects of the early stages can be repressed—well, it took a Freud to really spell those out. Modernity and postmodernity are not without their geniuses; the perennial philosophy is not without its limitations and inadequacies; a more complete spectrum of consciousness will necessarily include and balance all of their insights and discoveries. But the general nature of the waves in the great River of Life: the perennial philosophers were often right on the money.

I will often refer to the perennial philosophy (and the Great Nest) as the "wisdom of premodernity." This is not pejorative. Nor does it mean that you can find no trace of the perennial philosophy in modernity or postmodernity (although, frankly, it is rare). It simply means that the perennial philosophy originated in what we call premodern times. Also—and this is an important point that often confuses people—to say that premodernity had access to the entire Great Nest of Being does not mean that everybody in premodernity was fully awakened to every level in the Great Nest. In fact, the shamans, yogis, saints, and sages who had awakened to the higher levels of soul and spirit were always extremely rare. The average individual (as we will see in chapter 12) spent much of his or her time at prerational, not transrational, levels of consciousness. Still, "wisdom" means the *best* that any era has to offer, and sensitive scholars have often found that the perennial philosophers—from Plotinus to Shankara to Fa-tsang to Lady Tsogyal—are a storehouse of extraordinary wisdom.

Reaching out to them is more than an embrace of some important truths. It is a way to affirm our continuity with the wisdom of the ages; a way to acknowledge our own ancestors; a way to transcend and include that which went before us, and thus flow with the current of the Kosmos; and most of all, a way to remind ourselves that even if we are standing on the shoulders of giants, we are standing on the shoulders of GIANTS, and we would do well to remember that.

What I have tried to do, therefore, in presenting the basic waves of the Great Nest, is to look first to the perennial philosophy for the general contours of the various levels; and then to significantly supplement that understanding with the many refinements (and sometimes corrections) offered by modernity and postmodernity. Take Aurobindo, for example (see chart 2b). Notice that he referred to the intermediate levels as the lower mind, the concrete mind, the logical mind, and the higher mind. Aurobindo gave verbal descriptions of all of these basic structures, which are very useful. But those intermediate levels are also the structures that have been intensely investigated by Western developmental and cognitive psychology, and backed with considerable amounts of clinical and experimental evidence. I have therefore tended to use, for the intermediate levels, terms taken from that research, such as the rule/role mind, concrete operational thinking, and formal operational thinking. But all of these various codifications of the developmental levels are simply different snapshots taken from various angles, using different cameras, of the great River of Life, and they are all useful in their own ways. (Of course, blurred or bad photos are not very useful, and we can reject any research that doesn't measure up to decent standards. I have tried to include, in the charts, only the work of great photographers.)

In all of the charts, the correlations I have given among the various stages and theorists are very general, meant only to get us in the right ballpark (and initiate more refined and careful correlations). Still, many of these correlations have been given by the theorists themselves, and on balance I believe most of them are accurate to within plus-or-minus 1.5 stages. This is true for the higher (transpersonal) stages as well, although the situation becomes more difficult. First of all, as we approach the upper reaches of the spectrum of consciousness, orthodox Western psychological research begins to abandon us, and we increasingly must draw on the great sages and contemplatives, East and West, North and South. Second, cultural surface features are therefore often dramatically different, making the search for any cross-cultural deep features more demanding. And third, few practitioners of one system are conversant with the details of others, thus fewer cross-systematic comparisons have been made. Nonetheless, substantial and impressive studies, some of which we will see below, have made a great deal of headway in these important correlations, and I have reported many of these results in the charts. That there is a general cross-cultural *similarity* of these higher, transrational, transpersonal stages is a sure sign that we are photographing some very real currents in a very real River.

The Great Nest Is a Potential, Not a Given

It is not necessary to picture the basic structures or basic holons as being permanently fixed and unchanging essences (Platonic, Kantian, Hegelian, or Husserlian). They can, in part, be understood as habits of evolution, more like a Kosmic memory than a pregiven mold.[4] But either way, a crucial point remains: the fact that the great yogis, saints, and sages have *already* experienced many of the transpersonal realms (as we will see) shows us unmistakably that we *already* have the potentials for these higher levels present in our own makeup. The human organism and its brain, in its present form, has the capacity for these higher states. Perhaps other states will emerge in the future; perhaps new potentials will unfold; possibly higher realizations will dawn. But the fact remains that *right now* we have at least these extraordinary transpersonal realms already available to us. And whether we say that these higher potentials have been eternally given to us by God, or that they were first created by the evolutionary pioneering saints and sages and then bequeathed to the rest of us as morphogenetic fields and evolutionary grooves, or that they are Platonic Forms forever embedded in the Kosmos, or that they showed up by blind dumb chance mutation and vapidly mindless natural selection, doesn't change in the least the simple fact that those higher potentials are now available to all of us.

The basic structures or basic holons that I generally present—and that are listed in the far-left column in each of the charts—represent a master template taken from premodern, modern, and postmodern sources, using each to fill in the gaps in the others. For comparison, charts 2a and 2b show some of the basic levels as conceived in other systems. Under the "General Great Chain" I have listed the most common five: matter, body (in the sense of living, vital bodies, the emotional-sexual level), mind (including imagination, concepts, and logic), soul (the supraindividual source of identity), and spirit (both the formless ground and nondual union of all other levels). These levels, as I said, are like colors in a rainbow, so I have drawn them overlapping. But even that is misleading; a more accurate representation would be a series of concentric spheres, with each senior sphere enfolding and embracing its juniors (as in fig. 1). The model here is not rungs in a ladder each piled on top of the other, but holons in a holarchy like atoms/molecules/cells/organisms, with each senior enfolding its juniors.

At the same time—and this cannot be emphasized too strongly—the higher levels in the Great Nest are *potentials*, not absolute givens. The lower levels—matter, body, mind—have already emerged on a large scale, so they already exist full-fledged in this manifest world. But the higher structures—psychic, subtle, causal—are not yet consciously manifest on a collective scale; they remain, for most people, potentials of the human bodymind, not fully actualized realities. What the Great Nest represents, in my opinion, is most basically a great *morphogenetic field* or *developmental space*—stretching from matter to mind to spirit—in which various potentials unfold into actuality. Although for convenience I will often speak of the higher levels as if they were simply given, they are in many ways still plastic, still open to being formed as more and more people coevolve into them (which is why, as I said, the basic structures are more like Kosmic habits than pregiven molds). As these higher potentials become actualized, they will be given more form and content, and thus increasingly become everyday realities. Until then, they are, in part, great and grand potentials, which nonetheless still exert an undeniable attraction, still are present in many profound ways, still can be directly realized by higher growth and development, and still show a great deal of similarity wherever they appear.[5]

STRUCTURES AND STATES

The most classic, and probably the oldest, of the sophisticated versions of the Great Nest is that of Vedanta (chart 2b), which also includes the extremely important distinctions between states, bodies, and structures. A *state* means a state of consciousness, such as waking, dreaming, and deep sleep. A *structure* is a sheath or level of consciousness, of which the Vedanta gives five of the most important: the material level, the biological level, the mental level, the higher mental, and the spiritual. A *body* is the energetic support of the various states and levels of mind, of which Vedanta gives three: the gross body of the waking state (which supports the material mind); the subtle body of the dreaming state (which supports the emotional, mental, and higher mental levels); and the causal body of deep sleep (which supports the spiritual mind).[6]

Notice that a given state of consciousness—such as waking or dreaming—can in fact house several different structures or levels of consciousness. In Western terms we would say that the waking *state* of consciousness can contain several quite different *structures* of consciousness, such as sensorimotor, preoperational, concrete operational, and formal operational. In other words, although states of consciousness are important, structures of consciousness give much more detailed information about the actual status of any individual's growth and development, and thus a full-spectrum approach would want to include both states and structures.

In my own system, the *structures* are of two major types: the basic structures (which we have already introduced) and the structures in the various developmental lines (which we will examine below). Structures, in both psychology and sociology, are simply *stable patterns* of events. Psychological structures can be divided and subdivided in numerous ways—deep and surface, levels and lines, enduring and transitional—and I use all of those distinctions.[7] But, as I said, I most often use only two: the structures in the basic levels of consciousness (such as sensation, impulse, image, rule, formop, vision-logic, psychic, subtle, etc.) and the structures in the developmental lines of consciousness (such as the stages of cognition, affect, needs, morals, and so on). In short, structures are the *holistic patterns* that are found in both the *levels* of development and the *lines* of development.

The major *states* are also of two general types: natural and altered. The *natural states of consciousness* include those identified by the perennial philosophy—namely, waking/gross, dreaming/subtle, and deep sleep/causal. According to the perennial philosophy, the waking state is the home of our everyday ego. But the dream state, precisely because it is a world created entirely by the psyche, gives us one type of access to states of the soul. And the deep sleep state, because it is a realm of pure formlessness, gives us one type of access to formless (or causal) spirit. Of course, for most people, the dream and deep sleep state are less real, not more real, than waking reality, which is true enough from one angle. But according to the perennial philosophy, these deeper states can be entered with full consciousness, whereupon they yield their extraordinary secrets (as we will see). In the meantime, we can simply note that the perennial philosophy maintains that waking, dreaming, and deep sleep states offer one type of access to the gross ego, the subtle soul, and causal spirit, respectively.

(I often subdivide the subtle states into a lower or "psychic" realm and the "subtle" realm proper, because the lower subtle or psychic, lying as it does right next to the gross realm, often involves an intense embrace or sense of union with the entire gross realm, as in *nature mysticism*; whereas the subtle proper so transcends the gross realm that it usually involves purely transcendental states of *deity mysticism*. The causal, of course, is the realm of unmanifest cessation, and is the home of *formless mysticism*. Integrating all of them is *nondual mysticism*. We will be examining all of these higher, transpersonal realms throughout this book, so most questions about their exact meaning will be cleared up by further reading.)

The importance of these three (or four) natural states is that every human being, at no matter what stage or structure or level of development, *has available the general spectrum of consciousness*—ego to soul to spirit—at least as temporary states, for the simple reason that all humans wake, dream, and sleep.

An *altered state of consciousness* is a "non-normal" or a "nonordinary" state of consciousness, including everything from drug-induced states to near-death experiences to meditative states.[8] In a *peak experience* (a temporary altered state), a person can briefly experience, while awake, any of the natural states of psychic, subtle, causal, or nondual awareness, and these often result in direct *spiritual experiences* (such as nature mysticism, deity mysticism, and formless mysticism; see below). *Peak experiences can occur to individuals at almost any stage of development.* The notion, then, that spiritual and transpersonal states are available only at the higher stages of development is quite incorrect.

Nonetheless, although the major states of gross, subtle, causal, and nondual are available to human beings at virtually any stage of growth, *the way in which those states or realms are experienced and interpreted* depends to some degree on the stage of development of the person having the peak experience. This means, as I suggested in *A Sociable God*, that we can create a grid of the types of spiritual experiences that are generally available to individuals at different stages of growth.

For example, let us simply call the earlier stages archaic, magic, mythic, and rational. A person at any of those stages can have a temporary peak experience of the psychic, subtle, causal, or nondual. This gives us a grid of around sixteen different types of spiritual experiences.

To give a few examples: A person at the magic stage of development (which cannot easily take the role of other) might have a subtle-level peak experience (of, say, a radiant God-union), in which case that person will tend to experience God-union as applying only to himself (since he cannot take the role of other and thus realize that all people—in fact, all sentient beings—are equally one with God). He will thus tend to suffer massive ego-inflation, perhaps even psychotic in its dimensions. On the other hand, a person at the mythic level (which has expanded identity from egocentric to sociocentric, but which is very concrete-literal and fundamentalist) will experience subtle God-union as being a salvation that is given, not exclusively to him (as the egocentric does), but exclusively to those who embrace the particular myths ("If you want to be saved, you must believe in my God/dess, which is the one and only true Divinity"); thus this person might become a born-again fundamentalist, set upon converting the entire world to his or her version of a revealed God. The subtle-level experience is very real and genuine, but *it has to be carried somewhere*, and it is carried, in this case, in an ethnocentric, fundamentalist, mythic-membership mind, which dramatically limits and ultimately distorts the contours of the subtle domain (as did, even more so, the previous egocentric stage). A person at the formal-reflexive level would tend to experience subtle God-union in more reason-based terms, perhaps as rational Deism, or as a demythologized Ground of Being, and so on.

In other words, a given peak experience (or temporary state of consciousness) is usually *interpreted* according to the general stage of development of the individual having the experience. This gives us, as I said, a grid of around sixteen very general types of spiritual experience: psychic, subtle, causal, and nondual states poured into archaic, magic, mythic, and rational structures. In *A Sociable God* I gave examples of all of these, and pointed out their importance (and we will return to them later in this book).[9]

But all of those peak experiences, no matter how profound, are merely temporary, passing, transient states. In order for higher development to occur, those *temporary states must become permanent traits*. Higher development involves, in part, the conversion of altered states into permanent realizations. In other words, in the upper reaches of evolution, the transpersonal potentials that were only available in temporary *states* of consciousness are increasingly converted into enduring *structures* of consciousness (states into traits).

This is where *meditative states* become increasingly important. Unlike natural states (which access psychic, subtle, and causal states in the natural sleep cycle, but rarely while awake or fully conscious) and unlike spontaneous peak experiences (which are fleeting), meditative states access these higher realms in a deliberate and prolonged fashion. As such, they more stably disclose the higher levels of the Great Nest, higher levels that eventually become, with practice, *permanent realizations*.[10] In other words, psychic, subtle, causal, and nondual states can all become *enduring structures in one's own makeup,* which is why those labels (psychic, subtle, causal, and nondual) are also used to refer to the highest of the *basic structures* in the Great Nest of Being. As they emerge permanently in an individual's development, their potentials, once available only in passing states, become enduring contours of an enlightened mind.

THE BASIC LEVELS IN OTHER SYSTEMS

As I said, charts 2a and 2b give the Great Nest and its basic structures or levels as conceived in some other systems. I am not claiming that these are all identical structures, levels, or waves, only that they share many important similarities across a developmental space, and this *developmental space*, we will see, is what is so interesting—and so important for an integral psychology.

It appears that the oldest of any of these systems originated in India and thereabouts, perhaps as early as the first or second millennium BCE (although tradition claims a much older date). The chakra system, the Vedanta sheaths and states, the Buddhist vijnanas, the Kashmir Shaivite vibratory levels, and Aurobindo's superconscient hierarchy all come out of this historically unsurpassed river of consciousness research. Following soon thereafter, and possibly due to migration (but just as likely due to the universal existence of these potentials), the Mesopotamian/Middle Eastern river begins its mighty journey, which would include Persian, North African, Palestinian, and Grecian streams. The most influential of these would unfold as the Neoplatonic tradition, represented by currents from Plotinus to Kabbalah to Sufism to Christian mysticism (all of which are represented on the charts).

Although it has become fashionable among pluralistic relativists to bash the perennial philosophy (and anything "universal" other than their own universal pronouncements on the importance of pluralism), a less biased look at the evidence shows a rather striking set of very general commonalities among the world's great wisdom traditions. And why should this surprise us? The human body everywhere grows 206 bones, two kidneys, and one heart; and the human mind everywhere grows the capacities for images, symbols, and concepts. Likewise, it seems, the human spirit everywhere grows intuitions of the Divine, and these, too, show many similarities in deep, not surface, features. Some traditions were more complete than others; some were more precise. But putting them all together gives us a general map of the incredibly wide spectrum of human possibilities.

At this point, people who are uncomfortable with level and stage conceptions tend to become suspicious: is consciousness and its development really just a series of linear, monolithic stages, proceeding one after another, in ladder-like fashion? The answer is, not at all. As we will see, these basic waves in the Great Nest are simply the general levels through which numerous different developmental lines or streams will flow— such as emotions, needs, self-identity, morals, spiritual realizations, and so on—all proceeding at their own pace, in their own way, with their own dynamic. Thus, overall development is absolutely not a linear, sequential, ladder-like affair. It is a fluid flowing of many streams through these basic waves. We will soon examine many of these streams. But first we need to finish our account of the basic waves and their emergence.

DATES OF EMERGENCE OF THE BASIC WAVES

In the far-left column of chart 3a, I have included the average ages of emergence of the basic structures of consciousness up to the formal mind. Research suggests that these ages are relatively similar for most people in today's world, simply because—I have hypothesized— collective development or evolution on the whole has reached the formal level (whereas levels higher than the formal, which collective evolution has not reached, must be accessed by one's own efforts—again, in part because they are higher potentials, not givens).[11]

The traditions often divide life's overall journey into the "Seven Ages of a Person," where each age involves adaptation to one of the seven basic levels of consciousness (such as the seven chakras: physical; emotional-sexual; lower, middle, and higher mental; soul; and spirit), and each of the seven stages is said to take seven years. Thus, the first seven years of life involve adaptation to the physical realm (especially food, survival, safety). The second seven years involve adaptation to the emotional-sexual-feeling dimension (which culminates in sexual maturation or puberty). The third seven years of life (typically adolescence) involves the emergence of the logical mind and adaptation to its new perspectives. This brings us to around age twenty-one, where many individuals' overall development tends to become arrested.[12] But if development continues, each seven-year period brings the possibility of a new and higher level of consciousness evolution, so in chart 3a I have listed in brackets these general ages next to the higher basic structures. Of course, these are the most general of generalizations, with exceptions abounding, but they are rather suggestive.

Why "seven ages" and not, say, ten? Again, exactly how to divide and subdivide the number of colors in a rainbow is largely a matter of choice. However, the perennial philosophers and psychologists have found that, no matter how many minute subdivisions we might make for various purposes (such as perhaps thirty for very specific and detailed stages of certain types of meditation), nonetheless there is a sense in talking about *functional groupings* of the basic waves in the Great Nest. That is, there is a sense in which the material levels and sublevels (quarks, atoms, molecules, crystals) are all material and not biological (none of them can sexually reproduce, for example). Likewise, there is a sense in which the mental levels and sublevels (images, symbols, concepts, rules) are all mental and not, say, psychic or subtle. In other words, even if we find it useful on occasion to distinguish dozens (or even hundreds) of minute gradations in the colors of a rainbow, there is also good reason to say there are basically just six or seven major colors in most rainbows.

This is what the perennial philosophy means by the "Seven Ages of a Person" or the seven main chakras or basic structures. For various reasons, I have found that although around two dozen basic structures can be readily identified (e.g., form, sensation, perception, exocept, impulse, image, symbol, endocept, concept, rule . . .), nonetheless they can be condensed into around seven to ten *functional groupings* which reflect easily recognizable stages (as we will see throughout this volume). These functional groupings of basic structures I represent with some very general names, which are also listed on the left column in all the charts: (1) sensorimotor, (2) phantasmic-emotional (or emotional-sexual), (3) rep-mind (short for the representational mind, similar to general preoperational thinking, or "preop"), (4) the rule/role mind (similar to concrete operational thinking, or "conop"), (5) formal-reflexive (similar to formal operational, or "formop"), (6) vision-logic, (7) psychic, (8) subtle, (9) causal, and (10) nondual.[13] Again, these are simple orienting generalizations, but they offer us a convenient way to deal with a great deal of data and evidence. But none of these generalizations need stop us from using maps that are either more detailed or more simplified, as the occasion warrants.

COGNITIVE DEVELOPMENT AND THE GREAT NEST OF BEING

The Great Nest is actually a great holarchy of being and knowing: levels of reality and levels of knowing those levels. That is, the perennial philosophers found both ontology and epistemology to be important, as inseparable aspects of the great waves of reality. Modernity found it necessary to differentiate ontology and epistemology, which would have been quite welcome had modernity or postmodernity completed the development and *integrated* those differentiations, whereas all that happened was that those differentiations completely fell apart; and modernity, trusting only its own isolated subjectivity, embraced epistemology alone, whereupon ontology fell into the black hole of subjectivism, never to be heard from again.

The Great Chain, to the degree modernity recognized it at all, thus became merely a hierarchy of levels of knowing—that is, *a hierarchy of cognition*, such as investigated by Piaget. That is not so much wrong as it is terribly partial, leaving out the levels of reality that would ground the cognition (or, just as sadly, acknowledging only the sensorimotor level of reality, to which all cognition must be faithful in order to be judged "true"). Nonetheless, if for the moment we focus just on cognition—and because it is certainly true that the Great Chain is in part a great spectrum of consciousness—the question then becomes: in individuals, *is the development of the Great Chain the same as cognitive development?*

Not exactly. To begin with, you certainly can think of the Great Nest as being, in part, a great spectrum of consciousness, which it is. One of the dictionary definitions of "cognitive" is "relating to consciousness." Therefore, in dictionary terms anyway, you could think of the development of the Great Nest (which in individuals involves the unfolding of

higher and more encompassing levels of consciousness) as being generally quite similar to cognitive development, as long as we understand
that "cognition" or "consciousness" runs from subconscious to self-
conscious to superconscious, and that it includes interior modes of
awareness just as much as exterior modes.

The problem, as I was saying, is that "cognition" in Western psychology came to have a very narrow meaning that excluded most of the
above. It came to mean *the apprehension of exterior objects*. All sorts
of "consciousness" or "awareness" (in the broad sense) were therefore
excluded (e.g., emotions, dreams, creative visions, subtle states, and
peak experiences). If the *contents* of consciousness were not some sort
of *objective-empirical object* (a rock, a tree, a car, an organism), then
that consciousness was said *not* to possess cognitive validity. So much
for all the really interesting states and modes of consciousness.

In the hands of such as Piaget, the meaning of cognition was nar-
rowed even further, to types of logico-mathematical operations, which
were claimed to underlie all other developmental lines in all other domains. At that point, consciousness as "cognition" had been reduced to
perceiving nothing but the flat and faded surfaces of empirical objects
(what we will be calling "flatland"). Put simply, any awareness that saw
something other than the world of scientific materialism was not a true
awareness, was not a "true" cognition.

In that sense, the development of the Great Nest in individuals is most
certainly *not* a "cognitive development." And yet, if we look a little
closer at the Piagetian scheme—and at what most subsequent psychologists have meant by "cognitive development"—we can find some very
interesting (and very important)—if limited—similarities.

First of all, the Western psychological study of cognitive development
still involves the study of some sort of *consciousness*, however narrow
and restricted on occasion. Thus, what Piaget studied as formal operational thought—which was conceived as a mathematical structure (the
INRC grouping)—is one legitimate way to slice the stream of consciousness at that point, but it hardly exhausts the snapshots we can take of
consciousness at that particular bend in the River. Numerous other and
equally valid perspectives exist for defining consciousness at that stage,
from role taking to epistemological styles to worldviews to moral drives.
But in focusing on cognitive development, Piaget was at least highlight-
ing the central importance of *consciousness development*, even if in a
sometimes narrow way.

That importance is underscored by the fact that, when specific developmental lines are studied—such as moral development, self development, and role-taking development—it has almost always been found that *cognitive development is necessary (but not sufficient) for these other developments.* In other words, *before* you can develop morals, or a self-perspective, or some idea of the good life, you have to be able to consciously register those various elements in the first place. Consciousness is thus necessary, but not sufficient, for these other developments.

And that is exactly the claim of the Great Nest theorists. The levels of the Great Nest (the basic structures of consciousness) are the levels through which the various developmental lines will proceed, and without the basic waves, there is nothing for the various boats to float on. This is why the basic structures (whether conceived as the sheaths in Vedanta, the levels of consciousness in Mahayana, the ontological levels of the sefirot of Kabbalah, or the stages of the soul's growth toward God in Sufism) are the backbone, the crucial skeleton, on which most other systems hang.

Thus, although they can by no means be equated, cognitive development (as studied by Western psychologists) is perhaps the closest thing we have to the Great Chain or the spectrum of consciousness (at least up to the levels of the formal mind; beyond that most Western researchers recognize no forms of cognition at all). For this reason—and while keeping firmly in mind the many qualifications and limitations—I sometimes use cognitive terms (such as conop and formop) to describe some of the basic structures.

Still, because cognitive development does have a very specific and narrow meaning in Western psychology, I also treat it as a separate developmental line apart from the basic structures (so that we can preserve the ontological richness of the basic holons, and not reduce them to Western cognitive categories). Charts 3a and 3b are correlations of the basic structures with the cognitive stages disclosed by various modern researchers.

One of the most interesting items in those charts is the number of Western psychologists who, based on extensive empirical and phenomenological data, have detected several stages of *postformal* development—that is, stages of cognitive development beyond linear rationality (i.e., beyond formal operational thinking, or formop). Although "postformal" can refer to any and all stages beyond formop, it usually applies only to mental and personal, not supramental and transpersonal, stages. In other words, for most Western researchers, "postformal" refers to the first major stage beyond formop, which I call *vision-logic*.[14] As shown in charts 3a–b, most researchers have found two to four stages of post-formal (vision-logic) cognition. These postformal stages generally move beyond the formal/mechanistic phases (of early formop) into various stages of relativity, pluralistic systems, and contextualism (early vision-logic), and from there into stages of metasystematic, integrated, unified, dialectical, and holistic thinking (middle to late vision-logic). This gives us a picture of the *highest mental domains* as being dynamic, developmental, dialectical, integrated.

Few of those researchers, however, move into the *transmental* domains (of psychic, subtle, causal, or nondual occasions—transrational and transpersonal), although many of them increasingly acknowledge these higher levels. For the contours of these levels we must often rely, once again, on the great sages and contemplatives, as several of the charts make clear.

In this regard, a hotly disputed topic is whether the spiritual/transpersonal stages themselves can be conceived as higher levels of cognitive development. The answer, I have suggested, depends on what you mean by "cognitive." If you mean what most Western psychologists mean—which is a mental conceptual knowledge of exterior objects—then no, higher or spiritual stages are *not* mental cognition, because they are often supramental, transconceptual, and nonexterior. If by "cognitive" you mean "consciousness in general," including superconscious states, then much of higher spiritual experience is indeed cognitive. But spiritual and transpersonal states also have many other aspects—such as higher affects, morals, and self-sense—so that, even with an expanded definition of cognitive, they are not *merely* cognitive. Nonetheless, "cognition" in the broadest sense means "consciousness," and thus cognitive developments of various sorts are an important part of the entire spectrum of being and knowing.

THE COGNITIVE LINE

Charts 3a and 3b list some of the best-known and most influential researchers in cognitive development. Piaget's studies are pivotal, of course. Even with all of their shortcomings, Piaget's contributions remain a stunning accomplishment; certainly one of the most significant psychological investigations of this century. He opened up an extraordinary number of avenues of research: following the pioneering work of James Mark Baldwin (see below), Piaget demonstrated that each level of development has a different worldview, with different perceptions, modes of space and time, and moral motivations (discoveries upon which the work of researchers from Maslow to Kohlberg to Loevinger to Gilligan would depend); he showed that reality is not simply given but is in many important ways constructed (a structuralism that made possible poststructuralism); his *méthode clinique* subjected the unfolding of consciousness to a meticulous investigation, which resulted in literally hundreds of novel discoveries; his psychological researches had immediate influence on everything from education to philosophy (Habermas, among many others, stands greatly in his debt). Few are the theorists who can claim a tenth as much.

The major inadequacy of Piaget's system, most scholars now agree, is that Piaget generally maintained that cognitive development (conceived as logico-mathematical competence) is the only major line of development, whereas there is now abundant evidence that numerous different developmental lines (such as ego, moral, affective, interpersonal, artistic, etc.) can unfold in a relatively independent manner. In the model I am presenting, for example, the cognitive line is merely one of some two dozen developmental lines, none of which, as lines, can claim preeminence. (We will examine these other lines in the next chapter.)

But as for the cognitive line itself, Piaget's work is still very impressive; moreover, after almost three decades of intense cross-cultural research, the evidence is virtually unanimous: Piaget's stages up to formal operational are universal and cross-cultural. As only one example, *Lives across Cultures: Cross-Cultural Human Development* is a highly respected textbook written from an openly liberal perspective (which is often suspicious of "universal" stages). The authors (Harry Gardiner, Jay Mutter, and Corinne Kosmitzki) carefully review the evidence for Piaget's stages of sensorimotor, preoperational, concrete operational, and formal operational. They found that cultural settings sometimes alter the *rate* of development, or an *emphasis* on certain aspects of the stages—but not the stages themselves or their cross-cultural validity.

Thus, for sensorimotor: "In fact, the qualitative characteristics of sensorimotor development remain nearly identical in all infants studied so far, despite vast differences in their cultural environments." For preoperational and concrete operational, based on an enormous number of studies, including Nigerians, Zambians, Iranians, Algerians, Nepalese, Asians, Senegalese, Amazon Indians, and Australian Aborigines: "What can we conclude from this vast amount of cross-cultural data? First, support for the universality of the structures or operations underlying the preoperational period is highly convincing. Second, the qualitative characteristics of concrete operational development (e.g., stage sequences and reasoning styles) appear to be universal [although] the rate of cognitive development . . . is not uniform but depends on ecocultural factors." Although the authors do not use exactly these terms, they conclude that the deep features of the stages are universal but the surface features depend strongly on cultural, environmental, and ecological factors (as we will later put it, all four quadrants are involved in individual development). "Finally, it appears that although the rate and level of performance at which children move through Piaget's concrete operational period depend on cultural experience, children in diverse societies still proceed in the same sequence he predicted."[15]

Fewer individuals in any cultures (Asian, African, American, or otherwise) reach formal operational cognition, and the reasons given for this vary. It might be that formal operational is a genuinely higher stage that fewer therefore reach, as I believe. It might be that formal operational is a genuine capacity but not a genuine stage, as the authors believe (i.e., only some cultures emphasize formal operational and therefore teach it). Evidence for the existence of Piaget's formal stage is therefore strong but not conclusive. Yet this one item is often used to dismiss *all* of Piaget's stages, whereas the correct conclusion, backed by enormous evidence, is that all of the stages up to formal operational have now been adequately demonstrated to be universal and cross-cultural.

I believe the stages at and beyond formop are also universal, including vision-logic and the general transrational stages, and I will present substantial evidence for this as we proceed. At the same time, as we will see when we get to the discussion on childhood spirituality (in chapter 11), the early stages are exactly the stages of Piaget's studies that have consistently held up to cross-cultural evidence. This will help us to see these early stages in a more accurate light, I believe.

As for the cognitive line itself, its overall study has been fruitfully carried forward by Michael Commons and Francis Richards, Kurt Fischer, Juan Pascual-Leone, Robert Sternberg, Gisela Labouvie-Vief, Herb Koplowitz, Michael Basseches, Philip Powell, Suzanne Benack, Patricia Arlin, Jan Sinnott, and Cheryl Armon, to name a prominent few (all of whom are represented on the charts).[16]

Although there are important differences between these researchers, there are also many profound similarities. Most of them have found that cognitive development moves through three or four major stages (with numerous substages): sensorimotor, concrete, formal, and postformal.

The sensorimotor stages usually occur in the first two years of life, and result in a capacity to perceive physical objects. Cognition then slowly begins to learn to represent these objects with names, symbols, and concepts. These early symbols and concepts tend to suffer various sorts of inadequacies (objects with similar predicates are equated; there is more water in a tall glass than in a short one, even if it is the same water; concepts are confused with the objects they represent; and so on). These inadequacies lead to various sorts of "magical" displacements and "mythical" beliefs. This is why, on all the charts, you will see so many researchers referring to these early stages with names like magic, animistic, mythic, and so on.

This is *not* to say that all magic and all myths are merely early cognitive inadequacies, but that some of them clearly are—if I eat the eye of a cat, I will see like a cat; a rabbit's foot brings good luck; if I don't eat my spinach, God will punish me, etc. There is a world of difference between mythic symbols taken to be concretely and literally true—Jesus really was born from a biological virgin, the earth really is resting on a Hindu serpent, Lao Tzu really was nine hundred years old when he was born—and mythic symbols imbued with metaphor and perspectivism, which only come into existence with formal and postformal consciousness. Unless otherwise indicated, when I use the word "mythic" it refers to preformal, concrete-literal mythic images and symbols, some aspects of which are in fact imbued with cognitive inadequacies, for these myths claim as empirical fact many things that can be empirically disproved—e.g., the volcano erupts because it is personally mad at you; the clouds move because they are following you. These preformal mythic beliefs, scholars from Piaget to Joseph Campbell have noted, are always egocentrically focused and literally/concretely believed.

For the same reason, these early stages are referred to by names such as preconventional, preoperational, egocentric, and narcissistic. Because children at the sensorimotor and preoperational stages cannot yet easily or fully take the role of other, they are locked into their own perspectives. This "narcissism" is a normal, healthy feature of these early stages, and causes problems only if it is not substantially outgrown (as we will see).

As cognitive capacity grows, these researchers generally agree, consciousness begins more accurately to relate to, and operate on, the sensorimotor world, whether that be learning to play the violin or learning to organize classes in order of their size (although many "mythic adherences" still remain in awareness). These *concrete operations* are carried out by *schemas* and *rules*, which also allow the self at this stage to adopt various *roles* in society, and thus move from the egocentric/preconventional realm to the sociocentric/conventional.

As consciousness further develops and deepens, these concrete categories and operations begin to become more generalized, more abstract (in the sense of being applicable to more and more situations), and thus more universal. *Formal operational* consciousness can therefore begin to support a *postconventional* orientation to the world, escaping in many ways the ethnocentric/sociocentric world of concrete (and mythic-membership) thought.

Although, largely under the onslaught of anti-Western cultural studies (with a strong relativistic prejudice), "rationality" has become a derogatory term, it is actually the seat of an extraordinary number of positive accomplishments and capacities (including the capacities used by the antirational critics). Rationality (or reason in the broad sense) involves, first and foremost, the capacity to take perspectives (hence Jean Gebser calls it "perspectival-reason"). According to Susanne Cook-Greuter's research, preoperational thinking has only a first-person perspective (egocentric); concrete operational adds second-person perspectives (sociocentric); and formal operational goes further and adds third-person perspectives (which allow not only scientific precision but also impartial, postconventional, worldcentric judgments of fairness and care). Thus reason can "norm the norms" of a culture, subjecting them to criticism based on universal (non-ethnocentric) principles of fairness. Perspectival-reason, being highly reflexive, also allows sustained introspection. And it is the first structure that can imagine "as if" and "what if" worlds: it becomes a true dreamer and visionary.

As important as formal rationality is, these researchers all acknowledge the existence of yet higher, *postformal* stages of cognition—or a higher reason—which takes even more perspectives into account (fourth- and fifth-person perspectives, according to Cook-Greuter). Bringing together multiple perspectives while unduly privileging none is what Gebser called *integral-aperspectival*, which involves a further deepening of worldcentric and postconventional consciousness. There is general agreement that these postformal (or vision-logic) developments involve at least two or three major stages. Growing beyond abstract universal *formalism* (of formop), consciousness moves first into a cognition of dynamic relativity and *pluralism* (early vision-logic), and then further into a cognition of unity, holism, dynamic dialecticism, or universal *integralism* (middle to late vision-logic), all of which can be seen quite clearly on charts 3a and 3b (and others we will discuss later).[17]

As "holistic" as these vision-logic developments are, they are still mental realm developments. They are the very highest reaches of the mental realms, to be sure, but beyond them lie supramental and properly transrational developments. I have therefore included Sri Aurobindo and Charles Alexander as examples of what a full-spectrum cognitive developmental model might include. (In chapter 9, we will investigate this overall cognitive line as it moves from gross to subtle to causal.) Notice that Aurobindo uses decidedly cognitive terms for almost all of his stages: higher mind, illumined mind, overmind, supermind, and so on. In other words, the spectrum of consciousness is in part a spectrum of genuine cognition, using "cognition" in its broadest sense. But it is not just that, which is why Aurobindo also describes the higher affects, morals, needs, and self identities of these higher levels. But his general point is quite similar: cognitive development is primary and is necessary (but not sufficient) for these other developments.

SUMMARY

Such, then, is a brief introduction to the basic levels in the Great Nest of Being. The Great Nest is simply a great *morphogenetic field* that provides a *developmental space* in which human potentials can unfold. The basic levels of the Great Nest are the basic waves of that unfolding: matter to body to mind to soul to spirit. We saw that these basic levels (or structures or waves) can be divided and subdivided in many legitimate ways. The charts give around sixteen waves in the overall spectrum of consciousness, but these can be condensed or expanded in numerous ways, as we will continue to see throughout this presentation.

Through these general waves in the great River, some two dozen different developmental streams will flow, all navigated by the self on its extraordinary journey from dust to Deity.

2

The Developmental Lines
or Streams

THROUGH THE BASIC *levels* or waves in the Great Nest flow some
two dozen relatively independent developmental *lines* or streams.
These different developmental lines include morals, affects, self-identity,
psychosexuality, cognition, ideas of the good, role taking, socio-emo-
tional capacity, creativity, altruism, several lines that can be called "spiritual" (care, openness, concern, religious faith, meditative stages), joy,
communicative competence, modes of space and time, death-seizure,
needs, worldviews, logico-mathematical competence, kinesthetic skills,
gender identity, and empathy—to name a few of the more prominent
developmental lines for which we have some empirical evidence.[1]

These lines are "relatively independent," which means that, for the
most part, they can develop independently of each other, at different
rates, with a different dynamic, and on a different time schedule. A person can be very advanced in some lines, medium in others, low in still
others—all at the same time. Thus, *overall development*—the sum total
of all these different lines—shows no linear or sequential development
whatsoever. (It is that fact which finally undid the Piagetian scheme.)

However, the bulk of research has continued to find that *each developmental line itself* tends to unfold in a sequential, holarchical fashion:
higher stages in each line tend to build upon or incorporate the earlier
stages, no stages can be skipped, and the stages emerge in an order that
cannot be altered by environmental conditioning or social reinforce-

ment. So far, considerable evidence suggests that this is true for all of the developmental lines that I mentioned.[2]

For example, in the widely regarded text *Higher Stages of Human Development* (edited by Charles Alexander and Ellen Langer), the works of thirteen top developmental psychologists—including Piaget, Kohlberg, Carol Gilligan, Kurt Fischer, Howard Gardner, Karl Pribram, and Robert Kegan—are presented, and of those thirteen, all of them except one or two present models that are hierarchical in part, including Gilligan for female development. These conclusions are based on massive amounts of experimental data, not merely on theoretical speculations. This is not to say that all of these developmental lines are *only* hierarchical; many of their features are not (see below). But crucial aspects of all of them appear to be hierarchical in important ways. Furthermore, there is a general consensus that no matter how different the developmental lines might be, not only do most of them unfold holarchically, *they do so through the same set of general waves*, which include: a physical/sensorimotor/preconventional stage, a concrete actions/conventional rules stage, and a more abstract, formal, postconventional stage.[3]

In learning to play a musical instrument, for example, one first physically grapples with the instrument and learns to relate to it in a sensorimotor fashion. One then learns to play a simple song or two, gradually mastering the concrete operations and rules of using the instrument. As one becomes proficient in playing the musical keys and scales, the skills become more abstract, and one can increasingly apply the abstract skills to new and different songs. Almost all of the developmental lines—from cognitive to ego to affective to moral to kinesthetic—proceed through those three broad stages. If we allow for the fact that there might be yet higher or transpersonal stages of development, and if we simply call all of those "post-postconventional," then that would give us four broad stages, levels, or waves—sensorimotor, conventional, postconventional, and post-postconventional (precon to con to postcon to post-postcon)—through which most of the developmental lines proceed.

And what are those four broad waves? Nothing but a simplified version of the Great Nest of Being, moving from body (sensorimotor) to mind (conventional and postconventional) to spirit (post-postconventional). Of course, those four broad stages are just a succinct summary of what research has found; in most of the cases—cognitive, self, and moral, for example—development actually goes through five, six, seven or more stages, and in virtually every case, those stages, as far as they go, match in a very general fashion the levels in the Great Nest.

In other words, the reason that most of the developmental lines proceed through a largely universal, invariant, holarchical sequence is that they are following the largely universal, invariant, Great Holarchy of Being—they are following the general morphogenetic field so clearly suggested in the charts. *The Great Nest is most basically that general morphogenetic field or developmental space.* It simply represents some of the basic waves of reality that are available to individuals; and as different talents, capacities, and skills emerge in individuals, they tend to follow, in a general way, the contours of the Great Nest, they migrate through that developmental space. Again, it is not that these levels are etched in concrete or set in stone; they are simply some of the stronger currents in the great River of Life; and when pieces of wood are dropped in that River, they tend to follow the currents already operating. Just so for the individual potentials that emerge in human development: they tend to follow the currents in the great River of Life, they follow the waves in the Great Holarchy. This, at any rate, is what the preponderance of empirical evidence has consistently suggested.

But to return to an equally important point: the various streams, even if they migrate across a similar field, do so in a relatively independent manner. A person can be highly evolved in some lines, medium in others, and low in still others. This means, as I said, that overall development follows no linear sequence whatsoever.

All of this can be represented as in figure 2, which is what I call an "integral psychograph." The levels in the Great Nest are shown on the

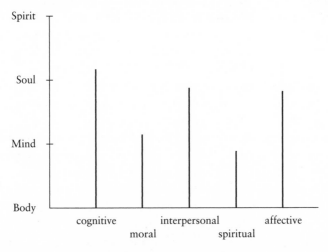

FIGURE 2. *The Integral Psychograph*

vertical axis, and through those levels run the various lines. (Of the two dozen or so lines, I give five as examples: cognitive, moral, interpersonal, spiritual, and affective. I have listed "spirit" both as the highest level and as a separate developmental line, reflecting the two most common definitions of "spirituality" [see chapter 10]). Since the Great Nest is actually a holarchy (as shown in fig. 1), we can more accurately represent the integral psychograph as in figure 3.

This does not mean that all, or even most, of the important aspects of development are hierarchical. In my system, each basic structure or wave actually consists of both hierarchy (or increasing holistic capacity) and heterarchy (or nonhierarchical interaction among mutually equivalent elements). The relation *between* levels is hierarchical, with each senior level transcending and including its juniors, but not vice versa (molecules contain atoms, but not vice versa; cells contain molecules, but not vice versa; sentences contain words, but not vice versa), and that "not vice versa" establishes an *asymmetrical hierarchy of increasing holistic capacity* (which simply means that the senior dimension embraces the junior, but not vice versa, so that the senior is more holistic and encompassing). But *within* each level, most elements exist as mutually equivalent and mutually interacting patterns. Much of develop-

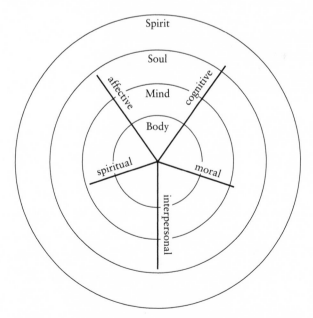

FIGURE 3. *The Integral Psychograph as a Holarchy*

ment—at least half of it—involves various types of nonhierarchical, heterarchical processes of competence articulation and application. These nonhierarchical processes, of course, are not indicated on the charts, which focus on migratory development; but their profound importance should not on that account be forgotten.

Thus *holarchy*, as I use the term, includes a balance of both *hierarchy* (qualitatively ranked levels) and *heterarchy* (mutually linked dimensions). Theorists who attempt to use only one or the other of those types of relations have consistently failed to explain development at all.

We will return to the nature of the developmental streams and give several examples. But first, a look at the self that is navigating those streams.

3

The Self

L EVELS AND LINES are navigated by the self. Although I will subdivide that simple scheme in a moment, those three items—the basic waves, the developmental streams, and the self as the navigator of both—appear to be central to an integral model. We have examined the basic levels or waves, and we will shortly return to the developmental lines or streams and examine them more closely. But at this point we need to look at the self, and the role it plays in the overall evolution of consciousness.[1]

THE SELF AS THE NAVIGATOR OF THE WAVES AND STREAMS

If you get a sense of your self right now—simply notice what it is that you call "you"—you might notice at least two parts to this "self": one, there is some sort of observing self (an inner subject or watcher); and two, there is some sort of observed self (some objective things that you can see or know about yourself—I am a father, mother, doctor, clerk; I weigh so many pounds, have blond hair, etc.). The first is experienced as an "I," the second as a "me" (or even "mine"). I call the first the *proximate self* (since it is closer to "you"), and the second the *distal self* (since it is objective and "farther away"). The both of them together— along with any other source of selfness—I call the *overall self*.

These distinctions are important because, as many researchers have noted—from Sri Ramana Maharshi to Robert Kegan—during psychological development, *the "I" of one stage becomes a "me" at the next.* That is, what you are identified with (or embedded in) at one stage of development (and what you therefore experience very intimately as an "I") tends to become transcended, or disidentified with, or de-embedded at the next, so you can see it more objectively, with some distance and detachment. In other words, the *subject* of one stage becomes an *object* of the next.

For example, a young infant is identified almost solely with its body—the body is the infant's self or subject (the proximate I), and thus the infant cannot really stand back and objectively observe its body. It simply *is* a bodyself, and as a body it looks at the world. But when the infant's verbal and conceptual mind begins to emerge, the infant will start to identify with the mind—the mind becomes the self or subject (the proximate I), and the infant can then, for the first time, start to see its body objectively (as a distal object or "me")—the body is now an object of the new subject, the mental self. Thus, the subject of one stage becomes an object of the next.

(And, the perennial philosophers add, at the very upper reaches of the spectrum of consciousness, your individual I—your separate self or inner subject—becomes an object of the ultimate I, which is none other than radiant Spirit and your own true Self. According to the mystics, you are one with God as ultimate Subject or pure Consciousness—a pure Emptiness that, as absolute Witness, I-I, or Seer, can never itself be seen, and yet paradoxically exists as Everything that is seen: the Spirit that transcends all—and thus can never be seen—and includes all—and thus is everything you are looking at right now. We will pursue this in chapter 8.)

The *overall self*, then, is an amalgam of all of these "selves" insofar as they are present in you right now: the proximate self (or "I"), the distal self (or "me"), and at the very back of your awareness, that ultimate Witness (the transcendental Self, antecedent Self, or "I-I"). All of those go into your sensation of being a self in this moment, and all of them are important for understanding the development or evolution of consciousness.

Precisely because the overall self contains several different streams (and all sorts of *subpersonalities*, which we will discuss below), the overall self does *not* show a sequential or stage-like development. However, modern research has consistently shown that *at least one aspect of the self does undergo relatively sequential or stage-like development, and that is the proximate self.*[2] Jane Loevinger, for example, in some highly respected and widely repeated research (including in non-Western countries), has found substantial evidence that "ego development" proceeds through almost a dozen stages of clearly recognizable growth (up to what I call the centaur; see chart 1a). What Loevinger calls "ego development" is quite similar to what I refer to as proximate-self development.[3] And proximate-self development is, in my view, at the very heart of the evolution of consciousness. *For it is the proximate self that is the navigator through the basic waves in the Great Nest of Being.*

The basic structures or basic waves themselves are devoid of a sense of self. This point has been made by perennial philosophers from Plotinus to Vasubandhu to Padmasambhava to Saint Teresa. The basic structures are simply the waves of being and knowing that are available to the self as it develops toward its highest potentials. Each time the self (the proximate self) encounters a new level in the Great Nest, it first *identifies* with it and consolidates it; then disidentifies with it (*transcends* it, de-embeds from it); and then includes and *integrates* it from the next higher level. In other words, the self goes through a *fulcrum (or a milestone) of its own development.* These major milestones of self development have been investigated by researchers such as James Mark Baldwin, Clare Graves, Jane Loevinger, John Broughton, Erik Erikson, Susanne Cook-Greuter, Don Beck, and Robert Kegan, to name a prominent few, all of whom are represented on the charts. (Again, these researchers are not investigating identical currents, but simply currents that run close together in the Great River and thus share certain similarities—similarities in the nature of the proximate-self sense.)

To say that the self has identified with a particular wave in the Great Rainbow does not, however, mean that the self is rigidly stuck at that level. On the contrary, the self can be "all over the place" on occasion. Within limits, the self can temporarily roam all over the spectrum of consciousness—it can regress, or move down the holarchy of being and knowing; it can spiral, reconsolidate, and return. Moreover, because the self at every stage of its development has fluid access to the great natural states of consciousness (psychic, subtle, causal, and nondual), it can have temporary peak experiences of any or all of those transpersonal realms, thus momentarily leaping forward into greater realities.

Still, empirical evidence has consistently demonstrated that the self's *center of gravity*, so to speak, tends to hover around one basic level of consciousness at any given time. This means, for example, that if you give individuals a test of ego development, about 50 percent of their answers will come from one level, and about 25 percent from the level immediately above or below it. In my view, the reason this happens is that, each time the self identifies with a particular level of consciousness, it experiences the loss of that level as a death—literally, as a type of death-seizure, because the very *life* of the self is identified with that level.[4] Letting go of that level is therefore experienced only with great difficulty. In fact, I believe that each of the major milestones of self-development is marked by a difficult life-death battle, involving the death (or the disidentifying with, or the transcendence) of each level, which can often be quite traumatic (see chart 1a; we will examine these milestones or fulcrums of self-development in chapter 8).[5] The only reason the self eventually accepts the *death* of its given level is that the *life* of the next higher level is even more enticing and ultimately satisfying. The self therefore disidentifies with (or de-embeds from) its present level, "dies" to an exclusive identity with that level, and identifies with (or embraces and embeds in) the life of the next higher level, until its death, too, is accepted. (And according to the perennial philosophy, when all deaths have been died, the result is only God, or an awakening to the what the Sufis call the Supreme Identity of self and spirit.)

The proximate self, then, is the navigator of the waves (and streams) in the great River of Life. It is the central source of identity, and that identity expands and deepens as the self navigates from egocentric to sociocentric to worldcentric to theocentric waves (or precon to con to postcon to post-postcon levels of overall development)—an identity that ranges from matter to id to ego to God.

(Incidentally, when we say that identity expands from, say, egocentric to sociocentric to worldcentric, this does not mean that somebody at the worldcentric or postconventional level has no ego at all; on the contrary, somebody at worldcentric has a very mature ego. It simply means that the person can take *multiple perspectives* no longer confined to *just* his own ego, and thus he can make moral judgments based on the considerations of fairness, justness, and care, regardless of race, color, sex, or creed. He will still act in his own self-interest where that is appropriate, but the sphere of his consideration is immeasurably expanded, and his own self-interest will increasingly include the interests of others, since they fall into the orbit of his own expanded identity. See chapter 9, section "Morals.")

As the central navigator through the Great Nest, the self is the locus of such important functions as *identification* (what to call "I"), *will* (or choices that are free within the constraints and limitations of its present level),[6] *defenses* (which are laid down hierarchically),[7] *metabolism* (which converts states into traits),[8] and most important of all, *integration* (the self is responsible for balancing and integrating whatever elements are present).[9] (As for the Buddhist objections to the self, see endnote).[10]

CONCLUSION

What each of us calls an "I" (the proximate self) is both a *constant function* and a *developmental stream*. That is, the self has several *functional invariants* that constitute its central activity—it is the locus of identity, will, metabolism, navigation, defenses, and integration, to name the more important. And this self (with its functions) also undergoes *its own development* through the basic waves in the Great Nest (the stages of which we will examine in chapter 8: material self to bodily self to mental self to soul self to selfless Self). Especially significant is the fact that, as the locus of integration, the self is responsible *for balancing and integrating all of the levels, lines, and states in the individual.*

In short, the self as navigator is a juggling act of all of the elements that it will encounter on its extraordinary journey from subconscious to self-conscious to superconscious—a journey we will soon follow in detail.

4

The Self-Related Streams

T HE SELF NAVIGATES through the basic waves of the Great Nest by using the self's capacity to *identify* with each wave and ride it to some sort of completion. The self has the capacity to intimately identify with a level of consciousness, become competent at that level, and then disidentify with it (and integrate it) in order to step up to the next higher and wider sphere and identify with it (and so on until its capacity for growth is exhausted).

Each time the self's center of gravity orbits around a new level of consciousness, it has, of course, a new and different outlook on life. Precisely because each basic level in the Great Nest has a different architecture, the self at each level *sees a different world*: it faces new fears, has different goals, suffers new problems. It has a new set of needs, a new class of morals, a new sense of self. I call all of those developmental lines the *self-related lines or streams*, because they are all intimately connected with the self and its extraordinary journey through the great waves.

Thus, there are the developmental lines in general (cognitive, affective, aesthetic, kinesthetic, mathematical, etc.), and, as a subset of those, there are the developmental lines that are especially and intimately associated with the self, its needs, its identity, and its development—and those are the self-related lines.

In fact, the self-related stages are generated, in part, precisely from the self's *identifying with a particular level of consciousness*. To give a simplistic example: when the self identifies with the conventional mind (when the self's major level of consciousness is late conop), its sense of self (à la Loevinger) is a *conformist role*, its moral sense (à la Kohlberg) is starting to become *conventional*, and its major need (à la Maslow) is for *belongingness* (you can see these on the charts). All of those specific roles, morals, and needs come into play when the self's center of gravity is at the late rule/role mind, and they are supported largely by the *exclusive identification* of the self with that level of consciousness.[1] From that particular level in the Great Spectrum, that is what the world looks like.

Many of those stages—such as morals, self-identity, and self-needs—are listed in charts 4a–c and 5a–c. Charts 4a–c contain the self-related stages that are most intimately connected with *self identity* (such as Loevinger's ego development and Erikson's psychosocial stages), and charts 5a–c contain the self-related stages of *morals and perspectives*, or the different types of outlook (and worldviews) that the self has at each of the basic levels of consciousness. We will discuss them in that order.

THE SELF-STAGES (CHARTS 4A–C)

Early pioneers in the study of the stages of self-development (and those who have considerably influenced my own view) include James Mark Baldwin, John Dewey, G. H. Mead, C. Cooley, Anna Freud, Heinz Werner, Edith Jacobson, Harry Stack Sullivan, Heinz Hartmann, Rene Spitz, Erich Neumann, Edward F. Edinger, Clare Graves, and Erik Erikson.[2] More recent theorists (also instrumental in my view) include Jane Loevinger, John Broughton, Otto Kernberg, Jacques Lacan, Heinz Kohut, Margaret Mahler, James Masterson, Robert Kegan, and Susanne Cook-Greuter (among others to be discussed).

Erikson, coming from within the psychoanalytic tradition, posed such a profoundly far-reaching extension of its concepts that it actually helped to undermine psychoanalytic reductionism. His "psychosocial stages," ranging from birth through adolescence to old age, struck an immediately sympathetic chord not only with the public but with many other researchers—he was clearly on to something of importance. In Erikson's scheme, quite reminiscent of the "seven ages of a person," there are seven or eight major ages (or stages) of a person's life (see chart 4a). Echoing a truth that was already beginning to surface from Baldwin's and Piaget's studies (and which was explicit in the German Idealists' vision, which greatly influenced both Baldwin and Piaget), each stage of development sees a different world—with different needs, different tasks, different dilemmas, different problems and pathologies. Instead of reducing all of life's problems to something that went wrong in the first age of a person, there are six or seven other ages, equally important, sometimes more important. Erikson's highest stages were not quite transpersonal (they were often horizontal unfoldings of a personal sort);[3] still, it would never be quite as easy to reduce all significant life events to the first age of a person.

Clare Graves was one of the first (along with Baldwin, Dewey, and Maslow) to take a developmental scheme and show its extraordinary applicability in a wide range of endeavors, from business to government to education. Graves proposed a profound and elegant system of human development, a system that subsequent research has refined and validated, not refuted. "Briefly, what I am proposing is that the psychology of the mature human being is an unfolding, emergent, oscillating spiraling process marked by progressive subordination of older, lower-order behavior systems to newer, higher-order systems as man's existential problems change. Each successive stage, wave, or level of existence is a state through which people pass on their way to other states of being. When the human is centralized in one state of existence"—that is, when the self's *center of gravity* hovers around a given level of consciousness—"he or she has a psychology which is particular to that state. His or her feelings, motivations, ethics and values, biochemistry, degree of neurological activation, learning system, belief systems, conception of mental health, ideas as to what mental illness is and how it should be treated, conceptions of and preferences for management, education, economics, and political theory and practice are all appropriate to that state."[4]

Graves outlined around seven major "levels or waves of human existence," ranging from autistic, magical, and animistic, through sociocentric/conventional, to individualistic and integrated, as shown in chart 4c. As is usually the case with Western researchers, he recognized no higher (transpersonal) levels, but the contributions he made to the prepersonal and personal realms were profound.

It should be remembered that virtually all of these stage conceptions—from Abraham Maslow to Jane Loevinger to Robert Kegan to Clare Graves—are based on extensive amounts of research and data. These are not simply conceptual ideas and pet theories, but are grounded at every point in a considerable amount of carefully checked evidence. Many of the stage theorists that I am presenting (such as Piaget, Loevinger, Maslow, and Graves) have had their models checked in First,

Second, and Third World countries (as we saw with Piaget). The same is true with Graves's model; to date, it has been tested in over fifty thousand people from around the world, and there have been no major exceptions found to his scheme.[5]

Of course, this does not mean that any of these schemes give the whole story, or even most of it. They are all, as I said, partial snapshots of the great River of Life, and they are all useful when looking at the River from that particular angle. This does not prevent other pictures from being equally useful, nor does it mean that these pictures cannot be refined with further study. What it does mean is that any psychological model that does not include these pictures is not a very integral model.

Graves's work has been carried forward, refined, and significantly extended by Don Beck. *Spiral Dynamics*, written with his colleague Christopher Cowan (they founded the National Values Center), is a superb application of developmental principles in general (and Gravesian ones in particular) to a wide range of sociocultural problems. Far from being mere armchair analysts, Beck and Cowan participated in the discussions that led to the end of apartheid in South Africa (and then went on, using the same developmental principles, to design the "hearts and minds" strategy for the South African rugby union team, which won the 1995 World Cup). The principles of Spiral Dynamics have been fruitfully used to reorganize businesses, revitalize townships, overhaul education systems, and defuse inner-city tensions. Beck and Cowan have had this extraordinary success because, in a world lost in pluralistic relativism, they have brought the clarity—and the reality—of dynamic developmentalism.

The situation in South Africa is a prime example of why the idea of developmental levels (each with its own worldview, values, and needs) can actually reduce and even alleviate social tensions, not exacerbate them (as critics often charge). Spiral Dynamics sees human development as proceeding through eight general value MEMES or deep structures: *instinctive* (uroboric), *animistic/tribalistic* (typhonic-magic), *power gods* (magic-mythic), *absolutist-religious* (mythic), *individualistic-achiever* (rational-egoic), *relativistic* (early vision-logic), *systematic-integrative* (middle vision-logic), and *global-holistic* (late vision-logic), as shown in chart 4b. These are not rigid levels but fluid and flowing waves, with much overlap and interweaving, resulting in a meshwork or dynamic spiral of consciousness unfolding.

The typical, well-meaning liberal approach to solving social tensions is to treat every value as equal, and then try to force a leveling or redistribution of resources (money, rights, goods, land) while leaving the values untouched. The typical conservative approach is take its particular values and try to foist them on everybody else. The developmental approach is to realize that there are many different values and worldviews; that some are more complex than others; that many of the problems at one stage of development can only be defused by evolving to a higher level; and that only by recognizing and facilitating this evolution can social justice be finally served. Moreover, by seeing that each and every individual has all of these MEMES potentially available to them, the lines of social tension are redrawn: not based on skin color, economic class, or political clout, but on the *type* of worldview from which a person, group of persons, clan, tribe, business, government, educational system, or nation is operating. As Beck puts it, "The focus is not on types *of* people, but types *in* people." This removes skin color from the game and focuses on some of the truly underlying factors (developmental values and worldviews) that generate social tensions, and this is exactly what happened to help dismantle apartheid in South Africa.[6]

(We will return to Beck at the end of this chapter for some fascinating examples, so if these sections on self development seem dry and abstract, they will hopefully come alive with numerous examples and applications.)

Jane Loevinger's impressive research focused specifically on ego development (see chart 4a); it brought a great deal of precision to the field and sparked an explosion of further developmental studies. She found that ego (proximate-self) development moves through about ten discernible stages, the names of which tend to tell the story: autistic, symbiotic, impulsive, self-protective, conformist, conscientious-conformist, conscientious, individualistic, autonomous, and integrated. Her research has been repeated in several different cultures now, and continues to garner wide support. Susanne Cook-Greuter has refined and extended Loevinger's research, and is forging her own original and important model of self development (chart 4c).[7]

Robert Kegan (chart 4c) seems to be everybody's favorite developmentalist (count me in). He discusses a broad range of developmental issues with insight, exactitude, sensitivity, and care. Kegan's approach is especially important, in my view, because he so clearly elucidates the nature of embedding (identifying) and de-embedding (transcending), which marks each major wave of self development. His books *The Evol-*

ving Self and *In Over Our Heads* show why a developmental approach is so important (and why Kegan is everybody's favorite son).

Juan Pascual-Leone brings a much-needed Continental (hermeneutic, phenomenological, dialectical) orientation to developmental studies, weaving together the work of Piaget, Jaspers, Husserl, Scheler, Merleau-Ponty, and Heidegger (who have likewise influenced my view)—plus his own highly original formulations—into a powerful system of dynamic dialecticism (charts 3b and 4b).[8]

John Broughton's research is of great significance, I believe, especially in terms of delineating the developmental stages of self and its epistemology (chart 4a). Following the lead of James Mark Baldwin (see below), Broughton has contributed not only a good deal of important research, but a much-needed series of theoretical counterbalances to the narrowness of the Piagetian tradition.[9]

As examples of researchers who follow the self-stages into the transpersonal domains, I have included Rudolf Steiner (chart 4b), Michael Washburn (4a), and Jenny Wade (4a); Stan Grof's levels can be seen in chart 2a.[10] Steiner (1861–1925) was an extraordinary pioneer (during that "genesis period" of Fechner, Jung, James, etc.) and one of the most comprehensive psychological and philosophical visionaries of his time. The founder of anthroposophy, he authored over two hundred books on virtually every conceivable subject.[11] Michael Washburn has presented a very clear version of a Romantic view of higher development involving a recapture of earlier lost potentials; and Jenny Wade, who is one of the most competent developmentalists now writing, has presented an excellent overview of the unfolding of eight major waves of consciousness, spanning the entire spectrum.

Once again, although there are many important differences between these theories of the stages of self-development, one can't help but also notice the many profound similarities. The very names that these theorists have given to the self-stages tend to tell the story. Using only the terms from the theorists listed in charts 4a–c: Consciousness starts out largely autistic and undifferentiated from the material world. It then differentiates its bodily self from the material environment and emerges as an instinctive, impulsive self, but one that is still magically and animistically involved with the environment, and still struggling for egocentric power over the environment. As the conceptual mind begins to emerge, it differentiates from the body, and thus the self adds increasingly mental capacities to its sensory ones, and hence begins to move out of the narcissistic, first-person, safety/security/power orbit and into more widely intersubjective, communal, and social circles.

As rule thinking and the capacity to take the role of others emerge, *egocentric* gives way to *sociocentric*, with its initially conformist and conventional roles, mythic-absolutist beliefs, and often authoritarian ways. A further growth of consciousness differentiates the self from its embeddedness in sociocentric and ethnocentric modes, and opens it to formal, universal, worldcentric, postconventional awareness, which is an extraordinary expansion of consciousness into modes that are beginning to become truly global.

This postconventional stance is deepened with postformal development, which, most researchers agree, moves through *relativistic individualism* (where a belief in pluralism tends to lead to isolated, hyper-individualism) to *global holism* (which moves beyond pluralism to universal integration), so that the personal self becomes a more truly integrated, autonomous self. (Which I call the *centaur*. "Centaur" is a term used by Erikson to denote a mature mind-and-body integration, where "human mind" and "animal body" are harmoniously one. We might say that it is the highest of the personal realms, beyond which lie more transpersonal developments).

If consciousness continues its evolutionary spiral beyond the centaur, it can stably move into transpersonal, post-postconventional realms (psychic, subtle, causal, and nondual). A few of the modern Western pioneers studying these higher realms include Johann Fichte, Friedrich Schelling, Georg Hegel, Arthur Schopenhauer, Henri Bergson, Friedrich Nietzsche, Carl Jung, Martin Heidegger, Karl Jaspers, Edmund Husserl, Gustav Fechner, Henry James Sr., Ralph Waldo Emerson, Rudolf Steiner, Vladimir Solovyov, Josiah Royce, Annie Besant, Frederic Myers, Nikolai Berdyaev, Aldous Huxley, Erich Fromm, Roberto Assagioli, James Mark Baldwin, William James, and Abraham Maslow.[12]

MORALS AND PERSPECTIVES (CHARTS 5A–C)

Each time the self's center of gravity identifies with a new and higher basic wave in the unfolding Great Nest, it doesn't just have a new sense of *identity*, it has a new and higher *view* of the world, with a wider and more encompassing set of *morals* and *perspectives*, many of which are listed in charts 5a–c.

The pivotal figure here is Lawrence Kohlberg (chart 5a), whose work, building on that of Baldwin, Dewey, and Piaget, demonstrated that moral development goes through six or seven stages (spanning preconventional to conventional to postconventional to post-postconventional). The individual starts out amoral and egocentric ("whatever I want" is what is right), moves to sociocentric ("what the group, tribe, country wants" is what is right), to postconventional (what is fair for all peoples, regardless of race, color, creed). Kohlberg's highest stage—what he called stage seven—is "universal-spiritual" (post-postconventional).

Deirdre Kramer (chart 5a) has given a powerful overview of world-view development (preformal to formal to pluralistic to integral). Kitchener and King have done important and influential work on reflective judgment (from representation to relativism to synthesis; chart 5a). William Perry's work on social perspectives, which develop from rigidly dualistic to relativistic/pluralistic to synthetic committed (chart 5a), has been widely hailed by other researchers and is especially appreciated by college students, since it outlines their typical angst-ridden developments with great care. Robert Selman's studies on role-taking have elucidated crucial aspects of the development of the self and its intersubjective capacities (chart 5c). Carol Gilligan (chart 5c) outlined a hierarchy of female moral development ("selfish" to "care" to "universal care," yet another version of egocentric to sociocentric to worldcentric), which had an enormous influence on the popular culture to precisely the degree it was widely misinterpreted (as implying that only males go through hierarchical stages; the idea that women do not go through hierarchical development became one of the most influential cultural myths of the last two decades). Torbert's levels of action-inquiry have proven especially useful in business (chart 5a). Blanchard-Fields's work offers a significant overview of the evolution of perspectives, from egocentric to multiple to integrative (chart 5a). John Rawls's moral positions line up in a hierarchy (chart 5c), as do Cheryl Armon's stages of the Good (chart 5b) and Howe's important work on moral character structures (chart 5c).[13]

In other words, what all of these theories have in common is a general view of morals and perspectives evolving from preconventional to conventional to postconventional (to post-postconventional)—yet more general evidence for the Great Nest and its often universal currents.[14] Nonetheless, it should be emphasized that these different self-related developmental streams still retain a relatively independent character. For example, research continues to suggest that cognitive development is necessary but not sufficient for interpersonal development, which is necessary but not sufficient for moral development, which is necessary but not sufficient for ideas of the Good.[15] That underscores the fact that, once again, even though most of the individual developmental lines undergo a sequential holarchical unfolding, overall development itself does not.

OBJECTIONS

One criticism that has constantly been raised by advocates of pluralistic relativism is that any stage conception—such as Kohlberg's or Loevinger's—is inherently Eurocentric, marginalizing, and sexist. These are important concerns. However, over the last decade and a half these criticisms have been carefully investigated, and for the most part they have proven unfounded. Kohlberg's moral stages, for example, were claimed to be biased against women. "At this point there is little support for the claim that Kohlberg's theory is biased against females," reports the widely respected textbook *Social and Personality Development.* "Nor is there much evidence that females travel a different moral path and come to emphasize a morality of care more than males do. In fact, there is evidence to the contrary: when reasoning about real-life moral dilemmas that they have faced, *both* males and females raise issues of compassion and interpersonal responsibility about *as often as* or *more often than* issues of law, justice, and individual rights" (emphasis in original). In short, "Research has consistently failed to support the claim that Kohlberg's theory is biased against women."[16]

How about the claim that Kohlberg's research is Eurocentric, with a Western bias that marginalizes other cultures? "Similar findings have emerged from studies in Mexico, the Bahamas, Taiwan, Indonesia, Turkey, Honduras, India, Nigeria, and Kenya. . . . So it seems that Kohlberg's levels and stages of moral reasoning are 'universal' structures . . . [and] Kohlberg's moral stages do seem to represent an invariant sequence."[17] As another researcher summarizes the evidence: "Comprehensive reviews of cross-cultural studies suggest that Kohlberg's theory and method are reasonably culture-fair and do reflect moral issues, norms, and values relevant in other cultural settings. Further, these data also support the developmental criteria implied by his stage model [giving] impressive support for his developmental theory and its nonrelativistic stance. . . ."[18]

Theories such as Kohlberg's have demonstrated their nonrelativistic stance precisely because, I would claim, those stages are surfing the waves of the nonrelativistic Great Holarchy, preconventional to conventional to postconventional to post-postconventional. These waves are flowing across a morphogenetic field and developmental space that spans insentient matter to superconscient spirit, while remaining, at every stage, fully grounded in that Spirit which is the suchness and isness of the entire display.

SPIRAL DYNAMICS: AN EXAMPLE OF THE WAVES OF EXISTENCE

We return now to Spiral Dynamics for a brief overview of one version of the self-streams and their waves of unfolding. Remember that this is simply one series of photos of the Great River; there are actually numerous different streams proceeding relatively independently through the basic waves; and individuals can simultaneously be at many different waves in their various streams (as shown in the integral psychograph, figs. 2 and 3). Spiral Dynamics does not include states of consciousness, nor does it cover the higher, transpersonal waves of consciousness.[19] But for the ground it covers, it gives one very useful and elegant model of the self and its journey through what Clare Graves called the "waves of existence."

Beck and Cowan (who have remained quite faithful to Graves's system) refer to these levels of self-existence as ^{V}MEMEs. A ^{V}MEME is at once a psychological structure, value system, and mode of adaptation, which can express itself in numerous different ways, from worldviews to clothing styles to governmental forms. The various ^{V}MEMEs are, in a sense, the "different worlds" available to the self as it develops along the great spiral of existence, driven by both its own internal dynamics and shifting life conditions. And each ^{V}MEME is a holon, which transcends and includes its predecessors—a development that is envelopment. I have included a "Graves Diagram" (fig. 4), which is a diagram Clare Graves himself used to indicate this nesting envelopment (what we would call a holarchy).

Beck and Cowan use various names and colors to refer to these different self-world levels, of which there are around eight or nine. But these are not just passing phases in the self's unfolding; they are permanently

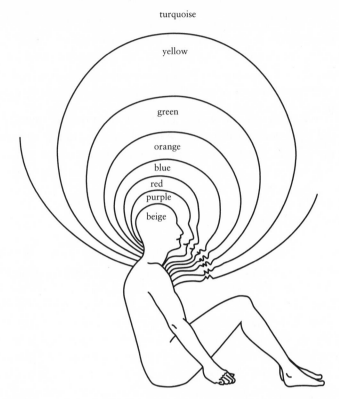

turquoise
yellow
green
orange
blue
red
purple
beige

FIGURE 4. *Graves Diagram: Holons of Increasing Development*

available capacities and coping strategies that can, once they have emerged, be activated under the appropriate life conditions (e.g., survival instincts can be activated in emergency situations; bonding capacities are activated in close human relationships, and so on). Moreover, as Beck puts it, "The Spiral is messy, not symmetrical, with multiple admixtures rather than pure types. These are mosaics, meshes, and blends."[20]

The first six levels are "subsistence levels" marked by "first-tier thinking." Then there occurs a revolutionary shift in consciousness: the emergence of "being levels" and "second-tier thinking." Here is a brief description of all eight waves, the percentage of the world population at each wave, and the percentage of social power held by each.[21]

1. *Beige: Archaic-Instinctual.* The level of basic survival; food, water, warmth, sex, and safety have priority. Uses habits and instincts just to

survive. Distinct self is barely awakened or sustained. Forms into *survival bands* to perpetuate life.

Where seen: First human societies, newborn infants, senile elderly, late-stage Alzheimer's victims, mentally ill street people, starving masses, shell shock. 0.1 percent of the adult population, 0 percent power.

2. *Purple: Magical-Animistic.* Thinking is animistic; magical spirits, good and bad, swarm the earth leaving blessings, curses, and spells that determine events. Forms into *ethnic tribes*. The spirits exist in ancestors and bond the tribe. Kinship and lineage establish political links. Sounds "holistic" but is actually atomistic: "there is a name for each bend in the river but no name for the river."

Where seen: Belief in voodoo-like curses, blood oaths, ancient grudges, good luck charms, family rituals, magical ethnic beliefs and superstitions; strong in Third World settings, gangs, athletic teams, and corporate "tribes." 10 percent of the population, 1 percent of the power.

3. *Red: Power Gods.* First emergence of a self distinct from the tribe; powerful, impulsive, egocentric, heroic. Mythic spirits, dragons, beasts, and powerful people. Feudal lords protect underlings in exchange for obedience and labor. The basis of *feudal empires*—power and glory. The world is a jungle full of threats and predators. Conquers, outfoxes, and dominates; enjoys self to the fullest without regret or remorse.

Where seen: The "terrible twos," rebellious youth, frontier mentalities, feudal kingdoms, epic heroes, James Bond villains, soldiers of fortune, wild rock stars, Attila the Hun, *Lord of the Flies*. 20 percent of the population, 5 percent of the power.

4. *Blue: Conformist Rule.* Life has meaning, direction, and purpose, with outcomes determined by an all-powerful Other or Order. This righteous Order enforces a code of conduct based on absolutist and unvarying principles of "right" and "wrong." Violating the code or rules has severe, perhaps everlasting repercussions. Following the code yields rewards for the faithful. Basis of *ancient nations*. Rigid social hierarchies; paternalistic; one right way and only one right way to think about everything. Law and order; impulsivity controlled through guilt; concrete-literal and fundamentalist belief; obedience to the rule of Order. Often "religious" [in the mythic-membership sense; Graves and Beck refer to it as the "saintly/absolutistic" level], but can be secular or atheistic Order or Mission.

Where seen: Puritan America, Confucianist China, Dickensian England, Singapore discipline, codes of chivalry and honor, charitable good deeds, Islamic fundamentalism, Boy and Girl Scouts, "moral majority," patriotism. 40 percent of the population, 30 percent of the power.

5. *Orange: Scientific Achievement.* At this wave, the self "escapes" from the "herd mentality" of blue, and seeks truth and meaning in individualistic terms—hypothetico-deductive, experimental, objective, mechanistic, operational—"scientific" in the typical sense. The world is a rational and well-oiled machine with natural laws that can be learned, mastered, and manipulated for one's own purposes. Highly achievement-oriented, especially (in America) toward materialistic gains. The laws of science rule politics, the economy, and human events. The world is a chessboard on which games are played as winners gain preeminence and perks over losers. Marketplace alliances; manipulate earth's resources for one's strategic gains. Basis of *corporate states.*

Where seen: The Enlightenment, Ayn Rand's *Atlas Shrugged*, Wall Street, the Riviera, emerging middle classes around the world, cosmetics industry, trophy hunting, colonialism, the Cold War, fashion industry, materialism, liberal self-interest. 30 percent of the population, 50 percent of the power.

6. *Green: The Sensitive Self.* Communitarian, human bonding, ecological sensitivity, networking. The human spirit must be freed from greed, dogma, and divisiveness; feelings and caring supersede cold rationality; cherishing of the earth, Gaia, life. Against hierarchy; establishes lateral bonding and linking. Permeable self, relational self, group intermeshing. Emphasis on dialogue, relationships. Basis of *collective communities* (i.e., freely chosen affiliations based on shared sentiments). Reaches decisions through reconciliation and consensus (downside: interminable "processing" and incapacity to reach decisions). Refresh spirituality, bring harmony, enrich human potential. Strongly egalitarian, antihierarchy, pluralistic values, social construction of reality, diversity, multiculturalism, relativistic value systems; this worldview is often called *pluralistic relativism.* Subjective, nonlinear thinking; shows a greater degree of affective warmth, sensitivity, and caring, for earth and all its inhabitants.

Where seen: Deep ecology, postmodernism, Netherlands idealism, Rogerian counseling, Canadian health care, humanistic psychology, liberation theology, World Council of Churches, Greenpeace, animal rights, ecofeminism, postcolonialism, Foucault/Derrida, politically correct, diversity movements, human rights issues, ecopsychology. 10 percent of the population, 15 percent of the power.

With the completion of the green meme, human consciousness is poised for a quantum jump into "second-tier thinking." Clare Graves referred to this as a "momentous leap," where "a chasm of unbelievable depth of meaning is crossed." In essence, with second-tier consciousness, one can think both vertically and horizontally, using both hierarchies and heterarchies; one can, for the first time, *vividly grasp the entire spectrum of interior development*, and thus see that each level, each meme, each wave is crucially important for the health of the overall spiral.

As I would word it, since each wave is "transcend and include," each wave is a fundamental ingredient of all subsequent waves, and thus each is to be cherished and embraced. Moreover, each wave can itself be activated or reactivated as life circumstances warrant. In emergency situations, we can activate red power drives; in response to chaos, we might need to activate blue order; in looking for a new job, we might need orange achievement drives; in marriage and with friends, close green bonding.

But what none of those memes can do, on its own, is fully appreciate the existence of the other memes. Each of those first-tier memes thinks that its worldview is the correct or best perspective. It reacts negatively if challenged; it lashes out, using its own tools, whenever it is threatened. Blue order is very uncomfortable with both red impulsiveness and orange individualism. Orange achievement thinks blue order is for suckers and green bonding is weak and woo-woo. Green egalitarianism cannot easily abide excellence and value rankings, big pictures, or anything that appears authoritarian, and thus it reacts strongly to blue, orange, and anything post-green.

All of that begins to change with second-tier thinking. Because second-tier consciousness is fully aware of the interior stages of development—even if it cannot articulate them in a technical fashion—it steps back and grasps the big picture, and thus second-tier thinking appreciates the necessary role that all of the various memes play. Using what we would recognize as vision-logic, second-tier awareness thinks in terms of the overall spiral of existence, and not merely in the terms of any one level.

Where the green meme uses early or beginning vision-logic in order to grasp the numerous different systems and contexts that exist in different cultures, second-tier thinking goes one step further and begins to *inte-*

grate those pluralistic systems into integral and holistic spirals and holarchies (Beck and Cowan themselves refer to second-tier thinking as operating with "holons"). These holarchies include both interior and exterior levels of development, in both vertical and horizontal dimensions, resulting in a multileveled, multidimensional, richly holarchical view.

There are two major waves to this second-tier thinking (corresponding to what we would recognize as middle and late vision-logic):

7. *Yellow: Integrative.* Life is a kaleidoscope of natural hierarchies [holarchies], systems, and forms. Flexibility, spontaneity, and functionality have the highest priority. Differences and pluralities can be integrated into interdependent, natural flows. Egalitarianism is complemented with natural degrees of excellence where appropriate. Knowledge and competency should supersede rank, power, status, or group. The prevailing world order is the result of the existence of different levels of reality (memes) and the inevitable patterns of movement up and down the dynamic spiral. Good governance facilitates the emergence of entities through the levels of increasing complexity (nested hierarchy).

8. *Turquoise: Holistic.* Universal holistic system, holons/waves of integrative energies; unites feeling with knowledge [centaur]; multiple levels interwoven into one conscious system. Universal order, but in a living, conscious fashion, not based on external rules (blue) or group bonds (green). A "grand unification" is possible, in theory and in actuality. Sometimes involves the emergence of a new spirituality as a meshwork of all existence. Turquoise thinking uses the entire spiral; sees multiple levels of interaction; detects harmonics, the mystical forces, and the pervasive flow-states that permeate any organization.

Second-tier thinking: 1 percent of the population, 5 percent of the power.

With only 1 percent of the population at second-tier thinking (and only 0.1 percent at turquoise), second-tier consciousness is relatively rare because it is now the "leading edge" of collective human evolution. As examples, Beck and Cowan mention items ranging from Teilhard de Chardin's noosphere to the growth of transpersonal psychology, with increases in frequency definitely on the way—and even higher memes still in the offing. . . .

At the same time, it might be noted that second-tier thinking has to emerge in the face of much resistance from first-tier thinking. In fact, as we will see in chapter 13, a version of the postmodern green meme, with its pluralism and relativism, has actively fought the emergence of more integrative and holarchical thinking. (It has also made developmental studies, which depend on second-tier thinking, virtually anathema at most universities, which is why the researchers presented throughout this book—and in the charts—are heroes and heroines by any definition, who have often pursued their studies in the most hostile of environments.) And yet without second-tier thinking, as Graves, Beck, and Cowan point out, humanity is destined to remain victims of a global "auto-immune disease," where various memes turn on each other in an attempt to establish supremacy.

At the same time, it is from the large fund of green memes (and sometimes orange) that the second tier emerges.[22] It is from the pluralistic perspectives freed by green that integrative and holistic networks are built. This book is therefore an invitation to those greens who find it appropriate to move on, not by abandoning green, but by enriching it.

HORIZONTAL TYPOLOGIES

Finally, a word about "horizontal" typologies, such as Jungian types, the Enneagram, Myers-Briggs, and so forth. For the most part, these are not vertical levels, stages, or waves of development, but rather different types of orientations *possible at each of the various levels.* Some individuals find these typologies to be very useful in understanding themselves and others. But it should be understood that these "horizontal" typologies are of a fundamentally different nature than the "vertical" levels—namely, the latter are universal stages through which individuals pass in a normal course of development, whereas the former are types of personalities that may—or may not—be found at any of the stages.

For example, we saw that cognitive development goes through the stages of sensorimotor, preoperational, and concrete operational, leading up to formal. According to the evidence to date, there are no major exceptions to those stages (see chapter 1). Thus, we can include those stages, and others like them, in any integral psychology with a fair amount of confidence. But we have no such confidence with the horizontal typologies. They simply outline some of the *possible* orientations that may, or may not, be found at any of the stages, and thus their inclusion is based more on personal taste and usefulness than on universal evidence: all individuals do not necessarily fit a particular typology, whereas all individuals do go through the basic waves of consciousness.

This doesn't mean that horizontal typologies are useless; on the contrary, they can be quite helpful for various purposes. The Enneagram, for example, is a sophisticated system that classifies people into nine basic personality types (the reformer, the helper, the motivator, the individualist, the investigator, the loyalist, the enthusiast, the leader, the peacemaker, the reformer).[23] The way to use such typologies is to realize that these nine different types can exist at each of the major levels of consciousness development.

Thus, to use the example of Spiral Dynamics for the vertical levels and the Enneagram for the horizontal, you can have Enneagram type 3 (the motivator) at the purple level, the red level, the blue level, the orange level, the green level, and so on. In this example, nine types at eight levels gives us a typology of seventy-two different personality types—and you can start to see what a truly multidimensional psychology might look like!

But that is simply one example of the multiple waves and streams—and types—that can be found in the great River of Life. None of them have the final answer; all of them have something important to tell us.

CONCLUSION TO PART ONE

Waves, streams, and self. In Part One, we have briefly looked at the basic levels or waves of development (matter to body to mind to soul to spirit), the individual lines or streams of development (cognition, morals, identity, worldviews, values, etc.), and the self that navigates them both. We have seen the importance of "transcend and include," and thus the importance of honoring and embracing each and every wave and stream in the Great Nest of Being.

But as we look more carefully at the overall levels of consciousness, we can't help but notice that, with a few exceptions, the vast majority of modern researchers do not include, or even acknowledge, the higher, transpersonal, spiritual levels. Glancing through the charts, which span the entire spectrum, it is striking how many modern researchers stop somewhere around the centaur and vision-logic, and ignore or even deny the transpersonal and transcendental waves of superconscious development.

In premodern times, while it is true that much, or even most, of spirituality was magic, mythic, and prerational, nonetheless the most highly evolved yogis, saints, and sages had access to the transrational, transpersonal, transcendental realms—they embraced, in their own way and in their own terms, the entire Great Nest of Being, subconscious to self-conscious to superconscious. Those very rare souls evidenced not only a capacity for second-tier thinking (as evidenced in their extensive developmental models; see chapter 12), but they also transcended the thinking mind altogether in superconscious and supramental states. And by and large they were supported by the entire culture in their attempts to do so. This is why we say that the *wisdom of premodernity* was embodied in the Great Nest of Being. And even if the *average* individual did not awaken to the higher levels in the Nest, it was clearly understood that these higher potentials were available to any who wished to pursue a path of awakening, liberation, or enlightenment. Premodernity acknowledged these higher, transpersonal, spiritual realms, whereas modernity, for the most part, denies them altogether.

What's going on here? How could something universally widespread at one point in our collective history become resolutely erased at the next? It's a staggering scenario, fully comparable, in its own way, to the extinction of the dinosaurs. The most pervasive notion in human history and prehistory (namely, the existence of some sort of spiritual dimension) was simply pronounced, with the thundering authority of science, put with a zeal that was inversely proportional to its believability, to be a massive collective hallucination. The spiritual dimension, it was solemnly announced, was nothing but a wish-fulfillment of infantile needs (Freud), an opaque ideology for oppressing the masses (Marx), or a projection of human potentials (Feuerbach). Spirituality is thus a deep confusion that apparently plagued humanity for approximately a million years, until just recently, a mere few centuries ago, when modernity pledged allegiance to sensory science, and then promptly decided that the entire world contained nothing but matter, period.

The bleakness of the modern scientific proclamation is chilling. In that extraordinary journey from matter to body to mind to soul to spirit, scientific materialism halted the journey at the very first stage, and proclaimed all subsequent developments to be nothing but arrangements of frisky dirt. Why this dirt would get right up and eventually start writing poetry was not explained. Or rather, it was explained by dumb chance and dumb selection, as if two dumbs would make a Shakespeare. The sensorimotor realm was proclaimed the only real realm, and it soon came to pass that mental health would be defined as adaptation to that "reality." Any consciousness that saw something other than matter was obviously hallucinating.

The only word that can adequately define this cultural catastrophe is "horrifying." Still, if these higher spiritual and transpersonal dimensions are in fact *inherent potentials of the human bodymind*, then even this extensive cultural repression would not be strong enough to cure the soul of wonder or empty it of grace; not strong enough to hide the mystery of transcendence, ecstasy and liberation, radiant God and beloved Goddess.

If there is ever to be a truly integral psychology (or any sort of integral studies), this extraordinary rupture between premodernity and modernity—spiritual and material—needs to be confronted head on. Although there is a slow movement in the modern and postmodern world to reintroduce some sort of spirituality, nonetheless the "official" and most widespread worldview of the modern West is that of scientific materialism. And clearly, we cannot have an integral view of the levels of consciousness if modernity and modern science denies the existence of most of them. "Integral" means, if it means anything, the integration of all that is given to humanity; and if modernity insists instead on trashing everything that came before it, then the integral enterprise is derailed from the start. At the same time, it will do no good, as Romantics wish, to attempt a return to yesteryear, an attempt to "resurrect" the past with a "resurgence of the real," for modernity brought its own important truths and profound insights, which need to be harmonized as well; and yesteryear, full truth be told, just wasn't all that swell.

If we are to move forward to the bright promise of an integral approach, we need a way to honor *both* the strengths and the weaknesses of *both* premodernity and modernity. If we can find a coherent way to honor truths both ancient and modern, a truly integral approach might become more than a passing dream.

PART TWO

PATH
From Premodern to Modern

A TRULY INTEGRAL PSYCHOLOGY would surely wish to include the religious or spiritual dimensions of men and women. And yet, for the most part, the great systems of spirituality—Christianity, Judaism, Islam, Buddhism, Hinduism, Taoism, indigenous religions—are part of the legacy of premodernity. This is not to say that these religions don't exist or have influence in the modern world; only that their roots and foundations were largely laid in premodern times and their worldviews are deeply molded by premodern currents. Further, the actual historical epoch called "modernity" (especially the Enlightenment in the West) specifically defined itself as "antireligion." The scientific empiricism of the Enlightenment often set out to destroy the "superstitions" that, it felt, composed most of the tenets of organized religion.

If an integral psychology truly wishes to embrace the enduring insights of both "religious" premodernity and "scientific" modernity, there needs to be some way to reconcile, in a very general way, their antagonistic stances toward spirituality.

Therefore, in Part Two, we will take a very brief look at the great transition from the premodern to the modern worldviews, attempting to point out that they *both* possessed many strengths and many weaknesses, and that an integral approach might best proceed by taking the enduring insights from both and jettisoning their limitations. I believe that there is no other way to generate a truly integral approach. Virtually every attempt at an integral model that I have seen suffers from either not appreciating the strengths of the ancient traditions, or not understanding the important contributions of modernity; I will try, as best I can, to outline both.

We will then return, in Part Three, and attempt to pull the pieces together—honoring both premodern and modern—and thus suggesting a constructive postmodern approach to an integral psychology.

5

What Is Modernity?

SOMETHING UNHEARD OF

WHAT SPECIFICALLY DID modernity bring into the world that the premodern cultures by and large lacked? What made modernity so substantially *different* from the cultures and epochs that preceded it? Whatever it was, it very likely will be an essential feature of any comprehensive or integral psychology.[1]

There have been many answers offered to the question, What is modernity? Most of them are decidedly negative. Modernity, it is said, marked the death of God, the death of the Goddess, the commodification of life, the leveling of qualitative distinctions, the brutalities of capitalism, the replacement of quality by quantity, the loss of value and meaning, the fragmentation of the lifeworld, existential dread, polluting industrialization, a rampant and vulgar materialism—all of which have often been summarized in the phrase made famous by Max Weber: "the disenchantment of the world."

No doubt there is some truth to all of those claims, and we need to give them sufficient consideration. But clearly there were some immensely positive aspects of modernity as well, for it also gave us the liberal democracies; the ideals of equality, freedom, and justice, regardless of race, class, creed, or gender; modern medicine, physics, biology, and chemistry; the end of slavery; the rise of feminism; and the universal rights of humankind. Those, surely, are a little more noble than the mere "disenchantment of the world."

No, we need a specific definition or description of modernity that allows for all of those factors, both good (such as liberal democracies) and bad (such as the widespread loss of meaning). Various scholars, from Max Weber to Jürgen Habermas, have suggested that what specifically defined modernity was something called "the differentiation of the cultural value spheres," which especially means the differentiation of art, morals, and science. Where previously these spheres tended to be fused, modernity differentiated them and let each proceed at its own pace, with its own dignity, using its own tools, following its own discoveries, unencumbered by intrusions from the other spheres.

This differentiation allowed each sphere to make profound discoveries that, if used wisely, could lead to such "good" results as democracy, the end of slavery, the rise of feminism, and the rapid advances in medical science; but discoveries that, if used unwisely, could just as easily be perverted into the "downsides" of modernity, such as scientific imperialism, the disenchantment of the world, and totalizing schemes of world domination.

The brilliance of this definition of modernity—namely, that it differentiated the value spheres of art, morals, and science—is that it allows us to see the underpinnings of *both* the good news and the bad news of modern times. It allows us to understand both the *dignity* and the *disaster* of modernity.

Premodern cultures certainly possessed art, morals, and science. The point, rather, is that these spheres tended to be relatively "undifferentiated." To give only one example, in the Middle Ages, Galileo could not freely look through his telescope and report the results because art and morals and science were all fused under the Church, and thus the morals of the Church defined what science could—or could not—do. The Bible said (or implied) that the sun went around the earth, and that was the end of the discussion.

But with the differentiation of the value spheres, a Galileo could look through his telescope without fear of being charged with heresy and treason. Science was free to pursue its own truths unencumbered by brutal domination from the other spheres. And likewise with art and morals. Artists could, without fear of punishment, paint nonreligious themes, or even sacrilegious themes, if they wished. And moral theory was likewise free to pursue an inquiry into the good life, whether it agreed with the Bible or not.

For all those reasons and more, these *differentiations* of modernity have also been referred to as the *dignity* of modernity, for these differentiations were in part responsible for the rise of liberal democracy, the end of slavery, the growth of feminism, and the staggering advances in the medical sciences, to name but a few of these many dignities.

The "bad news" of modernity was that these value spheres did not just peacefully separate, they often flew apart completely. The wonderful *differentiations* of modernity went too far into actual *dissociation*, fragmentation, alienation. The dignity became a disaster. The growth became a cancer. As the value spheres began to dissociate, this allowed a powerful and aggressive science to begin to invade and dominate the other spheres, crowding art and morals out of any serious consideration in approaching "reality." Science became *scientism*—scientific materialism and scientific imperialism—which soon became the dominant "official" worldview of modernity.

It was this scientific materialism that very soon pronounced the other value spheres to be worthless, "not scientific," illusory, or worse. And for precisely that reason, it was scientific materialism that *pronounced the Great Nest of Being to be nonexistent.*

According to scientific materialism, the Great Nest of matter, body, mind, soul, and spirit could be thoroughly reduced to *systems of matter alone*; and matter—or matter/energy—whether in the material brain or material process systems—would account for all of reality, without remainder. Gone was mind and gone was soul and gone was spirit—gone, in fact, was the entire Great Chain, except for its pitiful bottom rung—and in its place, as Whitehead famously lamented, there was reality as "a dull affair, soundless, scentless, colorless; merely the hurrying of material, endlessly, meaninglessly." (To which he added, "Thereby, modern philosophy has been ruined.")

And so it came about that the modern West was the first major civilization in the history of the human race to deny substantial reality to the Great Nest of Being. And it is into this massive denial that we wish to attempt to reintroduce consciousness, the within, the deep, the spiritual, and thus move gently toward a more integral embrace.

THE FOUR QUADRANTS

There is, I believe, a simple way to understand this scientific reductionism—and a simple way to reverse it.

As I was comparing and contrasting the many systems listed in the charts, I noticed that, virtually without exception, they fell into four general classes. It eventually became apparent that these four classes represented the interior and the exterior of the individual and the collective, as can be seen in figure 5. The upper half of the diagram is individual, the lower half is communal or collective; the left half is interior (subjective, consciousness), and the right half is exterior (objective, material).

Thus, the Upper-Left quadrant represents the *interior of the individual*, the subjective aspect of consciousness, or individual awareness, which I have represented with the cognitive line, leading up to vision-logic. (Fig. 5 represents developments, starting with the Big Bang, up to today's average mode of consciousness; it does not cover transpersonal developments, which we will discuss in more detail later.) The full Upper-Left quadrant includes the entire spectrum of consciousness as it

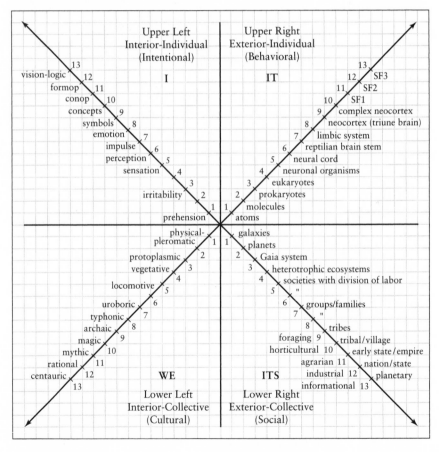

FIGURE 5. *The Four Quadrants*

appears in any individual, from bodily sensations to mental ideas to soul and spirit. The integral psychograph is a graph of this quadrant. *The language of this quadrant is I-language*: first-person accounts of the inner stream of consciousness. This is also the home of aesthetics, or the beauty that is in the "I" of the beholder.

The Upper-Right quadrant represents the *objective or exterior correlates* of those interior states of consciousness. Without worrying at the moment about the exact relation of interior mind and objective brain, we can simply note that the two are, at the least, intimately correlated. Thus, as you can see on figure 5, simple cells (prokaryotes and eukaryotes) already show "irritability," or an active response to stimuli. Neuronal organisms possess sensation and perception; a reptilian brain stem adds the capacity for impulses and instinctual behavior; a limbic system adds emotions and certain rudimentary but powerful feelings; a neocortex further adds the capacities to form symbols and concepts, and so on. (SF1, SF2, and SF3 represent higher structure-functions of the brain correlated with higher cognitions, as we will see.) Researchers that study this quadrant focus on brain mechanisms, neurotransmitters, and organic computations that support consciousness (neurophysiology, cognitive science, biological psychiatry, etc.). *The language of this quadrant is it-language*: third-person or objective accounts of the scientific facts about the individual organism.

But individuals never exist alone; every being is a being-in-the-world. Individuals are always part of some collective, and there are the "insides" of a collective and the "outsides." These are indicated in the Lower-Left and Lower-Right quadrants, respectively. The Lower Left represents the *inside of the collective*, or the values, meanings, worldviews, and ethics that are shared by any group of individuals. In figure 5 I have represented all of these with *worldviews,* such as magic, mythic, and rational (which we will discuss later). *The language of this quadrant is we-language*: second-person or I-thou language, which involves mutual understanding, justness, and goodness—in short, how you and I will arrange to get along together. This is the *cultural* quadrant.

But culture does not hang disembodied in midair. Just as individual consciousness is anchored in objective, material forms (such as the brain), so all cultural components are anchored in exterior, material, institutional forms. These *social* systems include material institutions, geopolitical formations, and the forces of production (ranging from foraging to horticultural to agrarian to industrial to informational). Because these are objective phenomena, *the language of this quadrant, like that of the objective individual, is it-language.*

Since both the Upper-Right and Lower-Right quadrants are objective "its," they can be treated as one general domain, and this means that the four quadrants can be summarized as the "Big Three" of I, we, and it. Or the aesthetics of "I," the morals of "we," and the "its" of science. The Beautiful, the Good, and the True; first-person, second-person, and third-person accounts; self, culture, and nature; art, morals, and science.[2]

In other words, the four quadrants (or simply the Big Three) are actually *the underpinnings of the modern differentiation of the value spheres* of art, morals, and science. Where premodernity had tended to fuse, or not clearly differentiate, the Big Three, modernity clearly differentiated them and set each free to pursue its own path. This differentiation was part of the dignity of modernity, which, in allowing each domain to pursue its own truths, allowed each to make stunning and far-reaching discoveries, discoveries that, even the harshest critics agree, set modernity apart from premodernity.

But something else set modernity apart. The differentiation of the Big Three went too far into the dissociation of the Big Three: the dignity drifted into disaster, and this allowed an imperialistic science to dominate the other spheres and claim that they possessed no inherent reality of their own (scientism, scientific materialism, one-dimensional man, the disenchantment of the world). Gone was mind and soul and spirit, and in their place, as far as the eye could see, the unending dreariness of a world of its: "a dull affair, soundless, scentless, colorless; merely the hurrying of material, endlessly, meaninglessly."

And so it came about that virtually the entire spectrum of consciousness, and certainly its higher levels (soul and spirit), were reduced to permutations and combinations of matter and bodies. Put bluntly, all "I's" and "we's" were reduced to "its," to objects of the scientific gaze, which, no matter how long or hard it looked, could find nothing resembling the Great Nest of human possibilities, but saw only endless patterns of process its, scurrying here and there.

CONCLUSION: THE INTEGRAL TASK

Thus, it seems that premodernity had at least one great strength that modernity lacked: it recognized the entire Great Nest of Being, which is basically a general map of higher human potentials. But premodernity also had at least one great weakness: it did not fully differentiate the value spheres at any of the levels in the Great Nest. Thus, among other things, objective-scientific investigation of the spectrum was hampered; the specific and often local cultural expressions of the Great Nest were taken to be universally valid; and the moral injunctions recommended to all were tied to those limited cultural expressions. Giordano Bruno might have experienced many of the upper levels of the Great Nest, but because the value spheres were not fully differentiated at large and their individual freedoms were not protected by law and custom, the Inquisition cheerfully burned him at the stake.

Modernity, on the other hand, did manage to differentiate the Big Three of art, morals, and science, on a large scale, so that each began to make phenomenal discoveries. But as the Big Three dissociated, and scientific colonialism began its aggressive career, all "I's" and all "we's" were reduced to patterns of objective "its," and thus all the interior stages of consciousness—reaching from body to mind to soul to spirit— were summarily dismissed as so much superstitious nonsense. The Great Nest collapsed into scientific materialism—into what we will be calling "flatland"—and there the modern world, by and large, still remains.

Our job, it thus appears, is to take the strengths of both premodernity and modernity, and jettison their weaknesses.

6

To Integrate Premodern and Modern

O NE OF OUR AIMS is to integrate the enduring truths of premodern
    and modern approaches to psychology and consciousness. We
have seen that the essence of the premodern worldview is the Great Nest
of Being, and the essence of modernity is the differentiation of the value
spheres of art, morals, and science. Thus, in order to integrate premodern and modern, we need to *integrate the Great Nest with the differentiations of modernity*. This means that each of the levels in the traditional
Great Nest needs to be carefully differentiated according to the four
quadrants. To do so would honor *both* the core claim of ancient spirituality—namely, the Great Nest—and the core claim of modernity—
namely, the differentiation of the value spheres. And this would offer a
foundation that might help us move toward a more integral psychology.

This can be represented, in a very simplistic fashion, as in figure 6,
where I have differentiated each of the levels in the Great Nest according
to the four quadrants. Modern science has already provided us with an
impressive description of the evolution or development of the Right-
Hand quadrants—atoms to molecules to cells to organisms, foraging to
agrarian to industrial to informational. And in our own discussion we
have seen numerous examples of the evolution or development in the
interior quadrants—the waves, streams, worldviews, morals, and so
forth.

But, *unlike modernity*, we wish to include *all* of the levels in the four
quadrants, reaching from body to mind to soul to spirit (and not simply
deny the higher levels). And, *unlike premodernity*, we wish to include *all*

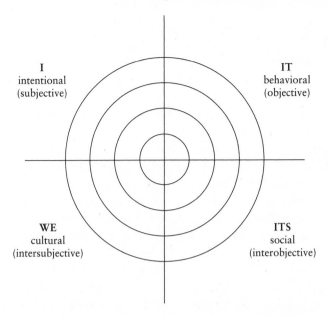

I
intentional
(subjective)

IT
behavioral
(objective)

WE
cultural
(intersubjective)

ITS
social
(interobjective)

FIGURE 6. *The Great Nest with the Four Quadrants*

of the quadrants at each of those levels (and not fuse them indiscriminately).

Thus, the job of an integral psychology (as a subset of integral studies) is to *coordinate and integrate the research findings in all of the levels in all of the quadrants.* Integral psychology obviously focuses on the Upper-Left quadrant, but the whole point of the integral approach is that for a full understanding of this quadrant, it needs to be seen in the context of all the others. This "all-level, all-quadrant" integration was denied to premodernity (which was all-level but not all-quadrant) and denied to modernity (which was all-quadrant but not all-level). Those two grave inadequacies deserve a closer look.

PREMODERNITY AT ITS BEST: ALL-LEVEL

The traditional Great Chain dealt almost exclusively with the Upper-Left quadrant, or the spectrum of consciousness as it appears in individual men and women (body to mind to soul to spirit). Although the Great Chain also referred to ontological spheres (or levels) of reality, those spheres were not clearly differentiated into the four quadrants, at least not on a wide scale. Thus, there was little or no understanding of the way in which consciousness is correlated with brain states, neurophysiology, and neurotransmitters (not reducible to brain states, but not purely "transcending" them, either). There was little or no understanding of how a person's view of the world—and a person's experience of the spectrum of consciousness—is profoundly colored and molded by the background cultural contexts in which the person lives. There was little or no understanding of how the material mode of production (foraging, horticultural, agrarian, industrial, informational) deeply affects the contours of an individual's consciousness and dramatically alters everything from gender roles to suicide rates to eating habits.

The traditional Great Chain, in short, focused mostly on the Upper-Left quadrant and almost totally ignored the differentiated details of the other quadrants, from objective brain states to intersubjective cultural contexts to interobjective social forces. It thus was a great, massive, *static* system, not yet clearly understood according to the differentiation of pluralistic cultural contexts, and their further integration into globally evolving systems—an understanding provided by modernity and postmodernity (as we will further see in chapter 12).[1] A Plotinus might personally develop and evolve all the way up the Great Chain, but the detailed correlations with the other quadrants were simply not well understood (precisely because they were not well differentiated at large).In particular, the Upper-Right quadrant (the material organism), because it is material, was placed by the perennial philosophers on the very lowest rung in the Great Chain (matter), as they failed to see that material forms are related to conscious states as exterior and interior, not merely lower and higher. Traditionally, every level above matter was usually viewed as "transcendent" to matter, *totally beyond it*, existing either in some sort of heaven or in some nonearthly estate, and this gave the Great Chain its largely "otherworldly" feel. Instead of seeing that the evolution of consciousness involves, on the *interior*, an increase in the *quality* of consciousness, and on the *exterior*, an increase in the *complexity* of matter (so that the human brain has more neural connections than there are stars in the universe: as the most complex piece of matter in existence, it is correlated with the highest degree of consciousness in the Kosmos)—instead of understanding that intimate correlation, with spirit being *interior* to nature, not perched on top of nature, the traditional Great Chain invited a rejection and devaluing of *this* world.

Moreover, when modern science discovered some of these intimate relations between "transcendent consciousness" and "material brain," the traditional Great Chain took a colossal hit from which it never recovered. If "otherworldly consciousness" is actually correlated with "this-worldly organism," might not all so-called metaphysical realities actually be aspects of *this* world? Do we even need any of those "spiritual" realities at all? Isn't everything given right here, to be seen with our senses, scientifically sharpened? In fact, isn't the belief in any sort of spiritual realities the way that men and women project their own potentials and thus remain alienated from themselves? Isn't religion nothing but the opiate of the masses?

In short, the strength of the traditional Great Chain was that it was admirably all-level, stretching from matter to body to mind to soul to spirit. But because it was not all-quadrant, it was ill-prepared to cope with modernity, and in fact was one of the first great casualties of the modern gaze.

MODERNITY AT ITS BEST: ALL-QUADRANT

The rise of modernity, I suggested, was marked by two profound events, one of which was wonderful and one of which was wretched. The good news: modernity managed, for the first time on a large scale, to fully differentiate the four quadrants (or simply the Big Three of art, morals, and science), which contributed to the many dignities of modernity.

And dignities they were. The differentiation of "I" and "we" meant that the individual I would no longer be merely subservient to the collective We (church, state, monarchy, herd mentality): the universal rights of man were everywhere proclaimed, which eventually led to the liberation movements from abolition to feminism. The differentiation of "I" and "it" meant that objective reality could no longer crush individual choice and taste, which, among other things, freed art from representation. The differentiation of "we" and "it" meant that science's investigation of objective truth was no longer subservient to dictates of church or state, which contributed to the stunning discoveries in physics, medicine, biology, and technology that, within the span of a mere few centuries, would, among other things, extend average lifespan around the world a staggering several decades. Truly, the differentiation of the value spheres allowed each to make colossal advancements previously undreamed of.

And thus we say that modernity at its best was all-quadrant. But it was not, alas, all-level, because, almost from the start, the major philosophers of the Enlightenment were committed to what we would recognize as an empirical-scientific outlook, in any of its many forms:

sensationalism, empiricism, naturalism, realism, materialism. And there was good reason for this empirical slant. If you look at figure 5, notice that all of the Left-Hand realities have Right-Hand correlates. Interior feelings, for examples, do have some sort of correlate in the objective limbic system. Formal operational thinking does seem to go with a neo-cortex, and so on. Thus, instead of trying to investigate the interior do-mains—which, after all, can be very slippery to pin down—let us focus our attention on the Right-Hand world of empirical, sensorimotor reali-ties, from material objects to concrete social institutions to brain states. Those all have simple location; they can been seen with the senses or their extensions; they are all subject to quantification and measurement; they are therefore ideally suited to the scientific method, or some sort of controlled, objective, empirical investigation.

And that is exactly what the Enlightenment—and official moder-nity—set out to do. But the inherent downsides of this approach are perhaps obvious: it is all too easy to go from saying that all interior states have exterior, objective, material correlates, to saying that all inte-rior states are nothing but material objects. In its understandable zeal to correlate all otherworldly "metaphysical" realities with this-worldly "empirical" realities (a legitimate agenda, since all Left-Hand events do indeed have Right-Hand correlates, as you can see in fig. 5), modernity inadvertently collapsed all interiors into exteriors (a disaster of the first magnitude). All subjective truths (from introspection to art to conscious-ness to beauty) and all intersubjective truths (from morals to justice to substantive values) were collapsed into exterior, empirical, sensorimotor occasions. Collapsed, that is, into dirt. Literally. The great nightmare of scientific materialism was upon us (Whitehead), the nightmare of one-dimensional man (Marcuse), the disqualified universe (Mumford), the colonization of art and morals by science (Habermas), the disenchant-ment of the world (Weber)—a nightmare I have also called flatland.

FLATLAND

Flatland is simply the belief that *only the Right-Hand world is real*—the world of matter/energy, empirically investigated by the human senses and their extensions (telescopes, microscopes, photographic plates, etc.). All of the interior worlds are reduced to, or explained by, objective/exterior terms.

There are two major forms of this flatland belief: subtle reductionism and gross reductionism. *Subtle reductionism* reduces all Left-Hand interiors to the Lower-Right quadrant; that is, reduces all "I's" and all "we's" to systems of interwoven "its" (systems theory is the classic example). *Gross reductionism* goes one step further and reduces all material systems to material atoms.

Contrary to what many popular Romantic writers have claimed, the thinkers of the Enlightenment were predominantly subtle reductionists, not gross reductionists. They believed, as scholars from Arthur Lovejoy to Charles Taylor have demonstrated, in "the great Universal System" of nature, a systems view of reality if ever there was one—but a systems view that allowed *only Right-Hand realities*.[2] The "crime of the Enlightenment" was not its gross reductionism (although there was plenty of that, as there has been ever since Democritus of Abdera), but rather its persuasive subtle reductionism, which gutted the interior dimensions and laid them out to dry in the blazing sun of scientific materialism and exterior holism: I's and we's were reduced to systems of its. As Foucault summarized the nightmare: men and women were seen as "objects of information, never subjects in communication." That subtle reductionism was applied to the interior dimensions of reality (such as soul and spirit), whereupon they promptly disappeared from view.

The many pop writers who claim that the major crime of the Enlightenment was gross reductionism and atomism, then claim that the cure for the Western flatland is *systems theory*, fail to see that systems theory is precisely part of the disease we are trying to overcome. Systems theory simply offers us holistic its instead of atomistic its, whereas both of those need to be integrated with the interior domains of the I and the we—the domains of consciousness and culture, aesthetics and morals, appreciated in their own terms. Dynamical systems theory, in all its many forms, is simply the Lower-Right quadrant, whereas we need all four quadrants without privileging any.

Thus, it is still quite common to hear statements such as: "Recently the ecologist C. S. Holling has discussed the conflict between 'two streams of science' and the confusion it creates for politicians and the public. One stream is experimental, reductionistic, and narrowly disciplinary. It is familiar to us as the scientific ideal. The less familiar stream is interdisciplinary, integrative, historical, analytical, comparative, and experimental at appropriate scales. Examples given of the first form are molecular biology and genetic engineering. The second form is found in evolutionary biology and systems approaches in populations, ecosystems, landscapes, and global systems. One stream is a science of parts, the other a science of the integration of parts."

And both are a science of flatland.

I am not saying systems theory is unimportant; I am saying it is true but partial, and being partial, it is not a genuine holism, but merely an exterior/objectivistic holism, which needs desperately a supplement of the soul to be fully complete—needs, that is, the entire interior dimensions as disclosed *in their own terms,* by their own methods, with their own truths, in their own way. So in our quest for an integral holism (which includes both the interior holism of I and we and the exterior holism of it and its), we want to *honor all four quadrants,* and not merely privilege one of them in a reductionism blatant or subtle.

In short, modernity heroically managed to differentiate the cultural value spheres (or the four quadrants)—so that, at its best, modernity was indeed all-quadrant, and that enduring contribution we can certainly honor. But then, instead of moving forward to integrate them, modernity all too often allowed that important and necessary *differentiation* to fall into unnecessary and pathological *dissociation*: art and morals and science fragmented, and this allowed an aggressive science to colonize and dominate the other spheres, so that, in "official reality," nothing was ultimately true except the truths of science, and the truths of science were all about frisky dirt. The entire interior and subjective realms—*including the entire Great Nest of Being and all of its levels, body to mind to soul to spirit*—were all rudely collapsed into their sensorimotor correlates, which is to say, they were murdered. Strained through the mesh of the monological gaze, shredded to fit the monochrome madness, all interior and subjective states—from feeling to intuition to states of consciousness to superconscious illumination—were pronounced epiphenomena at best, hallucinations at worst, and the modern world settled back, triumphant in its conquering stance, to fashion a life of dust and dirt, shadows and surfaces, scientific facts and valueless veneers.

CONCLUSION

What is required, then, if we can speak in extremely bold generalizations, is to take the enduring truths of the perennial traditions (namely, the Great Nest of Being), and combine that with the good news of modernity (namely, the differentiation of the value spheres), which means that each and every level of the Great Chain is differentiated into at least four dimensions: subjective or intentional, objective or behavioral, intersubjective or cultural, and interobjective or social—each with its own independent validity claims and equally honored forms of truth, from science to aesthetics to morals, as suggested in figure 6 (and simplified in fig. 7). This would take the best of ancient wisdom and integrate it with the best of modernity, while avoiding the downside of the ancient outlook (its lack of differentiation, pluralism, and contextualism) and the downside of modernity (its catastrophic collapse into flatland).[3]

And *that* marriage would allow us to move forward to the bright promise of a *constructive postmodernity*: the integration of art, morals, and science, at every level of the extraordinary spectrum of consciousness, body to mind to soul to spirit. That integration, I am suggesting, would involve the very best of premodernity (which was all-level), the best of modernity (which was all-quadrant), and the best of postmodernity (which, as we will see, involves their integration)—"all-level, all-quadrant."

It is toward just such an integral model that we can now turn.

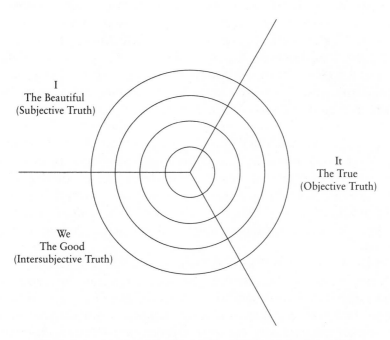

FIGURE 7. *Levels of the Good, the True, and the Beautiful*

7

Some Important Modern Pioneers

INTRODUCTION TO AN INTEGRAL APPROACH

A N INTEGRAL APPROACH to the Kosmos would be free to investigate the many levels and lines in all of the quadrants, without attempting unwarrantedly to reduce any of them to the others.

If you look at figure 5, notice that all of the entities or holons in the Right-Hand quadrants possess *simple location*. You can see all of them with your senses (or their extensions). You can see rocks, villages, organisms, ecosystems, planets, and so on. But *none of the holons in the Left-Hand quadrants possess simple location*. You cannot see, running around in the exterior world, any feelings, concepts, states of consciousness, interior illuminations, cultural values, and so forth. None of those exist in physical or sensorimotor space. They exist in emotional space, conceptual space, spiritual space, the space of mutual understanding, the space of shared values and meanings, and so forth. Although those have correlates in the objective, physical world, they cannot be *reduced* to those correlates without completely destroying their own intrinsic contours.

When it comes to individual subjective consciousness (such as waves, streams, and states), their physical correlates (from brainwaves to neurotransmitters) all exist in sensorimotor space, and thus they can be arranged in hierarchies that emphasize *quantity* or size (organisms are bigger than cells, which are bigger than molecules, which are bigger than atoms). These Right-Hand hierarchies are not hierarchies of value—cells are not better than molecules, atoms are not better than quarks—but merely hierarchies of size and physical enclosure. But the subjective, interior, or Left-Hand correlates all exist in inner spaces that unfold in hierarchies of *quality* (compassion is *better* than murder; love is *better* than hate; postconventional is better than conventional which is better than preconventional, in terms of the moral depth and care extended to others).

Thus, an integral approach allows us to map the exterior correlates of interior states, without attempting to reduce one to the other. After all, compassion might be morally better than hatred, but serotonin is *not* better than dopamine; and thus if we reduce consciousness to neurotransmitters, we completely lose all value and meaning. In other words, we fall into flatland, where all Left-Hand meaning and significance are collapsed into valueless facts and meaningless surfaces—"a dull affair, soundless, scentless, colorless; merely the hurrying of material, endlessly, meaninglessly."

An integral approach, then, does not wish to reduce I and We to systems of interwoven Its. An integral approach does not wish to commit subtle reductionism; it does not wish to reduce interior holism to exterior holism (both rather includes them both). It does not reduce all art, beauty, morals, and consciousness to a flatland system of processes, data bits, neurotransmitters, a web of life, or any other system of holistic objects. It wishes to include, in a nonreductionistic fashion, the interior domains of subjective and intersubjective waves and streams and states, spanning body to mind to soul to spirit, even though the latter all have objective correlates of various sorts that can (and should) be approached in third-person, scientific, it-language terms.

You can see some of these important correlations in figure 8. The interior waves of the full spectrum of consciousness, as they appear in an individual—from body (feelings) to mind (ideas) to soul (luminosity) to spirit (all-pervading)—are listed in the Upper-Left quadrant. These cannot be reduced to material dimensions (because, unlike matter, they do not possess simple location). Nonetheless, feelings, mental ideas, and spiritual illuminations *all have physical correlates* that can be measured by various scientific means, from EEG machines to blood chemistry to PET scans to galvanic skin response. These physical correlates are represented by dotted lines on the Right-Hand quadrants.[1]

Thus, for example, certain archaic behavioral impulses have correlates in the reptilian brain stem. Various emotional states and feelings have correlates in states of limbic system arousal. Conceptual thinking

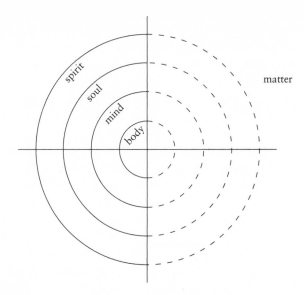

FIGURE 8. *Correlations of Interior (Consciousness) States
with Exterior (Material) States*

shows activity particularly in the frontal cortex. Various meditative states show pronounced changes in brainwave patterns (e.g., high amplitude theta and delta waves, hemispheric synchronization).[2] From bodily feelings to mental ideas to spiritual illuminations (Left Hand), there are at least some physical correlates (Right Hand) for all of the states and stages of consciousness evolution.

And why don't we simply go all the way and say that consciousness is therefore nothing but a byproduct of complex brain structures, connectionist systems, digital processes, computational biocircuits, or some such? Because none of those Right-Hand correlates have any value gradations, which are the essence of the Left-Hand domains themselves.

For example, different brainwave patterns can be registered by an EEG machine; but nothing on the machine says that one pattern is *better* than another, only that they are *different*. Thus, ethnocentric prejudice and worldcentric fairness will both register brainwave patterns on the EEG machine; but nothing on the machine says, or can say, that one of those brainwaves is better, or more valuable, or more beautiful than another. None of those value gradations show up, or can show up, on the machine registering the Right-Hand correlates, because in the Right-Hand world you only have gradations of size and simple location, not gradations of value, depth, and meaning.

Thus, to the extent that we reduce states of consciousness to brain states, we lose all values. We end up in the disqualified universe. If we reduce joy to serotonin and morals to dopamine, if we reduce consciousness to neuronal pathways and awareness to connectionist systems, we completely erase value, meaning, depth, and Divinity from the face of the Kosmos itself: we fall into flatland, we fall into subtle reductionism.[3]

(You can see a schematic representation of flatland in fig. 13 on page 182. All the interior domains of the I and we have been reduced to their corresponding its, leaving the mind dangling in midair, with no understanding of how it is related to the external world and to its own organic roots—the infamous "mind-body" problem that we will investigate in chapter 14.)

The *realities* of the Left-Hand domains—from stages of consciousness development to degrees of moral growth—are all discovered, not by looking carefully at any exterior objects, but by investigating the interior domains themselves, whereupon it becomes obvious (as research into these domains shows) that some levels and stages of growth are better, higher, deeper, more encompassing, and more liberating—moving from egocentric to sociocentric to worldcentric—and although all of those interior waves have exterior correlates in organic brain functions (which can and should be studied), they cannot be reduced to those correlates without completely destroying the very factors that define them.

Thus, let us honor the differentiations (and dignity) of modernity, without falling into the dissociations (and disaster) of modernity. Thanks to the differentiations of modernity, we can investigate any structure or state of consciousness using first-person (Upper-Left), second-person (Lower-Left), *and* third-person (Right-Hand) approaches, honoring the Big Three on every level (body to mind to soul to spirit), as indicated in figure 8. We can, for example, investigate meditative states using first-person or phenomenal accounts (the accounts of those actually doing the meditating), while also investigating any effects meditation has on brainwave activity, blood chemistry, immune functions, and neurophysiology. We can examine the ways in which various cultural backgrounds, linguistic practices, and ethical systems affect meditative states; and the types of social institutions and practices that are most conducive to those states. We can, in short, adopt an "all-quadrant, all-level" approach.[4]

EXEMPLARS

What I would like to do in this section is introduce several modern pioneers in an integral approach, an approach that, in important ways, attempts to be "all-quadrant, all-level." What all of these pioneers have in common is that they were fully cognizant of the important differentiations of modernity, and therefore they were increasingly aware of the ways in which science could supplement (not replace) religion, spirituality, and psychology. All of them, as we will see, used modern discoveries in the Big Three to elucidate the Great Nest. (All of them, in other words, were offering important elaborations of fig. 7.)

Early modern pioneers of an integral approach abound, such as Goethe, Schelling, Hegel, Fechner, and James. The early pioneers increasingly had access to scientific data on evolution, and thus increasingly understood something about the Great Nest that the premodern pioneers usually did not: it shows development not just in individuals, but in the species; not just ontogenetically, but phylogenetically. In this century, although pioneers also abound—from Steiner to Whitehead to Gebser—I would like particularly to mention James Mark Baldwin, Jürgen Habermas, Sri Aurobindo, and Abraham Maslow.

James Mark Baldwin

Of the four, James Mark Baldwin (1861–1934) is the most pivotal, and history might well find him to be America's greatest psychologist. A contemporary of James and Peirce, Baldwin forged an integral psychology and philosophy that is only now being recognized for its scope and profundity. He was the first great developmental psychologist in modern history; he was the first to clearly define a stage of development; he sought to integrate introspective phenomenology with scientific evolutionary epistemology; he believed that the three great modes of experience were aesthetic, moral, and scientific (the Big Three!), and he proposed *detailed developmental stages in each of those domains* (in other words, he was one of the first to trace development in all quadrants); he was also one of the first to outline stages of religious development. His cognitive developmental scheme was taken up by Piaget and Kohlberg; his studies on dialogical interaction were furthered by Dewey and Mead; his evolutionary epistemology was embraced by Karl Popper and Donald Campbell; his influence, in short, is almost impossible to overestimate. The only reason his name is a not a household word is that, shortly after his death, the positivist and behaviorist schools would raise flatland to a dogmatic belief, and integral studies of any sort were scrubbed from the curriculum.

Baldwin went through three main phases in his own development:

mental philosophy (of the Scottish school), evolutionary psychology, and developmental epistemology. In all of this, he was determined to include and equally honor the scientific, the moral, and the aesthetic, without trying to reduce any of them to the others or privilege any of them unwarrantedly. He included what he called "the metaphysic of intuition, the ontology of introspection" (i.e., the very real realities of the Left-Hand domains), along with a rigorous commitment to scientific experimentation. He at first found that the philosophy of Spinoza could best accommodate this integration, since Spinoza equally honored the interior/mental and the exterior/bodily; but it was the static nature of Spinoza's system that rendered it incapable of coming to grips with evolution. Baldwin came to the conclusion that "no consistent view of mental development in the individual could possibly be reached without a doctrine of the . . . development of consciousness."[5] Moreover, this developmental view had to be constructed without a retreat to mere empiricism, which badly misconstrues mental structures. Baldwin: "The older view of the soul was of a fixed substance, with fixed attributes. . . . The genetic [developmental] idea reverses all this. Instead of a fixed substance, we have the conception of a growing, developing activity. Functional psychology succeeds faculty psychology."[6] Baldwin made a deep study of the German Idealists, and found further evidence of the importance of a developmental approach.

Baldwin began this second phase (evolutionary psychology) with a reassessment of the research tools necessary: "How can the development of the mental order of phenomena be fruitfully investigated? The quantitative method, brought over into psychology from the exact sciences, must be discarded; for its ideal consisted in reducing the more complex to the more simple, the whole to its parts, the later-evolved to the earlier-existent, thus denying or eliminating just the factor which constituted or revealed what was truly genetic [developmental]."[7] Baldwin added to scientific investigation the tools of philosophical epistemology, or an analysis of the types of structures that could be empirically investigated, and this eventually led to his third phase, developmental epistemology (represented in his acknowledged classic, *Thought and Things: A Study of the Development and Meaning of Thought, or Genetic Logic*).

Baldwin came to see consciousness as developing through a half-dozen qualitatively distinct stages or levels of consciousness (see chart 11), each of which hierarchically differentiates and reintegrates the lower elements on a higher level: the *prelogical* (similar to sensorimotor), the *quasilogical* (preop and early conop), the *logical* (formop), the *extralogical* (vision-logic), and finally, the *hyperlogical*, which we might call supralogical or translogical, for it represents a satori-like nondual awareness that transcends the subject and object dualism. This highest stage, as Baldwin put it, is "a form of contemplation . . . in which the immediacy of experience constantly seeks to reestablish itself. In the highest form of such contemplation, a form which comes to itself as genuine and profound aesthetic experience, we find a synthesis of motives, a mode in which the strands of the earlier and diverging dualisms are merged and fused . . . an experience whose essential character is just its unity of comprehension, [wherein] consciousness has its completest and most direct and final apprehension of what reality is and means."[8] This experience is of waking reality as a whole, immediately apprehended (what we would recognize as psychic-level cosmic consciousness, or union with the entire empirical world: "nature mysticism"). As Baldwin often pointed out, in this unity consciousness, all of the dualisms that were created during development (such as inner/outer, mind/body, subject/object, true/false, and good/bad) are transcended and united in an experience of completeness. And he stressed that this was hyperlogical, not prelogical. Through those half-dozen or so basic levels of consciousness, Baldwin traced the lines and stages of moral, aesthetic, religious, scientific, and self development.

In its general completeness, it was an integral psychology and philosophy the likes of which have rarely been equaled. Others, such as Aurobindo, would grasp the many stages of spiritual development with greater precision (what Baldwin called "hyperlogical" actually consists of at least four distinct levels of consciousness); others would display a more powerfully philosophical mind (Habermas, for example); still others would make more contributions to an experimental psychology. But few combined all of them with the rigor, depth, and breadth of Baldwin.

Baldwin's influence, as I said, was considerable. His stage-by-stage account of the dialectical development of self and other (in all three major domains—moral, aesthetic, scientific) had a major impact on the social sciences. Kohlberg's account is typical: "As I read more deeply into Baldwin, I realized that Piaget had derived all the basic ideas with which he started in the twenties from Baldwin: assimilation, accommodation, schema, and adualism, 'egocentricity,' or undifferentiated character of the child's mind. I saw, too, that Piaget's overall enterprise, the creation of a genetic epistemology and ethics which would use epistemology to pose problems for developmental psychology and use developmental observation to help answer epistemological questions, had also been Baldwin's."[9] But unlike Piaget, Baldwin's genius was his integral vision: he refused to reduce all development to cognitive development, which is why, as an overall system, Baldwin's is much more credible and enduring, as John Broughton and others have pointed out.

In moral development, psychologists and sociologists were generally agreed, by the early 1900s, that moralization proceeds through three broad stages. As McDougall put it in 1908: "The fundamental problem of social psychology is the moralization of the individual by society. This moralization proceeds through, first, the stage in which the operation of the instinctive impulses is modified by the influence of rewards and punishments; second, the stage in which conduct is controlled in the main by anticipation of social praise and blame; and third, the stage in which conduct is regulated by an ideal that enables man to act in a way that seems right to him, regardless of the praise or blame of his immediate environment."[10] These are, of course, the three broad stages now most often known as preconventional, conventional, and postconventional. As Kohlberg points out, "The Dewey-McDougall levels [just outlined] are described from the standpoint of the relation of the self to society. They do not clearly reflect the child's qualitative cognitive and epistemological growth. Our data suggested that Baldwin's three-level distinctions [adual, dualistic, and ethical] defined 'stages' (or sublevels) in the basic series, preconventional, conventional, and postconventional (autonomous-ethical)."[11] In other words, by also using Baldwin's developmental levels, Kohlberg was able to suggest a six-stage scheme of moral development, a scheme that research so far has found to be largely invariant and universal.[12]

Baldwin also presented one of the first, and still one of the most sophisticated, accounts of the stages of religious development. In order to do so, Baldwin had first to argue (successfully, I believe) that religious or spiritual interests were an independent domain, not reducible to economic, scientific, or moral interests. Rather, "Religious motivations stand alongside theoretical, moral, and aesthetic interests as one of the irreducible and, when properly understood, ubiquitous motivations of persons."[13] This pioneering line of research was later taken up most notably by James Fowler.

Perhaps most interesting of all is the fact that Baldwin saw consciousness development leading to, and culminating in, an experience of a type of profound unity consciousness, which was for Baldwin a supremely aesthetic experience that simultaneously united both the highest morals and the highest science.[14] This is, of course, a version of aesthetic idealism (derived from Kant, Schelling, Schiller), but which Baldwin reworked into his own system called *pancalism*, a word which meant that this cosmic consciousness is "all-comprehensive, with no reference outside of itself."

This unity experience is prefigured in the contemplation of a beautiful artwork. The artwork itself exists in the objective, exterior world, and *as an object* can be studied by scientific investigation. But the beauty and the value of the artwork is an interior and *subjective state*, brought to the art by the viewer (although anchored in objectively real features of the work). Thus, when you contemplate an artwork that you love and value, you are joining the subjective and objective worlds—the worlds of values and facts, morals and science, Left and Right—in a unified embrace.

Furthermore—and this is the crucial addition—according to Baldwin, "It is the nature of such synthetic experience to move beyond specific aesthetic objects of contemplation to reality itself as a whole. Such synthetic experience includes the idea of God, but now seen as referring to that organic or spiritual whole within which self and world can finally be known."[15] This aesthetic strand, too, undergoes stage by stage development, culminating in the consummate experience of cosmic consciousness.

Baldwin, in short, was one of the first great modern researchers who, in essence, took the Great Nest of Being and Knowing—prelogical body to logical mind to translogical spirit—and differentiated each of those levels into aesthetic, moral, and scientific modes of experience, and further, showed the development of each of those lines through each of those major levels. His accomplishment is not likely to be soon equaled.

Jürgen Habermas

Jürgen Habermas (born 1929) has, in the course of his distinguished career, applied his integral vision across a wide variety of domains—philosophy, psychology, anthropology, evolutionary theory, linguistics, politics (see chart 10). Habermas's overall model has three tiers. First is a theory of communication ("universal pragmatics"), which serves as the starting point for an account of the development of subjective (aesthetic), intersubjective (moral), and objective (scientific) consciousness (i.e., the Big Three; this developmental account of the individual is the second tier). The third tier, based on the first two, is an account of sociocultural evolution as a reconstruction of historical materialism, and a synthesis of systems theory, lifeworld, scientific, aesthetic, and moral domains.[16]

Habermas is the most comprehensive developmental philosopher now working. However, lamentably, he leaves out and totally ignores any of the stages of I, we, and it consciousness beyond vision-logic. As I would put it, Habermas is all-quadrant, but not quite all-level. Moreover, in placing his reliance on linguistically generated structures of understanding, Habermas places an unfortunate wedge between human and nonhuman nature, so that his approach to nature is essentially instrumental. In short, we might say that his integral view is inadequate to both the prerational and the transrational domains—inadequate to both nature and spirit (a major flaw, some would say). Nonetheless, for the ground it covers, his work has already assured him a place in history as being at least one of the half-dozen most important thinkers of this century, and it appears that no integral view can hope to succeed that ignores his profound contributions.

Sri Aurobindo

Aurobindo (1872–1950) was India's greatest modern philosopher-sage, and the magnitude of his achievements is hard to convey convincingly. His "integral yoga" is a concerted effort to unite and integrate the ascending (evolutionary) and descending (involutionary) currents in human beings, thus uniting otherworldly and this-worldly, transcendent and immanent, spirit and matter. He covered much of the scope of India's vast spiritual heritage and lineages, and brought many of them together into a powerful synthesis. He was also one of the first truly great sages to have access to the evolutionary record (disclosed by the differentiations of modernity), which allowed him to expand his system from a dynamic developmentalism of ontogeny (which all great perennial philosophers possessed) to one of phylogeny as well. Aurobindo's integral yoga, we might say, was India's first great synthesis of the truths of the premodern Great Nest with the truths brought by the differentiations of modernity.

Aurobindo's overall model of consciousness consists basically of three systems: (1) the surface/outer/frontal consciousness (typically gross state), consisting of physical, vital, and mental levels of consciousness; (2) a deeper/psychic/soul system "behind" the frontal in each of its levels (inner physical, inner vital, inner mental, and innermost psychic or soul; typically subtle state); and (3) the vertical ascending/descending systems stretching both above the mind (higher mind, illumined mind, intuitive mind, overmind, supermind; including causal/nondual) and below the mind (the subconscient and inconscient)—all nested in Sat-Chit-Ananda, or pure nondual Spirit.[17]

Aurobindo's greatest shortcoming is a shortcoming faced by all theorists, namely, the unavailability of the important discoveries made since his time. Aurobindo was most concerned with the transformations of consciousness (Upper Left) and the correlative changes in the material body (Upper Right). Although he had many important insights on the social and political system, he did not seem to grasp the actual interrelations of cultural, social, intentional, and behavioral, nor did his analysis at any point proceed on the level of intersubjectivity (Lower Left) and interobjectivity (Lower Right). He did not, that is, fully assimilate the differentiations of modernity. But the levels and modes that Aurobindo did cover make his formulations indispensable for any truly integral model.

Abraham Maslow

Abraham Maslow (1908–1970) is well known enough that I will only make a few passing comments. Like all truly great integral thinkers—from Aurobindo to Gebser to Whitehead to Baldwin to Habermas—he was a developmentalist. He was one of the first to gather substantial empirical and phenomenological evidence suggesting that each level in the Great Nest has a different need, that these needs emerge hierarchically and prepotently, and that each of us carries the potential for all of these levels-needs (see chart 7). Instrumental in founding both the Third Force (Humanistic-Existential Psychology) and the Fourth Force (Transpersonal), Maslow's ideas had an extraordinary impact on education, business, and values research.

Maslow's work fell into temporary disrepute during the eighties, when an extreme postmodernism, dominating both academia and the counterculture, made all forms of holarchy subservient to what certainly seemed to be a form of flatland dogmatism. But as the world awakens from that reductionism, Maslow's pioneering works are there to greet all who would genuinely embrace a more integral and holarchical view.

All of these integral thinkers are simply a few of the pioneering geniuses that can help guide us to even further integral visions. No matter how great any of them were, each new generation has a chance to move the integral vision forward in a substantial way, simply because new information, data, and discoveries are constantly being made. Hegel's towering brilliance was utterly bereft of exposure to Asian traditions. Schelling had no access to substantial anthropological data. Aurobindo missed the meticulous studies of modern cognitive science. Habermas is of a generation that never quite grasped the transpersonal revolution. Likewise, whatever contributions any of us might make will only be the shoulders, we can hope, upon which others will soon stand.

PART THREE

FRUITION

An Integral Model

A TRULY INTEGRAL PSYCHOLOGY, I have suggested, would involve the very best of premodernity (the Great Nest), modernity (the differentiation of the value spheres), and postmodernity (their integration across all levels in the Great Nest)—"all-level, all-quadrant." We can now begin to pull these strands together.

8

The Archeology of Spirit

OVERVIEW

THE FOREGOING SECTIONS introduced us to a few of the many theorists and the many strands of research that need to be embraced, in a general way, for any current integral view.

They also introduced the major components, as I see them, of the evolution of consciousness: the *basic levels*, structures, or waves in the Great Nest (matter, body, mind, soul, spirit); the *developmental lines* or streams (moral, aesthetic, religious, cognitive, affective, etc.) that move relatively independently through the great waves; the *states*, or temporary states of consciousness (such as peak experiences, dream states, and altered states); the *self*, which is the seat of identity, will, and defenses, and which has to navigate, balance, and integrate all the various levels, lines, and states that it encounters; and the *self-related lines*, which are the developmental lines most intimately connected with the self (such as the self's central identity, its morals, and its needs). In short: waves, streams, states, self, and self-streams.

Altered states are very important, and certainly get much of the attention, but for them to contribute to *development* they must become structures/traits. Self-streams are crucial, but they are a subset of streams in general. Thus, in the simplest of terms, we can say that development comes down to waves, streams, and self.

THE BASIC WAVES

I have included, in charts 1a and 1b, a summary of some of the major components of an integral model.[1] We have already discussed some of these features, and I mean for all of that discussion to be included here. But I will simply make a few further comments about this model based on some of the items in the charts, and specifically with a view toward an "all-level, all-quadrant" approach.

On the left side, in each of the charts, are the basic structures, levels, or waves in the Great Nest of Being and Knowing.[2] What is worth keeping in mind is that, taken together, the basic levels in virtually every major system, ancient and modern, Eastern and Western, simply describe a vast *morphogenetic field*, or developmental space, and one that is *migratory*—it grades holarchically, transcending and including, nests within nests indefinitely, inviting a development that is envelopment.

Further, these different migratory conceptions listed on the charts show a remarkable harmony, not in specifics, but in the developmental space they portray. We have seen that scholars such as Huston Smith have made this argument for the perennial philosophy; what is not as often appreciated is that modern researchers (working on the stages from sensorimotor to formal to postformal) have reached quite similar conclusions. As Francis Richards and Michael Commons put it, after surveying the developmental research and data from Fischer, Sternberg, Kohlberg, Armon, Pascual-Leone, Powell, Labouvie-Vief, Arlin, Sinott, Basseches, Koplowitz, and Alexander (all of whom are represented on the charts): "The stage sequences [of all of these theorists] can be aligned across a common *developmental space*. The harmony of alignment shown suggests a possible reconciliation of [these] theories. . . ."[3]

What I have done is to take the results of that research, along with dozens of other modern theorists, and attempted to integrate it with the best of the perennial philosophers, to arrive at a master template of a *full-spectrum developmental space*, reaching from matter to body to mind to soul to spirit. (The holarchical nature of this unfolding is discussed in an endnote.)[4] As we have seen, these are the basic waves of being and knowing through which the various developmental streams will flow, all of which are balanced and (ideally) integrated by the self in its remarkable journey from subconscious to self-conscious to superconscious.

But, of course, this tortuous journey is not without its perils.

THE SELF AND ITS PATHOLOGIES

Column two in chart 1a gives the "general self-sense"—some of the general names I often use for the developmental stages of the proximate self (bodyego, persona, ego, centaur, soul). Notice that I have drawn a continuing arrow for each of them. There is a persistent confusion in the literature about whether, for example, the ego is retained or lost in higher development. Most transpersonal researchers refer to the higher stages as being "beyond ego" or "transegoic," which seems to imply the ego is lost. But this confusion is almost entirely semantic. If by ego you mean an *exclusive* identification with the personal self, then that *exclusiveness* is mostly lost or dissolved in higher development—that "ego" is largely destroyed (and the higher stages are correctly called transegoic). But if by ego you mean a functional self that relates to the conventional world, then that ego is definitely retained (and often strengthened). Likewise, if you mean—as psychoanalysis does—that an important part of the ego is its capacity for detached witnessing, then that ego is definitely retained (and almost always strengthened)—when Jack Engler says that "Meditation increases ego strength," he is absolutely right.[5] Also, if by ego you mean—as ego psychology does—the psyche's capacity for integrating, then that ego is also retained and strengthened.[6]

In short, the *exclusiveness* of an identity with a given self (bodyego, persona, ego, centaur, soul) is dissolved or released with each higher stage of self growth, but the important *functional capacities* of each are retained, incorporated (holarchically), and often strengthened in succeeding stages. The period of exclusive identification is what is indicated by the solid line in column two (a period that eventually comes to an end with higher growth). But the functional capacities of that stage remain as important subholons in subsequent stages, and that I have indicated with the continuing arrow. (In other words, the solid line indicates when each of those selves is the proximate self, or I; when its major dominant phase is over and consciousness moves on, that self becomes part of the distal self, or me.)

I'll briefly mention the following items in chart 1a, then we will look at them more closely in the next three sections. Column three ("specific aspects") indicates in more detail the nature of the proximate self at each of its stages and substages.[7] Column four ("defenses") gives some of the major defense mechanisms that can develop at each of the basic waves. "Possible pathology" refers in a very general way to the types and levels of pathology that can occur as the self navigates each of the basic waves. "Fulcrums" refers to the major milestones in the self's development—in other words, what happens to the proximate self when its center of gravity is at a particular level of consciousness.[8] And "treatment" is a summary of the types of psychological and spiritual therapies that appear to be most helpful for the different types of pathologies that beset the different levels of consciousness.

As we saw, each time *the center of gravity* of the self moves through a basic level of the Great Nest, it goes through a *fulcrum* (or a milestone) of its own development: it first identifies with a new level, then disidentifies with and transcends that level, then includes and integrates that level from the next higher level.[9] Throughout this discussion I have often summarized the Great Nest as possessing nine basic levels (as functional groupings: sensorimotor, phantasmic-emotional, rep-mind, rule/role mind, formal-reflexive, vision-logic, psychic, subtle, and causal/nondual—you can see these listed on the left column in each of the charts), and therefore I outline the *nine correlative fulcrums* that the self goes through in a complete evolution or development through the entire Great Nest. (Based on empirical research, such as Stan Grof's, I also include the birth fulcrum, F-0, which gives us ten or so major, qualitatively distinct milestones in the self's journey from conception to enlightenment.)

Each time the self (the proximate self) steps up to a new and higher sphere in the Great Nest, it can do so in a relatively healthy fashion—which means it smoothly differentiates and integrates the elements of that level—or in a relatively pathological fashion—which means it either *fails to differentiate* (and thus remains in fusion/fixation/arrest) or it *fails to integrate* (which results in repression, alienation, fragmentation). Each level of the Great Nest has a qualitatively different architecture, and thus each fulcrum (and pathology) likewise has a qualitatively different texture. We can now look more closely at these different pathologies faced by the self on its jostling journey through the great River.

LOWER PATHOLOGIES (F-0 TO F-3)

One of the major breakthroughs in depth psychology of the last several decades has been the realization that there are not just different *types* of psychopathology (e.g., obsessive-compulsive disorders, phobias, anxiety, depression) but also different *levels* of psychopathology (e.g., neurotic, borderline, and psychotic). These different levels of pathology are correlated, in part, with the three major stages of early self-development (particularly as disclosed by the pioneering research of Rene Spitz, Edith Jakobson, Margaret Mahler, and others). A developmental miscarriage at any of these stages can contribute to a corresponding level of pathology.[10] These are not, of course, rigid and discrete levels like the floors in a building, but overlapping waves of self-development and the many things that can go wrong at each of those general waves.[11]

These three early waves of self-development can be summarized fairly simply. The self starts out relatively undifferentiated from its environment.[12] That is, it cannot easily tell where its body stops and the physical environment begins (this is the start of fulcrum-1). Somewhere during the first year, the infant learns that if it bites a blanket, it does not hurt, but if it bites its thumb, it hurts: there is a difference between body and matter. The infant differentiates its body from the environment, and thus its identity switches from fusion with the material world to an identity with the emotional-feeling body (which begins fulcrum-2). As the conceptual mind begins to emerge and develop (especially around 3 to 6 years), the child eventually differentiates the conceptual mind and the emotional body (this is fulcrum-3). The proximate self's identity has thus gone from matter to body to early mind (and we can see that it is well on its way through the waves in the Great Nest).

Each of those self-stages (or fulcrums) ideally involves both *differentiation* and *integration* (transcendence and inclusion). The self differentiates from the lower level (e.g., body), identifies with the next higher level (e.g., mind), and then integrates the conceptual mind with the feelings of the body. A failure at any of those points results in a pathology—a malformation, crippling, or narrowing of the self in its otherwise ever-expanding journey. Thus, if the mind fails to differentiate from bodily feelings, it can be overwhelmed with painfully strong emotions (not simply feel strong emotions, but be capsized by them), histrionic mood swings are common, there is great difficulty with impulse control, and developmental arrest often occurs that that point. On the other hand, if mind and body differentiate but are not then integrated (so that *differentiation* goes too far into *dissociation*), the result is a classic neurosis, or the *repression* of bodily feelings by mental structures (ego, superego, harsh conscience).

Thus, the differentiation-and-integration process can go wrong at each and every self-stage (or fulcrum), and the *level* of the fulcrum helps determine the *level* of pathology. In fulcrum-1, if the self does not correctly differentiate from, and integrate its images of, the physical environment, the result can be psychosis (the individual cannot tell where his body stops and the environment begins, he hallucinates, and so on). In fulcrum-2, if the emotional bodyself has difficulty differentiating itself from others, the result can be narcissism (others are treated as extensions of the self) or borderline disorders (others are constantly invading and disrupting the self's fragile boundaries). In fulcrum-3, as we just saw, a failure to differentiate leaves a *fusion* with the labile emotional self, whereas a failure to integrate leads to a *repression* of the emotional self by the newly emerging mental-egoic self (classic psychoneurosis).

Another way to say the same thing is that each level of self development has different types of defenses. The self, at every level, will attempt to defend itself against pain, disruption, and ultimately death, and it will do so *using whatever tools are present at that level*. If the self has concepts, it will use concepts; if it has rules, it will use rules; if it has vision-logic, it will use vision-logic. At the first fulcrum (as you can see in chart 1a), the self only has sensations, perceptions, and exocepts (which are the early forms of sensorimotor cognition), along with the very earliest of impulses and images; thus the archaic self can defend itself in only the most rudimentary ways, such as fusing with the physical environment, hallucinatory wish fulfillment (in images), and perceptual distortion. At fulcrum-2, the self has the added tools of more intense feelings, emotions, and newly emerging symbols, and thus it can defend itself in more elaborate ways, such as splitting (dividing the self and the world into "all good" and "all bad" representations), projecting its feelings and emotions onto others, and fusing itself with the emotional world of others. By the time of fulcrum-3, the self has added elaborate concepts and beginning rules, and these very powerful mental tools can be used to forcefully repress the body and its feelings, displace its desires, create reaction formations, and so on. (Many of these defenses are listed in chart 1a, and the research behind them is discussed in the endnote.)[13] In short, the level of defenses, the level of self development, the level of pathology—all are facets of the same migratory unfolding across the qualitatively distinct waves in the Great Nest.

Likewise, in each of those cases, a somewhat different treatment has been found to be most helpful. Starting with fulcrum-3 and moving down the spectrum: With typical neurosis (F-3), the treatment involves relaxing and undoing the repression barrier, recontacting the repressed or shadow feelings, and reintegrating them into the psyche, so that the ongoing flow of consciousness unfolding can more smoothly continue.

These therapeutic approaches are generically called *uncovering techniques* because they attempt to uncover and reintegrate the shadow. This "regression in service of the ego" temporarily returns consciousness to the early trauma (or simply puts it back in touch with the alienated feelings, drives, or impulses), allows it to befriend and reintegrate the alienated feelings, and thus restores a relative harmony to the psyche. These approaches include classic psychoanalysis, aspects of Gestalt Therapy, the shadow facet of Jungian therapy, Gendlin's focusing, and aspects of ego psychology and self psychology, among others.[14]

(In therapies that acknowledge the higher or transpersonal domains, this healing regressive spiral is often used as a prelude to evolutionary and progressive transcendence to higher levels, as indicated in fig. 9. This curative spiral is not a regression to a higher ground, but to a lower one, which helps reset the foundations for a surer transcendence.)[15]

Moving down to the borderline level of pathology (F-2), the problem is not that a strong self represses the body, but that there isn't enough of a strong self to begin with. Techniques here are therefore called *structure building*: they attempt to build up the self's boundaries and fortify ego strength. There is little repressed material to "uncover," because the self has not been strong enough to repress much of anything. Rather, the aim of therapy here is to help complete the separation-individuation stage (F-2), so that the person emerges with a strong self and clearly differentiated-integrated emotional boundaries. These F-2 approaches

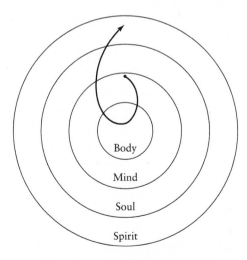

FIGURE 9. *The Curative Spiral*

include aspects of object relations therapy (Winnicott, Fairbairn, Guntrip), psychoanalytic ego psychology (Mahler, Blanck and Blanck, Kernberg), self psychology (Kohut), and numerous integrations of those approaches (such as those of John Gedo and James Masterson).

The earliest fulcrums (F-0 and F-1) have, until recently, resisted treatment (except for medication/pacification), precisely because they are so primitive and difficult to access. However, recent avant-garde (and highly controversial) treatments, ranging from Janov's primal scream to Grof's holotropic breathwork, have claimed various sorts of success, by again "temporarily regressing" to the deep wounds, reexperiencing them in full awareness, and thus allowing consciousness to move forward in a more integrated fashion.

INTERMEDIATE (F-4 TO F-6) AND HIGHER (F-7 TO F-9) PATHOLOGIES

As we move into the intermediate and higher fulcrums, we see the same overall process: because each of the basic waves in the Great Nest has a different architecture, each level of self development has a *qualitatively different* level of pathology, different types of defenses, and a correspondingly different type of treatment.[16] In fulcrum-4 (typically ages 6–12), the rule/role mind begins to emerge and the self's center of gravity starts to identify with that wave. The self begins to take the role of others, and therefore begins to shift from egocentric/preconventional to sociocentric/conventional. If something goes wrong at this general wave, we get a "script pathology"—all of the false, misleading, and sometimes crippling scripts, stories, and myths that the self learns. Therapy (such as cognitive therapy) helps the individual to uproot these false ideas about itself and replace them with more accurate, healthy scripts. In fulcrum-5, as the self-reflexive ego emerges, and the center of gravity begins to shift from conventional/conformist to postconventional/individualistic, the self is faced with "identity versus role confusion": how is the self to discover who or what it is, once it no longer depends on society (with its conventional ethics, rules, and roles) to make decisions for it? In fulcrum-6, the panoramic view of vision-logic brings existential issues and problems to the forefront, along with the possibility of a more fully integrated bodymind (or centauric self). In fulcrum-7, the transpersonal domains begin to come into focus, not simply as passing peak experiences, but as new and higher structures—with new and higher possible pathologies (as we will see below).

I have dealt with these nine or ten levels of pathology, defenses, and treatments in various books, and Rowan, among others, has given an extensive discussion of pathologies and treatments at each of these fulcrums.[17] For this simple overview, all we need note is that each level of the Great Nest has a qualitatively different architecture, and thus each wave of self-development, self-pathology, and treatment likewise has a qualitatively different tone. If you acknowledge any of the basic stages of development, you can probably also acknowledge that something can go wrong with any of them, thus producing qualitatively different pathologies and treatments.

The nine or ten general levels of therapy that I outlined are meant to be suggestive only; they are broad guidelines as to what we can expect, based on the extensive evidence compiled by numerous different schools of developmental psychology and contemplative spirituality. There is, needless to say, *a great deal of overlap between these therapies*. For example, I list "script pathology" and "cognitive therapy" as being especially relevant to fulcrum-4, which is where the self identifies, for the first time, with the rule/role mind and thus can begin to take the *role* of others and learn the *rules* of its society. As we saw, if something goes wrong during this general developmental period, the result is a "script pathology," a series of distorted, demeaning, unfair ideas and scripts about oneself and others. Cognitive therapy has excelled in rooting out these maladaptive scripts and replacing them with more accurate, benign, and therefore healthy ideas and self-concepts. But to say cognitive therapy focuses on this level of consciousness development is *not* to say it has no benefit at other levels, for clearly it does. The idea, rather, is that the farther away we get from this level, the less relevant (but never completely useless) cognitive therapy becomes. Developments in fulcrums 1 and 2 are mostly preverbal and preconceptual, so conceptual reprogramming does not directly address these levels; and developments beyond fulcrum-6 are mostly transmental and transrational, so mental reprogramming, in and of itself, is limited in its effectiveness.

So it is not that a given therapy applies only to one level of development, but that, in focusing on one or two levels, most forms of therapy increasingly lose their effectiveness when applied to more distant realms. All too often, one particular psychotherapeutic approach (psychoanalysis, Gestalt, neurolinguistic programming, holotropic breathwork, Transactional Analysis, biological psychiatry, yoga, etc.) is used for *all* types of psychopathologies, often with unfortunate results. Rather, the one thing we learn from the existence of the multiple levels of the spectrum of consciousness is just how many different dimensions of existence there are, and how a sensitivity to these multiple dimensions demands a multiplicity of treatment modalities.

Also, it is generally true, as I first suggested in *The Spectrum of Consciousness*, that the therapies of one level will acknowledge and often use the therapies from lower levels, but they are reluctant to recognize any level higher than their own. Thus, classical psychoanalysis will recognize the importance of instinctual and emotional drives, but downplay the importance of cognitive scripts themselves. Cognitive therapists emphasize the importance of those scripts but downplay or ignore the importance of the total psychophysical organism (or centaur), which humanistic and existential therapists emphasize. And many existential therapists vehemently deny the importance or even existence of the transpersonal and transrational levels. By assigning each therapy a general level on the overall spectrum of consciousness, I am also taking those particular facts into account—the therapy at one level will usually acknowledge and even use all of the therapies from lower levels, but rarely from any higher (whose existence, in fact, they often pathologize).

TYPICAL THERAPY

Not often will a therapist see a client so evolved as to present problems from all nine or ten fulcrums. Most adults' center of gravity is somewhere around mythic, rational, or centauric; and they have occasionally had psychic or subtle peak experiences (which they may or may not have trouble integrating). Typical individual therapy therefore tends to involve strengthening boundaries (F-2), contacting and befriending shadow feelings (F-3), cognitive rescripting (F-4), and Socratic dialogue (F-5 and F-6), with specific issues of getting in touch with one's feelings (F-3), dealing with belongingness needs (F-4), self-esteem (F-5), and self-actualization (F-6). Sometimes these are accompanied by issues of integrating peak experiences and spiritual illuminations (psychic, subtle, causal, or nondual), which need to be carefully differentiated from prerational magic and mythic structures. (See *Eye to Eye* for suggestions on differentiating between preformal magic and mythic and postformal psychic and subtle.)

As we have seen, intense regressive therapies (Grof, Janov) attempt to reexperience aspects of the earliest fulcrums (pre-, peri-, and neonatal; F-0 and F-1). Psychoanalytic ego psychology and self psychology tend to deal with the next but still rather early fulcrums (especially F-2 and F-3). Cognitive and interpersonal therapy tend to focus on beliefs and scripts (F-4 and F-5).[18] Humanistic-existential therapies tend to deal with all those issues *and* on actualizing an authentic self, existential being, bodymind integration, or centaur (F-6).[19] And transpersonal therapies, while addressing all of those personal fulcrums, also include various approaches to the higher spiritual domains (F-7, F-8, F-9; we will discuss these below; some good introductions to transpersonal psychology/therapy are listed in the endnote).[20]

Is there a common thread to all these levels of treatment? A common thread to psychoanalytic, cognitive, humanistic, transpersonal? In a very general sense, yes. It is this: *awareness in and of itself is curative.* Every therapeutic school we have mentioned attempts, in its own way, to allow consciousness to encounter (or reencounter) facets of experience that were previously alienated, malformed, distorted, or ignored.[21] This is *curative* for a basic reason: *by experiencing these facets fully,* consciousness can genuinely acknowledge these elements and thereby let go of them: see them as an object, and thus differentiate from them, de-embed from them, *transcend them*—and then integrate them into a more encompassing, compassionate embrace.

The curative catalyst, in every case, is bringing awareness or consciousness to bear on an area of experience that is (or has been) denied, distorted, falsified, or ignored. Once that area enters (or reenters) consciousness, then it can rejoin the ongoing flow of evolutionary unfolding, instead of remaining behind, stuck in a distorted or alienated loop and sending up painful symptoms (anxiety, depression, phobias) as the only indication of its imprisonment. Encountering (or reencountering) these disturbed or ignored facets allows them to be differentiated (transcended) and integrated (included) in the ongoing waves of ever-expanding consciousness.

In short, in the grand morphogenetic migration from matter through body through mind through soul through spirit, facets of consciousness can be split off, distorted, or neglected at any of those waves—facets of the body can be repressed, elements of the mind can be distorted, aspects of the soul can be denied, the call of spirit can be ignored. In each case, those alienated facets remain as "stick points" or lesions in awareness, split off or avoided—a fragmentation that produces pathology, with the type of pathology depending in large part on the level of the fragmentation. Contacting (or recontacting) those facets, meeting them with awareness, and thus experiencing them fully, allows consciousness to differentiate (transcend) and integrate (include) their important voices in the overall flow of evolutionary unfolding.

SUBPERSONALITIES

I mentioned that the self contains numerous *subpersonalities*, and nowhere does this become more obvious or significant than in pathology, diagnosis, and treatment. Authorities on subpersonalities point out that the average person often has around a dozen or more subpersonalities, variously known as parent ego state, child ego state, adult ego state, topdog, underdog, conscience, ego ideal, idealized ego, false self, authentic self, real self, harsh critic, superego, libidinous self, and so on.[22] Most of these are experienced, in part, as different vocal or subvocal voices in one's inner dialogue. Sometimes one or more subpersonalities become almost completely dissociated, which can result, in extremes, in multiple personality disorder. For most people, however, these various subpersonalities simply vie for attention and behavioral dominance, forming a type of subconscious society of selves that must be negotiated by the proximate self at any of its stages.

Each of these subpersonalities can be at a different level of development in any of its lines. In other words, subpersonalities can form at virtually any of the fulcrums: archaic subpersonalities (F-0, F-1), magical subpersonalities (F-2, F-3), mythic subpersonalities (F-3, F-4), rational subpersonalities (F-5, F-6), and even soul subpersonalities (F-7, F-8).[23]

Thus, considerable research suggests that not only can the various developmental lines unfold relatively independently, so can any of the various subpersonalities. For *both* of these reasons, *a person can therefore have facets of his or her consciousness at many different levels* of morals, worldviews, defenses, pathologies, needs, and so forth (which can be mapped on an integral psychograph, as in figs. 2 and 3). For example, the child ego state is usually generated at F-2 and F-3 (with preconventional morals, magic worldview, and safety needs), which becomes perfectly obvious when a person is gripped by a child ego state (e.g., explosive temper tantrum, with egocentric demands, narcissistic worldview), which can blow through the personality, commandeer it for minutes or hours, and then pass as quickly as it came, returning the person to his or her more typical, average self (which may be otherwise quite highly evolved).

Thus, when I outline nine or ten general levels of consciousness, worldviews, pathology, treatment, and so on, that does not in any way mean that a person is simply at one stage, with one type of defense, one type of pathology, one type of need, and one type of treatment. The dozen or more subpersonalities can each be at a different level, so that the individual has numerous types and levels of needs, defenses, and pathologies (e.g., from borderline to neurotic to existential to spiritual), and will therefore respond to a wide variety of therapeutic endeavors.

Subpersonalities, in their benign form, are simply functional self-presentations that navigate particular psychosocial situations (a father persona, a wife persona, a libidinal self, an achiever self, and so on). Subpersonalities become problematic only to the degree of their dissociation, which runs along a continuum from mild to moderate to severe. The difficulty comes when any of these functional personalities are strongly dissociated, or split from access to the conscious self, due to repeated trauma, developmental miscarriages, recurrent stress, or selective inattention. These submerged personae—with their now-dissociated and fixated set of morals, needs, worldviews, and so on—set up shop in the basement, where they sabotage further growth and development. They remain as "hidden subjects," facets of consciousness that the self can no longer *disidentify* with and transcend, because they are sealed off in unconscious pockets of the psyche, from which they send up symbolic derivatives in the form of painful symptoms.

The curative catalyst, again, is to bring awareness to bear on these subpersonalities, thus objectifying them, and thus including them in a more compassionate embrace. Generally speaking, individuals will present a symptomatology where one or two subpersonalities and their pathologies are dominant (a harsh inner critic, a prone-to-failure underdog, a low-self-esteem ego state, etc.), and thus therapy tends to focus on these more visible issues. As dominant pathologies are alleviated (and their subpersonalities integrated), less noticeable ones will often tend to emerge, sometimes forcefully, and therapeutic attention naturally gravitates to them. These subpersonalities can include both more primitive selves (archaic, magic) and any newly emerging transpersonal selves (soul, spirit).

Likewise, the various subpersonalities are often context-triggered: a person will do fine in one situation, only to have another situation trigger panic, depression, anxiety, and so on. Alleviating the dominant problem in one area will often allow less noticeable pathologies to surface, and they can then be worked through. The therapeutic ingredient—bring awareness to bear—helps the individual become more conscious of the subpersonalities, thus converting them from "hidden subjects" into "conscious objects," where they can be reintegrated in the self and thus join the ongoing flow of consciousness evolution, instead of remaining fixated at the lower levels where they were originally dissociated. For no matter how numerous the subpersonalities, it is the task of the proximate self to fashion some sort of integration or harmony in the chorus of voices, and thus more surely wend its way to the Source of them all.

THE ARCHEOLOGY OF THE SELF

We can give a simplified summary of the above discussion on the stages of self and pathology by using figure 10. This is again the Great Nest, but this time drawn to show *degrees of interior depth*. In other words, figures such as 1 and 6 show that the higher spheres transcend and include the lower; figure 10 shows that the higher spheres are *experienced* as being interior to, and deeper than, the lower, which are experienced, in comparison, as superficial, shallow, and exterior. Thus, the body is experienced as being inside the physical environment; the mind is experienced as being inside the body; the soul is experienced interior to the mind, and deep within the soul is pure spirit itself, which transcends all and embraces all (thus transcending inside and outside).

Figure 10 shows this archeology of Spirit, as the more superficial layers of the Self are peeled off to expose increasingly deeper and more profound waves of consciousness. This involves the *emergence* of ever-greater potentials, which therefore leads us forward, not backward, and shows us future evolution and growth, not past evolution and regression. This is an archeology of depth, to be sure, but a depth that plumbs the future, not the past; that reaches into a greater tomorrow, not a dusty yesterday; that unearths the hidden treasures of involution, not the fossils of evolution. We dig within in order to go beyond, not back.

A summary of this archeological expedition:

At the beginning of F-1, on the shallowest surface of Spirit, the self is still largely undifferentiated from the material world (as Piaget put it, "The self is here *material*, so to speak"); problems at this stage can therefore contribute to a disturbing lack of self-boundaries, infantile au-

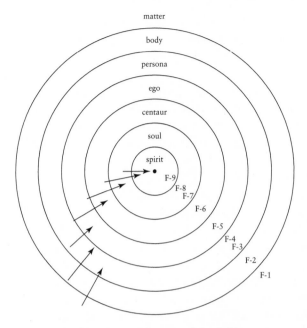

FIGURE 10. *Layers of the Self*

tism, and some forms of psychosis. The worldview of this stage is *archaic*, and this archaic consciousness, if not differentiated (transcended) and integrated (resolved), can lead to primitive pathologies. The trip to the Self is sabotaged at its first step, and the repercussions are severe.[24]

In F-2 (the separation-individuation stage), the emotional bodyself differentiates itself from the emotions and feelings of others. Problems at this stage can contribute to borderline and narcissistic conditions, where the self treats the world and others as mere extensions of itself (narcissism), or the world invades and painfully disrupts the self (borderline); both due to the fact that the world and the self are not stably differentiated. The worldview of this stage is *magical*—the self can magically order the world around in omnipotent fantasy, the environment is full of animistic displacements (not as a sophisticated form of panentheism, but as anthropomorphic impulse projections), and "word magic" reigns. Fixation at this magical level (and magical subpersonalities) is a large part of the cognitive repertoire of the borderline and narcissistic conditions.

With F-3, the early mental self (the early ego or persona) first begins to emerge and differentiate from the body and its impulses, feelings, and emotions, and attempts to integrate these feelings in its newly conceptual self. Failure at this crucial fulcrum (often summarized as Oedipal/Electra) can contribute to a classic neurosis: anxiety, depression, phobias, obsessive-compulsive disorders, and excessive guilt at the hands of the newly internalized superego. The conceptual self is frightened of, and overwhelmed by, the feelings of the body (especially sex and aggression), and in its misguided attempt to defend itself against these feelings, merely ends up sending them underground (as impulsive subpersonalities), where they cause even more pain and terror than when faced with awareness.

All of these early fulcrums (F-1 to F-3) remain heavily egocentric and preconventional (as for possible childhood spiritual experiences, see chapter 10). Fixation to their narcissistic modes keeps consciousness circling on the surface of the Self, and the journey to the Depths is derailed at some of the most superficial archeological layers.

This early mental self is at first a simple name self, then a rudimentary self-concept, but it soon expands into a full-fledged *role self* (or persona) with the emergence of the rule/role mind and the increasing capacity to take the role of other (F-4). The worldview of both late F-3 and early F-4 is *mythic*, which means that these early roles are often those found displayed in the mythological gods and goddesses, which represent the *archetypal roles* available to individuals. That is, these are simply some of the collective, concrete roles available to men and women—roles such as a strong father, a caring mother, a warrior, a trickster, the anima, animus, and so forth, which are often embodied in the concrete figures of the world's mythologies (Persephone, Demeter, Zeus, Apollo, Venus, Indra, etc.). Jungian research suggests that these archetypal mythic roles are *collectively* inherited; but, let us note, for the most part they are *not* transpersonal (a confusion common in Jungian and New Age circles).[25] These mythic roles are simply part of the many (sub)personalities that can exist at this preformal mythic level of consciousness development; they are preformal and collective, not postformal and transpersonal. A few "high archetypes," such as the Wise Old Man, the Crone, and the mandala, are sometimes *symbols* of the transpersonal domains, but do not necessarily carry direct experience of those domains.[26] In any event, we are here focusing on the concrete-literal mythic level itself.

These preformal, archetypal roles are bolstered by the specific cultural roles that the child begins to learn at this stage—the specific interactions with family, peers, and social others. As these cultural scripts are learned, various problems and distortions can arise, and these contribute to what we have generically been calling script pathology. Since the worldview of this level is *mythic* (mythic-membership), therapy at this level, by whatever name, often involves uprooting these myths and replacing them with more accurate, less self-damaging scripts and roles. Even the Jungian approach, which sometimes overvalues mythic displays, proceeds in a similar fashion, by differentiating-and-integrating mythic motifs and thus both honoring them and transcending them.[27]

But what is really happening here? In moving from preconventional and narcissistic to conventional and mythic-membership, consciousness has profoundly deepened from egocentric to sociocentric. It has expanded from *me* to *we*, and thus plumbed new depths on its archeological journey to the Self. It is slowly abandoning the pale and primitive surfaces, becoming less narcissistic, less of the shallows, less of the surface, and diving instead into the deep, where individual selves are increasingly united in that common Self which shines throughout the entire display, and in the move from egocentric-magic to sociocentric-mythic, the heart of the all-encompassing Self is increasingly intuited.

With the emergence of formal-reflexive capacities, the self can plunge yet deeper, moving from conventional/conformist roles and a mythic-membership self (the persona), to a postconventional, global, worldcentric self—namely, the mature ego (conscientious and individualistic, to use Loevinger's version). No longer just *us* (my tribe, my clan, my group, my nation), but *all of us* (all human beings without exception, regardless of race, religion, sex, or creed). Consciousness cuts loose from its parochial surfaces and dives into that which is shared by a global humanity, insisting on forms of compassion that are universal, impartial, just and fair for all.

Problems at this stage (F-5) often center around the incredibly difficult transition from conformist roles and prescriptive morality, to universal principles of conscience and postconventional identities: who am I, not according to mom or dad or society or the Bible, but according to my own deepest conscience? Erikson's "identity crisis" is a classic summary of many of the problems of this stage.[28]

As vision-logic begins to emerge, postconventional awareness deepens into fully universal, existential concerns: life and death, authenticity, full bodymind integration, self-actualization, global awareness, holistic embrace—all summarized as the emergence of the *centaur* (e.g., Loevinger's autonomous and integrated stages). In the archeological journey to the Self, the personal realm's exclusive reign is coming to an end, starting to be peeled off a radiant Spirit, and that universal radiance begins increasingly to shine through, rendering the self more and more transparent.

As usual, the more we go within, the more we go beyond. In the extraordinary archeology of Spirit, the deeper the level, the wider the embrace—the within that takes you beyond. Within the world of matter is the body, but the vital body goes beyond matter in so many ways: its feelings respond while rocks do not; its perceptions recognize a world while insentience sleeps; its emotions move a body while dirt awaits in silence. Likewise, the mind exists within the vital body, but the mind goes beyond the body in so many ways: while the body feels its own feelings, the cognition of the mind takes the role of others, and thus expands consciousness from egocentric to sociocentric to worldcentric; the mind knits together past and future, and thus rises above the impulsiveness of the body's instincts; while the mind conceives the world of what might be and what should be, the body slumbers in its naive present.

Likewise, looking deep within the mind, in the very most interior part of the self, when the mind becomes very, very quiet, and one listens very carefully, in that infinite Silence, the soul begins to whisper, and its feather-soft voice takes one far beyond what the mind could ever imagine, beyond anything rationality could possibly tolerate, beyond anything logic can endure. In its gentle whisperings, there are the faintest hints of infinite love, glimmers of a life that time forgot, flashes of a bliss that must not be mentioned, an infinite intersection where the mysteries of eternity breathe life into mortal time, where suffering and pain have forgotten how to pronounce their own names, this secret quiet intersection of time and the very timeless, an intersection called the soul.

In the archeology of the Self, deep within the personal lies the transpersonal, which takes you far beyond the personal: always within and beyond. Experienced previously only in peak experiences, or as a background intuition of immortality, wonder, and grace, the soul begins now to emerge more permanently in consciousness. Not yet infinite and all-embracing, no longer merely personal and mortal, the soul is the great intermediate conveyor between pure Spirit and individual self. The soul can embrace the gross realm in nature mysticism, or it can plumb its own depths in deity mysticism. It can confer a postmortem meaning on all of life, and deliver grace to every corner of the psyche. It offers the beginning of an unshakable witnessing and equanimity in the midst of the slings and arrows of outrageous fortune, and breathes a tender mercy on all that it encounters. It is reached by a simple technique: turn left at mind, and go within.

A sickness of the soul is sickness indeed. The pathologies that beset psychic and subtle development are numerous and profound. The first and simplest are those that result from abrupt psychic and subtle peak experiences, before they have become permanent realizations and basic waves in one's own awareness. As we have seen, a person at the archaic, magic, mythic, rational, or centauric level can "peek"-experience any of the higher states (psychic, subtle, causal, nondual). In some cases these are so disruptive that, especially in a person with F-1 or F-2 deficiencies, they can trigger a psychotic break.[29] In others, the result is a spiritual emergency.[30] In yet others, the peak experience is a beneficial, life-altering occasion.[31] But in all of these cases, understanding the experience depends upon understanding both the level *from which* the experience originates (psychic, subtle, causal, nondual) and the level *at which* it is experienced and interpreted (archaic, magic, mythic, rational, centauric; or, more accurately, the level of development of the self and all of the self-related lines, including morals, needs, worldviews, and so on. As we saw, a transpersonal peak experience is experienced and interpreted very differently at, for example, different moral stages, and all of these various levels and lines need to be taken into account when assessing the nature and treatment of any spiritual emergency). In other words, an integral psychograph of the individual is the best guide in this—or any other—therapeutic endeavor.

Beyond nonordinary states and temporary peak experiences is permanent realization, and as adaptation to the soul realms begins, any number of pathologies can develop.[32] The self can be overwhelmed by the light, painfully lost in the love, inundated with a largess that its boundaries cannot contain. Alternatively, it can simply swell its ego to infinite proportions (especially if there are any F-2 or narcissistic-borderline residues). It can develop a split between its upper and lower realms (especially between the soul and the body). It can repress and dissociate aspects of the soul itself (producing F-7 and F-8 subpersonalities; not lower impulses trying to come up, but higher impulses trying to come down). It can remain fused with the soul when it should begin to let go of it. And the earliest, simplest pathology of all: denying the existence of one's very own soul.

A growing body of literature is increasingly attuned to the diseases of the soul, using the techniques of both traditional spiritual disciplines and modern psychotherapy (several such approaches are listed in the endnote).[33] For the more traditional techniques—which are also part of any integral therapy—I have listed in the charts the path of shamans/yogis, the path of saints, the path of sages, and the path of siddhas (dealing with psychic, subtle, causal, and nondual, respectively), which I will also address in an endnote.[34]

In the archeology of the Self, we are at the point where the soul has emerged from the interior depths of the mind and pointed the way to a greater tomorrow. But, like Moses, the soul can see from afar, but never actually enter, the Promised Land. As Teresa would say, after the butterfly (soul) emerged from the death of the chrysalis (ego), so now the little butterfly must die. When the soul itself grows quiet, and rests from its own weariness; when the witness releases its final hold, and dissolves into its ever-present ground; when the last layer of the Self is peeled into the purest emptiness; when the final form of the self-contraction unfolds in the infinity of all space; then Spirit itself, as ever-present awareness, stands free of its own accord, never really lost, and therefore never really found. With a shock of the utterly obvious, the world continues to arise, just as it always has.

In the deepest within, the most infinite beyond. In ever-present awareness, your soul expands to embrace the entire Kosmos, so that Spirit alone remains, as the simple world of what is. The rain no longer falls on you, but within you; the sun shines from inside your heart and radiates out into the world, blessing it with grace; supernovas swirl in your consciousness, the thunder is the sound of your own exhilarated heart; the oceans and rivers are nothing but your blood pulsing to the rhythm of your soul. Infinitely ascended worlds of light dance in the interior of your brain; infinitely descended worlds of night cascade around your feet; the clouds crawl across the sky of your own unfettered mind, while the wind blows through the empty space where your self once used to be. The sound of the rain falling on the roof is the only self you can find, here in the obvious world of crystalline one taste, where inner and outer are silly fictions and self and other are obscene lies, and ever-present simplicity is the sound of one hand clapping madly for all eternity. In the greatest depth, the simplest what is, and the journey ends, as it always does, exactly where it began.

A FULL-SPECTRUM THERAPY

A few points might be emphasized in this archeology of the Self. As indicated in column two in chart 1a, these general waves of self development (material self, bodyself, persona, ego, centaur, soul) are not rigidly discrete rungs in a ladder, but overlapping streams of self unfolding, and they exist as functional subholons in subsequent development (barring pathology, such as being split off into dissociated subpersonalities). Although each fulcrum itself is fairly discrete, the functional capacities of each self remain in subsequent development, and this is indicated by the continuing arrows that are drawn in both chart 1a and figure 10. (Later, we will return to this idea and show yet another reason that these various "selves" can overlap and coexist to some degree; see *Different Lines of the Self* in chapter 9).

The point is simply that the average adult comes to therapy with, to use a simplified version, a physical body, a libidinal/emotional body, one or more body-images, one or more personae or conventional roles, one or more ego states—with dissociations at any of those levels producing dissociated complexes and subpersonalities at those levels—and a fledgling soul and spirit awaiting a more genuine birth.[35] A full-spectrum therapist works with the body, the shadow, the persona, the ego, the existential self, the soul and spirit, attempting to bring awareness to all of them, so that all of them may join consciousness in the extraordinary return voyage to the Self and Spirit that grounds and moves the entire display.

In short, a full-spectrum therapist is an archeologist of the Self. But, as we saw, this is an archeology that unearths the future, not the past. This profound archeology digs into the within in order to find the beyond, the emergent, the newly arising, not the already buried. These ever-deeper sheaths pull us forward, not backward; they are layers of Eros, not Thanatos; they lead to tomorrow's births, not yesterday's graves.

(In this unfolding of higher potentials, should any aspect of the Self that has *already emerged* be repressed, lost, or alienated, then we need, therapeutically, to "regress in service of the self"—we need to return to the past, return to the more superficial and shallow layers—to the material self, the libidinal self, the early distorted scripts, and so on—and recontact those facets, release their distortions, reintegrate them in the ongoing stream of consciousness unfolding, and thus resume the voyage to the real depths undistracted by those surface commotions of much sound and fury, signifying, if not nothing, then nothing much. Most "depth psychology"—Freudian, for example—is really "superficial psychology," plumbing not the depths but the shallows of the Self.)

But to say that the deeper waves of the Self are archeologically uncovered is absolutely not to say they are simply pregiven, like a buried treasure chest fully existing and awaiting excavation. It simply means that these deeper waves are all basic potentials of the human (and sentient) condition. Each individual *discovers* the depths that are collectively given to all of us (we all have bodies and minds and souls and spirits, and none of us created those); but each individual discovers the depths by *creating* the surface features of each wave that will be *uniquely* his or hers (what you do with the body, mind, soul, and spirit: that is truly up to you). As always, we have to make the future that is given us; and the full-spectrum therapist is an assistant in this extraordinary voyage that is both discovery and creation.

DEPTH AND HEIGHT

Finally, an important word about all these metaphors of "depth," "height," "ascent," "descent," and so on. In the first part of this presentation, I often used the metaphor of "higher" levels and waves, with an ascent of consciousness. Now I have switched to "depth," and a diving into the within. The fact is, all of these metaphors are useful, because they all emphasize different aspects of a consciousness that is greater than any conceptualizations. Yet time and again I have seen discussions come to a crashing halt because somebody didn't like "height" or "ascent," somebody else loathed "within," somebody else "depth." Surely we can appreciate the partial truths that all of these metaphors convey.

Huston Smith, in *Forgotten Truth*, points out that the traditions usually refer to greater levels of reality as *higher*, and greater levels of the self as *deeper*, so that the higher you go on the Great Nest of Being, the deeper you go into your own selfhood. I have just taken that approach in the Archeology of the Self. This is a completely valid approach, because, like all good metaphors, it takes something that we already know and applies it to something as yet unfamiliar, to help us better grasp the latter. In this case, we all know that the body is experienced as being within the physical environment, and we all know that the mind is experienced as being within the body. This metaphor of depth, of moving within, is thus a wonderful hint that the soul, too, is experienced as being within the mind, and yet also moves far beyond it, and that spirit is within and utterly beyond the soul, transcending all, embracing all. The metaphor of "layers of depth" or "sheaths of the Self" (as found in Vedanta, for example, or Teresa's seven interior castles) is a lovely metaphor, and it powerfully reminds us that what the vulgar world takes to be "deep" is often very shallow.

The metaphor of height is equally lovely. Although, as Huston reminds us, "height" is often used for levels of reality, in the final analysis levels of reality and levels of consciousness are two phrases for the same thing, and thus we can usefully speak of the ascent of consciousness, the heights of the soul and spirit, the moving beyond that is transpersonal and superconscious. This metaphor, too, is grounded in something that we know already: every time we move beyond a narrow concern to a broader perspective, we feel we have risen above the situation. There is a sense of being free, a sense of release, an increase in spaciousness, a transcendence. To move from egocentric to ethnocentric to worldcentric to theocentric is to ascend into greater and wider and higher spheres of release and embrace, transcendence and inclusion, freedom and compassion. Sometimes this ascent is also felt concretely, as when, for example, kundalini energy literally moves up the spinal line. The metaphor of vertical height also works well because in many spiritual experiences, we sense that Spirit is *descending* from above into us (a factor emphasized in many spiritual practices, from Aurobindo's descent of the supermind to the Gnostics' descent of the holy spirit). We reach up to Spirit with Eros; Spirit reaches down to us with Agape. These, too, are wonderful metaphors.

But we must be very careful to specify which metaphors we are using, because "depth" in each of them means something exactly opposite. With the depth or archeology metaphor, "depth" means a greater reality; with the ascent metaphor, depth means a lower reality. For example:

Working with the ascent metaphor, we can speak, as Assagioli did, of "height psychology" and "depth psychology." In this case, both "height" and "depth" are judged according to their relation to the average rational-ego. Anything *lower* than the ego (archaic impulses, vital emotions, magic-mythic fantasies) are part of "depth psychology" (which actually means lower, primitive psychology), and anything *higher* than the ego (soul and spirit) are part of "height psychology." In this metaphor, *evolution* is the ascent of consciousness from matter to body to mind to soul to spirit, and *involution* is the descent of consciousness through any of those vehicles. *Regression* is moving backward in the line of evolution, whereas *development* is moving forward in that line.[36] (In the depth metaphor, regression is moving toward the surfaces, and development is moving toward the depths: same thing, different metaphor.)[37]

I will continue to use all of those metaphors, and the context will make clear what is meant. (Figure 10 uses depth; figures 1 through 9 emphasize height.) The fact is, all of those metaphors are true in their own ways. Every within is a beyond, and a full-spectrum therapist is a guide to the ever-increasing depths that reveal ever-greater heights.

FOUR-QUADRANT OR INTEGRAL THERAPY

Notice that the above factors focused almost exclusively on interior developments in an individual (the Upper-Left quadrant). Those conclusions, while valid, need to be set in the context of the other quadrants, even when trying to understand individual development and pathology. All four quadrants mutually interact (they are embedded in each other), and thus *all* of them are required in order to understand pathologies in *any* of them.

We have seen that the subjective events in individual consciousness (UL) are intimately interrelated with objective events and mechanisms in the organism (UR), such as events in the brain stem, the limbic system, the neocortex, brainwave patterns (alpha, beta, theta, and delta states), hemispheric synchronization, neurotransmitter levels and imbalances, and so on.[38] All of those Upper-Right-quadrant factors need to be carefully included in any understanding of individual psychopathology. This includes the partial truths of biological psychiatry, which focuses on pharmacology and medicinal treatments of psychopathology (although we needn't reduce all consciousness to events in the Upper-Right quadrant).

Likewise, we need to look specifically at the larger cultural currents (Lower Left) and social structures (Lower Right) that are inseparable from individual consciousness development. What good does it do to adjust and integrate the self in a culture that is itself sick? What does it mean to be a well-adjusted Nazi? Is that mental health? Or is a maladjusted person in a Nazi society the only one who is sane?

All of those are crucial considerations. A malformation—a pathology, a "sickness"—in any quadrant will reverberate through all four quadrants, because every holon has these four facets to its being. So a society with an alienating mode of production (LR)—such as slave wages for dehumanizing labor—will reflect in low self-esteem for laborers (UL) and an out-of-whack brain chemistry (UR) that might, for example, institutionalize alcohol abuse as self-medication. Similarly, a cultural worldview that devalues women will result in a tendency to cripple individual female potential and a brain chemistry that could definitely use some Prozac.

And so on around the four-quadrant circle. Cripple one quadrant and all four tend to hemorrhage. We are fast approaching an understanding that sees individual "pathologies" as but the tip of an enormous iceberg that includes self-stages, cultural worldviews, social structures, and spiritual access to depth.[39] Individual therapy is by no means unimportant, but in many ways it is but a small slice of a dysfunctional (not yet integral) world. This is why a truly integral therapy is not only individual but cultural, social, spiritual, and political.

In the simplest terms, an integral therapy would therefore attempt to address as many facets of the quadrants as is pragmatically feasible in any given case. Mike Murphy's *Future of the Body* is an excellent compendium of an integral view, as is Tony Schwartz's *What Really Matters*. I outline aspects of an integral approach in *The Eye of Spirit*. Murphy and Leonard's *The Life We Are Given* is a practical guide to one type of integral practice, and is highly recommended.[40]

But anybody can put together his or her own integral practice. The idea is to simultaneously exercise all the major capacities and dimensions of the human bodymind—physical, emotional, mental, social, cultural, spiritual. In *One Taste*, I outline my own recommendations for one such integral ("all-level, all-quadrant") therapy; here are some examples, going around the quadrants, with some representative practices from each:

UPPER-RIGHT QUADRANT (INDIVIDUAL, OBJECTIVE, BEHAVIORAL)—

Physical
> DIET—Atkins, Eades, Ornish; vitamins, hormones
> STRUCTURAL—weightlifting, aerobics, hiking, Rolfing, etc.

Neurological
> PHARMACOLOGICAL—various medications/drugs, where appropriate
> BRAIN/MIND MACHINES—to help induce theta and delta states of consciousness

UPPER-LEFT QUADRANT (INDIVIDUAL, SUBJECTIVE, INTENTIONAL)—

Emotional
> BREATH—t'ai chi, yoga, bioenergetics, circulation of prana or feeling-energy, qi gong
> SEX—tantric sexual communion, self-transcending whole-bodied sexuality

Mental

THERAPY—psychotherapy, cognitive therapy, shadow work

VISION—adopting a conscious philosophy of life, visualization, affirmation

Spiritual

PSYCHIC (shaman/yogi)—shamanic, nature mysticism, beginning tantric

SUBTLE (saint)—deity mysticism, yidam, contemplative prayer, advanced tantric

CAUSAL (sage)—vipassana, self-inquiry, bare attention, centering prayer, Witnessing, formless mysticism

NONDUAL (siddha)—Dzogchen, Mahamudra, Shaivism, Zen, Eckhart, nondual mysticism, etc.

LOWER-RIGHT QUADRANT (SOCIAL, INTEROBJECTIVE)—

Systems—exercising responsibilities to Gaia, nature, biosphere, and geopolitical infrastructures at all levels

Institutional—exercising educational, political, and civic duties to family, town, state, nation, world

LOWER-LEFT QUADRANT (CULTURAL, INTERSUBJECTIVE)—

Relationships—with family, friends, sentient beings in general; making relationships part of one's growth, decentering the self[41]

Community Service—volunteer work, homeless shelters, hospice, etc.

Morals—engaging the intersubjective world of the Good, practicing compassion in relation to all sentient beings

The general idea of integral practice is clear enough: *Exercise body, mind, soul, and spirit in self, culture, and nature.* (That is, try to exercise the full spectrum in the I, we, and it domains.) Pick a basic practice from each category, or from as many categories as pragmatically possible, and practice them concurrently. The more categories engaged, the more effective they all become (because they are all intimately related as aspects of your own being). Practice them diligently, and coordinate your integral efforts to unfold the various potentials of the bodymind—until the bodymind itself unfolds in Emptiness, and the entire journey is a misty memory from a trip that never even occurred.

9

Some Important Developmental Streams

W E HAVE LOOKED BRIEFLY at the basic levels or waves, the self navigating those waves, and some of the problems that the self can encounter when it does so. We turn our attention now to the developmental lines or streams.

It is, of course, up to the self to integrate all these various streams, and we have already followed the general story of the self and its overall development. Now we are simply taking a separate look at some of the more important lines that the self has to balance on its overall journey.[1] Each developmental stream—from morals to aesthetics to interpersonal relationship to cognition—represents an important facet of the great River of Life, and thus, in integrating these streams, the self is learning to be at home in the Kosmos. All of these developmental lines can be entered on an individual's psychograph (figs. 2 and 3), which is actually a graph of one's "at-home-ness" with the world. The deeper each stream, the more of the Kosmos it embraces, until it embraces the All, and is thus released into the Ground and Suchness of the entire display.

MORALS

In charts 1a and 5c, "Moral Span" refers to the stream of moral development, which in my scheme includes not only principles of moral judgment (Kohlberg) and care (Gilligan)—or how one reaches a moral decision—but also moral span, or those deemed worthy of being included in the decision in the first place. As with most streams, this runs from egocentric to ethnocentric to worldcentric to theocentric (or, more accurately, "pneumocentric," or spirit-centered, so as not to confuse the transpersonal realm with mythic theism). Each of those increasingly greater moral depths encompasses within itself a larger moral span (from "me" to "us" to "all of us" to "all sentient beings").[2]

Nowhere is the amazing expansion of consciousness more apparent than in the self's identity and its morals, an expansion that is mostly lost if we focus on flatland and describe psychology in nothing but Right-Hand terms, where there is simply the organism (UR) and its interaction with its environment (LR): the brain processes information through emergent connectionist systems, and driven by its self-organizing autopoietic mechanisms interwoven with its ecosystem, selects those responses that are more likely to get the brain and its genetic material passed forward in time.

All of which is true, and all of which misses the interior facts: What is it that you call *yourself*? With what do you identify this self of yours? For that *identity* expands from egocentric to ethnocentric to worldcentric to pneumocentric—you actually feel that you are *one with* each of those expanding worlds—and none of that is spotted by "organism-and-environment" schemes, which recognize only identities based on exterior quantitative entities (and not interior qualitative shifts).

This expanding identity is directly reflected in moral awareness (subjective identity is reflected in intersubjective morals: not just organism and environment, but self and culture). For you will treat as yourself those *with whom you identify*. If you identify only with you, you will treat others narcissistically. If you identify with your friends and family, you will treat them with care. If you identify with your nation, you will treat your countrymen as compatriots. If you identify with all human beings, you will strive to treat all people fairly and compassionately, regardless of race, sex, color, or creed. If your identity expands to embrace the Kosmos, you will treat all sentient beings with respect and kindness, for they are all perfect manifestations of the same radiant Self, which is your very own Self as well. This comes to you in a direct realization of the Supreme Identity, precisely because identity can span the entire spectrum of consciousness, matter to body to mind to soul to spirit, with each expansion bringing a greater moral embrace, until the All itself is embraced with passionate equanimity.

And where is the selfish gene in all of that? Only by focusing on the Upper-Right quadrant could so narrow a view of human reality gain credence. Since truth in any domain always carries certain types of advantages (wisdom has many rewards), it is fairly easy to find a few ways that these rewards translate into sexual payoffs (which they sometimes do), and thus it is easy to pretend that all these higher truths are nothing but elaborately clever ways to get laid.

And when the limited usefulness of that neo-Darwinian game becomes apparent, it is easy enough to shift the entire concept of natural selection to that of "memes" (which are basically holons in any quadrant—intentional, behavioral, social, or cultural), and simply apply natural selection to anything that endures in time—a cultural trait, a social institution, a dress style, a philosophical idea, a music style, and so on. True as all that may be, it continues to ignore the central and crucial issue, which is not: How do holons or memes, once they have emerged, remain in existence? (yes, they are *selected* by evolutionary pressures of various sorts), but rather: Where do the *new* memes come from in the first place? Granted that successful memes are those that are selected once they have emerged, why and how do they emerge at all?

In other words, *creativity*, by any other name, is built into the very fabric of the Kosmos. This creativity—Eros is one of its many names—drives the emergence of ever higher and ever wider holons, a drive that shows up, in the interior domains, *as an expansion of identity* (and morals and consciousness) from matter to body to mind to soul to spirit. And the proof of *that* sequence is found, not by staring at the physical organism and its environment, but by looking into the subjective and intersubjective domains. But humanity has *already* done that very carefully for at least several thousand years, the general results of which are presented in charts 1 through 11.

In flatland, as we have seen, the Right-Hand world of objective entities and systems is thought to be the only "really real" world, and thus all *subjective* values are said to be merely personal, or idiosyncratic, or based on emotional preferences, but possess no grounding in reality itself. But if we reject the limitations of flatland, it becomes obvious that the subjective and intersubjective domains are simply the interiors of holons at every level in the Kosmos. Subjectivity is an *inherent* feature of the universe. Of course there are personal preferences within the subjective domains, but those domains themselves, and their general waves of unfolding, are as real as DNA, and even more significant. The expansion of moral identity is simply one of the more obvious manifestations of these profound waves of consciousness unfolding.

MOTIVATION: LEVELS OF FOOD

"Levels of Food" (chart 1b) refers to the levels of *need*, drive, or fundamental motivation (which may be conscious or unconscious). As I suggested in *Up from Eden* and *A Sociable God*, needs arise due to the fact that every structure (in both levels and lines) is a *system of relational exchange* with the same level of organization in the world at large, resulting in a holarchy of "food"—physical food, emotional food, mental food, soul food.[3]

Physical needs reflect our physical relationships and exchanges with the material universe: food, water, shelter, and so on. Emotional needs reflect our relationships with other emotional beings, and consist in an exchange of emotional warmth, sexual intimacy, and caring. Mental needs reflect our exchanges with other mental creatures: in every act of verbal communication, we exchange a set of symbols with others. (Monks who take vows of both celibacy and silence report that the lack of communication is much more painful than the lack of sex: these are genuine needs and drives, based on relational exchange.) And spiritual needs reflect our need to be in relationship with a Source and Ground that gives sanction, meaning, and deliverance to our separate selves (the unsatisfaction of those needs is described, one way or another, as hell).

In *Up from Eden* I discuss these levels of need and motivation in detail (giving eight general levels of motivation, not the simple four I am using here), and correlate them with similar conceptions, such as Maslow's, along with examples of how oppression and repression *distort relational exchanges*, resulting in pathology (physical illness, emotional illness, mental illness, spiritual illness; all of the pathologies that we discussed in chapter 8 are not just disruptions of the self, but disruptions of relational exchange with others). Although we may discern many different types and levels of needs, all genuine needs simply reflect the *interrelationships* necessary for the life of any holon (at any level).

WORLDVIEWS

"Worldview" (chart 1b) refers to the way the world looks at each of the basic waves in the Great Nest. When you only have sensations, perceptions, and impulses, the world is archaic. When you add the capacity for images and symbols, the world appears magical. When you add concepts, rules, and roles, the world becomes mythic. When formal-reflexive capacities emerge, the rational world comes into view. With vision-logic, the existential world stands forth. When the subtle emerges, the world becomes divine. When the causal emerges, the self becomes divine. When the nondual emerges, world and self are realized to be one Spirit.

But not in any sort of pregiven, fixed fashion. A worldview unfolds in a particular culture with its specific (and often local) surface features.[4] In general, "worldview" refers to the Lower-Left quadrant, or all of the intersubjective practices, linguistic signs, semantic structures, contexts, and communal meanings that are generated through shared perceptions and collective values—in short, "culture." This cultural dimension (Lower Left) is distinct from (but not separable from) the *social* dimension (Lower Right), which involves the exterior, concrete, material, institutional forms of collective life, including modes of techno-economic production, collective social practices, architectural structures, social systems, the written and spoken media of communication (print, television, internet), geopolitical infrastructures, family systems, and so on.

Worldviews are particularly important because all individual, subjective consciousness *arises within* the clearing created by cultural or intersubjective structures. For example, somebody at Kohlberg's moral stage 2 (morals are part of intersubjective structures) who faces a personal ethical dilemma will have all of his thoughts governed, in the main, by the deep features of moral stage 2. He will *not* have a moral-stage-5 thought cross his mind. Thus, he is not "free" to think anything he wants. His subjective thoughts *arise in a space or clearing* that is created by, and largely controlled by, *the intersubjective structures of his cultural worldview* (including the moral stage of his individual self). As we saw, even if this person has a peak experience of a transpersonal realm, that experience will be largely interpreted and carried by the intersubjective structures which have developed in his own case. (Failing to see that subjective experiences *arise in the space created by intersubjective structures* is one of the main liabilities of many forms of spiritual and transpersonal psychology, and especially those that focus merely on altered or nonordinary states.)[5] Of course, individuals can, to some degree, transcend aspects of their own given culture; and when that happens, they seek out others with whom to share the new insights—thus creating a new culture. The point is that subjectivity and intersubjectivity—in fact, all four quadrants—are mutually arising and mutually interdependent.

AFFECT

"Affect" (chart 1b) refers to the developmental line of affects, or "emotions" and "feelings" in the broadest sense. There are two rather different meanings of the word "emotion" in the perennial philosophy, and I use both. One, emotion refers to a *specific level* of consciousness: the pranamayakosha, or the level-sheath of emotional-sexual energy (the basic structure of "impulse/emotion" on the charts). Two, it refers to the energetic *feeling tone* of any and all of the basic structures across the entire spectrum. (These are listed in "Affect" in chart 1b.) I have often been accused of limiting "feeling" or "emotion" to the first definition and ignoring the second, but this is clearly incorrect. In *The Atman Project*, for example, I listed "affective tone" for each of the basic structures in the overall spectrum. Consciousness itself is more of a "feeling-awareness" than it is a "thinking-awareness," and there are levels of that feeling-awareness, or experiential vividness, across the Great Nest.

(One of the real problems in humanistic/transpersonal circles is that many people confuse the warmth and heart-expanse of postconventional awareness with the merely subjective feelings of the sensory body, and, caught in this pre/post fallacy, recommend merely bodywork for higher emotional expansion, when what is *also* required is postformal cognitive growth, not simply preformal cognitive immersion. Obviously bodywork has an important and foundational role to play in growth and therapy, but the elevation of preformal sensations to postformal love has caused endless problems in the human potential movement.)[6]

GENDER

"Gender Identity" (chart 1b) follows the development of gender from its biological roots (which are biological givens, not cultural constructions), through conventional formations (which *are* cultural constructions, mostly), into transgender orientations (which are largely transdifferentiated and transconventional). Research continues to confirm that the *deep features* of the basic waves and most of the self-related streams (morals, needs, role capacities) are *gender-neutral* (i.e., they are essentially the same in men and women). However, men and women can negotiate these same structures and stages "in a different voice" (which is usually summarized by saying men tend to translate with an emphasis on agency, women on communion, although both use both).[7]

In *The Eye of Spirit* I argued that we need an "all-level, all-quadrant" approach to feminism and gender studies, or an "integral feminism." Many feminists unfortunately resist an integral approach because they often acknowledge only one quadrant (usually the Lower Left, or the cultural construction of gender), while denying the others (such as biological factors, since they suspect that of being another version of "biology is destiny," which it would be if the Upper-Right quadrant were the only quadrant in existence. But biological factors are profoundly molded by cultural values, social institutions, and personal intentions; thus acknowledging some biological factors is not sexist but realistic). This narrow focus is unfortunate, but it needn't stop others from moving ahead with a more integral feminism, and many have, such as Joyce Nielsen, Kaisa Puhakka, and Elizabeth Debold.[8]

AESTHETICS

"Art" (chart 8) refers to levels of aesthetic experience, and we can see here a very important phenomenon that applies to most forms of development. Namely, you can analyze a given activity (such as art) on the basis of both the level it *comes from* and the level it *aims at*—or the level producing the art and the level depicted in the art. (As with any mode of consciousness, you can analyze the level of the *subject* of consciousness—the level of selfhood—and level of reality of the *object* of consciousness, as explained in several endnotes.)[9] For example, art produced *by* the mental level can take as its object something in the material, mental, or spiritual realms, and you get a quite different art in each case. The resultant artwork is thus a combined product of the structures that are producing the art and the structures that are depicted in the art (i.e., the level of self producing the art, and level of reality depicted in the art). This gives us a grid of a very large number of different types of art, of which I have listed only a few representative samples on chart 8.[10]

To show what is involved in this dual analysis, notice that the earliest prehistoric artists (e.g., the cave painters of the Paleolithic), although presumably "closer" to nature and the sensorimotor realm, never painted nature in the way that moderns would. The Paleolithic artists do not use perspective, nor is their art empirical or "accurate" in any sense we moderns would accept (figures overlap each other with no concern for spatial separation, there is no depth perception, etc.). A plausible reason is that they were painting the sensorimotor realms *from* the magical structure, which lacks the capacity for spatial perspective. Likewise, in the mythic era, nature was never portrayed in perspective either, but always as part of a mythic-literal background. Only with the rise of modernity (starting in the Renaissance), and the widespread use of perspectival-reason, did perspective itself come to be seen and thus painted in art. We might say, only as consciousness gained some distance from nature could it paint nature more realistically.

For the same reason, only with the (anti)modern reaction of Romanticism could emotional feelings become the object of expressive art. It was only with the widespread differentiation of mind and body that the body realms could be clearly perceived by the mind and thus portrayed. (And when the modern differentiation went too far into dissociation, that painful pathology could also become part of the existential expressivist themes of art.)

The same dual analysis (level of the subject producing the art and level of the object being portrayed) can be done with modes of knowing (and, in fact, with all modes of consciousness).[11] Rationality, for example, can take as its object the sensorimotor realms (producing empiric-analytic knowledge), the mental realms themselves (producing phenomenology and hermeneutics), or the spiritual realms (producing theology, mandalic reason, and so forth). This is important to realize because with modernity, some very high levels (e.g., reason) confined their attention to some very low realms (e.g., matter), with the result that modernity looked like nothing but regression, whereas it was only "half" regressive: a higher subject confining its attention to a lower object—a deeper self in a shallower world (the good news and bad news of modernity).[12]

Aesthetics is an extremely important developmental stream because it is one of the preeminent subjective streams (which doesn't mean "unreal" or merely idiosyncratic; it means very real as subjective ontology). We saw that Baldwin and Habermas, among others, recognized that development must be traced in at least three irreducible modes—aesthetic, moral, and scientific (i.e., the Big Three).[13] As I pointed out in *The Eye of Spirit*, all of the numerous developmental streams are basically variations of the Big Three. Some developmental lines emphasize the subjective components (e.g., self-identity, affects, needs, aesthetics); some emphasize the intersubjective components (worldviews, linguistics, ethics); and some the objective components (exterior cognition, scientific cognition, Piagetian cognitive line, etc.).[14] None of these can finally be separated from the others, but each developmental stream tends to be oriented toward a particular quadrant (e.g., aesthetics toward the subjective, morals toward the intersubjective, and cognition toward the objective). By emphasizing the importance of following developments in all four quadrants (or simply the Big Three), we can strive for a truly integral model. The holons in all four quadrants evolve, and a comprehensive model would attempt to honor all of those evolutionary streams.

DIFFERENT TYPES OF COGNITIVE LINES

Notice that in chart 3b ("Cognitive Development"), I have listed "overall cognitive lines." This refers to an alternative way to conceptualize cognitive development once we move from a monolithic one-axis model to an integral model of states, waves, and streams.[15] As indicated on the chart, we can picture not one uniform line of cognitive development, with each stage stacked on top of its predecessors like so many bricks, but several relatively independent lines of cognitive development, each developing alongside the others like columns in a beautiful mansion. Based primarily on the fact of *natural states of consciousness*—that is, on the undeniable existence and availability of gross/waking, subtle/ dreaming, and deep sleep/causal states to individuals at almost every stage of their development—we can reasonably postulate that those states/realms might also have their own developmental lines. This would mean that we could trace the development of different types of cognition (gross, subtle, and causal) as they appear throughout a person's life. Instead of one appearing only after another, they would all develop simultaneously, at least in certain ways. Some examples:

The main characteristic of gross cognition is that it *takes as its object the sensorimotor realm*. This line of cognition would begin with sensorimotor development itself, move into concrete operational, and then both peak and begin to trail off at formal operational cognition. It tends to start trailing off at formal, and especially postformal, operations, because both of those increasingly take the world of thought as an object, and thus increasingly move into subtle cognition. We might say, then, that the gross (or more technically, the gross-reflecting) line of cognition runs from sensorimotor to preop to conop to formop and trails off at vision-logic. This cognitive line develops, as most lines do, from preconventional to conventional to postconventional, but it doesn't easily continue beyond that into postformal and post-postconventional waves, simply because in those higher stages the sensorimotor world, although not in any way abandoned, ceases to be the dominant object of awareness.

The main characteristic of subtle cognition is that it *takes as its object the world of thought*, or the mental and subtle realms altogether. This developmental line also begins in infancy (and probably in prenatal states; it is said to be the main cognitive mode in most of the bardos, as well as sleep with dreams and meditative states of savikalpa samadhi). This subtle line of cognition involves precisely all those perceptions whose study has been downplayed by Western cognitive psychologists: first and foremost, states of imagination, reverie, daydreams, creative visions, hypnogogic states, etheric states, visionary revelations, hypnotic states, transcendental illuminations, and dozens of types of savikalpa samadhi (or meditation with form). What they all have in common, even in infancy and childhood, is that they take as their referents, not the material world of sensorimotor occasions, but the interior world of images, thoughts, visions, dreams. . . .[16]

We would generally expect the subtle-cognitive stream to have available to it the same basic waves as most other streams: preconventional, conventional, postconventional, and post-postconventional (or egocentric, sociocentric, worldcentric, and pneumocentric), but the point is that it is a developmental line reaching all the way back to infancy, and not simply jumping out at a higher, adult stage.

(In chart 3b I have shown subtle-cognition picking up importance at formal and beyond, but that is just an arbitrary indication. In fact, I suspect what we will find is that subtle-cognition shows a U-development, being more present in early childhood and then temporarily waning as conop and formop come to the fore, then picking up prominence again in the postformal stages, up to the causal. At the same time, we needn't get unduly Romantic over these implications, because the subtle cognition present in childhood is still a largely preconventional, egocentric cognition, no matter how otherwise vivid and imaginative [see chap. 11]. Still, the importance of looking at this as a developmental line is that childhood subtle-cognition could then be acknowledged and honored, which would also presumably have benefits at the postformal stages.)

The main characteristic of causal cognition is that *it is the root of attention* (and the capacity for Witnessing).[17] This line, too, can be traced to early childhood, although it comes increasingly to the fore in the postformal stages. (For the important reasons that the early infantile fusion states should not be confused with the higher enlightened states or Ground, see the endnote).[18] But this line, also, if recognized and honored, could be strengthened from its first appearances in childhood forward, presumably with multiple benefits then and later.[19]

DIFFERENT LINES OF THE SELF

We can apply the same type of modeling to the self and its development, suggesting that these three great realms—gross, subtle, and causal—are home to three different lines of self, which I generically call ego, soul, and Self (or frontal, deeper psychic, and Witness).[20] Just as we did with cognition, we can treat these three modes of self as relatively independent developmental lines, so that they do not develop one after the other, but alongside each other. That relationship is shown in column two in chart 4b and in figure 11.

Of course, most streams can and do develop relatively independently of each other—the various streams often progress at their own pace through the major waves—which is why overall development follows no linear sequence whatsoever. This section continues that theme, but more radically, for I am suggesting—just as with cognition—that what has traditionally been considered *one stream* (in this case, the self) might actually be *several different streams*, each developing relatively independently.

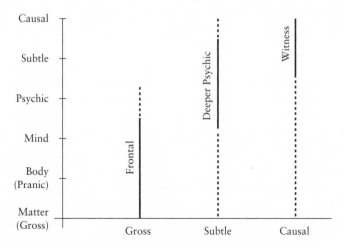

FIGURE 11. *The Development of the Frontal (or Ego), the Deeper Psychic (or Soul), and the Witness (or Self)*

We have already seen that the major stages of the self stream—such as bodyself, persona, ego, centaur—*depend* on the competences developed by the previous stages in that overall stream. Once those selves emerge, they overlap; but a great deal of research strongly confirms that they emerge in a generally hierarchical fashion (as indicated in column two in chart 1a and again in fig. 10).[21]

All of that is still true. The present conception does not replace that but complements it: the realms of gross, subtle, and causal can develop, to some degree, independently of each other; and thus the frontal, the soul, and the Self can develop, to some degree, alongside each other. What researchers have been measuring as sequential self development is still accurate, but what they are measuring is the *frontal self* (bodyself to ego to centaur), and not the soul or spirit, which can develop, to some degree, *alongside* all of that, following their own holarchies and nests within nests, none of which is obvious in frontal terms.[22]

The ego (or frontal) is the self that adapts to the gross realm; the soul (or deeper psychic) is the self that adapts to the subtle realm; and the Self (or Witness) is the self that adapts to the causal realm. The frontal includes all of the self-stages that *orient consciousness to the gross realm* (the material self, the bodyself, the persona, the ego, and the centaur— all of which can be generically called "the ego"). The frontal is the self that depends on the line of gross cognition (sensorimotor to preop to conop to formop), and the frontal is therefore the self-stream responsible for orienting and integrating consciousness in the gross domain.

Alongside those developments, the soul (the psychic/subtle self) can follow its own trajectory, unfolding in its own holarchical stream. The soul or deeper-psychic line includes all the self-streams that *adapt consciousness to the many facets of the subtle sphere*. The soul is the self that depends on the subtle line of cognition (which includes, as we saw, imagination, reverie, daydreams, creative visions, hypnogogic states, etheric states, visionary revelations, hypnotic states, transcendental illuminations, and numerous types of savikalpa samadhi),[23] and thus the soul is the self-stream that orients and integrates consciousness in the subtle domain. In chart 4b, I have indicated the U-development that the subtle sometimes seems to go through: present early in development (as "trailing clouds"), then fading out as frontal (egoic) development starts to get under way, only to reassert itself in the postformal stages. (Since most theorists contest this U-development, I have left it out of fig. 11. We will return to this topic in chap. 11.)

Alongside both of those general-realm developments, the Self (or Witness) can follow its own unfolding stream.[24] The Witness is the self that depends upon the causal line of cognition (the capacity for attention, detached witnessing, equanimity in the face of gross and subtle fluctuations, etc.), and thus it is the self that orients and integrates consciousness in the causal domain. Just as important, this Self is responsible for the overall integration of all the other selves, waves, and streams. It is the Self that shines through the proximate self at any stage and in any domain, and thus it is the Self that drives the transcend-and-include Eros of every unfolding. And it is the Self supreme that prevents the three realms—gross, subtle, and causal—from flying apart in the first place. For, even though the three domains can show relatively independent development, they are still held together, and drawn together, by the radiant Self, the purest Emptiness that can impartially reflect, and therefore embrace, the entire manifest domain.

Although with higher development, the center of gravity of consciousness increasingly shifts from ego to soul to Self, nonetheless all of those are the necessary and important vehicles of Spirit as it shines in the gross, subtle, and causal realms. Thus, all three of them can be, and usually are, simultaneously present in various proportions throughout development, and the highest development itself simply involves their seamless integration as a chorus of equally valued voices of Spirit in the world.

INTEGRAL PSYCHOLOGY

Thus, the simplest generalization of an integral psychology is that it involves waves, streams, and states, ego, soul, and spirit.

When it comes to integral therapy, this means several things. First, although overall development still shows an unmistakable morphogenetic drift to deeper domains (ego to soul to spirit), the therapist can be alert to ways to recognize and strengthen the soul and spirit as they increasingly make their appearance, not simply after the ego, but within it and alongside it. Integral and transpersonal therapy works *concurrently* with the frontal, soul, and spirit, as they each unfold alongside each other, carrying their own truths, insights, and possible pathologies. Attunement to these different dimensions of consciousness can facilitate their more graceful unfolding.[25]

But this is not to suggest that gross-realm work (bodywork, ego strengthening) can be bypassed in favor of soul or spirit work, because without a strong ego as a foundation, the higher realms cannot be carried as a permanent, stable, integrated realization. Instead, the higher realms are relegated to transient peak experiences, temporary revelations, or even dissociated into spiritual emergencies. An individual who is at moral stage 2 in the frontal line of moral development can "holographically experience" all the transpersonal realms he desires, but he will *still* have to develop to moral stage 3, then 4, then 5, in order to begin to actualize those experiences in a *permanent,* nondistorted, postconventional, worldcentric, global, and bodhisattvic fashion. In fact, failure of the therapist to follow (and encourage) frontal line development, while merely encouraging altered states, can contribute to the client's failure to permanently integrate the higher and lower domains into a full-spectrum realization.

Thus, even though gross, subtle, and causal lines (and selves) can exist alongside each other in many ways, still, with continuing evolution and integral development, the *center of gravity* continues to shift holarchically toward the deeper layers of the Self (ego to soul to spirit), and around these deeper waves consciousness is increasingly organized. Concerns of the ego, while rarely disappearing, tend to fade from immediacy; the soul comes to the foreground more often. But then it, too, eventually tends to fade, becoming thinner and more transparent, as the center of gravity shifts more and more toward spirit. All of the lower selves, as functional capacities, continue to exist, holarchically enfolded in higher waves; they all continue to serve functional capacities, face their own problems, respond to their own treatments; but they increasingly lose their power to commandeer consciousness and claim it for their own.

Thus, for an overall integral development, the center of gravity of consciousness still moves through the nine fulcrums in the Great Nest, but it is a cacophony of many voices, many streams, often overlapping, always intertwining. But none of the major waves of consciousness can be totally bypassed on that account. The frontal cannot be bypassed,[26] vision-logic cannot be bypassed,[27] the subtle cannot be bypassed[28]—not for permanent, enduring, integral development and awakening. All these waves and streams are headed toward the ocean of One Taste, pulled through that great morphogenetic field by the force of "gentle persuasion toward Love"—pulled, that is, by Eros, by Spirit-in-action, by the Love that moves the sun and other stars.

10

Spirituality: Stages or Not?

ONE OF THE THORNIEST of questions is whether spirituality itself necessarily unfolds in stages. This is an extremely touchy issue. Nonetheless, as I have often suggested, this question depends in large measure on how we define "spirituality." There are at least five very different definitions, two of which seem to involve stages, and three of which do not. All of them appear to be legitimate uses of the word "spirituality," but it is absolutely necessary to specify which you mean. In fact, I think these are five very important aspects of the broad phenomenon we call "spirituality," and all of them deserve to be included to some degree in any integral model.

Here are the common definitions: (1) Spirituality involves the highest levels of any of the developmental lines. (2) Spirituality is the sum total of the highest levels of the developmental lines. (3) Spirituality is itself a separate developmental line. (4) Spirituality is an attitude (such as openness or love) that you can have at whatever stage you are at. (5) Spirituality basically involves peak experiences, not stages.

1. *Spirituality involves the highest levels of any of the developmental lines.* In this definition, "spirituality" basically means the transpersonal, transrational, post-postconventional levels of *any* of the lines, such as our highest cognitive capacities (e.g., transrational intuition), our most developed affects (e.g., transpersonal love), our highest moral aspirations (transcendental compassion for all sentient beings), our most evolved self (the transpersonal Self or supraindividual Witness), and so

on.[1] In this usage, spirituality (or this particular aspect of spirituality) definitely follows a sequential or stage-like course, because it is, by definition, the post-postconventional stages in any of the developmental streams. This is a very common usage, reflecting those aspects of spirituality that embody the very highest capacities, the noblest motives, the best of aspirations; the farther reaches of human nature; the most highly evolved, the growing tip, the leading edge—all of which point to the highest levels in any of the lines.

2. *Spirituality is the sum total of the highest levels of the developmental lines.* This is similar to the previous definition, but with a slightly different (yet important) twist. This definition emphasizes the fact that, even though the individual lines unfold hierarchically, the *sum total* of the highest stages of those lines would show no such stage-like development. Like "overall development" and "overall self" development, "overall spiritual development" would *not* be stage-like. (Say there are ten developmental lines. Say that the post-postconventional stages of those lines are the ones we are calling "spiritual." One person might develop post-postcon capacities in lines 2 and 7. Another person, in lines 3, 5, 6, 8, and 9. Another person, in lines 1 and 5. Each of those lines is hierarchical, but the sum total obviously follows no set sequence at all.) Every person's spiritual path, in other words, is radically individual and unique, even though the particular competences themselves might follow a well-defined path. (Notice, however, that with this definition, precisely because the developmental lines *themselves* are still stage-like, the development in each of those lines could be tested for.) I believe that this definition, like all of them, points to some very real and important aspects of spirituality, aspects that any complete definition of spirituality would want to include.

3. *Spirituality is itself a separate developmental line.* Obviously in this case spiritual development would show some sort of stage-like unfolding, since a developmental line, by definition, shows development.[2] I have drawn together some two dozen theorists, East and West, in charts 6a–c, who present convincing and sometimes massive evidence that at least some aspects of spirituality undergo sequential or stage-like development. This includes most of the various meditative paths East and West. In all of these cases, these aspects of spirituality show holarchical sequential development (although again, that does not preclude regressions, spirals, temporary leaps forward, or peak experiences of any of the major states).

Daniel P. Brown's extensive work on the cross-cultural stages of meditative development deserves special mention as being the most meticulous and sophisticated research to date (chart 6b). What he and his
coworker Jack Engler found is that "The major [spiritual] traditions we
have studied *in their original languages* present an unfolding of meditation experiences in terms of a *stage model*: for example, the Mahamudra
from the Tibetan Mahayana Buddhist tradition; the Visuddhimagga
from the Pali Theravada Buddhist tradition; and the Yoga Sutras from
the Sanskrit Hindu tradition [these were subsequently checked against
Chinese and Christian sources]. The models are sufficiently similar to
suggest an *underlying common invariant sequence of stages*, despite vast
cultural and linguistic differences as well as styles of practice. . . . The
results strongly suggest that the stages of meditation are in fact of cross-
cultural and universal applicability (at a deep, not surface, analysis)."[3]

Their work is included in *Transformations of Consciousness*, along
with an in-depth study by Harvard theologian John Chirban of the
stages of spiritual development evidenced by saints in Eastern Orthodox
Christianity (see chart 6c). Chirban's conclusion: "Although each saint
describes his own experience (often in his own unique way), basic parallels emerge as one compares the stages of the saints with one another.
This sameness confirms the catholicity of their experience . . ."—and the
catholicity (or universal applicability) of the basic waves of consciousness themselves, which are similarly reflected in these numerous cross-
cultural sources. Whether one is looking at Saint Teresa, Muhyiddin Ibn
'Arabi, Lady Tsogyal, Saint Dionysius, Patanjali, Hazrat Inayat Kahn,
or Mahamudra (all listed in charts 6a–c), one is again struck by the
broadly similar morphogenetic field or developmental space over which
their stages migrate.

"Highest Yoga Tantra," which, next to Dzogchen, is said to be the
highest of the Buddha's teachings, possesses an unsurpassed grasp of the
extraordinary interrelation between conscious states and bodily energies
(chart 6b). According to this teaching, in order to master the mind, one
must concomitantly master the body's subtle energies—ch'i, prana,
rLung, ki—and this yoga is an exquisite system of harnessing these subtle energies at every stage of development, right up to and including the
enlightened state of Clear Light Emptiness. Highest Yoga Tantra outlines
this overall consciousness evolution in terms of seven very clear-cut
stages, each with a very striking phenomenological sign that accompan-
ies the stage when it emerges. Thus, in meditation, when concentration
reaches the point that the first basic structure (or skandha) is tran-

scended, there arises in awareness a mirage-like appearance. When all five gross-realm basic structures are transcended, and subtle-realm consciousness emerges, there appears a vision like a "clear autumn moonlight." As subtle consciousness is transcended and one enters very subtle (or causal) consciousness, formless cessation appears as "the thick blackness of an autumn night," and so on (chart 6b).

Although these interior visions show a great deal of deep structural similarity with other meditative systems, several critics have, over the years, scolded me for implying that there are strong similarities between, for example, the Buddhist Dharmakaya (and Emptiness) and the Vedanta causal body (and nirguna Brahman). And yet—as only one example—according to Highest Yoga Tantra, one type of the Dharmakaya is experienced in *deep dreamless sleep* (formlessness); the Sambhogakaya, in the *dream state*; and the Nirmanakaya, in the *waking state*. But notice: according to Vedanta, the causal body is experienced in deep dreamless sleep, the subtle body is experienced in the dream state, and the gross body in the waking state. Therefore, if you believe that there are similarities in deep dreamless sleep between individuals, it follows that there are some profound similarities between the Buddhist Dharmakaya and the Hindu causal body. (And likewise, similarities between the Buddhist Sambhogakaya and Hindu subtle body, and the Nirmanakaya and gross body.)

Of course there are many important differences between these Buddhist and Hindu notions, and those need to be rigorously honored. And yet—simultaneously—there seem to be important and profound similarities, and these cannot be cavalierly dismissed, as pluralists and relativists do. In all of my writings I have tried to emphasize both—certain similarities in deep features, important differences in surface features.

One of the major difficulties in coming to terms with a *stage conception* is that most people, even if they are in fact progressing through stages of competence, *rarely experience anything that feels or looks like a stage*. In their own direct experience, "stages" make no sense at all. With respect to cognitive development, for example, you can videotape children at a preop stage (where they will claim that when you pour an identical amount of water from a short glass into a tall glass, the tall glass has more water), and you can show them the videotape when they are at the conop stage (where it is "completely obvious" that the same amount of water is present in each glass), and they will accuse you of doctoring the videotape, because nobody could be that stupid, and certainly not them. In other words, they just went through a monumental stage in development, yet they actually experienced not the slightest thing that told them that an extraordinary milestone had just occurred.

So it is with stages in general. We spot them only by standing back from unreflective experience, comparing our experiences with others, and seeing if there are any common patterns. If these common patterns check out in numerous different settings, then we are justified in assuming that various stages are involved. But in all cases, these stages are the product of direct investigation and research, not abstract philosophizing. And when it comes to spiritual experience, all of the great wisdom traditions in charts 6a–c have found that some very important spiritual competences *follow a stage model*, not in a rigidly clunk-and-grind fashion, but as unfolding waves of subtler and subtler experiences, and that when you compare these experiences over a large number of people, certain similarities in unfolding occur. In other words, we have some stages.

My model has often been accused of being based solely on the Eastern meditative traditions. A quick glance at charts 6a–c is enough to dispel that misconception. I would in particular like to draw attention to the work of Evelyn Underhill. Her masterpiece, *Mysticism*, first published in 1911, is still in many ways an unsurpassed classic for the elucidation of the Western mystical and contemplative traditions. Underhill divides Western mysticism into three broad hierarchical stages (with numerous substages), which she calls *nature mysticism* (a lateral expansion of consciousness to embrace the stream of life), *metaphysical mysticism* (culminating in formless cessation), and *divine mysticism* (which she divides into dark night and union). These are in many ways quite similar to my own nature mysticism, deity mysticism, and formless/nondual mysticism. These *stages of spirituality* are deeply important, whether they appear East or West, North or South, and no account of spirituality is complete without them.

4. *Spirituality is an attitude (such as openness or love) that you can have at whatever stage you are at.* This is probably the most popular and common definition. Nonetheless, it has proven very difficult to define or even state in a coherent fashion. We can't easily say that the requisite attitude is love, because love, according to most research, tends (like other affects) to unfold from egocentric to sociocentric to worldcentric modes; and therefore this attitude is *not* fully present at all of the levels, but rather itself develops (do we really want to call egocentric love "spiritual"?). "Openness" might work, but again the question becomes: does

the capacity for openness itself simply show up fully formed, or does it develop? And just how "open" can a preconventional individual be, when he or she cannot even take the role of other? "Integration" would fit the bill—the degree to which whatever lines are present are integrated and balanced—but in my system that is just another name for what the self does, and thus is not anything specifically "spiritual." At any rate, I believe this is a legitimate definition, but thus far, coherent examples of it have been scarce.

5. *Spirituality basically involves peak experiences.* That is certainly true in many cases, and peak experiences (or altered states of consciousness) do not usually show development or stage-like unfolding. They are temporary, passing, transient. Moreover, states, unlike structures, are mostly *incompatible.* You cannot be drunk and sober at the same time. (This is quite unlike structures, which, because they transcend and include, can coexist: cells and molecules can both exist together, the one embracing the other—which is why growth and development occur by way of structures, not states, although the latter are significant in themselves and can have a direct impact on development.) Therefore, if one's definition of spirituality is a peak experience, then that does not in itself involve a stage-like unfolding.

However, as I earlier suggested, you can examine peak experiences more closely and find that they generally involve psychic, subtle, causal, or nondual peak experiences interpreted through archaic, magic, mythic, or rational structures—and each of those show stage-like development. Still, this is an important definition of spirituality, and it goes to show that at virtually any stage of development, temporary peak experiences of the transpersonal realms are possible. However, to the extent these *temporary states* are converted to *enduring traits,* they become structures that show development. (I will include in the endnote a discussion of a plausible mechanism for this conversion: the self metabolizes temporary experience to produce holistic structure.)[4]

Those are five of the more common definitions of spirituality. The conclusion: not everything that we can legitimately call "spirituality" shows stage-like development. Nonetheless, many aspects of spirituality turn out, upon closer inspection, to involve one or more aspects that are developmental. This includes the higher reaches of the various developmental lines, as well as spirituality considered as a separate line itself. Peak experiences, however, do not show stage-like development, although both the structures that have the peak experiences, and the realms that are peaked into, show development if permanent realizations are acquired.

DOES PSYCHOLOGICAL DEVELOPMENT HAVE TO BE COMPLETED BEFORE SPIRITUAL DEVELOPMENT CAN BEGIN?

This depends, once again, almost entirely on how we define those terms. If spirituality is defined as a separate line of development, the answer is "No" (because it occurs alongside, not on top of, psychological development). If spirituality is defined as peak experience, the answer is also "No" (because that can occur at any time). But beyond that it gets a little trickier.

First of all, what many theorists mean by "psychological development" is the *personal* stages of development (precon, con, and postcon), and what they mean by "spiritual" is the *transpersonal* stages (postpostcon). *Using those definitions,* and when looking at *any one developmental line,* the psychological must generally be completed before the spiritual can stably emerge (simply because, as much research indicates, you can't have postcon without first having con, and so on).

However—and this is what has confused many theorists—because the developmental lines themselves can unfold independently, an individual can be at a very high spiritual stage (transpersonal or post-postcon) in one line and still be at a very low personal or psychological stage (con or precon) in others. For example, a person might be at a transpersonal level of cognition (perhaps attained by meditative development), and yet still be at a personal or psychological (con or precon) stage of moral development. Thus, even though, with these definitions, the spiritual comes only after the psychological in any given line, nonetheless all sorts of spiritual developments can occur before, alongside, or after, all sorts of psychological developments, precisely because the lines themselves are relatively independent. A person can be at a precon stage in one line, a postcon stage in another, and a post-postcon in three others, which, by these definitions, means two psychological levels and three spiritual levels, so obviously overall psychological development does *not* have to be completed before any sort of spiritual development can occur.

If one's idea of spirituality is peak experiences, those can occur anytime, any place, so overall psychological development does not have to be completed for those, either. But to the extent those states become traits, they, too, will of necessity enter the stream of development and swim in its morphogenetic currents, flowing through the waves in the great River of Life.

THE IMPORTANCE OF SPIRITUAL PRACTICE

Finally, let us note an item of great importance. Whether, in the end, you believe spiritual practice involves stages or not, authentic spirituality does involve *practice*. This is not to deny that for many people beliefs are important, faith is important, religious mythology is important. It is simply to add that, as the testimony of the world's great yogis, saints, and sages has made quite clear, authentic spirituality can also involve direct *experience* of a living Reality, disclosed immediately and intimately in the heart and consciousness of individuals, and fostered by diligent, sincere, prolonged spiritual practice. Even if you relate to spirituality as a peak experience, those peak experiences can often be specifically induced, or at least invited, by various forms of spiritual practice, such as active ritual, contemplative prayer, shamanic voyage, intensive meditation, and so forth. All of those open one to a direct experience of Spirit, and not merely beliefs or ideas about Spirit.

Therefore, don't just think differently, practice diligently. My own recommendation is for any type of "integral transformative practice" (as outlined in chapter 8); but any sort of authentic spiritual practice will do. A qualified teacher, with whom you feel comfortable, is a must. One might start by consulting the works of Father Thomas Keating, Rabbi Zalman Schachter-Shalomi, the Dalai Lama, Sri Ramana Maharshi, Bawa Muhaiyadeen, or any of the many widely acknowledged teachers in any of the great lineages.

At the same time, be wary of those spiritual paths that involve simply changing your beliefs or ideas. Authentic spirituality is not about translating the world differently, but about transforming your consciousness. Yet many of the "new paradigm" approaches to spirituality would simply have you change the way you think about the world: you are supposed to think holistically instead of analytically; you are supposed to believe, not in the Newtonian-Cartesian billiard-ball world, but in the world of systems theory and the great "web of life"; you are supposed to think in terms, not of patriarchal divisiveness, but of the holistic Goddess and Gaia.

All of those are important ideas, but they are merely ways to think about the Right-Hand world, not ways to transform the Left-Hand world. Most of these new-paradigm approaches recommend that we use vision-logic (or holistic thinking) in order to overcome our fragmented world. But, as we have repeatedly seen, cognitive development (such as vision-logic or network-thinking) is necessary, *but not sufficient*, for moral development, self-development, spiritual development, and so on. You can have full access to vision-logic and still be at moral stage one, with safety needs, egocentric drives, and narcissistic inclinations. You can totally master systems theory and completely learn the new physics, and still be very poorly developed in emotional, moral, and spiritual streams.

Thus, simply learning systems theory, or the new physics, or learning about Gaia, or thinking holistically, will not necessarily do anything to transform your interior consciousness, because none of those address the interior stages of growth and development. Open any book on systems theory, the new paradigm, the new physics, and so on, and you will learn about how all things are part of a great interconnected Web of Life, and that by accepting this belief, the world can be healed. But rarely will you find a discussion of the many *interior stages of the growth of consciousness* that alone can lead to an actual embrace of global consciousness. You will find little on preconventional, conventional, postconventional, and post-postconventional stages; nothing on what an enormous amount of research has taught us on the growth of consciousness from egocentric to sociocentric to worldcentric (or more specifically, the nine or so fulcrums of self unfolding); no hints about how these interior transformations occur, and what you can do to foster them in your own case—thus truly contributing to a worldcentric, global, spiritual consciousness in yourself and others. All you find is: modern science and matriarchal religions all agree that we are parts of the great Web of Life.

The ecological crisis—or Gaia's main problem—is not pollution, toxic dumping, ozone depletion, or any such. Gaia's main problem is that not enough human beings have developed to the postconventional, worldcentric, global levels of consciousness, wherein they will automatically be moved to care for the global commons. And human beings develop to those postconventional levels, not by learning systems theories, but by going through at least a half-dozen major interior transformations, ranging from egocentric to ethnocentric to worldcentric, at which point, and not before, they can awaken to a deep and authentic concern for Gaia. The primary cure for the ecological crisis is not learning that Gaia is a Web of Life, however true that may be, but learning ways to foster these many arduous waves of interior growth, none of which are addressed by most of the new-paradigm approaches.

In short, systems theory and the Web-of-Life theories do not generally transform consciousness because, hobbled with their subtle reductionism, they do not adequately address the interior stages of consciousness development—where the real growth occurs. They might be a fine place for one to start on the spiritual path—they are helpful in suggesting a more unified life—but they themselves do not appear to be an effective path to that life. They do not offer, in short, any sort of sustained interior practice that can actualize the higher and more global stages of consciousness. And, sadly, in claiming to offer a completely "holistic" view of the world, they often prevent or discourage people from taking up a genuine path of interior growth and development, and thus they hamper the evolution of just that global consciousness that they otherwise so nobly espouse.

11

Is There a Childhood Spirituality?

I S THERE A CHILDHOOD SPIRITUALITY?
By definitions 1 and 2, no. By definitions 3, 4, and 5, yes. Sort of.

EARLY STAGES

Definition 1 (spirituality is the highest level in any line) and definition 2 (spirituality is the sum total of the highest levels in all the lines) rule out almost any sort of childhood spirituality, simply because during infancy and childhood most developmental lines are preconventional and conventional. This does not preclude other types of spirituality; it simply says that *to the extent* you define spirituality as transrational, supramental, postformal, superconscious, and post-postconventional, then those are not significantly present in childhood.

Definition 3 (spirituality is a separate line of development) maintains that infancy and childhood definitely have a spirituality . . . but only the lowest stages of spirituality, which by most definitions do not look very spiritual at all. Even according to the theorists who propose this definition, the love is egocentric, the beliefs are narcissistic, the outlook is self-absorbed, the capacity to take the role of others (and thus genuinely care for others) is rudimentary or missing altogether. Nonetheless, this definition considers those to be the *early stages* of lines that can be called "spiritual" because they will, with further development, unfold into capacities that most people would clearly recognize as spiritual. James

Fowler's "stages of faith" is exactly this type of model. By this definition, then, we should not conclude that infants are saints or sages, or permanently in touch with authentic spiritual realities, but rather are on a long road to authentic spirituality via higher development (and here this reverts to definition 1 or 2: "real" or "authentic" spirituality involves the post-postconventional stages of development).

Definition 4, on the other hand, strongly maintains that infants and children are directly in touch with spiritual realities, or at least can be, because they can be in touch with the attitude that defines spirituality (openness, love, fluidity, etc.). Moreover, most people using this definition claim that children are *more* in touch with this quality of, say, openness or fluidity, than are adults, and that a genuine spirituality involves the *recapture* of this openness.

The problem with that definition, as we saw, is that it has had difficulty producing credible and coherent examples. Does the "openness" just show up fully formed, or does it develop? If it can't take the role of other, how "open" can it really be? If the openness is egocentric, no matter how spontaneous and fluid, is that really what we mean by "spiritual"? Is a joyful narcissist "spiritual"?

It appears that what most people have in mind with this definition is that children often have a more open contact with a certain feeling-dimension of being (the prana-maya-kosha, élan vital, emotional-etheric sheath, second chakra, etc.), and that is very likely true. Moreover, it is definitely true that aspects of that dimension can be repressed by the higher structures of the mind (ego, superego, conscience), which can result in various types of painful pathology. And that, finally, a *recapture* (in the form of regression in service of the ego) of that lost potential is required in order to heal the damage and regain a more fluid, flowing, feeling-ful outlook on life.

I agree with all of those points. The question is, why call the preconventional feeling-dimension by the term "spiritual," when, as research has repeatedly demonstrated, it is egocentric in relation to others? For the mind to be in touch with the feelings of the body is extremely important, but spirituality *also* involves being in touch with the feelings of *others*, and a positively massive amount of research has consistently demonstrated that such role-taking and perspectivism steadily *increases* from preop to conop to formop to postformal.

If your idea of spirituality is feeling good, then childhood might be Eden;[1] but if your idea *also* involves doing good, by taking the role of others, and projecting your consciousness through multiple perspectives and pluralistic outlooks so as to include compassion, caring, and altruism, then childhood is a realm of diminished expectations, no matter how wonderfully fluid and flowing its egocentrism. What is regrettable about the repression of childhood capacities is not that, for the most part, it involves the repression of higher, spiritual dimensions (e.g., the vijnana-maya-kosha), but that it involves the repression of lower but invaluable foundations (e.g., prana-maya-kosha), whose dissociation can cripple further development. Moreover, the *repression barrier* erected by the ego to prevent lower, prerational impulses from coming up, can also act, in later development, to prevent higher, transrational impulses from coming down. The defenses against id can defend against God, simply because a wall is a wall. But what the childhood ego essentially represses is the preconventional id, not the postconventional God.

ALTERED STATES AND TRAILING CLOUDS

Definition 5 (peak experiences), however, offers a credible definition and a modest amount of evidence that at least some children have some types of spiritual experiences. I believe that is true, and I have offered a grid of such experiences—namely, peak experiences of the psychic, subtle, causal, or nondual realm interpreted through an archaic, magic, mythic, or rational outlook—for most children, that means magic or mythic. I realize that many theorists strongly object to calling that "spiritual," and research such as Fowler's would deny any higher or authentic spirituality to those structures; but I think we can refer to them as spiritual peak experiences, as long as we are careful to specify the exact contours.[2]

The one aspect of infancy and childhood that, if it exists, might be genuinely spiritual is that aspect I call the "trailing clouds of glory" (from Wordsworth: "Not in entire forgetfulness . . . but trailing clouds of glory do we come. . . ."), namely, the deeper psychic (or soul) dimension that, some evidence tentatively suggests, is present from prenatal through the early years, but then fades as frontal (egoic) development gets under way.[3] The "trailing clouds of glory" refers in general to all the deeper psychic (or soul) awareness that the individual brings to this life and which is therefore present in some sense from conception forward (however you wish to construe that—as reincarnation, or simply as deeper potentials present from the start). Hazrat Inayat Khan probably put it best, representing the traditional view: "The crying of an infant is very often the expression of its longing for the angelic heavens [through which it has just passed on its way to earthly birth—what the Tibetans call the rebirth bardo]; the smiles of an infant are a narrative of its memories of heaven and of the spheres above."[4]

This deeper psychic awareness is, according to various theories, either (1) the soul descending from the bardo realms (the realms between death and rebirth), or (2) a deeper ground or potential that is necessarily lost and buried as the analytic ego develops (but can be regained in enlightenment or full spiritual realization).

The second option, although it initially sounds feasible, seems to fall apart in the details. This ground is said to be the same ground one regains in enlightenment, but if so, why would anybody ever abandon it? If this ground is regained, why does development do something it does in no other system, namely, start running backwards? Would a chicken regress to an egg in order to find itself? If this ground is reunited with the ego, so that *both together* constitute full development, that means that the ground itself *is not complete*, and how could something inherently not complete be the ground of full enlightenment? Could a part ever be the ground of the whole? This view—which, incidentally, I once embraced—seems to be largely inadequate in both theory and data.[5]

That leaves option number one, the bardo realms, as the major contender, even though it sounds quite far-fetched to the conventional mind. Nonetheless, there is a modest amount of evidence that is suggestive.[6] It appears that this deeper psychic being is increasingly submerged and forgotten as frontal or egoic development gets under way (see chart 4b), although if development continues into the actual psychic level (F-7), this deeper psychic being emerges (which often brings flashbacks of childhood, when this deeper psychic was "watching" from afar).[7] But whatever this deeper psychic capacity is, it is *not* the resurrection of a prerational infantile structure, but the discovery of a transrational structure.

We can say, then, that infants and children at the very least seem to have access to some types of spiritual experiences (as peak experiences), even though these are interpreted through frontal structures that are preconventional and egocentric (and not, as it were, very spiritual themselves). But in possibly being in touch with the deeper psychic (or soul) realm, infancy and childhood might evidence a connection with one type of spiritual dimension, even though, once again, it is of necessity interpreted and expressed through preconventional and egocentric channels, and thus is not spiritual in any pure sense.

12

Sociocultural Evolution

SPIRIT-IN-ACTION

I T NOW SEEMS APPARENT that there are at least four major inadequacies to the Great Chain as it was traditionally conceived, and in order to bring it into the modern and postmodern world—and develop a truly integral approach—these shortcomings need to be carefully addressed.[1]

The first, as we saw, is that the four quadrants were very seldom differentiated on an adequate scale. Thus, the great traditions rarely understood that states of consciousness (UL) have correlates in the organic brain (UR), a fact that has revolutionized our understanding of psychopharmacology, psychiatry, and consciousness studies. Likewise, the traditions evidenced little understanding that individual awareness (UL) is profoundly molded by both its background cultural worldviews (LL) and the modes of techno-economic production (LR) in which it finds itself. This left the Great Chain open to devastating critiques from the Enlightenment, from modern cognitive science, from neuropsychiatry, and from postmodern cultural and historical studies, among others, all of which demonstrated that consciousness is not merely a disembodied, transcendental noumenon, but is deeply embedded in contexts of objective facts, cultural backgrounds, and social structures. The Great Chain theorists had no believable response to these charges (precisely because they were deficient in these areas).

As we saw, each of the *vertical levels* of the Great Chain needs to be differentiated into at least four *horizontal dimensions* (intentional, behavioral, cultural, social). The Great Nest desperately needs to be modernized and postmodernized: it needs to recognize the importance of cultural background, relativistic surface structures and contexts, correlations with modern scientific discoveries, sensitivity to minorities that the mythic-agrarian structure often marginalized, the importance of pluralistic voices, and so on. Only as body, mind, soul, and spirit are differentiated into the Big Three can these objections be handled.

The second inadequacy is that the level of mind itself needs to be subdivided in the light of its *early development*. Here the contributions of Western psychology are decisive. To put it in a nutshell, the mind itself has at least four major stages of growth: *magic* (2–5 years), *mythic* (6–11 years), *rational* (11 onward), and integral-aperspectival or *vision-logic* (adulthood, if then). Precisely because the infantile and childish origins of the *preformal* levels of magic and mythic were not clearly understood, the traditions often confused them with the *postformal* states of psychic and subtle, and this pre/post fallacy haunts most of the perennial philosophy, injecting it not only with truly enlightened wisdom, but substantial stretches of superstition.

The third inadequacy: Because the traditional Great Chain theorists had a poor understanding of the early, infantile, prerational stages of human development, they likewise failed to grasp the types of *psychopathologies* that often stem from complications at these early stages. In particular, psychosis, borderline, and neurotic diseases often stem from problems at the early fulcrums of self-development, and can best be approached with an understanding of their developmental dimensions. Meditation—which is a way to carry development forward into the transpersonal—will not, as a rule, cure these prepersonal lesions (as hosts of American practitioners found out the hard way).

The fourth inadequacy in the traditional Great Chain is its lack of understanding of evolution, an understanding that is also a rather exclusive contribution of the modern West. This is easily remedied, because, as many theorists have pointed out, if you tilt the Great Chain on its side and let it unfold in time—instead of being statically given all at once, as traditionally thought—you have the outlines of evolution itself. Plotinus temporalized = evolution.

In other words, evolution to date—starting with the Big Bang—has unfolded approximately three-fifths of the Great Chain—matter, sensation, perception, impulse, image, symbol, concept, rule, and formal, in essentially the order suggested by the Great Nest. All that is required is to see that the Great Chain does not exist fully given and statically unchanging, but rather evolves or develops over great periods of time. And the fact is, despite the bluff of Western biologists, nobody really understands how higher stages emerge in evolution—unless we assume it is via Eros, or Spirit-in-action.

This also means, as I have often pointed out, that what the perennial philosophy took to be eternally unchanging archetypes can better be understood as formative habits of evolution, "Kosmic memories," as it were, and not pregiven molds into which the world is poured.[2] This dynamic orientation can bring the Great Nest of Being more into accord with evolutionary thinkers from Peirce to Sheldrake to Kaufmann, and it is a view that is definitely implicit in Great Nest theorists from Plotinus to Asanga and Vasubandhu.[3]

The point is that, once the Great Nest is plugged into an *evolutionary* and *developmental* view, it can happily coexist with much of the God of the modern West, namely, evolution.[4] Moreover, it raises the stunning possibility: if evolution has thus far unfolded the first three-fifths of the Great Nest, isn't it likely that it will continue in the coming years and unfold the higher two-fifths? If that is so, God lies down the road, not up it; Spirit is found by going forward, not backward; the Garden of Eden lies in our future, not our past.[5]

Be that as it may, when one moves from pluralistic relativism to universal integralism (e.g., when one moves from green to yellow/turquoise and begins to take advantage of second-tier constructions), one is open to such meta-systemic theories as presented in charts 9a and 9b—namely, overviews of social and cultural evolution.

COLLECTIVE EVOLUTION

In my definitions, "social" refers to the Lower-Right quadrant (the interobjective dimension, including forms of the techno-economic base, social systems, institutions, and physical structures), and "cultural" refers to the Lower-Left quadrant (the intersubjective dimension, including collective worldviews, ethics, values, and meaning). The preponderance of evidence clearly suggests that evolution occurs in both of these quadrants, as it certainly does in the others. But this needs to be qualified in several respects.

For example, to say that a given society is at a magical level of development does not mean that everybody in that society is at that level. It only means that the *average* level of consciousness is generally magical, and that, more specifically, the defining laws, principles of cultural organization, and mores of everyday reality stem predominantly from the magical worldview. But any number of people can be above or below that average in their own case. For example, some individuals in a magical culture (unlike a child at the magical structure—and here is one of the many places that strict onto/phylo parallels break down) can be at a mythic, mental, or higher level of development. Habermas believes, for instance, that even in hunting and gathering societies, a few people developed the capacities for formal operational thinking, and I have suggested that a few went even further and developed postformal and *psychic capacities* (and these were, of course, the shamans).[6] Thus, unlike a child at the magical level, a truly developed shaman in a magical culture, having evolved various postconventional capacities, would be able to authentically experience the transpersonal realms (mostly the psychic, but also, on occasion, subtle and perhaps causal) and interpret them through non-narcissistic and postconventional structures: in other words, an authentic spirituality by any definition.

That, of course, is speculation, and would represent a highly developed shamanic vision. As for the more typical or common shamanic journey, the available evidence suggests that it was a magic-level peak experience of the psychic domains, and thus it retained preformal imprints and interpretations, heavily involved, as magic often is, with power drives and needs. "Power" or "strong medicine" remains the dominant tone of many shamanic drives, reflecting, perhaps, the fact that in the typical hunting and gathering society, the major scarce resource, as Habermas pointed out, was power over nature, or simple safety needs, as Maslow might say.

Nonetheless, the profound importance of the shamanic voyage, in any of its versions, was that it was the first great discovery of, and exploration of, the transpersonal domains, and thus many shamanic insights, especially into the psychic realms, remained unsurpassed.[7] In particular, we may note that the shaman, as the first "psychotherapist," was the first to discover the extraordinary importance of transpersonal altered states of consciousness for ordinary healing, both physical healing and psychological healing—an insight that, disastrously, was one of the casualties of the modern flatland.

Still, the preponderance of evidence, when not subjected to an interpretation that is biased toward pluralistic relativism, suggests that, for the most part, both the average and the most advanced modes of development continued to deepen with subsequent evolution, and charts 9a and 9b outline some of the major contours of this evolutionary migration.

SOCIAL EVOLUTION

Lenski has laid out the forms of social evolution in a way that is now uncontested by most scholars: foraging, horticultural, maritime, agrarian, industrial, and informational. Systems theorists (and structural-functionalists, including Parsons, Merton, Luhmann, Alexander, Bellah) have shed an enormous light on social action systems, their maintenance and self-reproduction.[8] Marxists and neo-Marxists, despite the obvious failings of a system that attempts to reduce all quadrants to the Lower Right, have nonetheless outlined the many ways in which the techno-economic base profoundly influences the consciousness of men and women, and no integral theory can afford to overlook these important findings.[9]

The major drawback of systems theory (and Lower-Right theories in general) is their subtle reductionism: the attempt to reduce all interior domains (of the I and we) to objective it-domains—to information processing circuits, neuronal systems, social behavior, autopoietic self-maintenance systems, and "web of life" theories—all of which, to the extent they claim to be "holistic" and "all-encompassing," actually deny the lifeworld of the interior dimensions. Systems theory claims to offer a unified theory of everything, but in reducing all quadrants to the Lower Right, it actually leaves out "half" of the world, namely, the Left-Hand domains. As such, systems theory is actually part of the flatland project of modernity. It is part of the disease for which it claims to be the cure.

A genuine or integral holism would include both the exterior holism of systems theory and the interior holism of phenomenal consciousness, morals, values, waves, streams, and states, all embraced in their own terms, not forced into the molds of the others.

CULTURAL EVOLUTION

Evolution in the cultural domain is a sensitive topic, with potential for abuse when not handled with care. Still, the evidence for it continues to mount, and numerous theorists have embraced it in qualified forms. (As we saw in chapter 4, for several decades the green meme successfully fought any evolutionary thinking in academia, understandably concerned over its potential for abuse. But post-green developments have managed to combine green sensitivity to multiple perspectives with second-tier constructions.) In recent times, cultural evolution has been championed, in various ways, by Gerald Heard, Michael Murphy, W. G. Runciman, Sisirkumar Ghose, Alastair Taylor, Jean Houston, Duane Elgin, Jay Earley, Daniel Dennett, Jürgen Habermas, Robert Bellah, Ervin Laszlo, Kishore Gandhi, and Jean Gebser, to name a few.[10]

The pioneering work of Jean Gebser is paradigmatic: he sees cultural worldviews evolving—to use his words—from archaic to magic to mythic to mental to integral (see chart 9b). Gebser's masterpiece, *Ursprung und Gegenwart* (*The Ever-Present Origin*), is certainly one of the most brilliant surveys of cultural evolution ever written, and no integral theory, in my opinion, can hope to succeed without taking its meticulous formulations into account. It should be noted, however, that Gebser's "integral structure" refers basically to the overall vision-logic wave, and does not adequately cover the higher, truly transpersonal stages (psychic, subtle, causal, and nondual). Gebser's foremost American interpreter, Georg Feuerstein, agrees. "I must side with Wilber on this point. I think there is sufficient evidence to usefully group a wide range of what would be considered spiritual experiences into three main categories: those that are basically *psychic* (I propose *psychosomatic*), *causal* (I propose *psychospiritual*), and *nondual* (I propose *spiritual*)."[11] Thus Feuerstein's overall spectrum includes archaic, magic, mythic, mental, integral, psychic, causal, and nondual—a much more accurate full-spectrum view than Gebser's. Nonetheless, in the domain of average collective development—archaic to magic to mythic to rational to integral—Gebser is unsurpassed.

Habermas's attempt to reconstruct historical materialism on the basis of universal pragmatics and communicative action remains the most sophisticated of modern attempts to trace sociocultural evolution. The great advantage of Habermas's formulations is their attempt at a comprehensive scope: a truly all-quadrant, almost all-level, view (see chart 10). We saw that the major drawbacks in his approach include an inadequate coverage of both the prerational and the transrational domains, which unfortunately renders his scheme unstable with respect to both nature and spirit (a major liability). Still, in the intermediate realm of mind, Habermas is indispensable.

Fortunately, several theorists, who are equally familiar with the higher levels of consciousness, have used their expertise to trace consciousness evolution on the whole. Of these, particular mention might be made of the work of Jean Houston (especially *Life-Force*, a superb book based in part on the important work of Gerald Heard; see chart 9a), Duane Elgin (whose *Awakening Earth* is a masterful overview of consciousness evolution; see chart 9b), and Allan Combs (the only reason I have not listed Combs on the chart is that his wonderful book *The Radiance of Being* is a summary and overview of Gebser/Aurobindo/ Wilber, with many original insights, but without a radically new series of proposed stages, although he does offer his own model).[12]

Although the above scholars have made vital contributions to our understanding of sociocultural evolution, the entire topic itself remains deeply problematic to many theorists—especially to liberals (who suspect it of marginalizing tendencies), traditionalists (who do not understand why so much of religion was left behind by modern "evolution"), and Romantics (who often believe in devolution). Since evolution is one of the crucial ingredients—some would say *the* crucial ingredient—of the modern scientific worldview, and if we truly wish an integral embrace of premodern, modern, and postmodern, then we need a way to put the theory of evolution in a context that both honors its truths and curtails its abuses.

FIVE IMPORTANT HINTS

The crucial issue is this: In order for cultural evolution and morphogenesis to be embraced as an explanatory principle in human history, it faces exactly the profound objections that have led traditionalists, Romantics, and liberal social theorists to reject it. In other words, if evolution is operating in the human domain, how can we account for Auschwitz? And how dare we make judgments about some cultural productions being more evolved than others? How dare we make such value rankings? What kind of arrogance is that?

The traditionalists and today's perennial philosophers, for example, cannot believe in cultural evolution because of such modern horrors as Auschwitz, Hiroshima, Chernobyl. How can we say evolution is at work in humans when it produces such monsters? Better to deny evolution altogether than to get caught up in having to explain those obscenities.

The Romantic critics of evolution, on the other hand, are responding to what seems to be a universal human sympathy for a time prior to today's turmoils. Primal men and women, on the whole, did not suffer the disasters of modernity—no industrial pollution, little slavery, few property disputes, and so on. By any scale of quality, haven't we in fact gone downhill? Isn't it time to get back to nature, back to the noble savage, and thus find a truer self, a fairer community, a richer life?

The liberal social theorists likewise have every reason to recoil in horror from the notion of cultural evolution. Its unbelievably crude forms, such as Social Darwinism, are not just lacking in compassion; much more sinister, this type of crass "evolutionism," pressed into the hands of moral tyrants, would produce exactly the type of ruinous and barbaric notions of the superman, the master race, the coming human demigods, who would chillingly goose-step their way into history, who would in fact inscribe their beliefs on the tortured flesh of millions, would press their ideology into the gas chambers and let it all be settled there. Liberal social theorists, reacting to such horrors, naturally tend to look upon any sort of "social hierarchy" as a prelude to Auschwitz.

Obviously, if consciousness evolution is to be used as any sort of explanatory principle, it faces several stern difficulties. What is therefore required is a set of tenets that can explain *both* advance and regression, good news and bad news, the ups and downs of an evolutionary thrust that is nonetheless as active in humans as it is in the rest of the Kosmos. Otherwise, we face the extremely bizarre situation of driving a virulent wedge right through the middle of the Kosmos: everything nonhuman operates by evolution; everything human does not.

What are the principles that can rehabilitate cultural evolution in a sophisticated form, and thus reunite humanity with the rest of the Kosmos, and yet also account for the ups and downs of consciousness unfolding? Here are some of the central explanatory principles that I believe we need:

1. *The dialectic of progress.* As consciousness evolves and unfolds, each stage solves or defuses certain problems of the previous stage, but then adds new and recalcitrant—and sometimes more complex and more difficult—problems of its own. Precisely because evolution in all domains (human and otherwise) operates by a process of differentiation and integration, then each new and more complex level necessarily faces problems not present in its predecessors. Dogs get cancer; atoms don't. But this doesn't damn evolution altogether! It means evolution is good news, bad news, this dialectic of progress. And the more stages of evolu-

tion there are—the greater the depth of the Kosmos—the more things that *can* go wrong. Modernity can get sick in ways that foragers could not even imagine, literally.

So evolution inherently means that new potentials and new wonders and new glories are introduced with each new stage, but they are invariably accompanied by new horrors, new fears, new problems, new disasters. And any truly balanced account of history is a chronicle of the new wonders and the new diseases that unfolded in the unrelenting winds of the evolution of consciousness.

2. *The distinction between differentiation and dissociation.* Precisely because evolution proceeds by differentiation and integration, something can go wrong at each and every stage—the greater the depth of the Kosmos, the more diseases there can be. And, as we saw, one of the most prevalent forms of evolutionary pathology occurs when *differentiation* goes too far into *dissociation,* whether ontogenetically or phylogenetically. In human evolution, for example, it is one thing to differentiate the mind and body, quite another to dissociate them. It is one thing to differentiate culture and nature, quite another to dissociate them. Differentiation is the prelude to integration; dissociation is the prelude to disaster.

Human evolution (like evolution everywhere else) is marked by a series of important differentiations, which are absolutely normal and altogether crucial for the evolution and integration of consciousness (it is only by differentiation that an acorn grows into an oak). But at each stage, these differentiations can go too far into dissociation, which converts depth into disease, growth into cancer, culture into nightmare, consciousness into agony. And any balanced account of history is a chronicle not only of the necessary differentiations of consciousness evolution, but also of the pathological dissociations and distortions that all too often followed in their wake.

3. *The difference between transcendence and repression.* To say that evolution proceeds by differentiation and integration is to say that it proceeds by transcendence and inclusion. Each stage includes its predecessors, then adds its own defining and emergent qualities: it transcends and includes.

But for just that reason, with *pathology,* the senior dimension doesn't transcend and include; it transcends and represses, denies, distorts, disrupts. Each new and higher stage has exactly this choice: transcend and include, befriend, integrate, honor; or transcend and repress, deny, alienate, oppress. And any balanced account of history is a chronicle of the great transcendent occasions of human evolution, as well as of the grotesque repressions, oppressions, brutalities.

4. *The difference between natural hierarchy and pathological hierarchy.* During the evolutionary process, that which is whole at one stage becomes a part of the whole of the next: whole atoms become parts of molecules, whole molecules become parts of cells, whole cells become parts of organisms. . . . Each and every thing in the Kosmos is a whole/part, a holon, existing in a nested hierarchy or holarchy, an order of increasing wholeness and holism.

But that which transcends can repress. And thus normal and natural hierarchies can degenerate into pathological hierarchies, into dominator hierarchies. In these cases, an arrogant holon doesn't want to be *both* a whole and a part; it wants to be a whole, period. It does not want to be a part of something larger than itself; it does not want to share in the communions of its fellow holons; its wants to dominate them with its own agency. Power replaces communion; domination replaces communication; oppression replaces reciprocity. And any balanced account of history is a chronicle of the extraordinary growth and evolution of normal hierarchies, a growth that ironically allowed a degeneration into pathological hierarchies, which left their marks burned into the tortured flesh of untold millions, a trail of terror that accompanied the animal who not only can transcend but repress.

5. *Higher structures can be hijacked by lower impulses.* Tribalism, when left to its own devices, is relatively benign, simply because its means and its technologies are relatively harmless. You can only inflict so much damage on the biosphere, and on other humans, with a bow and arrow (and this lack of means does not necessarily mean presence of wisdom). The problem is that the advanced technologies of rationality, when hijacked by tribalism and its ethnocentric drives, can be devastating.

Auschwitz is not the result of rationality. Auschwitz is the result of the many products of rationality being used in irrational ways. Auschwitz is rationality hijacked by tribalism, by an ethnocentric mythology of blood and soil and race, rooted in the land, romantic in its dispositions, barbaric in its ethnic cleansing. You cannot seriously attempt genocide with a bow and arrow; but you can attempt it with steel and coal, combustion engines and gas chambers, machine guns and atomic bombs. These are not rational desires by any definition of rational; these are ethnocentric tribalisms commandeering the tools of an advanced consciousness and using them precisely for the lowest of the lowest motives. Auschwitz is the endgame, not of reason, but of tribalism.

Those are a handful of the distinctions that, I believe, are necessary to reconstruct the evolution of human consciousness in a much more satisfactory and compelling fashion, a fashion that can clearly account for the undeniable advances as well as the undeniable disasters of human history.[13] With this approach, and with these five or so distinctions, I believe we can begin to reunite humanity with the rest of the Kosmos, and not be saddled with a truly bizarre and rigid dualism: humanity over here, everything else over there.

No, it seems that we are part and parcel of a single and all-encompassing evolutionary current that is itself Spirit-in-action, the mode and manner of Spirit's creation. The same currents that run through our human blood run through swirling galaxies and colossal solar systems, crash through the great oceans and course through the cosmos, move the mightiest of mountains as well as our own moral aspirations—one and same current moves throughout the All, and drives the entire Kosmos in its every lasting gesture, an extraordinary morphogenetic field that exerts a pull and pressure which refuses to surrender until you remember who and what you are, and that you were carried to this realization by that single current of an all-pervading Love, and here "there came fulfillment in a flash of light, and vigor failed the lofty fantasy, but now my will and my desires were moved like a wheel revolving evenly, by the Love that moves the sun and other stars."

SPIRITUAL REVELATIONS: THE GROWING TIP OF EVOLUTION

With those five tenets, I believe we can more humanely approach the topic of evolution and draw upon its liberating insights. If, as we have seen, certain aspects of spirituality become more available in the higher stages of development, then an understanding of development—what it is, how to foster it—is part of the truly liberal agenda of liberty, freedom, equality. We have already examined the stages of individual ontogenetic development, and we are now surveying the correlative stages of phylogenetic/cultural development. In both cases, we need to be alert not only to the major emergents and positive advances, but also to the new pathologies, repressions, oppressions, and brutalities that each new evolutionary advance makes possible.

Up from Eden traces these cultural developments in both the *average mode* and the *most advanced mode* that typically defined a given era (see chart 9a). The general idea is simple: when the average level of consciousness of a given culture is, say, magical, what is the highest level of consciousness generally available?[14] We just saw that in magical times, the most highly evolved mode was generally shamanic. The shaman was *the growing tip of consciousness evolution* (reaching at least to the psychic domain, either as a permanent structural achievement or, at the very least, as a series of altered states and shamanic voyages).[15] The magical/shamanic mode was the dominant form of consciousness for the largest period of humanity's stay on earth thus far, reigning from perhaps as early as 500,000 years BCE to around 10,000 BCE, with its peak period probably from around 50,000 to 7000 BCE.[16]

As the average mode evolved from magic into mythic (beginning roughly around 10,000 BCE), and nature elementals and polytheistic figments increasingly gave way to a conception of one God/dess underlying the manifold world, the figure of the *saint* eventually became the dominant spiritual realizer. Often portrayed with haloes of light around the crown chakra (signifying the vivid awakening of the subtle realms of light and sound at and beyond the sahasrara), the saint was the great conveyor of growing-tip consciousness as it moved within and beyond nature mysticism to deity mysticism. These interior transcendental journeys—portrayed in brilliant manner by such exemplars as Saint John of the Cross, Ramanuja, Saint Teresa, Shinran, Saint Hildegard—disclosed depths of the soul, and heights of reality, that altered the very nature of consciousness at large, and left the world profoundly altered in its very structure.

As the average, collective mode of consciousness evolved from mythic to mental (beginning around the sixth century BCE), the most advanced mode evolved from subtle to causal, and the *sage*, more than the saint, embodied this growing tip of consciousness. Whereas the saint experienced divine interior luminosity, grace, love, and ecstasy, the sage experienced nothing. The sage, rather, was the first to push into the purely formless realm of sheer Emptiness, the causal of unmanifest absorption—nirvana, the cloud of unknowing, apophatic, nirvikalpa samadhi, nirodh, cessation. But far from being a literal "nothing" or stark blankness, Emptiness is the creative ground of all that is (hence "causal")—a vast Freedom and infinite Openness whose very discovery means Liberation from the world of form, suffering, sin, and samsara. Whereas, in the subtle, the soul and God find a communion or even union, in the causal, the soul and God both disappear into Godhead—the Atman that is Brahman, the Supreme Identity of the Sufi, "I and the Father are One," the separate self dissolves in Emptiness—and deity mysticism gives way to formless mysticism, the mysticism of the Abyss, the great Cloud of Unknowing, the Consciousness that is infinitely within and beyond the manifest world altogether.

But consciousness evolution is always "transcend and include," and having completely *transcended* the world of Form, consciousness awakens to a radical *embrace* of all Form: "That which is Form is not other than Emptiness, that which is Emptiness is not other than Form," says the *Heart Sutra*, in what is perhaps the most famous formula for this eternal, sacred equation. For pure Spirit (Emptiness) and the entire manifest world (Form) have become one eternal embrace. Shankara, one of India's great realizers, put this ultimate "transcend and include" as follows:

> The world is illusory,
> Brahman alone is real,
> Brahman is the world.

The World is illusory (transient, ephemeral, passing, finite, mortal), and it must be completely transcended in every way in order to find the sole reality of Spirit (Brahman). But once having completely let go of the world, and having plunged into the infinite Release of purest Spirit (unbounded, unlimited, timeless, formless reality), the finite world is then embraced and completely included in infinite Spirit, or the perfect union of manifest and unmanifest: Brahman *is* the world, and nondual mysticism takes it start with just that realization of One Taste.

The great Nondual traditions began around 200 CE, especially with such figures as Nagarjuna and Plotinus; but these traditions, particularly in their advanced forms as Tantra, began to flower in India around the eighth to the fourteenth century (coincident with the first collective or average-mode glimmers of vision-logic, exemplified in the West with Florence and the rise of Humanism, circa fourteenth century). It was during this time that Ch'an Buddhism saw its extraordinary rise in Tang and Song China (the seventh through the thirteenth centuries), and Padmasambhava brought Tantra to Tibet, which began its unparalleled flowering (especially the eighth through the eighteenth centuries).

These, too, are the most general of generalizations, but they are not without their usefulness. Among other things, distinguishing between average and most advanced allows us to avoid assuming that all the products of one era were generated by the same wave of consciousness. Scholars all too often look at a period in history and simply assume that everybody in that society was at the same level of consciousness (rather like looking back at our modern era and assuming Reagan and Krishnamurti were at the same level), and then proceed, on the basis of that assumption, to reach the most dubious conclusions. Deep ecologists often assume that in foraging cultures, everybody shared a shamanic consciousness, whereas the genuine shaman was a very rare bird—one shaman to a tribe, usually, and only one shaman in ten a true master (if that). Romantic theorists look back to ancient Egypt, notice that some adepts were clearly alive to the serpent power (kundalini), and then assume that the whole culture was awash in enlightened beings, whereas the number of kundalini adepts in any town could probably be counted on one hand (at most). It is then all too easy to assume that evolution has gone steadily downhill from these wonderful ancient days of rampant spirituality, whereas—if we actually follow the growing tip itself—spirituality has in many ways continued to deepen profoundly over the ages. Valentinus was amazing, but compare him to Eckhart. Magdelene was profound, but compare her to Saint Teresa of Ávila. Boethius was extraordinary, but compare him to Saint John of the Cross. And right up to Hakuin and Dogen, perhaps the most influential Japanese Zen adepts of all time; Sri Ramana Maharshi, one of India's greatest realizers (who died a mere few decades ago); and Aurobindo, her greatest philosopher-sage (also a mere few decades ago).

Further, by making that distinction (average and advanced), we can immediately see that, whereas some past epochs might look "very spiritual," their most common or *average mode* (such as magic or mythic) was actually *preformal,* not postformal. Only the fairly rare shaman, saint, or sage actually evolved into higher levels of psychic, subtle, or causal adaptation; and therefore the profoundly spiritual stages (psychic, subtle, causal)—*as a common, average mode of consciousness*—exist, if at all, in our collective future, not our past. Of course, any individual during any period—past, present, or future—can develop into the higher realms under his or her own power. But whole epochs of postformal spirituality, as a common attainment, were almost certainly never present at any point in past history. Scholars who mistake magic and mythic for authentic spirituality, and who therefore look at the past and think all forms of spirituality are behind us, are, I believe, in for a pleasant surprise. The *most advanced* figures of the past were plumbing the depths of the transpersonal levels, and those lie in our collective future, not our collective past.

In the extraordinary archeology of Spirit, those spiritual pioneers were ahead of their time, and they are still ahead of ours. They are thus voices, not of our past, but of our future; they point to emergents, not exhumations; they urge us forward, not backward. As the growing tip of humanity, they forged a future telos through which the trunk of humanity is now slowing heading, not as a rigid pregiven, but as a gentle persuasion. They are figures of the deepest layers of our own true Self, layers that whisper to us from the radiant depths of a greater tomorrow.

13

From Modernity to Postmodernity

N O EPOCH is without its geniuses, its wisdom, its enduring truths. Moreover, to ignore past truths seems to be the very definition of pathology. Therefore, an integral approach—a sane approach—would surely attempt to honor, acknowledge, and incorporate these enduring truths in the ongoing sweep of consciousness evolution.

From the premodern heritage, we have learned of the Great Nest of Being and Knowing, and found that it is a road map to Spirit, not in a pregiven way, but as a morphogenetic field of gentle persuasion. From the modern heritage, we have learned of the need to recognize and honor art, morals, and science, and let each pursue its own truths without violence from the others (a respect that contributed to the rise of the modern democracies, feminism, ecology, and the postconventional ideals of liberty, freedom, and equality).[1] We also learned of the modern discoveries of *evolution* in the quadrants (a notion that is at least compatible with the Great Chain tipped on its side and set loose across geological, biological, and cultural time). And we have mentioned the "bright promise" of a constructive postmodernity, which involves the integration of the best of premodernity (the Great Nest) and modernity (the differentiation and evolution of the Big Three), resulting in a more integral "all-level, all-quadrant" approach.

It is time now to finish this integral overview by looking, very briefly, at postmodernism itself—which is, after all, the leading edge of today's cultural evolution—and suggest exactly how it fits into an all-level, all-quadrant view.

Many people moan when "postmodern" anything is mentioned, so convoluted and indecipherable has postmodernese become. But these are important points, and I ask the reader to stick with me through this chapter, which I will try to make as painless as possible. We can then return, in the closing chapters, to a summary of what we have seen, and the implications for psychology, therapy, spirituality, and consciousness studies.

THE BRIGHT PROMISE

In trying to understand modernity, we asked the simple question: what made modernity different from the premodern era? We found many items (from industrialization to the liberation movements), but they could all be very generally summarized as the differentiation of the Big Three.

In attempting to understand postmodernity, let us ask again: what is it about postmodernity that makes it so different from modernity? We will see that there are also many items, but they can all be very generally summarized as an *attempt to be inclusive*—to avoid "marginalizing" the many voices and viewpoints that a powerful modernity often overlooked; to avoid a "hegemony" of formal rationality that often represses the nonrational and the irrational; to invite all races, all colors, all people, all genders into a rainbow coalition of mutual respect and mutual recognition. This inclusiveness is often simply called "diversity" (or "multiculturalism" or "pluralism"), and it is at the heart of the constructive postmodern agenda, in ways that we will explore throughout this chapter.

This attempt to be inclusive—holistic and embracing in the best sense—was in part a reaction to modernity's unfortunate slide into flatland, where the *dissociation* of the Big Three allowed a powerful science to colonize and dominate (and marginalize) all other forms of knowing and being. Postmodernity was a counterattempt to include the Big Three instead of merely differentiate and dissociate them. *Thus, where modernity differentiated the Big Three, postmodernity would embrace them—* the many I's and the many We's and the many Its—thus arriving at a more inclusive, integral, and nonexclusionary stance. And there, in a sentence, is the enduring truth, the integral truth, of the general postmodern movements.

But we will also see that, just as modernity has its downside, so too does postmodernity. The dignity of modernity slid into the disaster of modernity when the differentiation of the Big Three slid into their dissociation. Just so, the bright promise of a constructive postmodernity slid into a nihilistic deconstructive postmodernity when the pluralistic embrace turned into a rancid leveling of all qualitative distinctions. Postmodernity, attempting to escape flatland, often became its most vulgar champion.

In other words, postmodernity, just like modernity, has its good news and its bad news.

GOOD NEWS

The entry to postmodernism begins with an understanding of the intrinsic role that *interpretation* plays in human awareness. Postmodernism, in fact, may be credited with making interpretation central to both epistemology and ontology, to both knowing and being. Interpretation, the postmodernists all maintained in their own ways, is not only crucial for understanding the Kosmos, it is an aspect of its very structure. *Interpretation is an intrinsic feature of the fabric of the universe*: there is the crucial insight at the heart of the great postmodern movements.[2]

Interpretation: The Heart of the Postmodern

Many people are initially confused as to why, and how, interpretation is intrinsic to the universe. Interpretation is for things like language and literature, right? Yes, but language and literature are just the tip of the iceberg, an iceberg that extends to the very depths of the Kosmos itself. We might explain it like this:

As we have seen, all Right-Hand events—all sensorimotor objects and empirical processes and "its"—can be seen with the senses or their extensions. They all have simple location; you can actually point to most of them (rocks, towns, trees, lakes, stars, roads, rivers . . .).

But Left-Hand or interior events cannot be seen in that fashion. You cannot see love, envy, wonder, compassion, insight, intentionality, spiritual illumination, states of consciousness, value, or meaning running around out there in the empirical world. Interior events are not seen in an *exterior* or *objective* manner, they are seen by *introspection* and *interpretation*.

Thus, if you want to study *Macbeth* empirically, you can get a copy of the play and subject it to various scientific tests: it weighs so many grams, it has so many molecules of ink, it has this number of pages composed of these organic compounds, and so on. That's all you can know about *Macbeth* empirically. Those are its Right-Hand, objective, exterior aspects.

But if you want to know the *meaning* of the play, you will have to read it and enter into its interiority, its meaning, its intentions, its depths. And the only way you can do that is by *interpretation*: what does this sentence *mean*? Here, empirical science is largely worthless, because we are entering interior domains and symbolic depths, which cannot be accessed by exterior empiricism but only by introspection and interpretation. Not just objective, but subjective and intersubjective. Not just monological, but dialogical.

Thus, you might see me coming down the street, a frown on my face. You can see that. But what does that exterior frown actually mean? How will you find out? You will ask me. You will talk to me. You can see my surfaces, but in order to understand my interior, my depths, you will have to enter into the interpretive circle (the hermeneutic circle). You, as a subject, will not merely stare at me as an *object*, but rather you, as a subject, will attempt to understand me *as a subject*—as a person, as a self, as a bearer of intentionality and meaning. You will talk to me, and interpret what I say; and I will do the same with you. We are not subjects staring at objects; we are subjects trying to understand subjects—we are in the intersubjective circle, the dialogical dance.

This is true not only for humans, but for all sentient beings as such. If you want to understand your dog—is he happy, or perhaps hungry, or wanting to go for a walk?—you will have to *interpret* the signals he is giving you. And your dog, to the extent that he can, does the same with you. In other words, the *interior* of a holon can *only* be accessed by interpretation.

Thus, to put it bluntly, exterior surfaces can be *seen*, but interior depth must be *interpreted*. And precisely because this interior depth is an intrinsic part of the Kosmos—it is the Left-Hand dimension of every holon—then interpretation itself is an intrinsic feature of the Kosmos. Interpretation is not something added on to the Kosmos as an afterthought; it is the very opening of the interiors themselves. And since the depth of the Kosmos goes "all the way down," then, as Heidegger famously put it, "Interpretation goes all the way down."

Perhaps we can now see why one of the great aims of postmodernism was to *introduce interpretation as an intrinsic aspect of the Kosmos*. As

I would put it, every holon has a Left- and a Right-Hand dimension (as you can see in fig. 5), and therefore every holon has an objective (Right) and an interpretive (Left) component.

(How far "down" you wish to push interiors or consciousness is, of course, up to you. Some people push it down to mammals, others to reptiles, others to plants, others all the way down to atoms. I find this a completely relative issue: however much consciousness one holon has—say, an amoeba—a senior holon has a little more—say, a deer—and its senior has even more—say, a gorilla. The lower on the Great Nest, the less sentience a holon has, until it fades into the shades that we cannot detect. We will return to this topic in chapter 14; for now, the simple point is that, at least by the time we get to humans, interiors definitely exist, and they can only be accessed by introspection and interpretation.)[3]

The disaster of modernity was that it reduced all introspective and interpretive knowledge to exterior and empirical flatland: it attempted to erase the richness of interpretation from the script of the world. The attempt by postmodernism to reintroduce interpretation into the very structure and fabric of the Kosmos was in part a noble attempt to escape flatland, to resurrect the gutted interiors and interpretive modes of knowing. The postmodern emphasis on interpretation—starting most notably with Nietzsche, and running through Dilthey's *Geist* sciences to Heidegger's hermeneutic ontology to Derrida's "there is nothing outside the text [interpretation]"—is at bottom nothing but the Left-Hand domains screaming to be released from the crushing oblivion of the monological gaze of scientific monism and flatland holism. It was the bold reassertion of the I and the We in the face of faceless Its.

Moments of Truth in Postmodernism

Precisely because postmodernism is in many ways attempting to jettison flatland and its demeaning legacy, postmodern philosophy is a complex cluster of notions that are often defined almost entirely by what its proponents *reject*. They reject foundationalism, essentialism, and transcendentalism. They reject rationality, truth as correspondence, and representational knowledge. They reject grand narratives, metanarratives, and big pictures of any variety. They reject realism, final vocabularies, and canonical description.

Incoherent as the postmodern theories often sound (and often are), nonetheless most postmodern approaches share three important core assumptions:

1. Reality is not in all ways pregiven, but in some significant ways is a construction, an interpretation (this view is often called *constructivism*); the belief that reality is simply given, and not also partly constructed, is referred to as "the myth of the given."
2. Meaning is context-dependent, and contexts are boundless (this is often called *contextualism*).
3. Cognition must therefore unduly privilege no single perspective (this is called *integral-aperspectivism*).

I believe all three of those postmodern assumptions are quite accurate, and need to be honored and incorporated in any integral view.

But, as we will see in the bad news section, each of those assumptions has also been blown radically out of proportion by the extremist wing of postmodernism, with very unfortunate results. The extreme postmodernists do not just stress the importance of interpretation, they claim reality is *nothing but an interpretation*. They don't just emphasize the Left-Hand (or interpretive) aspects of all holons, *they attempt to completely deny reality to the Right-Hand (or objective) facets*. This, of course, is precisely the reverse disaster of modernity—not reducing all Left to Right, but reducing all Right to Left—and we can see, as is frequently the case, that extreme reactions are often the mirror images of what they loathe. The important features of the Kosmos that are interpretive are made the *only* features in existence. Objective truth itself disappears into arbitrary interpretations, said to be imposed by power, gender, race, ideology, anthropocentrism, androcentrism, speciesism, imperialism, logocentrism, phallocentrism, phallologocentrism, or one variety or another of utter unpleasantness.

But the fact that all holons have an interpretive as well as an objective component does *not* deny the objective component, it merely situates it. Thus, all Right-Hand exteriors, even if we superimpose conceptions upon them, nonetheless have various intrinsic features that are registered by the senses or their extensions, and in that general sense, all Right-Hand holons have some sort of objective reality. Even Wilfrid Sellars, generally regarded as the most persuasive opponent of "the myth of the given"—the myth of direct realism and naive empiricism, the myth that reality is simply given to us—maintains that, even though the manifest image of an object is in part a mental construction, it is *guided* in important ways by *intrinsic features* of sense experience, which is exactly why, as Thomas Kuhn said, science can make *real* progress.[4] A diamond will cut a piece of glass, no matter what words we use for "diamond," "cut," and "glass," and no amount of cultural constructivism will change that simple fact.

But that is the bad news. The point for now is that the postmodernists, in attempting to make room for those aspects of the Big Three that were excluded and marginalized by flatland, pointed out the *intrinsic* importance of interpretation, contextualism, and integralism, and in this regard, they were surely correct.

From Modern to Postmodern: The Linguistic Turn

The importance of constructivism, contextualism, and integral-aperspectivism came to the fore historically with what has been called *the linguistic turn* in philosophy—the general realization that language is not a simple representation of a pregiven world, but has a hand in the creation and construction of that world. With the linguistic turn, which began roughly in the nineteenth century, philosophers stopped using language to describe the world, and instead started looking at language itself.

Suddenly, language was no longer a simple and trusted tool. *Metaphysics* in general was replaced with *linguistic analysis*, because it was becoming increasingly obvious that language is not a clear window through which we innocently look at a given world; it is more like a slide projector throwing images against the screen of what we finally see. Language helps to create my world, and, as Wittgenstein would put it, the limits of my language are the limits of my world.

In many ways, "the linguistic turn" is just another name for the great transition from modernity to postmodernity. Where both premodern and modern cultures simply and naively used their language to approach the world, the postmodern mind spun on its heels and began to look at language itself. In the entire history of human beings, this, more or less, had never happened before.

In the wake of this extraordinary linguistic turn, philosophers would never again look at language in a simple and trusting way. Language did not merely report the world, represent the world, describe the world. Rather, language creates worlds, and in that creation is power. Language creates, distorts, carries, discloses, hides, allows, oppresses, enriches, enthralls. For good or ill, language itself is something of a demigod, and philosophy henceforth would focus much of its attention on that powerful force. From linguistic analysis to language games, from structuralism to poststructuralism, from semiology to semiotics, from linguistic intentionality to speech act theory—postmodern philosophy has been in large measure *the philosophy of language*, and it pointed out—quite rightly— that if we are to use language as a tool to understand reality, we had better start by looking very closely at that tool.[5]

And in this strange new world, most roads lead, sooner or later, to Ferdinand de Saussure.

Language Speaks

Most forms of postmodern poststructuralism trace their lineage to the work of the brilliant and pioneering linguist Ferdinand de Saussure. Saussure's work, and especially his *Course in General Linguistics* (1916), was the basis of much of modern linguistics, semiology (semiotics), structuralism, and hence poststructuralism, and his essential insights are as cogent today as they were when he first advanced them almost a century ago.

According to Saussure, a linguistic *sign* is composed of a material *signifier* (the written word, the spoken word, the marks on this page) and a conceptual *signified* (what comes to mind when you see the signifier), both of which are different from the actual *referent*. For example, if you see a tree, the actual tree is the referent; the written word "tree" is the signifier; and what comes to mind (the image, the thought, the mental picture or concept) when you read the word "tree" is the signified. The signifier and the signified together constitute the overall sign.

But what is it, Saussure asked, that allows a sign to mean something, to actually *carry meaning*? It can't be the word itself, because, for example, the word "bark" has a different meaning in the phrases "the bark of a dog" and "the bark of a tree." The word "bark" has meaning, in each case, because of its place in the entire phrase (a different phrase gives the same word a totally different meaning). Each phrase likewise has meaning because of its place in the larger sentence, and eventually, in the total linguistic structure. Any given word in itself is basically *meaningless* because the same word can have completely different meanings depending on the context or the structure in which it is placed.

Thus, Saussure pointed out, it is the *relationship between all of the words themselves* that stabilizes meaning. So—and this was Saussure's great insight—*a meaningless element becomes meaningful only by virtue of the total structure*. (This is the beginning of *structuralism*, virtually all schools of which trace their lineage in whole or part to Saussure. Present-day descendants include aspects of the work of Lévi-Strauss,

Jakobson, Piaget, Lacan, Barthes, Foucault, Derrida, Habermas, Loevinger, Kohlberg, Gilligan . . . it was a truly stunning discovery.)

In other words—and no surprise—every sign is a holon, a context within contexts within contexts in the overall network. And this means, said Saussure, that the entire language is instrumental in conferring meaning on an individual word.[6]

Meaning Is Context-Dependent

Accordingly—and here we begin to see the importance of *background cultural contexts* so stressed by postmodernists (especially starting with Heidegger)—meaning is created for me by vast networks of background contexts about which I consciously know very little. I do not fashion this meaning; this meaning fashions me. I am a part of this vast cultural background, and in many cases I haven't a clue as to where it all came from.

In other words—as we have often seen—every subjective intentionality (Upper Left) is *situated* in networks of intersubjective and cultural contexts (Lower Left) that are instrumental in the creation and interpretation of meaning itself. This is precisely why meaning is indeed context-dependent, and why the bark of a dog is different from the bark of a tree. This is also why individual states of consciousness must to some degree be interpreted within a cultural context, and why any truly postmodern view should attempt to move toward an *all-context sensitivity* (by stressing, for example, the endlessly holonic nature of consciousness).[7]

Not only is meaning in many important ways dependent upon the context in which it finds itself, these contexts are in principle *endless* or *boundless*. Thus there is no way finally to master and control meaning once and for all (because I can always imagine a further context that would alter the present meaning). Jonathan Culler has, in fact, summarized all of deconstruction (one of the most influential of the postmodern movements) in this way: "One could therefore identify deconstruction with the twin principles of the *contextual determination of meaning* and the *infinite extendability of context*."[8]

As I would put it, contexts are indeed endless precisely because reality is composed of holons within holons within holons *indefinitely*, with no discernible bottom or top. Even the entire universe right now is simply a part of the next moment's universe. Every whole is always a part, endlessly. And therefore every conceivable context is boundless. To say that the Kosmos is holonic is to say it is contextual, all the way up, all the way down.

Integral-Aperspectival

The fact that meaning is context-dependent—the second important truth of postmodernism, also called *contextualism*—means that a *multi-perspective* approach to reality is called for. Any single perspective is likely to be partial, limited, perhaps even distorted, and only by honoring multiple perspectives and multiple contexts can the knowledge quest be fruitfully advanced. And that "diversity" is the third important truth of general postmodernism.

Jean Gebser, whom we have seen in connection with worldviews, coined the term *integral-aperspectival* to refer to this pluralistic or multiple-perspectives view, which I also refer to as *vision-logic* or *network-logic*. "Aperspectival" means that no single perspective is privileged, and thus, in order to gain a more holistic or *integral* view, we need an *aperspectival* approach, which is exactly why Gebser usually hyphenated them: integral-aperspectival.

Gebser contrasted integral-aperspectival cognition with formal rationality (formop), or what he called "perspectival reason," which tends to take a single, monological perspective and view all of reality through that narrow lens. Where perspectival reason privileges the exclusive perspective of the particular subject, vision-logic *adds up all the perspectives*, privileging none, and thus attempts to grasp the integral, the whole, the multiple contexts within contexts that endlessly disclose the Kosmos, not in a rigid or absolutist fashion, but in a fluidly holonic and multidimensional tapestry.

This parallels almost exactly the Idealists' great emphasis on the difference between a reason that is merely formal, representational, or empiric-analytic, and a reason that is dialogical, dialectical, and network-oriented (vision-logic). They called the former *Verstand* and the latter *Vernunft*. And they saw Vernunft or vision-logic as being a higher evolutionary development than mere Verstand or formal rationality.[9]

Gebser, too, believed that vision-logic was an evolutionary development beyond formal rationality. Nor are Gebser and the Idealists alone. As we have repeatedly seen, many important theorists, from Jürgen Habermas to Carol Gilligan, view postformal, dialectical cognition as a higher and more embracing mode of reason than formop (as indicated on many of the charts). *To say cognitive development evolves from for-*

mal to postformal is to say that cultural evolution moves from modern to postmodern. This is, of course, a complex, four-quadrant affair, involving such important developments as industrial to informational; but the mode of cognition is a crucial element, and the postmodern world is, at its best, the postformal world.

This vision-logic not only can spot massive interrelationships, it is itself an intrinsic part of the interrelated Kosmos, which is why vision-logic does not just *represent* the Kosmos, but is a *performance* of the Kosmos. Of course, all modes of genuine knowing are such performances; but vision-logic is the first that can self-consciously realize this and articulate it. Hegel did so in one of the first and pioneering elaborations—vision-logic evolutionarily became conscious of itself in Hegel—and Saussure did exactly the same thing with linguistics.[10] Saussure took vision-logic and applied it to language, thus disclosing, for the first time in history, its network structure. The linguistic turn is, at bottom, vision-logic looking at language itself.

This same vision-logic would give rise to the extensively elaborated versions of systems theory in the natural sciences, and it would stand as well behind the postmodernists' recognition that meaning is context-dependent and contexts are boundless. In all of these movements and more, we see the radiant hand of vision-logic announcing the endless networks of holonic interconnection that constitute the very fabric of the Kosmos itself.

This is why I believe that the recognition of the importance of integral-aperspectival awareness is the third great (and valid) message of postmodernism in general.

BAD NEWS

All of which is well and good. But it is not enough, we have seen, to be "holistic" instead of "atomistic," or to be network-oriented instead of analytic and divisive. Because the alarming fact is that *any mode of knowing can be collapsed* and confined merely to surfaces, to exteriors, to Right-Hand occasions. And, in fact, almost as soon as vision-logic had heroically emerged in evolution, it was crushed by the flatland madness sweeping the modern world.

Language Collapses

Indeed, as we have repeatedly seen, the systems sciences themselves did exactly that. The systems sciences denied any substantial reality to the

"I" and the "we" domains (in their own terms), and reduced all of them to nothing but interwoven "its" in a dynamical system of network processes. This was vision-logic at work, but a crippled vision-logic, hobbled and chained to the bed of exterior processes and empirical its. This was a holism, but merely an exterior holism that perfectly gutted the interiors and denied any sort of validity to the extensive realms of Left-Hand holism (of the "I" and the "we"). The third-person shackles were no longer atomistic; the third-person shackles were now holistically interwoven.

Precisely the same fate awaited so much of the general postmodern agenda. Starting from the admirable reliance on vision-logic and integral-aperspectival awareness—and yet still unable to escape the intense gravity of flatland—these postmodern movements often ended up subtly embodying and even extending the reductionistic agenda. They were a new and higher form of reason, yes, but *reason still trapped in flatland.* They became simply another twist on flatland holism, material monism, monological madness. They still succumbed to the disaster of modernity even as they loudly announced they had overcome it, subverted it, deconstructed it, exploded it.

Depth Takes a Vacation

In fact, most postmodernism would eventually go to extraordinary lengths to *deny depth* in general. It is as if, suffering under the onslaught of flatland aggression, it identified with the aggressor. Postmodernism came to embrace surfaces, champion surfaces, glorify surfaces, and surfaces alone. There are only sliding chains of signifiers, everything is a material text, there is nothing under the surface, there is only the surface. As Bret Easton Ellis put it in *American Psycho*: "Nothing was affirmative, the term 'generosity of spirit' applied to nothing, was a cliché, was some kind of bad joke. . . . Reflection is useless, the world is senseless. Surface, surface, surface was all that anyone found meaning in . . . this was civilization as I saw it, colossal and jagged."

Robert Alter, reviewing William H. Gass's *The Tunnel*—a book claimed by many to be the ultimate postmodern novel—points out that the defining strategy of this postmodern masterpiece is that "*everything is deliberately reduced to the flattest surface.*" This is done by "denying the possibility of making consequential distinctions between, or meaningful rankings of, moral or aesthetic values. There is no within: murderer and victim, lover and onanist, altruist and bigot, dissolve into the same ineluctable slime"—the same sliding chains of equally flatland terms.

"Everything is reduced to the flattest surface. . . . *There is no within*"—a perfect description of flatland, a flatland that, beginning with modernity, was actually amplified and glorified with extreme postmodernity: "Surface, surface, surface was all that anyone found . . . ."

And Alter is exactly right that behind it all is the inability or refusal to make "consequential distinctions between, or meaningful rankings of, moral or aesthetic values." As we have often seen, in the Right-Hand world there are no values and no interiors and no qualitative distinctions—no states of consciousness, no realms of transpersonal awareness, no superconscious revelations, no spiritual illuminations—for those exist only in the Left-Hand domains. To collapse the Kosmos to Right-Hand surfaces is thus to step out of the real world and into the Twilight Zone known as the disqualified universe. Here there are no interior holarchies, no meaningful rankings of the I and the We, no qualitative distinctions of any sort—no depth, no divinity, no consciousness, no soul, and no spirit: "Surface, surface, surface is all that anyone found."[11]

Extreme postmodernism thus went from the noble insight that all perspectives need to be given a fair hearing, to the self-contradictory belief that no perspective is better than any other (self-contradictory because their own belief is held to be much better than the alternatives). Thus, under the intense gravity of flatland, integral-aperspectival awareness became simply *aperspectival madness*—the contradictory belief that no belief is better than any other—a total paralysis of thought, will, and action in the face of a million perspectives all given exactly the same depth, namely, zero.

At one point in *The Tunnel*, Gass himself, the author of this postmodern masterpiece, describes the *perfect postmodern form*, which serves "to raunchify, to suburp [sic] everything, to pollute the pollutants, explode the exploded, trash the trash. . . . It is all surface. . . . There's no inside however long or far you travel on it, no within, no deep."

No within, no deep. That may serve as a perfect credo for extreme postmodernism. Just as modernity often slid into dissociation, postmodernity often slid into surfaces.

CONCLUSION

The enduring contributions of the postmodern era—the world is in part a construction and interpretation; all meaning is context-dependent;

contexts are endlessly holonic—are truths that any comprehensive view would surely wish to embrace. All of these can be summarized, in the most general fashion, by saying that where modernity differentiated the Big Three, postmodernity would integrate them, thus arriving at an inclusive, integral, and nonexclusionary embrace. This integral agenda is the heart of a constructive postmodernity, and the heart of any truly integral psychology and spirituality.

But just as modernity's differentiations often slid into dissociation, so postmodernity's integral embrace often slid into aperspectival madness—into the *denial* of qualitative distinctions of any sort, the denial of holarchies altogether. And since the only way you get holism is via holarchies, in denying the latter, postmodernity effectively denied the former, and thus offered the world not holism but heapism: diversity run amok, with no way to integrate and harmonize the pluralistic voices. No stance is inherently better than any other; all hierarchies are marginalizing and should be rejected; all voices should be treated equally, with no marginalizing and no judging.

The inherent contradiction in that agenda is simply this: the very stance of postmodern pluralism—relying as it does on postformal vision-logic and integral-aperspectival cognition—is itself the product of at least five major stages of hierarchical development (sensorimotor to preop to conop to formop to postformal). From the very high developmental stance of postconventional, postformal, pluralistic awareness—which nobly wishes to treat all peoples fairly and justly—postmodernism then denied the importance of development altogether, denied that any stance is higher or deeper than another, denied in effect the claim that worldcentric is better than ethnocentric—in short, it completely denied its own stance. And yet it is only from the high developmental level of postformal and postconventional awareness that pluralism can be grasped in the first place! To deny development and evolution is to deny pluralism altogether and slide into nothing but a world of equivalent surfaces, where qualitative distinctions and holarchies have disappeared altogether. This is why postmodern pluralists have always had difficulty explaining why we should reject the Nazis and the KKK—if all stances are equal, why not embrace them? Aperspectival madness.

Thus, under the important truths of relativism, pluralism, and cultural diversity, postmodernism opened up the world to a richness of multiple voices, but then stood back to watch the multiple voices degenerate into a Tower of Babel, each voice claiming to be its own validity, yet few of them actually honoring the values of the others. Each was free to go its own way, whereupon everybody went in vigorously different ways. This did not ultimately liberate the many pluralistic voices, as was claimed, but merely sent them scurrying off, isolated and alienated, to the far corners of a fragmented world, there to suckle themselves in solitude, lost in the shuffle of equivalent surfaces. Attempting to escape flatland, deconstructive postmodernism became its most vocal champion.

Constructive postmodernism, on the other hand, takes up the multiple contexts freed by pluralism, and then goes one step further and weaves them together into mutually interrelated networks. (You can see this on virtually all of the charts. By whatever name, pluralistic relativism gives way to integral holism. See especially Deirdre Kramer, Gisela Labouvie-Vief, Jan Sinnott, Don Beck, Clare Graves, Susanne Cook-Greuter, Kitchener and King, Blanchard-Fields, William Perry, and Cheryl Armon, among others.) This integral-aperspectivism—this unity-in-diversity, this universal integralism—discloses global interconnections, nests within nests within nests, and vast holarchies of mutually enriching embrace, thus converting pluralistic heapism into integral holism.

(In the terms of Spiral Dynamics, the great strength of postmodernism is that it moved from orange scientific materialism to green pluralism, in a noble attempt to be more inclusive and sensitive to the marginalized others of rationality. But the downside of green pluralism is its subjectivism and relativism, which leaves the world splintered and fragmented. As Clare Graves himself put it, "This system sees the world relativistically. Thinking shows an almost radical, almost compulsive emphasis on seeing everything from a relativistic, subjective frame of reference." And however important these multiple contexts are for moving beyond scientific materialism, if they become an end in themselves, they simply prevent the emergence of second-tier constructions, which will actually reweave the fragments in a global-holistic embrace. It is the emergence of this second-tier thinking upon which any truly integral model will depend—and this is the path of constructive postmodernism.)

For an integral psychology, postmodernism means many things. First and foremost, it is a reaffirmation of what psychology is all about: the *constructing* and *creating* capacity of consciousness itself: the world is not merely reflected by consciousness, it is co-created by consciousness—the world is not merely a *perception* but an *interpretation*.[12] Interpretation is an intrinsic aspect of the Kosmos, "all the way down," because consciousness and interiors are an intrinsic aspect of the Kosmos, *all the way down*, and the only way you can get at interiors is via introspection and interpretation. That consciousness is endlessly holonic is the final message of postmodernism.

Therefore, any integral theory would be wise to include constructive, contextual, and integral-aperspectival dimensions in its own makeup. It is to this integral conclusion that we may now turn.

14

The 1-2-3 of Consciousness Studies

THE MIND-BODY PROBLEM

THE FIRST MAJOR PROBLEM that a truly integral (all-level, all-quadrant) approach helps to unravel is what Schopenhauer called "the world-knot," namely, the mind-body problem.

So let us start with a bold suggestion: a good deal of the mind-body problem is a product of flatland. Not the differentiation of mind and body, which is at least as old as civilization and never bothered anybody before; but the dissociation of mind and body, which is a peculiar lesion in the modern and postmodern consciousness, concomitant with the collapse of the Kosmos into flatland. For in flatland, we are faced with a truly unyielding dilemma as to the relation of mind and body: the mind (consciousness, feeling, thought, awareness)—in short, the Left-Hand domains—can find absolutely no room in the world described merely in Right-Hand terms (the material body and brain): the mind becomes the "ghost in the machine." We are then faced with two apparently absolute but contradictory truths: the truth of immediate experience, which tells me unmistakably that consciousness exists, and the truth of science, which tells me unmistakably that the world consists only of arrangements of fundamental units (quarks, atoms, strings, etc.) that possess no consciousness whatsoever, and no amount of rearranging those mindless units will result in mind.

Contrary to popular writers on the subject, the influential philosophers addressing the mind-body problem are more convinced than ever of its unyielding nature. There is simply no agreed-upon solution to this world-knot.[1] Much of the influential writing of the last several decades, in fact, has focused on the absolutely insuperable difficulties with the proposed solutions. As Keith Campbell summarized a vague and uneasy consensus, "I suspect we will never know how the trick is worked [the relation of mind and body]. This part of the Mind-Body problem seems insoluble. This aspect of humanity seems destined to remain forever beyond our understanding."[2]

Nonetheless, there have been many solutions offered, the two most influential being the *dualist* (interactionism) and the *physicalist* (scientific materialism). The dualist position was the most influential in the early part of the modern era (from Descartes to Leibniz), but the physicalist has been in the ascendancy ever since, and is now by far the dominant position.[3]

The physicalist (or materialist) approach claims that there is only the physical universe described best by physics and other natural sciences, and nowhere in that physical universe do we find consciousness, mind, experience, or awareness, and therefore those "interiors" are simply illusions (or, at best, byproducts without any genuine reality). Some versions of the physicalist approach allow for higher-level emergence of various complex systems (such as the brain, neocortex, autopoietic neuronal systems, etc.). But they point out that these higher-level systems are still objective realities with nothing that could be called consciousness or mind or experience, because experience has "qualia" or qualities, such as pain and pleasure, and those qualities are *not* properties of objective systems. Therefore there is no way that objective systems could give rise to those "mental" properties, and therefore those properties are simply illusory byproducts of complex systems, with no causal reality of their own.

(Using my terms, this argument says: objective systems are all described in it-language, whereas experience, consciousness, and qualia are all described in I-language, and thus if you believe that the world described by science is the "really real" world—and, after all, there are many good reasons to believe that science is our best hope of finding truth—then you naturally believe that qualia, experience, and consciousness are *not* "really real"—they are illusions or byproducts or secondary features of the real world disclosed by science.)

Although variations on physicalism are by far the most commonly accepted views, this is not so much because physicalism works well, but because the alternatives seem much worse. Even materialists acknowledge the massive problems with their own stance: Galen Strawson: "As an acting materialist, I . . . assume that experiential phenomena are realized in the brain. . . . [But] when we consider the brain as current physics and neurophysiology presents it to us, we are obliged to admit that we do not know how experience . . . is or even could be realized in the brain."[4] John Searle: "Criticisms of the materialist theory usually take a more or less technical form, but in fact, underlying the technical objections is a much deeper objection. . . . The theory in question has left out . . . some essential feature of the mind, such as consciousness or 'qualia' or semantic content. . . ."[5] Jaegwon Kim, whose "supervenience" theory is a very sophisticated emergent physicalism, concludes that the approach seems "to be up against a dead end."[6] Thomas Nagel concludes that "physicalism is a position that we cannot understand because we do not at present have any conception of how it might be true."[7] Colin McGinn states simply that we will *never* be able to resolve the issue of how consciousness emerges from a brain.[8] And that is the conclusion of the physicalists themselves!

The dualist therefore jumps on these insuperable difficulties in physicalism, and says to the materialists: We know that consciousness exists in some form, because it is one of the "hard-core" intuitions that humans possess, and therefore explaining it away will take some powerful explaining. We experience consciousness directly. But we do not directly experience quarks or atoms (or the fundamental units of the physical world). Therefore it is not necessary for me to proceed as you do, which is to start with quarks and then deduce that consciousness does not exist. It is necessary for you to start from consciousness and explain how you arrive at the ridiculous notion that it isn't there.

The dualist therefore maintains that, at the very least, there are two realities in the world: consciousness and matter. Neither can be reduced to the other; instead, they "interact" (hence the other common term for this position, interactionism). But then the dualist faces the age-old dilemma: how can two fundamentally different things influence each other? As everybody knows, ghosts walk through walls, they do not push walls around, so how can the ghostly mind actually have any real effect on the material body? The very move to show that mind cannot be reduced to matter leaves the dualist incapable of showing how mind can act on matter at all. And therefore the dualist has a very hard time explaining how, for example, I can even move my arm.

(The Idealists handled this by saying that mind and body are both forms of Spirit, and therefore they are not alien or ontologically different entities, but simply two different aspects of the same thing. This is an acceptable solution if one acknowledges Spirit, which most modern and postmodern philosophers do not, which is why this is not a commonly discussed option. We will return to this point shortly.)

Again, the dualists themselves point out the insuperable difficulties with their own position (which they hold mostly because the physicalist alternative is even worse). Geoffrey Madell notes that "interactionist dualism looks to be by far the only plausible framework in which the facts of our experience can be fitted" (because, we might say, interactionism at least acknowledges the undeniable realities of both I and it domains). Nonetheless, "the nature of the causal connection between the mental and the physical . . . is utterly mysterious" (how *does* the ghost move the wall?).[9] Sir Karl Popper states the central problem for dualism: "What we want is to understand how such nonphysical things as purposes, deliberations, plans, decisions, theories, tensions, and values can play a part in bringing about physical changes in the physical world."[10] The conclusion offered by dualist interactionism: that understanding, says Popper, "is unlikely to be achieved."[11]

WHAT DO WE MEAN BY "MIND" AND "BODY"?

Part of these difficulties, I am suggesting, is that both major positions have adopted the theoretical terms of flatland, and they attempt to juggle these terms to arrive at a solution, which has then been less than satisfactory, virtually all parties agree. If we instead use an "all-level, all-quadrant" approach, the first thing that we notice is that both "mind" and "body" have two very different meanings, showing that there are really four problems hidden in one. This can be followed fairly easily using figure 12.

To begin with, "body" can mean *the biological organism as a whole*, including the brain (the neocortex, the limbic system, reptilian stem, etc.)—in other words, "body" can mean the entire Upper-Right quadrant, which I will call "the organism." I will also refer to the organism as the "Body," capital *B*, as indicated in figure 12. Thus, the brain is in the Body, which is the commonly accepted scientific view (and an accurate description of the Upper-Right quadrant).

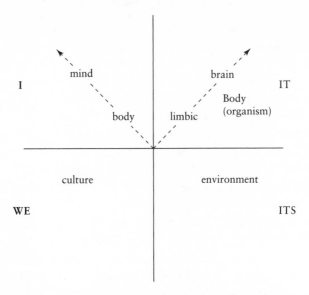

FIGURE 12. *Meanings of "Mind" and "Body"*

But "body" can also mean, and for the average person does mean, the subjective feelings, emotions, and sensations of the felt body. When the typical person says "My mind is fighting my body," he means his will is fighting some bodily desire or inclination (such as sex or food). In other words, in this common usage, "body" means the lower levels of one's own interior. In figure 12, I have labeled this as "body" in the Upper-Left quadrant, which simply means the feelings and emotions of the felt body (versus the Body, which means the entire objective organism).

Moving from body to mind, many scientific researchers simply identify "mind" with "brain," and they prefer to speak only of brain states, neurotransmitters, cognitive science, and so on. I will use the term "brain" to cover that meaning, which refers to the upper levels of the Upper-Right quadrant (e.g., the neocortex), as shown in figure 12.

On the other hand, when the average person says "My mind is fighting my body," he does not mean that his neocortex is fighting his limbic system. By "mind" he means the upper levels of his own interior, the upper levels of the Upper-Left quadrant (although he might not use exactly those terms)—in other words, his rational will is fighting his feelings or desires (formop is fighting the vital and sensorimotor dimensions). The mind is described in first-person phenomenal accounts and I-language, whereas the brain is described in third-person objective accounts and it-language. All of these are indicated in figure 12.

(There is a another general meaning for mind/body: "mind" can mean the interior dimension in general—or the Left Hand—and "body" the exterior dimension in general—or the Right Hand. I will specifically indicate that usage when it comes up.)

THE HARD PROBLEM

Here is the world-knot, the inherent paradox of flatland: the body is in the mind, but the brain is in the Body.

Both of those statements are true, but in flatland they appear contradictory, and those contradictions drive much of the world-knot.

The felt body is in the mind, as shown in figures 1, 3, and 8. That is, formop transcends and includes conop, which transcends and includes vital feelings and sensorimotor awareness: the mind transcends and includes the body (which is precisely why the mind can causally *operate on* the body, or why formop can operate on conop, which operates on sensorimotor, and so on, as every developmentalist knows). This "transcendent" part of the mind (e.g., my mind can move my arm) is what every physicalist *acknowledges* (and then tries to explain away by embracing only flatland), and what every dualist acknowledges and attempts to *incorporate* (but does so by turning it into a dualism that still accepts the flatland dissociation; see below).

With the collapse of the Kosmos into flatland (naturalism, physicalism, scientific materialism), the interior *realities* of the I-domain *are still felt* and *strongly intuited* (mind can control the body, a degree of free will is real, consciousness exists, there is a unity of experience), but these realities are faced with a world, thought to be ultimately real, in which there are only it-realities described by science. And in that world, the brain is simply part of the Body, part of the natural biological organism, and thus consciousness must somehow be a function of that brain. But there is absolutely nothing in that brain, as our authorities just told us, that even vaguely corresponds to the qualia or experiences or realities of the mind and consciousness. We must then either reduce consciousness to brain (and thus deny consciousness in its own terms), or accept the dualism as real, whereupon we can't even explain how I can move my arm (or how one reality affects the other).

I am suggesting that both those solutions occur within the flatland paradigm. The technical details I will reserve for an endnote.[12] In more general terms, we might simply note the following:

The materialist reduces the mind to the brain, and since the brain is indeed part of the organism, there is no dualism: the mind/body problem is solved! And that is correct—the brain is part of the organism, part of the physical world, so there is no dualism; nor are there any values, consciousness, depth, or divinity anywhere in the resultant universe. And that reductionism is exactly the "solution" that the physicalist imposes on reality, a solution still rampant in most forms of cognitive science, neuroscience, systems theory, and so on: reduce the Left to the Right and then claim you have solved the problem.

But the reason most people, even most scientists, are uneasy with that "solution"—and the reason the problem remains a problem—is that, even though materialism announces that there is no dualism, most people know otherwise, because they *feel* the difference between their mind and their body (between their thoughts and their feelings)—they feel it every time they consciously decide to move their arm, they feel it in every exercise of will—and they *also* feel the difference between their mind and their Body (or between the subject in here and the objective world out there). And the average person is right on both counts. To take them in that order:

There is a distinction between mind (formop) and felt body (vital and sensorimotor), and this can be experienced in the interior or Left-Hand domains. It is not a dualism, but is rather a case of "transcend and include," and almost every rational adult has a sense of the transcend part, in that the mind can, on a good day, control the body and its desires. All of that is phenomenologically true for the Left-Hand domains. But *none* of those *interior* stages of qualitative development (from body to mind to soul to spirit) are captured when "body" means Right-Hand organism and "mind" means Right-Hand brain—all of those qualitative distinctions are completely lost in material monism, which does not solve the problem but obliterates it.

The dualist, on the other hand, acknowledges as real both consciousness and matter, but generally despairs of finding any way to relate them. "Mind" in the general sense of "interiors" and "Body" in the general sense of "exteriors" seem to be separated by an unbridgeable gulf—a dualism between subject and object. And at the level of formal operational thinking (or reason in general), at which this discussion usually takes place, the dualists are right: inside and outside are a very real dualism, and attempts to deny that dualism can almost always be shown to be facile, a semantic sleight-of-hand that verbally claims that subject and object are one, but which still leaves the self looking at the world out there which seems as separate as ever.

This is where the *transrational stages of development* have so much to offer this discussion. In the disclosure known as satori, for example, it becomes clear that the subject and object are two sides of the same thing, that inside and outside are two aspects of One Taste. How to relate them is not the problem, according to the clear consensus of the many individuals who have tapped into this wave of development. The problem, rather, is that this genuinely nondual solution is not something that can be fully grasped at the rational level. In fact, simply stating, in a rational fashion, that subject and object are nondual leads to all sorts of intractable problems and paradoxes.[13] Besides, if this nondualism could be genuinely grasped in rational terms, then the great materialist and dualist philosophers (many of whom are acknowledged geniuses) would have figured this out long ago, and the mind-body problem would not be much of problem.

No, the reason that both sides of the argument have generally agreed that the mind-body problem is irresolvable, is not that they aren't smart enough to figure it out, but that it is only solved in postrational stages of development, stages which are generally suspect, ignored, or actively denied by most rational researchers. But in principle the problem is no different from this: A rationalist will maintain that there is a proof for the Pythagorean Theorem. A person at a prerational stage will not agree with, or even understand, that proof. Nonetheless, the rationalist is justified in making that claim, which is true enough to virtually anybody who develops to the rational level and studies geometry.

Just so with the nondual solution of the mind-body problem. Those who develop to the nondual stages of consciousness unfolding are virtually unanimous: consciousness and matter, interior and exterior, self and world, are of One Taste. Subject and object are *both* distinct realities *and* aspects of the same thing: a true unity-in-diversity. But that unity-in-diversity cannot be stated in rational terms in a way that makes sense to anybody who has not also had a transrational experience. Therefore the "proof" for this nondual solution can only be found in the further development of the consciousness of those who seek to know the solution. Although this solution ("you must further develop your own consciousness if you want to know its full dimensions") is not satisfactory to the rationalist (whether dualist or physicalist), nonetheless it is the only acceptable form of the solution according to a genuinely integral paradigm.[14] When we heard Campbell say that a solution to the mind-body problem is "forever beyond our understanding," we can amend that to: it is not beyond human understanding, it is simply beyond the rational stages of understanding. The solution is postrational, and fully available to all who wish to move in that direction.

TWO PHASES IN UNSNARLING THE KNOT

We can represent some of these dilemmas as in figure 13, which is a map of flatland. If you compare this map with that in figure 8, you will see that all of the interior domains (body, mind, soul, and spirit) have been collapsed to their exterior (physical) correlates, which alone are said to be ultimately real. This leaves the mind (or consciousness in general) hanging and dangling in midair. And that is exactly the problem.

More specifically, the insuperable problem (the world-knot) has been how to relate this mind to both the body (or the lower interior levels of feeling and desire) and to the Body (or the objective organism, brain, and material environment). As we saw, the physicalist reduces the mind to the brain or Body, and thus cannot account for the reality of the mind in its own terms, and the dualist leaves the mind dangling in midair, cut off from its own roots (in the body) and from the exterior world (of the Body)—hence the unacceptable dualism.

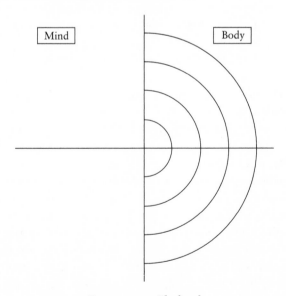

FIGURE 13. *Flatland*

Within the flatland paradigm depicted in figure 13, the problem is indeed unsolvable. The solution, I have suggested, involves an "all-level, all-quadrant" view, which plugs the mind back into its own body and intimately relates the mind to its own Body. And it does so, in the final analysis, through the disclosures of the postrational, nondual stages of consciousness development.

That means that part of this solution involves the existence of higher stages of development. But how do we proceed to unsnarl the world-knot if we have not yet reached these higher stages ourselves, and if we cannot expect that others will have done so? We can at least begin, I suggest, by acknowledging and incorporating *the realities of all four quadrants*. That is, if we cannot yet ourselves—in our own consciousness development—be "all-level" (matter to body to mind to soul to spirit), let us at least attempt to be "all-quadrant" (which means at least including the Big Three in our attempts to explain consciousness).

Thus, I am proposing two general phases for unsnarling the world-knot of the mind-body problem.[15] The first is a move from reductionistic accounts to all-quadrant accounts. This acknowledgment of the four quadrants (or simply the Big Three) allows an equal inclusion of *first-person* phenomenal accounts ("I"), *second-person* intersubjective backgrounds ("we"), and *third-person* physical systems ("it")—what we will call "the 1-2-3 of consciousness studies."

The second phase is then to move from "all-quadrant" to "all-level, all-quadrant." We will examine these two steps in that order.

STEP ONE: ALL-QUADRANT

It is not enough to say that organism and environment coevolve; it is not enough to say that culture and consciousness coevolve. All four of those "tetra-evolve" together.

That is, the objective organism (the Upper-Right quadrant), with its DNA, its neuronal pathways, its brain systems, and its behavioral patterns, mutually interacts with the objective environment, ecosystems, and social realities (the Lower Right), and all of those do indeed coevolve. Likewise, individual consciousness (Upper Left), with its intentionality, structures, and states, arises within, and mutually interacts with, the intersubjective culture (Lower Left) in which it finds itself, and which it in turn helps to create, so that these, too, coevolve. But just as important, subjective intentionality and objective behavior mutually interact (e.g., through will and response), and cultural worldviews mutually interact with social structures, as does individual consciousness and behavior. In other words, all four quadrants—organism, environment, consciousness, and culture—cause and are caused by the others: they "tetra-evolve."

(It does not matter "how" this happens; that "how," I am suggesting, is more fully disclosed at the postrational, nondual waves; at this point, it is only necessary to acknowledge that this interaction seems phenomenologically undeniable. Whether you think it is theoretically possible or not, your mind does interact with your body, your mind interacts with its culture, your mind interacts with the physical organism, and your organism interacts with your environment: they all "tetra-interact.")

As we have seen, the subjective features of consciousness (waves, streams, states) are intimately interrelated with the objective aspects of the organism (especially the brain, neurophysiology, and various organ systems in the individual), with the background cultural contexts that allow meaning and understanding to be generated in the first place, and with the social institutions that anchor them. As I suggested in *A Brief History of Everything*, even a single thought is inextricably embedded in all four quadrants—intentional, behavioral, cultural, and social—and cannot easily be understood without reference to them all.

Accordingly, in writings such as "An Integral Theory of Consciousness,"[16] I have stressed the need for an approach to consciousness that differentiates-and-integrates all four quadrants (or simply the Big Three of I, we, and it; or first-person, second-person, and third-person accounts: the 1-2-3 of consciousness studies).

That initially sounds like an impossibly tall order, but the fact is, for the first time in history we are actually at a point where we have enough of the pieces of the puzzle to at least begin such a project. Consider: in the Upper-Left quadrant of subjective consciousness, we have a body of research and evidence that includes the entire perennial philosophy (which offers three thousand years of meticulously gathered data on the interior domains) and a massive amount of modern research from developmental psychology. Much of that evidence is summarized in the charts, which are a startling testimony to the fact that, even if there are a million details yet to be worked out, the broad contours of the spectrum of consciousness have already been significantly outlined. The general similarities in all of those charts are most suggestive, and, from a bird's-eye view, hint that we are at least in the right ballpark.

The same can be said with a reasonable degree of confidence for the

Lower-Left quadrant (of intersubjective worldviews) and the Lower-Right quadrant (of the techno-economic base). A century or so of postmodernism has made the importance of pluralistic cultural worldviews and backgrounds abundantly clear (even rationally oriented theorists such as Habermas have agreed that all propositions are *always* in part culturally situated); moreover, scholars are in general agreement that cultural worldviews historically unfolded from archaic to magic to mythic to mental to global (although there is reasonable disagreement as to the respective values of those views). Likewise, in the Lower-Right quadrant, few scholars contest the evolutionary sequence of the social forces of production: foraging, horticultural, agrarian, industrial, informational. In both of those quadrants—cultural and social—although again a million details need to be worked out, the general contours are better understood today than at any other time in history.

Work in the Upper-Right quadrant—particularly in brain physiology and cognitive science—is yet in its infancy, and a fully integral view of consciousness will await more primary discoveries in this quadrant (which is one of the reasons I have written less about this quadrant than the others: cognitive science and neuroscience, despite the enthusiastic pronouncements of their proponents—the Churchlands, for example—is a babe in the woods). Still, our knowledge of this quadrant is growing as fast as babies usually do, and at this time we have enough knowledge to at least be able to situate neurophysiology in relation to the other dimensions of being, even as its contours continue to be elucidated.[17]

Thus, the time is certainly ripe for the beginning of an all-quadrant approach, or simply an approach that equally honors first-person phenomenal accounts, second-person intersubjective structures, and third-person scientific/objective systems: the 1-2-3 of consciousness studies.

There are many signs that this first phase is well under way. *The Journal of Consciousness Studies* regularly carries articles arguing for such balanced approaches, and several books have recently stated the case for such a balance in convincing terms. *The View from Within*, edited by Francisco Varela and Jonathan Shear, is a superb example. They defend a view that is predominantly a neurophenomenology, where first-person experience and third-person systems provide reciprocal constraints, often mediated through second-person positions. "It would be futile to stay with first-person descriptions in isolation. We need to harmonize and constrain them by building the appropriate *links* with third-person studies. (This often implies an intermediate mediation, a second-person position.) The overall results should be to move toward an integrated or global perspective on mind where neither experience [first-person, UL] nor external mechanisms [third-person, UR] have the final word. The global [integral] perspective requires therefore the explicit establishment of mutual constraints, a reciprocal influence and determination."[18] This is consonant with what I mean by saying that all quadrants are mutually determining (and "tetra-interacting").

Max Velmans's anthology *Investigating Phenomenal Consciousness* is another superb collection emphasizing an integral approach. It includes chapters by Alwyn Scott, Greg Simpson, Howard Shevrin, Richard Stevens, Jane Henry, Charles Tart, Francisco Varela, Wilber and Walsh, and Velmans. *Transpersonal Research Methods for the Social Sciences*, by William Braud and Rosemarie Anderson, is a fine collection of resources for what the authors call an "integral inquiry."

STEP TWO: ALL-LEVEL

I believe that the field needs to continue to flesh out that all-quadrant approach, and further, to move to the second phase, which is *all-level*.

Many of the all-quadrant approaches fully acknowledge the transpersonal domains of consciousness. Robert Forman, for example, points out that at least three transpersonal states need to be recognized: the pure consciousness event (or formless cessation), dual mystical consciousness (or permanent causal/witnessing awareness), and the nondual state (or permanent nondual realization).[19] Moreover, many of the all-quadrant approaches (including Jonathan Shear and Ron Jevning, Francisco Varela, James Austin, Robert Forman, Braud and Anderson, and others) have explicitly drawn much of their methodology from meditative and contemplative techniques.

Still, one is hard-pressed to find in many of those authors a full appreciation of the stage conceptions of consciousness development, such as the works of Baldwin, Habermas, Loevinger, Graves, Kohlberg, Wade, Cook-Greuter, Beck, Kegan, et al., even though, as we have seen, there is substantial evidence for their validity. It is not enough to simply note that first-person realities reciprocally influence and determine third-person mechanisms, and that both circulate through second-person intermediaries. It is also crucial to understand that *first-person consciousness develops*, and it does so through a variety of well-researched stages. Moreover, *second-person consciousness develops*, and this development, too, has been widely researched. Finally, *the capacity for third-person consciousness develops* (e.g., Piagetian cognition), and this has likewise been exhaustively studied.[20] Perhaps because many of the all-quadrant theorists have come from a phenomenological background, which in itself does not easily spot stages, they have tended to overlook the waves of consciousness unfolding in all four quadrants.[21] Be that as it may, a truly integral approach, in my opinion, will move from being merely all-quadrant to being all-level, all-quadrant. Or *1-2-3 across all levels*.

Obviously much work remains to be done. But a staggering amount of evidence—premodern, modern, and postmodern—points most strongly to an integral approach that is all-quadrant, all-level. The sheer amount of this evidence inexorably points to the fact that we stand today on the brink, not of fashioning a fully complete and integral view of consciousness, but of being able to settle, from now on, for nothing less.

15

The Integral Embrace

HOW THEN SHALL we see the world? An ancient era of resplendent wonder, a modernity gone merely mad? A postmodernity in pieces? Or perhaps evolution as unadulterated progress, today being the happiest days of all? Evolution, or devolution? The very fact that we recognize premodern, modern, and postmodern eras means we implicitly recognize some sort of development. Even the theorists who label themselves "postmodern" imply some sort of improvements over their modern predecessors, yes? How shall we balance the undeniable improvements in history with the equally undeniable horrors that also followed? And how can this balance allow us, finally, to embrace the best of premodern, modern, and postmodern, an embrace that might allow a genuinely integral psychology to emerge?

FROM PREMODERNITY

Each era has its enduring truths. Each has its pathological distortions.

Premodernity disclosed the Great Nest of Being in all of its radiant glory—and then often used that conception in a rigidly hierarchical fashion to justify the oppression of millions. Modernity differentiated the value spheres, ushering in everything from the liberal democracies to feminism—and then let those differentiations drift into dissociation, whereupon a rampant scientific materialism attempted to erase virtually every value originally freed by the differentiations: technical rationality nearly destroyed the humanity it had first made possible, and the modern disqualified universe settled like volcanic dust in a suffocating manner on all. And postmodernity, which set out nobly to deconstruct the nightmares of the modern flatland, ended up embracing and even amplifying them, so that not only was the integration offered by its own vision-logic not forthcoming, its integrative intent was set back decades.

While attempting to set aside the distortions of each epoch, we seek to honor the truths, for they are all truths of the human potential. To ignore past truths—in either phylogeny or ontogeny—is the very definition of pathology. Therefore, an integral approach—a sane approach—attempts to honor, acknowledge, and incorporate the enduring truths into the ongoing sweep of consciousness evolution, for they are the truths of our very own Self, even here and now.

From the premodern heritage, we have learned of the Great Nest of Being and Knowing, and found that it is a road map to Spirit, not in a rigid and predetermined fashion, but as a flowing morphogenetic field of gentle persuasion. The enduring truths of this ancient wisdom include the idea of levels or dimensions of reality and consciousness, reaching from matter to body to mind to soul to spirit, with Spirit fully and equally present at all of these levels as the Ground of the entire display. Each senior level transcends and includes its juniors, so that this Great Nest is a holarchy of extended love and compassionate embrace, reaching from dirt to Divinity, with no corner of the Kosmos left untouched by grace or care or luminosity.

The ancient sages taught us that, precisely because reality is multilayered—with physical, emotional, mental, and spiritual dimensions—reality is not simply a one-leveled affair lying around for all and sundry to see: you must be *adequate* to the level of reality you wish to understand. The soul is not running around out there in the physical world; it cannot be seen with microscopes or telescopes or photographic plates. If you want to see the soul, you must turn within. You must develop your consciousness. You must grow and evolve in your capacity to perceive the deeper layers of your Self, which disclose higher levels of reality: the great within that is beyond: the greater the depth, the higher the reality.

For an integral psychology, this means that we should attempt to honor the entire spectrum of consciousness, matter to body to mind to soul to spirit—by whatever names, in whatever guises, and in however many levels modern research can confirm (five, seven, twelve, twenty: the exact number matters less than the simple acknowledgment of the multidimensional richness involved). I have suggested around sixteen major waves, which can be condensed into nine or ten functional groupings (all shown in the charts), but all such cartographies are simply different approaches to the many waves in the great River of Life, matter to mind to spirit, which is the most precious legacy of the ancient wisdom.

For an integral psychology, this also means that a person's deepest drive—the major drive of which all others are derivative—is the drive to actualize the entire Great Nest through the vehicle of one's own being, so that one becomes, in full realization, a vehicle of Spirit shining radiantly into the world, as the entire world. We are all the sons and daughters of a Godhead that is the Goal and Ground of every gesture in the Kosmos, and we will not rest until our own Original Face greets us with each dawn.

The ancient adepts would have this Great Liberation be a permanent realization, not a passing glimmer—a permanent trait, not merely an altered state—and thus they left us with an extraordinary battery of spiritual practices, all of which have one thing in common: they help us to unfold the higher levels of the Great Nest of our own Divinity—they accelerate our development to Godhood. The more complete spiritual practices emphasize the *ascending currents*—taking us from body to mind to soul to spirit—as well as the *descending currents*—taking spiritual insights and expressing them in and through the incarnated body and blessed earth, thus integrating both the transcendental and immanent faces of Emptiness.

Whenever we moderns pause for a moment, and enter the silence, and listen very carefully, the glimmer of our own deepest nature begins to shine forth, and we are introduced to the mysteries of the deep, the call of the within, the infinite radiance of a splendor that time and space forgot—we are introduced to the all-pervading Spiritual domain that the growing tip of our honored ancestors were the first to discover. And they were good enough to leave us a general map to that infinite domain, a map called the Great Nest of Being, a map of our own interiors, an archeology of our own Spirit.

FROM MODERNITY

From modernity we take the enduring truths of the *differentiation* and the *evolution* of the Big Three (the Good, the True, and the Beautiful).[1] As the average mode of consciousness continued historically to grow and evolve—and because evolution operates in part by differentiation-and-integration—the perception of the Great Nest became increasingly differentiated and integrated on a widespread, cultural scale (and not just in a few individual pioneers). Differentiations seen in the past only by the most highly evolved became ordinary, common perceptions.[2]

As the Big Three of art, morals, and science began to differentiate and clarify on a widespread scale—I, we, and it; first-person, second-person, and third-person; self, culture, and nature; the Beautiful, the Good, and the True—each was allowed to yield its own truths unburdened by invasion from others. That modernity let these differentiations collapse into dissociation (so that scientific materialism could and did colonize the other spheres), condemns the pathological dissociation, not the dignity of the differentiations themselves, for they ushered in everything from democracy to feminism to the abolition of slavery to the rise of the ecological sciences to the worldwide increase in lifespan of over three decades: great dignities, indeed.

And thus, from modernity, we learn that each of the levels in the Great Nest needs to be differentiated into the four quadrants (or simply the Big Three), and done so on a widespread scale. From modernity we also learn that *each of those quadrants evolves*, and thus an integral psychology follows those developments as they appear in any individual.

For an integral psychology, this means that the basic levels of consciousness available to men and women need to be carefully differentiated into their various developmental lines. Through the levels or waves of the Great Nest (body, mind, soul, spirit) run numerous different developmental lines or streams (cognitive, moral, aesthetic, affective, needs, identities, perspectives, etc.). *It is the job of an integral psychology to track all of these various waves and streams as they unfold in any given individual.*

We called this overall picture "an integral psychograph" (see figs. 2 and 3). This approach allows us to determine, in a very general way, the evolving streams of an individual's consciousness as those streams move into ever-deeper, ever-higher waves, body to mind to soul to spirit, precon to con to postcon to post-postcon. It also allows us to more easily spot any "stick points"—any pathologies, fractured fulcrums, developmental miscarriages, dissociated subpersonalities, alienated facets of consciousness—and, by better understanding their genesis and texture, treat them more effectively. Although the various types of pathology and treatment will have some important differences (due to the qualitatively different architecture of each basic wave), nonetheless they all attempt to *bring the problem into consciousness*, so that it can rejoin the ongoing sweep of holarchical embrace, the ever-deeper unfolding that is consciousness evolution, prepersonal to personal to transpersonal, subconscious to self-conscious to superconscious.

Evolution does not isolate us from the rest of the Kosmos, it unites us with the rest of the Kosmos: the same currents that produced birds from dust and poetry from rocks produce egos from ids and sages from egos. Evolution in each quadrant is Spirit-in-action expressed in that mode, operating through gentle persuasion in the great morphogenetic field of increasing embrace. The evolutionary current of the Kosmos—this great River of Eros, binding human and nonhuman holons together in an ever-flowing caress—is indeed the Love that moves the sun and other stars. And modernity's enduring contributions—which disclosed the differentiation and evolution of the Big Three—simply allow us to track this evolving Love throughout its many waves and streams.

FROM POSTMODERNITY

Modernity's differentiation of the value spheres allowed postmodernity to see exactly how interrelated the four quadrants are. Every objective occasion has subjective and intersubjective components; every holon has four quadrants. The world is not merely an objective, Right-Hand occasion—it also has intrinsic depth, consciousness, the within, the interior, the Left-Hand worlds in all their glory. *Constructivism* means consciousness doesn't merely reflect the world, it helps construct it. *Contextualism* means that holons are nested, indefinitely. *Integral-aperspectivism* means that as many perspectives as humanly possible must be included in an integral embrace. That the Kosmos is endlessly holonic—there is the message of postmodernism.

For any integral studies, this means that we must take great care to ensure that the important differentiations of modernity are in fact integrated, that the Big Three do not fly apart; that subtle reductionism does not creep into the picture, yielding a flatland holism; and that any approach to consciousness is indeed a 1-2-3 approach, including and equally honoring first-person, second-person, and third-person accounts of consciousness: first-person or phenomenal accounts of the stream of consciousness as it is directly experienced by a person (Upper Left); second-person communication of those facts, set in particular linguistic structures, worldviews, and background contexts (Lower Left); and third-person scientific descriptions of the corresponding mechanisms, systems, and material networks, from brain structures to social systems (Right Hand).

That "all-quadrant" approach is the first step to a truly integral model. The second step adds an "all-level" approach, which investigates the *stages of development* of first-, second-, and third-person consciousness. In other words, it investigates the waves and streams, the levels and lines, in all of the quadrants.[3] The result is an "all-level, all-quadrant" approach to integral studies, across the spectrum of disciplines—science, history, religion, anthropology, philosophy, psychology, education, politics, business.

When it comes to the individual, the result is integral psychology, integral therapy, and integral transformative practice.

SPIRIT-IN-ACTION HAS COME TO AWAKEN

Should this "all-level, all-quadrant" approach succeed, we will have embraced some of the more enduring truths of premodernity (all-level), modernity (all-quadrant), and the postmodern integration (all-level, all-quadrant).

My aim in this book, while focusing specifically on an integral psychology, has also been an integral approach in general, attempting to take, not just the best of today's schools, but the best of premodern, modern, and postmodern insights, while jettisoning their extremist distortions. Obviously, as I said in the Introduction, this type of approach can only begin with the most general of generalizations—outrageous generalizations, some would say—but if we are to start on this endeavor, we must start somewhere, and this type of approach is, I suppose, as good as any. But the major aim of this book is to act as just that: a beginning, not an end; the start of a discussion, not the finish.

If we really are living in an integral-aperspectival era, then these types of integral attempts will become increasingly common. Some will be better, some worse; some felicitous, some virulent; some truly integral, some angling. But there will be many, many such attempts, and all of them, I suspect, will contribute to the great integral rainbow now beginning to shine, however tentatively, all over the globe.

For the fact is, this is the dawning of the age of vision-logic, the rise of the network society, the postmodern, aperspectival, internetted global village. Evolution in all forms has started to become conscious of itself.

Evolution, as Spirit-in-action, is starting to awaken on a more collective scale. Kosmic evolution is now producing theories and performances of its own integral embrace. This Eros moves through you and me, urging us to include, to diversify, to honor, to enfold. The Love that moves the sun and other stars is moving theories such as this, and it will move many others, as Eros connects the previously unconnected, and pulls together the fragments of a world too weary to endure.

Some would call these integral endeavors "powerful glimmers of a true Descent of the all-pervading World Soul." Others would simply say the time is ripe for such. But this much seems certain: less comprehensive endeavors are starting to lose their appeal; the allure of flatland, the call of fragmentation, the regressive pull of reductionism are becoming much less fascinating. Their power to enthrall the mind becomes weaker every day, as Eros works its subtle wonders in and through us all.

If we can believe the collective wisdom of the many ages of humankind, we can perhaps say:

This Eros is the same Spirit-in-action that originally threw itself outward to create a vast morphogenetic field of wondrous possibilities (known as the Great Nest). Out of itself, as matter, it began; out of itself, as life, it continued; out of itself, as mind, it began to awaken. The same Spirit-in-action differentiated itself into modes of the good and the true and the beautiful, as it continued its evolutionary play. And it is now the same Spirit-in-action, starting to become collectively conscious of itself, that has initiated an era of integral embrace—global village to communications internet to integral theories to network society—as it slowly binds together the fragments of a world that has forgotten how to care.

Just so, the same Spirit-in-action has written this book, and it is the very same Spirit-in-action who is now reading it. From subconscious to self-conscious to superconscious, the great Play continues and the grand River flows, with all of its glorious streams rushing to the ocean of One Taste, never really lost, never really found, this sound of the rain on the temple roof, which only alone is.

CHARTS

CHART 1A. WILBER CORRELATIONS

Correlative Basic Structures

subatomic; matter-atomic -molecular -polymer; sensation; perception; exocept; impulse/emotion; image; symbol; endocept; concept; rule/role (early, late, transition); formal (early, late, transition); vision-logic (early, middle, late); psychic (vision) (early, late); subtle (archetype) (early, late); causal (formless) (early, late); nondual (early, middle, late)

(bottom axis) sensorimotor | phantasmic-emotional | rep-mind | conop | formop | postformal

General Self-Sense

material self → bodyego → persona → ego → centaur → soul → spirit

Specific Aspects

pleromatic; uroboric; axial-body; pranic-body (typhonic); image-body (magical); name-self; concept-self (mythic); membership-self; early; middle; late; mature ego; centaur (existential, integrated self); psychic self; subtle self (soul); Pure Self (Witness); Nondual

Defenses

distortion / delusional proj. / hallucination / wish fulfillment; selfobject fusion; projection / splitting; isolation / repression / reaction form.; displacement / duplicitous transaction / covert; intentions; suppression / anticipation / sublimation; inauthenticity / deadening / aborted self-actualization / bad faith; psychic inflation / split-life goals / pranic disorder / yogic illness; failed integration / archetypal fragmentation; failed differentiation / Arhat's disease

Possible Pathology

psychosis; borderline; neurosis; script; ego; existential; psychic; subtle; causal

Fulcrum

BPM: F-0; F-1 (physical self); F-2 (emotional self); F-3 (self-concept); F-4 (role self); F-5 (mature ego); F-6 (centaur); F-7 (psychic); F-8 (subtle); F-9 (causal); Ground

Treatment

intense regressive therapies; pacification (Gedo: pacification); structure-building (Gedo: unification, optimal disillusion); uncovering (Gedo: interpretation); script analysis; introspection (Gedo: introspection); existential therapy; path of yogis; path of saints; path of sages

Moral Span (those deemed worthy of moral consideration)

autistic / symbolic / self-only; impulsive / magical / narcissism / hedonic; safety-power / mythic-membership / conformist / rational-reflexive; universal-global; panenhenic — all earthly beings (yogic); panentheistic — all sentient beings in all realms (saintly); always already (sage/siddha)

egocentric | sociocentric | worldcentric | shamanic | bodhisattvic | Buddhic

preconventional | conventional | postconventional | post-postconventional

"me" — locus of bodily self; "us" — locus of mythic-membership (family, group, tribe, nation); "all of us" — locus of World-rational universal pluralism (all humans without exception / all rational beings without exception); all earthly beings — locus of Soul (yogic); all sentient beings in all realms — locus of Brahma-lokas (realms without exception, saintly); all manifest and unmanifest reality — self-liberation in primordial awareness (sage/siddha)

CHART 1B. WILBER CORRELATIONS

General stage	Correlative Basic Structures	Affect	Levels of "Food" (relational exchange)	Gender Identity	Worldviews — name	Worldviews — general characteristics	(bracket)
sensorimotor	matter: -subatomic, -atomic, -molecular, -polymer	• reactivity		• morphological-genetic givens		• undifferentiated, pleromatic	egocentric
	sensation	• sensations					
	perception	• physiostates: touch, temperature, pleasure, pain	material exchange: -food, -labor	• undifferentiated	archaic		
	exocept				archaic-magical	• hallucinatory wish fulfillment; subject-object fusions; "selfobject"	
phantasmic-emotional	impulse/emotion	• protoemotions: tension, fear, rage, satisfaction	emotional exchange: -sex, -safety	• differentiated basic-gender identity	magical	• egocentric, word magic, narcissistic; locus of magic power = ego	
	image						
	symbol		power		magic-mythic	• omnipotence of ego challenged; security; ego omnipotence transferred to gods	ethnocentric
rep-mind	endocept	• 2° emotions: anxiety, anger, wishing, liking, safety	-belongingness, care	• gender conventionality	mythic	• concrete-literal myths; locus of magic power = deified Other	
	concept		mental exchange: -membership		mythic-rational	• rationalization of mythic structures	
conop	rule/role early	• 3° emotions: love, joy, depression, hate, belongingness	discourse	• gender consistency (norms)	rational	• demythologizing, formalizing	worldcentric
	rule/role late		-self-reflective exchange		formalism	• static universal formalism	
	transition					• static systems/contexts	
formop	formal early	• 4° emotions: universal affect, global justice, care, compassion, all-centric altruism	-autonomous exchange	• gender androgyny (trans-differentiated)	pluralistic	• pluralistic systems, dynamic-multiple contexts/histories	
	formal late				relativism	• integrates multiple contexts, paradigmatic	
	transition						
	vision-logic early				holistic	• cross-paradigmatic; dialectical	theocentric
postformal	vision-logic middle	• human love, world-centric altruism			integralism	developmentalism as World Process	
	vision-logic late		soul exchange: -psychic vision				
	psychic (vision) early	• awe, rapture, all-species love, compassion	-God communion	• archetypal	psychic (shamanic, yogic)	• union with World Process; nature mysticism; gross realm unity	
	psychic (vision) late						
	subtle (archetype) early	• ananda, ecstasy love-bliss, saintly commitment	-God union	• gender union (tantra)	subtle (archetypal, saintly)	• union with creatrix of gross realm; deity mysticism; subtle realm unity	
	subtle (archetype) late						
	causal early	• infinite freedom-release	spiritual exchange: -Godhead identity	• beyond gender	causal	• union with source of manifest realms; formless mysticism; causal unity	
	causal (formless) late	boddhisattvic-compassion			(formless, sage)		
	nondual early	• compassion	-sahaja	gender	nondual (siddha)	• union of form and formless, Spirit and World Process; nondual mysticism	
	nondual middle	• one taste					
	nondual late						

CHART 2A. BASIC STRUCTURES IN OTHER SYSTEMS

Basic Structures	Huston Smith levels (planes)	Plotinus	Buddhist Vijnanas	Stan Grof	John Battista	Chakras	General Great Chain	James Mark Baldwin
matter -subatomic			(levels of csness)	BPM: oceanic to birth		1. material	matter	
-molecular -polymer	body (terrestrial)	matter					body	
sensation		sensation	1–5, five senses	somatic	sensation			prelogical
perception		perception			perception			
exocept						2. emotional-sexual		
impulse/emotion		pleasure/pain images		aesthetic	emotion			
image	mind (intermediate)							
symbol		concepts, opinions		psychodynamic Freudian COEX systems		3. intentional-mind, power		quasi-logical
endocept							mind	
concept					cognition	4. community-mind, love		
rule/role early								logical
late		logical faculty	6. manovijnana (gross-reflecting mind)			5. verbal-rational mind		
transition					self-aware			
formal early								
late		creative reason		existential death-rebirth (cf BPM)				
transition			7. manas (higher mind)			6. psychic-mind, ajna (vision)		extra-logical
vision- early		world soul		astral-psychic extra-human			soul	
logic middle	soul (celestial)	soul		identifications archetypal		7. sahasrara, transcendental csness, light		
late					unition			hyper-logical
psychic early (vision)		nous	8. tainted alayavijnana (archetypal)	deity, luminosity		(higher shabd chakras, to cessation)		logical
late	spirit (infinite)			universal mind supracosmic			spirit	
subtle early (archetype) late		absolute		void		(release of all chakras in the Real)		
causal early (formless) late		one	9. nondual consciousness as suchness	ultimate	absolute			
nondual early middle late								

Cognitive line (Basic Structures): sensorimotor · phantasmic-emotional · rep-mind · conop · formop · postformal

CHART 2B. BASIC STRUCTURES IN OTHER SYSTEMS

Basic Structures	General Great Chain	Aurobindo	Kabbalah	Vedanta (state)	Vedanta (body)	Vedanta (sheaths)	William Tiller	Leadbetter (Theosophy)	Adi Da
matter -subatomic -atomic -molecular -polymer	matter	physical	Malkhut	waking	gross	1. material (anna-mayakosha)	physical	physical	1. physical body
sensation	body	sensation					etheric	etheric (fine physical)	
perception		perception							
exocept									
impulse/emotion		vital-emotional	Yesod			2. emotional-sexual (prana-mayakosha)	astral	astral (emotional)	2. emotional body
image									
symbol									
endocept	mind	lower mind	Netzach/Hod	dreaming	subtle		m-1 (lower mind)		
concept		concrete mind				3. middle mind (mano-mayakosha)		mental	3. lower mind willpower gross-mind
rule/role early / late		logical mind (reasoning)	Tiferet				m-2 (intellectual mind)		
transition								causal (higher mind)	
formal early / late		higher mind (systems)				4. higher mind (vijnana-mayakosha)			4. higher mind psychic opening
transition									
vision-logic early / middle / late	soul (psychic and subtle)	illumined mind	Chesed/Gevurah	deep sleep			m-3 (spiritual mind)	buddhic (illumined mind)	
psychic (vision) early / late		intuitive mind	Chokhmah/Binah			5. bliss mind (ananda-mayakosha)			5. supramental psychic/subtle
subtle (archetype) early / late	spirit (causal and nondual)	overmind	Keter	turiya	causal		spirit	atmic (universal spirit)	
causal (formless) early / late		supermind	Ayn		turiya	Brahman-Atman (turiyatita)		monad/logos	6. formless cessation, nirvikalpa
nondual early / middle / late		satchitananda	Ein Sof						7. sahaja bhava

sensorimotor · phantasmic-emotional · rep-mind · conop · formop · postformal

matter · body · mind

CHART 3A. COGNITIVE DEVELOPMENT

Average Age of Emergence	Correlative Basic Structures	Piaget	Commons & Richards	Kurt Fischer level	Alexander (levels of mind)
0–18 months (sensorimotor)	matter—subatomic, -atomic, -molecular, -polymer; sensation; perception	sensorimotor	1a sensorimotor actions; 1b sentential actions	1. single sensorimotor set (3–4 months); 2. sensorimotor mapping (7–8 months); 3. sensorimotor system (11–13 months)	1. sensorimotor
1–3 yrs (phantasmic-emotional)	exocept; impulse/emotion; image; symbol	preconceptual; preoperational	2a nominal actions	4. single representational set (20–24 months)	2. prana-emotion-desire
3–6 yrs (mind rep-)	endocept (conceptual); concept	intuitive (conceptual); preoperational	2b preoperational actions	5. representational mapping (4–5 yrs)	3. representational mind
7–8 (conop)	rule/role early	concrete operational – substage 1	3a primary actions	6. representational system (6–7.5 yrs)	
9–10	rule/role late	" – substage 2	3b concrete operations		
11–12	transition	transition [late conop/early formop (substage 1)]	4a abstract	7. abstract set (10–12)	
13–14 (formop)	formal early	formal operational – substage 2	4b formal	8. abstract mapping (11–15)	4. abstract mind
15–19	formal late	" " – substage 3			
19–21	transition	(transition – late formop/early polyvalent)	5a systematic	9. systems (19–21)	
open (postformal)	vision-logic early	(polyvalent logic – systems of systems)	5b meta-systematic	10. systems of systems (24–26)	
[21–28]	vision-logic middle		6a paradigmatic		
[28–35] (earliest expectable)	vision-logic late; psychic (vision) early		6b cross-paradigmatic		5. transcendental intuition
[35–42]	psychic late; subtle (archetype) early				
[42–49]	subtle late; causal (formless) early				6. root mind; 7. pure Self
[49–]	causal late; nondual early, middle, late				8. Brahman-Atman

CHART 3B. COGNITIVE DEVELOPMENT

Correlative Basic Structures	Overall Cognitive Lines	Pascual-Leone	Herb Koplowitz	Sri Aurobindo	Patricia Arlin	Gisela Labouvie-Vief	Jan Sinnott	Michael Basseches
matter -subatomic / -atomic / -molecular / -polymer								
sensation	gross							
perception		sensorimotor		physical	sensorimotor		sensorimotor	
exocept								
impulse/emotion				vital-emotional				
image								
symbol		preoperational			preoperational	symbolic	preoperational	
endocept				lower mind				
concept	gross-reflecting							
rule/role early				concrete mind	2a low concrete		concrete	1a preformal
late		late concrete			2b high concrete			
transition		early formal			3a low formal			
formal early		formal	formal	logical mind (reasoning)	3b high formal	intra-systemic	formal	1b formal
late		late formal						2 intermediate postformal
transition		pre-dialectical	systems	higher mind	4a postformal	inter-systemic	relativistic	3 general advanced
vision- early		dialectical	general systems	(systems)	4b–e late postformal (dialectical)	autonomous	unified-theory	4 advanced
logic middle	subtle	transcendental-thinking	unitary concepts					dialectical thinking
late			→					
psychic early (vision)				illumined mind				
late				intuitive mind				
subtle early (archetype)								
late	causal			overmind				
causal early (formless)				supermind				
late								
nondual early	nondual			satchitananda				
middle								
late								

Bottom axis (Correlative Basic Structures): sensorimotor — phantasmic-emotional — rep-mind — conop — formop — postformal

CHART 4A. SELF-RELATED STAGES

Notes at the pre/peri-natal level: Fulcrums (Wilber): "F-0 — pre and perinatal; deeper psychic trail"; Jenny Wade: "pre, peri, neonatal (possible transcendental)"

Correlative Basic Structures	Jane Loevinger (ego stages)	John Broughton (self epistemology)	Sullivan, Grant, and Grant (self-integration)	Fulcrums (Wilber)	Jenny Wade	Michael Washburn	Erik Erikson
matter -subatomic							
-atomic							
-molecular							
-polymer							
sensation	presocial						trust vs.
perception	autistic						mistrust
exocept							
impulse/emotion	symbiotic		1. differentiation of self & nonself	F-1	1. reactive	original embedment	autonomy vs.
image						bodyego	shame and doubt
symbol	impulsive					primal repression	
endocept		0. self "inside," reality "outside"	2. manipulative-demanding	F-2	2. naive		
concept	self-protective	1. big-person mind, little-person body		F-3	3. egocentric	mental	initiative vs. guilt & anxiety
rule/role early		2. naive subjectivism, mind and body differentiated	3. power: a. rules- "cons"			ego	industry vs.
rule/role late	conformist		b. rules- conformist	F-4	4. conformist		inferiority
formal transition	conscientious-conformist	3. persona vs. inner self	4. early individuation				
formal early			5. continuity	F-5	5. achievement/affiliative		identity vs. role confusion
formal late	conscientious	4. dualist or positivist cynical, mechanistic	6. self-consistency				intimacy/ isolation
transition	individualistic	5. inner observer differentiated from ego	7. relativity-integration				generativity/stagnation
vision (logic) early	autonomous	6. mind and body experiences of an integrated self		F-6	6. authentic	regression in service of transcendence	integrity/despair
logic middle	integrated						
logic late							
psychic (vision) early				F-7		regeneration in spirit	
psychic late							
subtle (archetype) early				F-8	7. transcendent		
subtle late							
causal early				F-9	8. unitary	integration	
causal (formless) late							
nondual early				nondual			
nondual middle							
nondual late							

General developmental levels (base axis): sensorimotor · phantasmic-emotional · rep-mind · conop · formop · formform · postformal

CHART 4B. SELF-RELATED STAGES

Correlative Basic Structures	Cognitive	Major Self Line	Neumann (mythological stages)	Neumann (psychological stages)	Scheler (structural hardware)	Pascual-Leone (ego development)	Karl Jaspers	Rudolph Steiner	Don Beck (Spiral Dynamics)
matter (-subatomic, -atomic, -molecular, -polymer)	sensorimotor	frontal (or ego)							
sensation	sensorimotor		pleroma	pleromatic uroboric fusion					
perception	sensorimotor		uroboros	alimentary uroboros	organismic survival			physical body	1. instinctive
exocept	sensorimotor			uroboric Mother wish-fulfillment					
impulse/emotion	phantasmic-emotional		the Great Mother	magic	instinctual effects			etheric body	2. magical-animistic
image	phantasmic-emotional			maternal incest body/self narcissism					
symbol	rep-mind		separation of the World Parents	Oedipus/Electra	associative memory			astral (emotion) body	
endocept	rep-mind		dragon fight	cs/uncs					
concept	rep-mind		birth of the Hero	overcoming instincts emergence of ego	practical intelligence			sensation-soul	3. power-gods
rule/role early	conop		slaying of Mother	differentiation of anima					
rule/role late	conop		slaying of Father	differentiation of animus					4. absolutist-religious
transition	conop		captive and treasure	mature ego					
formal early	formop		Transformation →	ego/self	creative-spiritual intelligence			rational-soul	5. individualistic-achiever
formal late	formop			integration					
transition	formop								
vision-logic early	postformal					1. existential self	1. empirical		6. relativistic
vision-logic middle	postformal					2. duality self	2. conceptual	consciousness-soul	7. systematic-integrative
vision-logic late	postformal					3. dialectical self	3. temporal		
psychic (vision) early		deeper psychic (or soul)				4. realized self (quaternity thinking)	4. true meditative thinking		8. global-holistic
psychic late									
subtle (archetype) early							meditative thinking	spirit-self	9. coral →
subtle late									
causal (formless) early		Witness (or Self)						spirit-life	
causal late									
nondual early								spirit-man	
nondual middle									
nondual late									

Pascual-Leone: stages of self development beyond phenomenological ego or ordinary adult ego = stages of transcendental ego (Kant, Husserl) or "ultraself."

Karl Jaspers: level-types of existential-phenomenological reduction, or meditative thinking

CHART 4C. SELF-RELATED STAGES

Correlative Basic Structures	Susanne Cook-Greuter: perspective	Susanne Cook-Greuter: self-sense	Susanne Cook-Greuter: characteristics	Clare Graves (ego types)	Robert Kegan	Fulcrums (Wilber)
matter -subatomic -molecular -polymer						
sensation						
perception	none	presocial	autistic, undifferentiated	1. autistic	0. incorporative	F-0 ‖ F-1 physical
exocept						
impulse/emotion	none	symbiotic	confused, confounded	2. magical animistic		
image						
symbol	1st person	impulsive	rudimentary		1. impulsive	F-2 emotional
endocept		self-protective	self-labeling	3. egocentric	2. imperial	F-3 mental: self-concept
concept			basic dichotomies, concepts			
rule/role early	2nd person	rule-oriented	early roles			role-self
rule/role late		conformist	simple roles	4. sociocentric	3. interpersonal	F-4 (persona)
transition	3rd person	self-conscious	introspection	5. multiplistic		
formal early		goal-oriented	historical self,		4. formal-institutional	ego (rational reflexive)
formal late		conscientious	many roles	6. relativistic/ individualistic		F-5
transition	4th person	individualistic	relativity of self			integrated:
vision-logic early		autonomous	self as system	7. systemic	5. postformal-interindividual →	F-6 centaur
vision-logic middle	5th person	ego-witnessing construct-witnessing	self as construct	(integrated)		
vision-logic late	6th person	witnessing	self transparent			
logic early	global	universal	ego			soul:
logic middle	cosmic	cosmic	transcendence →			F-7 psychic
logic late			→			
psychic (vision) early						
psychic (vision) late						
subtle (archetype) early						F-8 subtle
subtle (archetype) late						
causal (formless) early						spirit:
causal (formless) late						F-9 causal
nondual early						
nondual middle						nondual nondual
nondual late						

Cook-Greuter perspective groupings: preconventional, conventional, postconventional.

Basic Structures groupings (bottom axis): sensorimotor, phantasmic-emotional, rep-mind, conop, formop, postformal →

CHART 5A. THE SELF-RELATED STAGES OF MORALS AND PERSPECTIVES

Correlative Basic Structures (developmental level)	Kohlberg (moral judgment)	Torbert (levels of action-inquiry)	Blanchard-Fields (socioemotional development)	Kitchener & King (reflective judgment)	Deirdre Kramer (social-cognitive stages)	William Perry (self-outlook)
matter (-subatomic, -atomic, -molecular, -polymer)						
sensation						
perception						
exocept						
impulse/emotion (phantasmic-emotional)						
image				1. concrete category		
symbol	0. magic wish	1. impulsive		2. representational relations	1. undifferentiation	
endocept			1. one perspective			
concept	1. punishment/obedience	2. opportunist	2. dualist-absolutist	3. personal impressions	2. preformism	1. dualistic
rule/role early	2. naive hedonism					
rule/role late						2. early multiplicity
transition (conop→formop)	3. approval of others	3. diplomat	3. multiple outcomes	4. abstractions	3. formism/mechanism	3/4. multiplicity
formal early	4. law and order	4. technician	4. early multiple perspectives	5. relativism, contextualism	4. static relativism, pluralism	5. relativism, pluralism
formal late	4/5 transition	5. achiever	5. multiple perspectives	6. early synthesis	5. static systems	commitment:
transition (formop→postformal)	5. prior rights/social contract	6. existential	6. integrative multiple perspectives	7. synthesis	6. dynamic relativism, contextualism	6/7. early
vision-logic (vision- early)		7. ironist (transcendental) →			7. dynamic dialecticism ("integration of cultural and historical systems into evolving social structures")	
logic middle	6. universal ethical					8/9. middle, late
logic late						
psychic (vision) early	7. universal spiritual					
psychic late						
subtle (archetype) early						
subtle late						
causal (formless) early						
causal late						
nondual early						
nondual middle						
nondual late						

Kohlberg brackets: ← preconventional | conventional | postconventional | [post-postconventional] →

Piagetian stages (left axis): sensorimotor, phantasmic-emotional, rep-mind, conop, formop, postformal

CHART 5B. THE SELF-RELATED STAGES OF MORALS AND PERSPECTIVES

Top developmental arcs: **egocentric** → **ethnocentric** → **worldcentric** → **theocentric**

Correlative Basic Structures	Turner/Powell (social role-taking)	Cheryl Armon (stages of the good)	Peck (moral motivation)	Worldviews (Wilber) — name	Worldviews (Wilber) — general characteristics
-subatomic					
matter–atomic / –molecular / –polymer	level and type of role-taking:				
sensation				archaic	•undifferentiated, pleromatic
perception					
exocept					
impulse/emotion			amoral-impulsive	archaic-magical	•hallucinatory wish fulfillment; subject-object fusions; "selfobject"
image	identificatory			magical	•egocentric, word magic, narcissistic; locus of magic power = ego
symbol	nonreflexive				
endocept				magic-mythic	•omnipotence of ego challenged; security; ego omnipotence transferred to gods
concept	identificatory	1. radical egoism	expedient-self-protective	mythic (literal)	•concrete-literal myths; locus of magic power = deified Other
rule/role early	reflexive	2. instrumental egoism	conformist		
late	3rd party nonreflexive	3. affective mutuality	(irrational-conscientious)	mythic-rational	•rationalization of mythic structures; demythologizing, formalizing
transition	3rd party reflexive	4. individuality		rational	
formal early	interactive effect	4/5. subjective relativism		formalism	•static universal formalism
late	interactive	5. autonomy	rational-altruistic	pluralistic	•static systems/contexts
transition	empathy	6. universal holism		relativism	•pluralistic systems, dynamic-multiple contexts/histories
vision- early	social genius			holistic	•integrates multiple contexts, paradigmatic
logic middle				integralism	•cross-paradigmatic; dialectical developmentalism as World Process
late					
psychic early (vision) late				psychic (shamanic, yogic)	•union with World Process; nature mysticism; gross realm unity
subtle early (archetype) late				subtle (archetypal, saintly)	•union with creatrix of gross realm; deity mysticism; subtle realm unity
causal early (formless) late				causal (formless, sage)	•union with source of manifest realms; formless mysticism; causal unity
nondual early middle late				nondual (siddha)	•union of form and formless, Spirit and World Process; nondual mysticism

Cheryl Armon developmental band: **preconventional** — **conventional** — **postconventional**

Bottom developmental axis: sensorimotor → phantasmic-emotional → rep-mind → conop → formop → postformal

CHART 5C. THE SELF-RELATED STAGES OF MORALS AND PERSPECTIVES

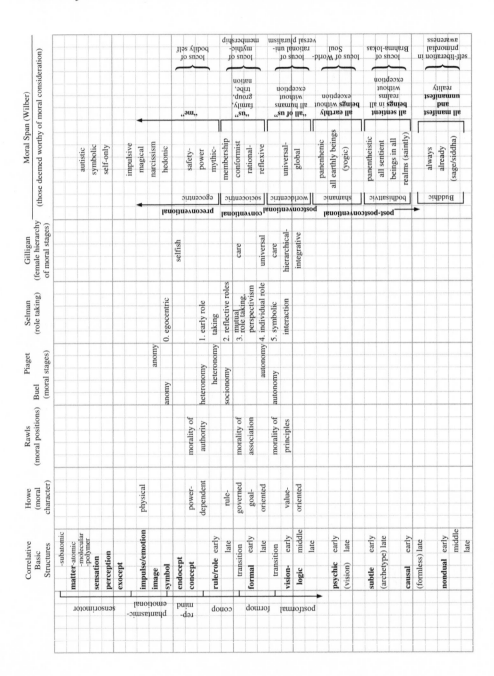

CHART 6A. STAGES OF SPIRITUALITY

Level	Correlative Basic Structures	Hazrat Inayat Khan (Sufism)	Mahamudra (stages of meditation)	Fowler (stages of faith)	Wilber	Underhill	Helminiak (spiritual development)	Funk (contact with Numinous)
sensorimotor	-subatomic							
	matter -atomic	matter						
	-molecular -polymer	(nasut)						
	sensation	vegetable						
	perception	animal			archaic			
phantasmic-emotional	exocept	mundane-person		0. preverbal, undifferentiated	archaic-magical			
	impulse/emotion	(bodily desires)			magical			libidinal, prepersonal
	image							
rep-mind	symbol		concepts	1. magical, projective	magic-mythic			
	endocept		and beliefs		mythic-literal			
	concept	material-person	of gross mind	2. mythic-literal	(mythic-membership)	conceptual		personal
conop	rule/role early	(earthly gain)				faith and beliefs		
	late			3. conventional				
	transition							
formop	formal early	artistic person	right	4. individual-reflexive			conformist	psychological
	late	(beyond conventions)	beliefs		rational-universal		conscientious-conformist	
	transition		foundations	5. conjunctive faith	integral-		conscientious	creative
postformal	vision- early		universal-	6. universalizing			compassionate	
	logic middle	idealistic	ethical practices	→	holistic (global)	contemplative illumination:	cosmic	(global)
	late	(universal principles)	meditation:					
	psychic early	djinn (genius)	access; 1. one-pointedness		nature mysticism; shamanic, yogic	1. nature mysticism		
	(vision) late	vision mind; (malkut)	gross union		gross-realm unity	union with stream of life		nature mysticism
	subtle early	soul (angelic)	subtle perception; luminosity		deity mysticism; luminosity, saintly	lateral expansion of csness; 2. metaphysical mysticism		
	(archetype) late	akasha-archetypal; arwah- divine; wahdat-witness	2. simplicity		subtle-realm unity	recollection (archetypal); luminosity		archetypal, theistic mysticism
	causal early	djabrut-cessation	cessation		formless mysticism; cessation	contemplation-divine love		
	(formless) late		emptiness		causal unity	divine ignorance (cessation)		
	nondual early	zat: absolute	3. one taste		nondual mysticism	3. divine mysticism - dark night		
	middle	consciousness	unity form/formless			- union		spirit, union
	late	nondual	4. non-meditation		constant consciousness			with absolute

CHART 6B. STAGES OF SPIRITUALITY

Domain	Correlative Basic Structures	Daniel Brown (cross-cultural stages of meditation)	Muhyiddin Ibn 'Arabi (stations of zikr)	St. Palamas	traditional samadhis (highest contemplative states)	seven stages of practice (Highest Yoga Tantra)	levels of csness (Highest Yoga Tantra)	phenomenological signs of appearance (Highest Yoga Tantra)
sensorimotor	subatomic							(1st dissolves into 2nd:)
	matter-atomic		mineral world				form (1st skandha)	
	-molecular						sensation (2nd)	mirage
	-polymer		vegetal world					(2nd dissolves into 3rd:)
	sensation						perception- impulse (3rd)	smoke
	perception							(3rd into 4th:)
	exocept		animal world				emotion- image (4th)	fireflies
emotional	impulse/emotion							(4th into 5th:)
	image						gross mental csness (5th)	flickering
mind	symbol							butterlamp
	endocept							
	concept							
conop	rule/role early		surface signs					
	rule/role late							
formop	transition							
	formal early	• preliminary	universal order				80 gross mental conceptions (overall gross csness)	steady
	formal late	practices						butterlamp
	transition							
postformal	vision-logic early		integral ideas					
	vision-logic middle							
	vision-logic late			vision	supramental meditative consciousness:			
	psychic (vision) early	• concentration with support	intellect in holy forms					
	psychic (vision) late	• transcending	vision-wholeness	recollection		winds dissolve: ① physical (gross) transcendence — in central channel		
	subtle (archetype) early	gross perception • subtle- perception	ascending sights	divine light	savikalpa	② verbal (subtle) transcendence — at heart	(dissolution of gross csness:) subtle csness / white appearance (luminosity)	clear autumn moonlight
	subtle (archetype) late	• luminosity	divine light bliss	theosis	luminosity, deity form archetypal form	③ mental (causal) transcendence — at drop in heart	red increase / very subtle	clear autumn sunlight
	causal early	• insight	witness-totality	formless	nirvikalpa-cessation jnana -nirodh, nirvana	④ (impure illusory body)	(causal) csness / black near- attainment (cessation)	thick blackness of autumn night
	causal (formless) late	• cessation • advanced	gnosis	illumination	post-nirvana stages:	5. actual clear light	clear- light	clear autumn dawn
	nondual early	insight	a returned one		sahaja -one taste	6. learner's union	emptiness	
	nondual middle	• Enlightenment: a,b,c			" -nonmeditation	7. Buddhahood		
	nondual late				post-Enlightenment: bhava			

CHART 6C. STAGES OF SPIRITUALITY

Correlative Basic Structures	General Great Chain	St. Teresa (seven stages of interior life)	Chirban (Eastern Orthodox Christianity)	St. Dionysius (pseudo)	Yoga Sutras of Patanjali	St. Gregory Nyssa	Alexander (TM)
matter -subatomic -atomic -molecular -polymer	matter						
sensation							
perception	body						
exocept							
impulse/emotion							
image							
symbol							
endocept	mind	1. humility					
concept		2. practice, prayer	image-- preliminary orientation metanoia--	**prayer of simplicity** (vocal)	cleansing, restraint, pranayana	darkness of sin	
rule/role early / late		3. exemplary life	turning toward spiritual	**prayer of mind** (subvocal)			
transition							
formal early / late			apatheia-- detachment	(purification)	recollection	faith in God	
transition				**prayer of recollection** (illumination)	dhyana		
vision- early / **logic** middle / late	soul	4. prayer of recollection, early visions	purification		one-pointedness		
psychic (vision) early / late		5. prayer of union (ego dies, soul emerges) luminosity	light-divine-- luminosity	**prayer of quiet** (unification)	subtle perception luminosity	light	
subtle (archetype) early / late			theosis-- oneness with God	**prayer of union**	shining forth oneness of buddhi		
causal (formless) early / late	spirit	6. cessation – formless		"glorious nothingness"	cessation (nirodh)	"not seeing" luminous darkness	transcendental csness Witness permanence
nondual early / middle / late		7. spiritual marriage		(**cloud of unknowing**)	raincloud		refined " unity csness

Bottom axis: sensorimotor — phantasmic-emotional — rep-mind — conop — formop — postformal

CHART 7. MISCELLANEOUS DEVELOPMENTAL LINES

	Correlative Basic Structures	Erotic Relationships (Fortune)	Needs (Maslow)	Levels of "Food" (relational exchange) (Wilber)	Modal Experience (Chinen)	Empathy (Benack)	Gender Identity (Wilber)	Affect (Wilber)
sensorimotor	-subatomic							
	matter -atomic -molecular -polymer	physical					• morphological-genetic givens	• reactivity
	sensation							• sensations
	perception	instinctual	physiological				• undifferentiated	• physiostates: touch, temperature, pleasure, pain
	exocept		beginning of safety					• protoemotions: tension, fear, rage, satisfaction
phantasmic-emotional	impulse/emotion	emotional		emotional exchange -sex			• differentiated basic-gender identity	
	image		safety					
	symbol			-safety, power				• 2° emotions: anxiety, anger, wishing, liking, safety
	endocept			-belongingness, care		unwilling to assume others' perspective		
rep-mind	concept	concrete		mental exchange -membership		unable to assume others' perspective	• gender conventionality	• 3° emotions: love, joy, depression, hate, belongingness
conop	rule/role early	mental	belongingness	discourse	1. enactment			
	rule/role late			-self-reflective exchange		willing to assume others' persp.	• gender consistency (norms)	• 4° emotions: universal affect, global justice, care, compassion, all-
	transition			exchange	2. reflection	able to assume others' perspective		
formop	formal early		self-esteem	-autonomous exchange	3. representation	perspective	• gender	
	formal late	abstract		exchange	4. pragmatic			
	transition	mental			5. hermeneutic			
postformal	vision- early		self-actualization				androgyny (trans-differentiated)	human love, world-centric altruism
	logic middle				6. attunement			
	late							
	psychic early	concrete	self-transcendence →	soul exchange -psychic vision				• awe, rapture, all-species love, compassion
	(vision) late	spirit		-God communion	7. enlightenment →		• archetypal gender union (tantra)	
	subtle early			-God union				• ananda, ecstasy love-bliss, saintly commitment
	(archetype) late							
	causal early	pure		spiritual exchange -Godhead identity			• beyond gender	• infinite freedom-release,
	(formless) late	spirit						bodhisattvic-compassion
	nondual early			-sahaja				
	middle							• one taste
	late							

CHART 8. MISCELLANEOUS

Correlative Basic Structures	Universal Waves of development (H. Gardner)	Art (Wilber)	Melvin Miller — teleological	Melvin Miller — ateleological	Melvin Miller — antiteleological
matter -subatomic					
-molecular / -polymer					
sensation					
perception					
exocept					
impulse/emotion		sensorimotor (initial aesthetic impact)			
image	event structuring	emotional-expressivist (feeling-expression)			
symbol	analog mapping	magical imagery (e.g., Paleolithic cave art, dream imagery, surrealist)			
endocept	digital mapping				
concept	notational systems / symbolic flowering				
rule/role early	rules, regulations	mythological-literal (e.g., concrete religious art, icons)	mythic-theism	stoicism	mechanism
rule/role late / transition	skill mastery				
formal early	self-critical	perspectival (naturalistic, empirical-representational, impressionist; conceptual, formal)	humanism	skepticism	nihilism
formal late / transition	relativism				
vision-logic early	integration of self and culture	aperspectival cubist, abstract	integrated theism	existentialism	pantheism
vision-logic middle					
vision-logic late		symbolist fantastic realist psychic perceptual			
psychic (vision) early		archetypal (e.g., thangka, bhakti expressivist)			
psychic (vision) late					
subtle (archetype) early					
subtle (archetype) late					
causal (formless) early					
causal (formless) late					
nondual early		nondual (e.g., Zen landscape)			
nondual middle					
nondual late					

Gardner developmental brackets: preconventional | conventional | postconventional | [post-postconventional]

Cognitive-line groupings (Correlative Basic Structures): sensorimotor, phantasmic-emotional, rep-mind, conop, formop, postformal

CHART 9A. SOCIOCULTURAL EVOLUTION

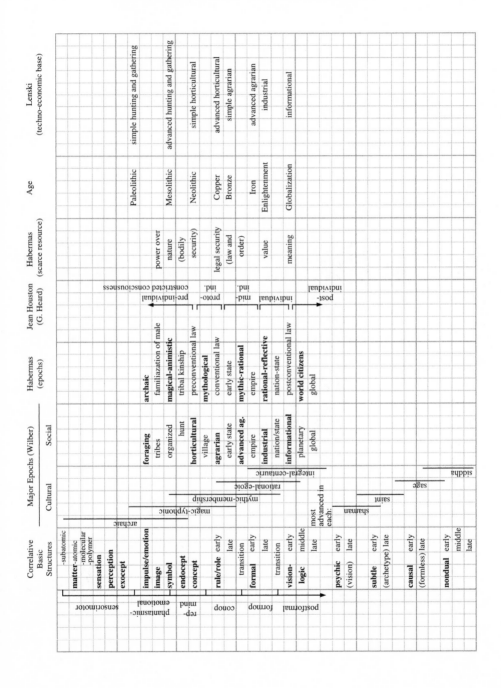

CHART 9B. SOCIOCULTURAL EVOLUTION

Correlative Basic Structures	Sociocultural (Wilber)	Jean Gebser	A. Taylor (levels of social organization)	Jay Earley	Robert Bellah (evolution of religious systems)	Duane Elgin era (consciousness)
matter -subatomic -molecular -polymer						
sensation						
perception						
exocept (archaic)	foraging	archaic			primitive	1. archaic humans (contracted consciousness)
impulse/emotion	tribes		S₁ – family, clan, band	1. tribal		
image (magic)		magic		hunting magic	archaic	2. hunter-gatherer (surface consciousness)
symbol						
endocept (mythic)	horticultural		S₂ – tribe, territorial	2. horticulture, villages, mythology		3. agrarian (depth)
concept	village agrarian	mythic			historic	
rule/role (rational) early	early state		S₃ – theocratic	3. empires, gods and heroes		
late	advanced ag.	mental	empires	4. medieval	early-modern	4. urban-industrial (dynamic)
formal early	empire		S₄ – national state	5. modern, democracy, individualism	modern	FUTURE:
late	industrial					
transition	nation	integral-aperspectival	S₅ – supra-national	6. global consciousness		5. global reconciliation (reflective)
vision-logic early (centauric)	informational			→		
middle	global					
late						
psychic (vision) early						6. global bonding (oceanic)
late						
subtle (archetype) early						7. global creativity (flow)
late						
causal (formless) early						8. global wisdom (integral)
late						
nondual early						
middle						
late						

sensorimotor · phantasmic-emotional · rep-mind · conop · formop · postformal

CHART 10. JÜRGEN HABERMAS

Correlative Basic Structures	Individual's Identity	Level of Communication	Idea of the Good Life	Domain of Validity	Ethics
-subatomic					
matter -atomic / -molecular / -polymer					
sensation					
perception					
exocept					
impulse/emotion					
image					
symbol (bodyego)	natural identity	actions and consequences of actions	1. hedonism under obedience	nature and social environment	naive hedonism
endocept					
concept			2. hedonism under exchange		
rule/role early (persona)	role identity	roles	3. concrete morality/primary groups	group of primary reference persons	specific order
late			4. " " / secondary groups	members of the political community	rational natural law
transition		systems of norms	5. civil liberties, legal freedom	all legal associates	formalistic ethics
formal early	identity				
late			6. moral freedom	all humans as private persons	universal ethics of speech
transition (ego)	ego identity	principles	7. political freedom		
vision- early (centaur)				all humans as world citizens	
logic middle					
late					
psychic early (vision)					
late					
subtle early (archetype) late					
causal early (formless) late					
nondual early / middle / late					

Bottom axis (basic structures groupings): sensorimotor — phantasmic-emotional — rep-mind — conop — formop — postformal

CHART 11. JAMES MARK BALDWIN

Correlative Basic Structures	Logical Mode (levels of consciousness)	Psychic Objects	Dualism	Aesthetic Stages	Religious Stages	Ethical Levels
-subatomic						
matter -atomic						
-molecular						
-polymer						
sensation	prelogical	sense	adualistic			
perception			animistic			
exocept		memory	present vs.	none	physical	adual
impulse/emotion			persisting		spontaneous	-projective
image		fancy	inner vs.		(magical)	-external
symbol		play	outer			necessity
endocept	quasi-logical					
concept		substantive		play		
rule/role early		content	mind vs. body	spontaneous	intellectual	dualistic
late			self vs. not self		ethical-1	-relativistic
transition					ethical-2	-instrumental
formal early	logical	judged-thought	truth vs. falsity	reflective →		
late						
transition						
vision- early	extra-logical	moral	good vs. bad		aesthetic-	ethical
logic middle					religious	-ideal
late					immediacy	-symnomic
psychic early	hyper-logical	aesthetic	pancalistic (nondual)			
(vision) late						
subtle early						
(archetype) late						
causal early						
(formless) late						
nondual early						
middle						
late						

Developmental lines (base axis): sensorimotor · phantasmic-emotional · rep-mind · conop · formop · postformal

Notes

Cross-references to notes in this section take the form (for example) "note 1.5," meaning note 5 for chapter 1. References to volumes in *The Collected Works of Ken Wilber* take the form "CW1," "CW2," and so on.

Note to the Reader

1. Quoted in translator's Preface, *Life after Death*, by G. Fechner, trans. H. Wernekke, written 1835, Chicago: Open Court Publishing, 1945. The book cover says *Life after Death*; the title page says *On Life after Death*; I am using the former, since that is what I first saw.
2. A. Zweig, "Gustav Theodor Fechner," in P. Edwards (ed.), *The Encyclopedia of Philosophy*, vol. 3.
3. Fechner, *Life after Death*, pp. 16–7.
4. Fechner, *Life after Death*, pp. 18.
5. A. Zweig, "Gustav Theodor Fechner," vol. 3.
6. This textbook has variously been called *System, Self, and Structure*; *Patterns and Process in Consciousness*; and *The 1-2-3 of Consciousness Studies*. The present book, *Integral Psychology*, is a highly condensed and edited version of the as yet unpublished two-volume work.

Part One

1. For a discussion of the importance of orienting generalizations and the way that I use them, see the Introduction to *Sex, Ecology, Spirituality*, 2nd ed. (CW6); and Jack Crittenden's Foreword to *The Eye of Spirit* (CW7).

Chapter 1. The Basic Levels or Waves

1. As we will see, I have numerous strong criticisms of the traditionalists, but their work is an indispensable starting point; see the works of F. Schuon, M. Pallis, A. Coomaraswamy, H. Corbin, S. Nasr. See also *The Eye of Spirit*; Huston Smith, *The World's Religions*; Roger Walsh, *The Spirit of Shamanism*.
2. Depending on how and what you count as a "level," I have listed anywhere

from sixteen basic structures (in boldface) to thirty (counting sublevels); as functional groupings, I usually give nine or ten (i.e., sensorimotor, emotional-sexual, rep-mind, conop, formop, vision-logic, psychic, subtle, causal, nondual). What all this means—and why these different counts are all legitimate—will become more obvious as the descriptions unfold. I should say that what we count as a stage depends first and foremost on empirical and phenomenological evidence, and as that evidence becomes richer, our stage conceptions become clearer (see the Introduction to *Transformations of Consciousness* for a discussion of the meaning of, and evidence for, "stages"). The sixteen or so basic structures/ stages presented in the charts are based on the textual reports of some three thousands years of meditative experience, coupled with recent psychological research; but they are always open to revision and clarification.

3. See *Sex, Ecology, Spirituality,* 2nd ed. (CW6), for an in-depth discussion of holons.

As Huston Smith points out in *Forgotten Truth* (see chart 2a), in the great traditions, the levels of consciousness (or levels of selfhood) are sometimes distinguished from the levels of reality (or planes of reality), and I also follow that distinction (see notes 1.5, 1.9, 1.10, 8.1, 8.2, 8.39, 12.12). However, for many purposes they can be treated together, as the being and knowing aspects of each of the levels in the Great Nest. In other words, the *basic structures of knowing* (the levels of consciousness/selfhood) and the *basic structures of being* (the planes/realms of reality) are intimately connected, and unless otherwise specified, both of these are indicated by the term *basic structures* or *basic levels* of the Great Nest. (Huston Smith indicates this by using the same figure of concentric circles to cover both levels of reality and levels of selfhood.) But the reason it is necessary to distinguish them is that a given level of selfhood can encounter a different level of reality, as we will see in subsequent discussions, and thus these need to be preserved as two independent variables. Nonetheless, there are advantages, in modern discourse, to emphasizing the epistemological component over the ontological, as I will point out in the following discussion. See notes 1.5, 1.9, 1.10, 8.1, 8.2, 8.39, 12.12.

4. See *Sex, Ecology, Spirituality,* 2nd ed. (CW6), and the Introduction to CW2 for a discussion of this topic.

5. This is similar to the Mahayana Buddhist notion of the alaya-vijnana, the "collective storehouse consciousness," which is present in every person, and which is said to be the repository of the memory traces (vasanas) of all past experiences, both of oneself and others (i.e., it is not just collective but transpersonal, embracing all sentient beings; in my system, it is the high-subtle to low-causal). It is said that, in higher stages of meditation, one can contact this transpersonal consciousness, which helps to release one from a narrow and restricted identity with the individual self. Thus, according to Mahayana Buddhism, the alaya-vijnana is: (1) a real transpersonal realm, an *actuality*, that exists in all people; (2) it is, however, rarely contacted in a conscious fashion, so for most people, that conscious contact is merely a *potential*; (3) as a collective storehouse, it is *evolving* and changing as more and more vasanas are collectively accumulated;

(4) thus its actual contours are constantly coevolving with people's experience—it is definitely *not* a pregiven, unchanging mold or eternal archetype; (5) *even though* it is constantly evolving, any individual, at any given time, by directly experiencing that realm, can be released from the constrictions of individuality; (6) thus, the fact that this subtle realm is evolving and changing does not mean that it cannot confer transpersonal liberation at any given time.

Of course, final liberation is said to be beyond even the subtle forms or vasanas, into the formless or causal (and then nondual). The causal is the only basic "level" that does not change and evolve, because it is purely formless. But even the nondual evolves in part, because it is a union of causal emptiness (which does not evolve) and the entire manifest world (which does).

To my mind, this conception (which is a reconstruction of the Buddhist view) is more adequate than that of eternally unchanging archetypal molds (see the Introduction to CW2 for a fuller discussion of this theme; some aspects of the Kosmos must still be assumed to be archetypal, but far fewer than the perennial philosophy generally imagined). In my opinion, all of the holons of existence (including the basic structures) are, in part, these types of evolutionary memories or habits. And, for the present discussion, it should be remembered that the higher levels are still evolving themselves, and thus they are great potentials, not pregiven absolutes, but this still does not prevent them from being able to release us from the constrictions of the lower realms.

6. See Eliot Deutsch, *Advaita Vedanta*. Incidentally, I use "the subtle realm" in two senses, broad and narrow. In the broad sense, I follow Vajrayana and Vedanta: matter is the gross realm, the unmanifest is the causal realm, and *everything in between* is the subtle realm (i.e., prana-maya-kosha, mano-maya-kosha, and vijnana-maya-kosha, or vital, mental, and beginning transmental). In the narrow sense, I use "subtle" for just the *highest reaches* of the overall subtle realm. Context will determine which is meant.

7. Structures in the general sense are used by all schools of psychology and sociology, and not simply in the narrow sense given them by the various schools of structuralism. The *Oxford Dictionary of Sociology* defines structure as "a term loosely applied to any recurring pattern." The *Penguin Dictionary of Psychology* gives: "an organized, patterned, relatively stable configuration." I specifically define a structure as a holistic pattern, and it is roughly synonymous with "holon." For my tangential relation with the actual school of structuralism, see the Introduction to CW2.

There are six types of structures that I have outlined: levels/lines, enduring/transitional, and deep/surface. The first set I have explained in the text (they are structures found in the basic levels and in the developmental lines). Enduring structures are ones that, once they emerge, remain in existence, fully functioning, but subsumed in higher structures (cognitive structures are mostly of this type). Transitional structures, on the other hand, tend to be *replaced* by their subsequent stages (e.g., ego stages and moral stages). The basic structures are *mostly* enduring structures; and the developmental lines consist *mostly* of transitional structures. All four of those types of structures have deep (universal) structures and surface (local) structures (although I now usually call these "deep features" and "surface features" to avoid confusion with Chomsky's formulations; also, deep and surface are a sliding scale: deep features can be those features shared by a group, a family, a tribe, a clan, a community, a nation, all humans, all species, all beings. Thus, "deep" doesn't necessarily mean "universal"; it means "shared with others," and research then determines how wide that group is—from a few people to genuine universals. The preponderance of research supports the claim that all of the basic structures, and most of the developmental lines, that I have presented in the charts, have some universal deep features). Commentators on my work have often confused deep structures with basic structures, and transitional structures with surface structures, no doubt due in part to lack of clarity in my exposition. But the six classes of structures (levels/lines, enduring/transitional, deep/surface) are distinct (yet overlapping) categories.

8. See in particular Charles Tart's exemplary work on states, *States of Consciousness*; B. Wolman, *Handbook of States of Consciousness*.

9. For the nature of the "nondual" state, see note 9.18. If we use around twenty basic structures, and four major states, we would have up to eighty different types of spiritual experience, and that is still very crude, since there are many different types (or subtypes) of states. Of course, the basic structures available to a person depend on his or her own developmental level (someone at the magic level can peak experience psychic, subtle, causal, or nondual, but will interpret them only in archaic or magical terms, *not* in mythic, rational, or centauric terms). As for the states, a person can peak experience any higher state that has not yet become a permanent structure—e.g., when individuals develop to the psychic level, they no longer have psychic peak experiences because the psychic is permanently available to them (but they can peak experience subtle, causal, and nondual). For further discussion of structures and states, see Wilber, "Paths beyond Ego in the Coming Decade" (in CW4 and in Walsh and Vaughan, *Paths beyond Ego*); numerous endnotes in *Sex, Ecology, Spirituality,* 2nd ed., such as chap. 14, note 17; *A Sociable God*; *The Eye of Spirit,* chap. 6, note 9; and notes 1.3, 1.5, 1.10, 8.1, 8.2, 8.39, 12.12.

10. A person at almost any stage of development can spontaneously in peak experiences (or naturally in the cycle of sleep) experience the psychic, subtle, causal, or nondual states; but those states/realms must be carried in, *and interpreted by*, the stage of development of the individual having the experience. Even if the peak experience itself is a "pure glimpse" of one of these transpersonal realms, it is either simultaneously or, soon thereafter, picked up and clothed in the subjective and intersubjective structures of the individual (i.e., it is carried in the preop, conop, formop, or vision-logic structure). As such, the full contours of the transpersonal realm are filtered, diluted, and sometimes distorted by the limitations of the lower structure (e.g., preop: its narcissism and egocentrism, its inability to take the role of others; conop: its concrete-literal mind, fundamentalistic and ethnocentric; formop: its tendency to rationally distance itself from nature and world).

It is only as a person *permanently* develops to the psychic level (i.e., has a permanent psychic basic structure) that the psychic realm is no longer of necessity distorted during its experience (and likewise with the subtle, causal, and nondual realms: only as they become basic structures, or realized patterns in consciousness, can they be experienced authentically). A person permanently awake to the psychic domain no longer has peak experiences of the psychic, just as we do not say of average adults, "They are having a verbal peak experience"—for they are permanently adapted to the verbal realm. Likewise, all the higher realms can become realizations that are *just as permanent.* Of course, a person at the psychic level could still have peak experiences of even higher realms—the subtle, causal, and nondual—but those will likewise be limited and distorted to some degree (until permanent growth to those higher levels occurs). A person at the subtle level (i.e., where the subtle realm has become not a passing peak experience but a permanent basic structure, or realized pattern in full consciousness) can have peak experiences of the causal and nondual. And so on—until "subject permanence," which is a continuous and permanent realization of that which witnesses the gross, subtle, and causal domains, at which point all of the higher realms—previously available to consciousness only as temporary peak experiences and nonordinary states—have become permanently available traits and structures. An enlightened being *still has access to subtle and causal levels* (since he or she still sleeps and dreams), which is why subtle and causal are also correctly referred to, at that point, as *enduring basic structures,* but they are constantly witnessed even as they continue to arise. See notes 1.3, 1.5, 1.9, 8.1, 8.2, 8.39, 12.12.

11. For further discussions of the idea that ontogenetic development up to formop is generally guaranteed (due to phylogenetic evolution to that point)—but beyond that you are on your own—see *Up from Eden, A Sociable God,* and *Transformations of Consciousness.* For a discussion of holons as Kosmic habits, see *Sex, Ecology, Spirituality,* 2nd ed.

12. The ages of emergence are generally true *only for the basic structures (and cognitive structures).* The ages of emergence of the self-related stages (e.g., identity, morals, needs, etc.) *vary considerably among individuals.* An adolescent with fully developed formop can be at moral stage 2, or 3, or 4, etc. The stages still occur in the same sequence, but their dates vary. The basic/cognitive structures are necessary, but not sufficient, for most other developments, and those other developments vary considerably as to their emergence, due to factors in all four quadrants (the four quadrants are introduced in Part Two).

13. The basic structures of each functional grouping are also shown in the charts (e.g., the "sensorimotor" functional grouping includes the basic structures of matter, sensation, perception, exocept; "phantasmic-emotional" includes impulse, protoemotion, image, symbol; "rep-mind" includes symbol, endocept, concept, early rule; and so on).

I have also subdivided many of the basic structures into early, middle, and late. Most researchers use "early" and "late"; a few prefer the terms "low" and "high." I myself prefer "low" and "high" (as used in *The Atman Project*) be-

cause the evidence suggests that in most cases the substages are actually enduring structures that are taken up and incorporated into subsequent structures
(they are enduring holons, not merely passing or transitional phases), and thus
"low" and "high" are more appropriate terms. Nonetheless, almost everybody
uses "early" and "late," and, although I will use both, I will generally follow
suit, as long as this qualification is kept in mind.

14. I use "postformal" both ways (as the first major stage beyond formop—namely,
vision-logic—and as *all* levels beyond formop), as context will tell; in this section, it means vision-logic.

15. Pp. 87–96.

16. See Commons et al., *Adult Development*, vols. 1 and 2; Commons et al., *Beyond Formal Operations*; Miller and Cook-Greuter, *Transcendence and Mature
Thought in Adulthood*; Alexander and Langer, *Higher Stages of Human Development*; Sinnott and Cavanaugh, *Bridging Paradigms*; Sinnott, *Interdisciplinary
Handbook of Adult Lifespan Learning*.

17. See the Introduction to CW4 and Wilber, *Boomeritis* (forthcoming).

Chapter 2. The Developmental Lines or Streams

1. Howard Gardner's important research on multiple intelligences is an example of
relatively independent developmental streams, and I am indebted to many of his
significant conceptions. Gardner is also one of the first to use the terms "waves"
and "streams," which I gratefully acknowledge. All of Gardner's books are
highly recommended. Chart 8 contains a summary of Gardner's research on
some of the universal waves of development (through which the various streams
unfold). For a more extended discussion of his important contributions, see *The
Eye of Spirit*.

   Perhaps the dominant theory in cognitive science at this moment is that of
modules—the idea that the brain/mind is composed of numerous, independent,
evolutionary modules, from linguistic to cognitive to moral. These modules are,
in many ways, quite similar to what I mean by relatively independent developmental lines or streams, with two strong qualifications. Modules are all described
in third-person it-language, thus overlooking (or even aggressively denying) first-
person phenomenal realities (as will be explained in the text, modules are Upper-
Right quadrant). Further, module theorists vehemently deny that there is any sort
of transcendental self or unity of consciousness. And yet, according to their own
theory and data, individuals are capable of being aware of these modules, and
can in fact override them on occasion. If you can override a module, you are not
just a module.

2. See Shaffer, *Social and Personality Development*; Commons et al., *Adult Devel-
opment*, vols. 1 and 2; Commons et al., *Beyond Formal Operations*; Sinnott and
Cavanaugh, *Bridging Paradigms*; Sinnott, *Interdisciplinary Handbook of Adult
Lifespan Learning*; Loevinger, *Ego Development*; Kegan, *The Evolving Self* and
In Over Our Heads; Beck, *Spiral Dynamics*; Wade, *Changes of Mind*; Miller and
Cook-Greuter, *Transcendence and Mature Thought in Adulthood*; Alexander

and Langer, *Higher Stages of Human Development*; Broughton, *Critical Theories of Psychological Development*; and Sroufe et al., *Child Development*.

For various related aspects of development, see also Cicchetti and Beeghly, *The Self in Transition*; Mendelsohn, *The Synthesis of Self* (4 vols.); Parsons and Blocker, *Aesthetics and Education*; Clarkin and Lenzenweger, *Major Theories of Personality Disorder*; Dawson and Fischer, *Human Behavior and the Developing Brain*; Mitchell, *Relational Concepts in Psychoanalysis*; Cashdan, *Object Relations Therapy*; Kramer and Akhtar, *Mahler and Kohut*; Dana, *Multicultural Assessment Perspectives for Professional Psychology*; Segal et al., *Uniting Psychology and Biology*; Siegler, *Children's Thinking*; Ausubel, *Ego Development and Psychopathology*; Ribaupierre, *Transition Mechanisms in Child Development*; Csikszentmihalyi, *The Evolving Self*; Murphy et al., *The Physical and Psychological Effects of Meditation*; Hedaya, *Understanding Biological Psychiatry*; Ellenberger, *The Discovery of the Unconscious*; Reed, *From Soul to Mind*; Messer and Warren, *Models of Brief Psychodynamic Therapy*; Kagan and Lamb, *The Emergence of Morality in Young Children*; Nucci, *Moral Development and Character Education*; Wren, *The Moral Domain*; Haan et al., *On Moral Grounds*; Flavell et al., *Cognitive Development*. See also notes 8.11 and 8.20.

Kohlberg and Armon (in Commons et al., *Beyond Formal Operations*) have identified three different types of stage models: *epigenetic* (e.g., Erikson); *soft stages* (e.g., Loevinger, Kegan, Perry, Gilligan, Fowler); and *hard stages* (e.g., Piaget, Kohlberg). Most of the stage models in existence are soft-stage models. We might add *micro-stage* models, which present stages of development that can recur with the acquisition of any new skill or trait. Unless specified, "stages" as I use the term includes all four. All of the developmental levels and lines that I presented have evidence that they belong to one or another of those stage conceptions. At the same time, the general *developmental space* shown in the charts indicates that hard stages are in part responsible, and those hard stages are essentially the basic waves in the Great Nest.

3. See note 2.2 for some of this extensive research; see *The Eye of Spirit* for a summary.

CHAPTER 3. THE SELF

1. I describe the self in first-person as the *self-sense*, and in third-person as the *self-system*, both of which are anchored in second-person, dialectical, intersubjective occasions. See *The Eye of Spirit*.

   For an excellent anthology of approaches to the self, organized around Kohut's contributions (but not limited to them), see Detrick and Detrick, *Self Psychology: Comparisons and Contrasts*. See also the works of Edinger, Neumann, Blanck and Blanck, Kernberg, Winnicott, Masterson, Jung, Assagioli, Almaas, Baldwin, Mead, Erikson, Graves, Loevinger, Broughton, Lacan, Cook-Greuter, and Kegan, most of whom are discussed in this and the next chapter, and many of whom are represented on the charts.

2. See Shaffer, *Social and Personality Development*; Kegan, *The Evolving Self* and

In Over Our Heads; Beck, *Spiral Dynamics*; Loevinger, *Ego Development*; Wade, *Changes of Mind*; Miller and Cook-Greuter, *Transcendence and Mature Thought in Adulthood*; Alexander and Langer, *Higher Stages of Human Development*; Commons et al., *Beyond Formal Operations* and *Adult Development* vols. 1 & 2; Broughton, *Critical Theories of Psychological Development*; Sinnott and Cavanaugh, *Bridging Paradigms*; Sinnott, *Interdisciplinary Handbook of Adult Lifespan Learning*; and Sroufe et al., *Child Development*.

3. In the continuum I-I to I to me to mine, Loevinger's "ego"—which she defines generally as the conscious self-concept or self-idea—is right between the proximate I and the distal me, and might be called the "I/me": it is the individual self insofar as it can immediately become an object of knowledge and thus be communicated to others. I generally include this "I/me" in the proximate self, but the whole point is that this scale is continuously sliding in development, as each I becomes a me until infinity (see *The Eye of Spirit*). For an expansion and clarification of Loevinger's ideas, see the important work of Susanne Cook-Greuter in, e.g., *Transcendence and Mature Thought in Adulthood* and Commons et al., *Adult Development* 2.

4. See *The Atman Project* (CW 2).

5. See *Transformations of Consciousness*.

6. See William James, *Principles of Psychology* and *The Will to Believe*; Rollo May, *Love and Will*; Assagioli, *The Act of Will*.

7. See, e.g., George Vaillant's wonderful *The Wisdom of the Ego* (1993). See also note 8.20.

8. For the mechanism of converting states to traits, see note 10.4.

9. More specifically, the self has numerous crucial functions: the (proximate) self is the locus of *identity* (an annexing of various elements to create a self-sense); the seat of *will* (the self is intrinsically involved in the good); a locus of *intersubjectivity* (the self is intrinsically a social, dialectical self, involved in justice and care); the seat of *aesthetic apprehension* (the self is intrinsically involved in the beautiful); the seat of *metabolism* (the self metabolizes experience to build structure); a locus of *cognition* (the self has an intrinsic capacity to orient to the objective world); the seat of *integration* (the self is responsible for integrating the functions, modes, states, waves, and streams of consciousness). These are largely functional invariants, and thus few of them are listed on the charts, which focus on diachronic elements; but the self and its functions seem to be absolutely crucial in any integral psychology.

10. Buddhists sometimes object that I am overlooking the Buddhist notion of anatta or "no-self," but I am actually using the Mahayana Buddhist doctrine of the relative reality of both the self and the dharmas; and I am here discussing the functions of the relatively real self-system. Along with Nagarjuna, I reject, as incomplete and incoherent, the Theravadin view of the self. See *Sex, Ecology, Spirituality*, 2nd ed. (CW6), chapter 14, note 1, for an extensive discussion of this topic. See also the discussion in the text, "The Self and Its Pathologies," in chap. 8 (page 91). See *Transformations of Consciousness* for a further discussion of the relative reality of the self and the pathologies that result when this self is not well formed.

CHAPTER 4. THE SELF-RELATED STREAMS

1. By "exclusive identification," I mean that the proximate self's center of gravity is predominantly at one general functional grouping (which generates a corresponding fulcrum of self-development, as explained in chap. 8). Since each basic wave, barring pathology, transcends and includes its predecessors, to say that the self is exclusively identified with, say, formop, means that the *overall self* includes all of the basic waves up to and including formop. Specifically, this usually means that the proximate self is organized around formop, and the distal self includes everything up to formop (from sensorimotor to conop). When the self's center of gravity shifts to vision-logic, formop becomes part of the distal self, and proximate self is organized around vision-logic; and so on through the morphogenetic field of the Great Nest.

2. Three of the most important of the self-related lines of development are those of self-identity (e.g., Loevinger), morals (e.g., Kohlberg), and needs (e.g., Maslow). I have previously (as in *Transformations of Consciousness*) referred to all of them, in shorthand, as "self-stages," but I now reserve "self-stages" (or "stages of self") *exclusively* for the self-identity or proximate-self line of development (e.g., Loevinger, Erikson, Kegan), and I use "self-related stages," "self-related streams," or simply "self-streams" for *all* of the self-related lines of development (proximate-self, morals, needs, etc.).

3. Several stage conceptions, such as Levinson's, deal with the "seasons" of horizontal translation, not stages of vertical transformation. Erikson's higher stages are a murky combination of both; I have simply listed them on the charts in their approximate placement.

4. C. Graves, "Summary Statement: The Emergent, Cyclical, Double-Helix Model of the Adult Human Biopsychosocial Systems," Boston, May 20, 1981.

5. Don Beck, personal communication; this data is on computer file in the National Values Center, Denton, Texas, and is open to qualified researchers.

6. See Beck and Linscott, *The Crucible: Forging South Africa's Future* for an excellent discussion of the role of evolutionary thinking for defusing social tension.

7. Jane Loevinger, *Ego Development*. Cook-Greuter and Miller, *Transcendence and Mature Thought in Adulthood*; see also Cook-Greuter's excellent chapter in Commons et al., *Adult Development 2*.

8. Start with Pascual-Leone's contributions to Commons et al., *Beyond Formal Operations* and Alexander and Langer, *Higher Stages of Human Development*.

9. See, for example, chap. 19 in *Beyond Formal Operations*; and *Critical Theories of Psychological Development*. For a good summary of Broughton's work, see Loevinger, *Ego Development*.

10. Grof's research has used techniques from psychedelic drugs to holotropic breathwork. His book *The Cosmic Game* is a summary of this work; see also *The Adventure of Self-Discovery*. M. Washburn, *The Ego and the Dynamic Ground* and *Transpersonal Psychology in Psychoanalytic Perspective*; J. Wade, *Changes of Mind*.

Incidentally, many people have assumed that because I wrote a partially critical review of *Changes of Mind* in *The Eye of Spirit* I somehow disagreed with
most of its points, which is not so. I found some fault with Wade's embrace of
Bohm's holonomic theories (although Jenny maintains that I read into that a
stronger agreement than she intended), but those are minor points. My main
criticism is that I found her model to be mostly a phase-2 type of model and not
enough phase-3 (which in any event is easy to correct; she only has to specify
that the different characteristics of each of her levels might in fact be relatively
independent lines—not only in different contexts, but simultaneously in a single
context [for the meaning of "phase-2" and "phase-3," see note 9.15]). Other
than that (and a few misrepresentations of my work), her model is a good summary of the most recent research on a developmental view of consciousness,
covering the eight or so basic levels of self and consciousness evolution, which
I have included in the self-related stages chart (chart 4a). Those who have recently attacked a developmental view of consciousness would do well to study
this book, since it suggests that they are perhaps out of touch with recent research, evidence, and theorizing. For an extended discussion of Grof, Washburn, and Wade, see *The Eye of Spirit*.

11. I am often asked about what I think of Steiner's writings. Although I have a
great deal of respect for his pioneering contributions, I have not found the details of his presentations to be that useful. I believe recent orthodox research
has offered better and more accurate maps of prepersonal to personal development, and I believe the meditative traditions offer more sophisticated maps of
transpersonal development. Still, one can only marvel at the amount of visionary material he produced, and his overall vision is as moving as one could imagine. See *The Essential Steiner*, edited by Robert McDermott.

12. More recent transpersonal theorists include Charles Alexander, Hameed Ali,
Rosemarie Anderson, Cheryl Armon, James Austin, John Battista, Michel
Bauwens, Charles Birch, Harold Bloomfield, Seymour Boorstein, Sylvia
Boorstein, William Braud, Crittenden Brookes, Haridas Chaudhuri, Allan Chi-
nen, John Cobb, Allan Combs, Susanne Cook-Greuter, Jack Crittenden, A. S.
Dalal, Olaf Deatherage, Elizabeth Debold, Han de Wit, Arthur Deikman, Steve
Dinan, Norman Don, Duane Elgin, John Enright, Mark Epstein, Joseph Fabry,
James Fadiman, Piero Ferucci, Jorge Ferrer, John Firman, Robert Forman, Rob-
ert Frager, Joel Funk, Gordon Globus, Joseph Goguen, Tom Greening, David
Ray Griffin, Christina Grof, Stanislav Grof, T George Harris, Arthur Hastings,
Steve Hendlin, J. Heron, Edward Hoffman, Jean Houston, Russ Hudson, Le-
land Johnson, Dwight Judy, Sam Keen, Sean Kelly, Herb Koplowitz, Jack Korn-
field, Joyce Kovelman, George Leonard, David Lukoff, Richard Mann, Robert
McDermott, Michael Mahoney, Gerald May, Arnold Mindell, Donald Moss,
Michael Murphy, John Nelson, Juan Pascual-Leone, Kaisa Puhakka, Kenneth
Ring, Don Riso, Gillian Ross, Donald Rothberg, John Rowan, Peter Russell,
Don Salmon, Andrew Samuels, Marilyn Schlitz, Stephen Schoen, Tony
Schwartz, Bruce Scotton, Deane Shapiro, Jonathan Shear, Maureen Silos, Kath-
leen Singh, Jan Sinnott, Jacquelyn Small, Surya Das, Charles Tart, Eugene Tay-

lor, L. Eugene Thomas, Keith Thompson, Robert Thurman, William Torbert, Ronald Valle, Leland van den Daele, Brian van der Horst, Francisco Varela, James Vargiu, Frances Vaughan, Miles Vich, Frank Visser, Jenny Wade, Roger Walsh, Michael Washburn, John Welwood, Edward Whitmont, Auguste Wildschmidt, Bryan Wittine, Benjamin Wolman, Robert Wuthnow, and Michael Zimmerman, among many others.

13. For good short introductions to most of the theorists in this paragraph, see Jane Loevinger, *Ego Development*, and relevant contributions to Commons et al., *Adult Development*, volumes 1 and 2; Commons et al., *Beyond Formal Operations*; Miller and Cook-Greuter, *Transcendence and Mature Thought in Adulthood*; Alexander and Langer, *Higher Stages of Human Development*.

14. See *The Eye of Spirit* for a discussion of this topic.

15. See Loevinger, *Ego Development*; Commons et al., *Adult Development*, volumes 1 and 2; Commons et al., *Beyond Formal Operations*; Miller and Cook-Greuter, *Transcendence and Mature Thought in Adulthood*; Alexander and Langer, *Higher Stages of Human Development*; Wilber, *The Eye of Spirit*.

16. D. Shaffer, *Social and Personality Development* (1994), pp. 423–24, 435. This does not mean that men and women do not have characteristically "different voices" in certain life situations. The claim of research such as Deborah Tannen's, for example, is that men and women tend to speak in different voices in many circumstances. I have summarized that research as: men tend to translate with an emphasis on agency, women with an emphasis on communion; men tend to transform with an emphasis on Eros, women with an emphasis on Agape (see *Sex, Ecology, Spirituality*, 2nd ed.). But I have also emphasized the fact that the basic structures of the Great Nest, and the various self-stages, are in themselves *gender-neutral*—they are not biased toward either sex, and the research just mentioned supports that claim. The fact that men and women might navigate the basic waves in the Great Holarchy with a different voice does not alter in the least the fact that they both face the same waves.

17. Shaffer, *Social and Personality Development*, pp. 417–18.

18. J. Vasudev, "Ahimsa, Justice, and the Unity of Life," in M. Miller and S. Cook-Greuter, *Transcendence and Mature Thought in Adulthood* (1994), p. 241. This does not mean that Kohlberg's model covers all the relevant moral issues in various cultures, only that it has proven to be universal in those stages that it does address. There is more to morals than moral reasoning—including moral affects and motivations—which are not covered well by Kohlberg's model (nor were they meant to be).

19. Although I know, from conversations with Don Beck, that he is very open to the ideas about transpersonal states and structures.

20. Don Beck, personal communication. See note 4.22.

21. Much of the following descriptions consist of direct quotes or paraphrasing from various publications of Graves, Beck, and Beck and Cowan. From C. Graves, "Human Nature Prepares for a Momentous Leap," *The Futurist*, April 1974; C. Graves, "Summary Statement"; Beck and Cowan, *Spiral Dynamics*; Don Beck, privately circulated papers and personal communication.

22. Jenny Wade, who has made a careful study of Graves, believes that orange (achievement) and green (affiliative) are not two different levels but two different choices offered to blue (conformist); so that both orange and green can advance directly to second-tier (authentic). In that conception, this book is an invitation to both orange and green to adopt second-tier perspectives.

At the same time, Spiral Dynamics—and developmental studies in general—indicate that many philosophical debates are not really a matter of the better objective argument, but of the subjective level of those debating. No amount of orange scientific evidence will convince blue mythic believers; no amount of green bonding will impress orange aggressiveness; no amount of turquoise holarchy will dislodge green hostility—unless the individual is ready to develop forward through the dynamic spiral of consciousness evolution. This is why "cross-level" debates are rarely resolved, and all parties usually feel unheard and unappreciated. This also alerts second-tier thinkers to look for ways to move the spiral, gently or by strategic rattling.

When I say, in the text, that green has often fought to prevent the emergence of second-tier thinking, I mean, of course, that all first-tier memes resist the emergence of second-tier consciousness. Scientific materialism (orange) is aggressively reductionistic toward second-tier constructs, attempting to reduce all interior stages to objectivistic neuronal fireworks. Mythic fundamentalism (blue) is often outraged at what it sees as attempts to unseat its given Order. Egocentrism (red) ignores second-tier altogether. Magic (purple) puts a hex on it.

Green accuses second-tier consciousness of being authoritarian, rigidly hierarchical, patriarchal, marginalizing, oppressive, racist, and sexist. In other words, it takes the pluralistic critique, which it developed and *correctly* aimed a pre-green positions (especially blue and orange, which are often guilty of all of the sins that green claims), and then incorrectly and inappropriately aims this pre-green critique at post-green developments, where it can be shown to be perhaps well-intentioned but misdirected (it generally distorts yellow and turquoise constructions, as second-tier researchers are quick to point out).

Green has been in charge of cultural studies for the past three decades. On the one hand, the pluralistic relativism of green has nobly enlarged the canon of cultural studies to include many previously marginalized peoples, ideas, and narratives. It has acted with sensitivity and care in attempting to redress social imbalances and avoid exclusionary practices. It has been responsible for basic initiatives in civil rights and environmental protection. It has developed strong and often convincing critiques of the philosophies, metaphysics, social practices, and sciences of the blue and orange memes, with their often exclusionary, patriarchal, sexist, and colonialistic agendas.

On the other hand, as effective as these critiques of pre-green stages have been, green has attempted to turn its guns on all post-green stages as well, with the most unfortunate results. In honorably fighting the rigid social hierarchies of blue, green has condemned all second-tier holarchies—which has made it very difficult, and often impossible, for green to move forward into more holistic, integral-aperspectival constructions.

On most of the self-related charts, you can see a movement from mythic absolutism and rational formalism (blue and orange), through stages of pluralism and relativism (green), to stages of integralism and holism (yellow and turquoise). The green meme, effectively challenging the absolutisms of blue and orange, then mistook all universals and all holarchies as being of the same order, and this often locked it tenaciously into first-tier thinking.

Still, it is from the *healthy* green ranks that second-tier emerges, as Spiral Dynamics points out, so most of my comments in my recent books have been directed toward green, as have my occasional polemical nudges, in an attempt to get green to look at its own premises more expansively. These jabs have not, in general, endeared me to greens, but they have jolted the conversation in ways that politeness consistently failed to do. (My first twelve books, over twenty years, were unfailingly polite, with not a single polemical sentence in any of them; my thirteenth book [SES] was polemical—as Miss Piggy put it, "I *tried* being nice.") Whether the polemical tone helped or hurt remains to be seen (see Introduction to CW7). But the message is simple enough: in order for green to make the jump into the hyperspace of second-tier, the following factors might be considered: (1) All systems are context-bound, according to green pluralism, so fully carry out that agenda: all relativities and all pluralities are therefore *also* context-bound: they themselves have wider and deeper contexts that bind them together into even larger systems—*therefore*, acknowledge these larger systems, and then begin to outline the universal-integral contexts binding them all together. (2) Systems evolve over space and time; therefore, trace this evolution and development. (3) The only way to do so is to include hierarchies with heterarchies (and thus arrive at holarchies). Once that happens, the important contributions of green can be taken up, embraced and included, in the ongoing unfolding of consciousness evolution. Green is not lost or denied, but included and enriched.

As for Spiral Dynamics, my only minor reservations are that it does not sufficiently include states of consciousness nor the higher, transpersonal structures of consciousness; and it is an example of a phase-2 model and not enough phase-3 (see note 9.15). That is, there is not enough sensitivity to the empirically demonstrated fact that different developmental lines can be at different levels in the same instance: not just that a person can be using a red meme in one circumstance and an orange meme in another, but that a person, in the *same* circumstance, can be cognitively orange and morally red. Finally, Spiral Dynamics does not sufficiently distinguish between enduring and transitional (see Introduction to CW7). From personal conversations, I believe Beck is open to all of these considerations.

Beck is also moving to incorporate the four quadrants into the Spiral Dynamics model, which he believes will help him more adequately distinguish between what he calls the healthy and unhealthy versions of the memes (the four quadrants are introduced in Part Two). Don writes that "The quadrants help differentiate the positive from negative versions of the ᵛMEMEs. They also show graphically why so many change initiatives are doomed to fail. Kids who are taken out of gang-infested neighborhoods and placed in an enrichment training program to enhance interior development, are often made worse when they are then dumped back into the same WE and ITS quadrants, which are toxic to the new level of development. Quadrants provide the missing element in the creation of healthy systems."

As another example of healthy/unhealthy VMEMEs, systems theory, which utilizes a yellow/turquoise meme, is often caught in flatland, where it recognizes only exterior systems described in it-language, and does not also acknowledge the interior stages described in I and We language (see chaps. 5, 6, and 7). Systems theory in itself is thus a partial, limited, flatland expression of second-tier thinking (and thus some of the examples of second-tier thinking given in *Spiral Dynamics* are actually unhealthy or not-fully-complete memes). I believe Beck is in substantial agreement with this view, and his new writings will reflect these minor adjustments. (As for the last three decades of cultural studies under green pluralism, see Wilber, *Boomeritis*, and Introduction to CW7.)

The point in all of this is that each meme—each level of consciousness and wave of existence—is, in its healthy form, *an absolutely necessary and desirable element* of the overall spiral, of the overall spectrum of consciousness. Even if every society on earth were established fully at the turquoise meme, every infant born in that society nonetheless starts at level 1, at beige, at sensorimotor instincts and perceptions, and must then grow and evolve through purple magic, red and blue myth, orange rationalism, green networking, and into yellow and turquoise vision-logic. All of those waves have important tasks and functions; all of them are taken up and included in subsequent waves; none of them can be bypassed; and none of them can be demeaned without grave consequences to self and society. *The health of the entire spiral is the prime directive, not preferential treatment for any one level.* No question about it: the higher the leading edge and the higher the governing body, the better—but only because second-tier consciousness can think of the health of the entire spiral.

23. See Riso and Hudson, *The Wisdom of the Enneagram*; and H. Palmer, *The Enneagram*. When we get to the discussion of subpersonalities, in chapter 8, this means that a subpersonality can be any *type* at any of the basic *levels*: a truly pluralistic society of selves!—nonetheless all navigated by the proximate self, which delivers a unity of experience to the ongoing flow of consciousness, however occasionally disrupted.

CHAPTER 5. WHAT IS MODERNITY?

1. See *The Marriage of Sense and Soul* for a fuller discussion of this theme.
2. Regarding the four quadrants, there is nothing magical about the number four; I am certainly not reifying it. The four quadrants are simply the results of some of the simplest distinctions that reality seems to make: inside/outside and singular/plural. But there are numerous, perhaps infinite, other dimensions that are also important. The only reason people have found the four quadrants so useful is that flatland doesn't even honor these simple distinctions, and thus, by compari-

son with the world of one-dimensional man, the four quadrants are positively complex.

The four quadrants (or simply the Big Three) are realities that are embedded even in ordinary language, which recognizes first-person (I), second-person (we), and third-person (it) perspectives, which is why, for example, individuals natively and easily understand the difference between art, morals, and science—and the need to include all three in any balanced approach to the world.

CHAPTER 6. TO INTEGRATE PREMODERN AND MODERN

1. See also the Introduction to CW 4 for a further discussion of this theme.
2. See Taylor's *Sources of the Self* for the concept of the great interlocking order; see Lovejoy's *The Great Chain of Being* for a discussion of the Enlightenment's belief in a systems view of reality; see *Sex, Ecology, Spirituality,* 2nd ed. (CW 6), for a discussion of systems theory, subtle reductionism, and their roots in the Enlightenment paradigm.
3. For premodernity's lack of pluralism and contextualism, see chap. 13; see also the Introduction to CW 4 and Wilber, *Boomeritis,* for a further discussion of this theme.

CHAPTER 7. SOME IMPORTANT MODERN PIONEERS

1. In figure 8, I have only indicated a few general waves in the Upper-Left quadrant, but the idea is that all of the levels, across all of the quadrants, can be investigated for their mutually constraining influences, thus arriving at a more integral, comprehensive model. See chap. 14.

    For very specific examples of levels of art, morals, and science—from body to mind to soul to spirit—see *The Marriage of Sense and Soul,* chap. 14.
2. For correlations of states/structures of consciousness and states/structures of organism-brain, see, e.g., Wade, *Changes of Mind;* Austin, *Zen and the Brain;* Alexander and Langer, *Higher Stages of Human Development;* Valerie Hunt, *Infinite Mind;* David Chalmers, *The Conscious Mind;* Laughlin et al., *Brain, Symbol, and Experience.* See also notes 14.1 and 14.17. Notice that, according to Ramana Maharshi, even complete spiritual Self-Realization has a *physical vibratory correlate* on the right side of the chest (i.e., every Left-Hand event, no matter how lofty, ascended, or transcendental, has a Right-Hand correlate).

    As for the traditional mind-body problem, it is given a fuller treatment in chap. 14. For the moment, a few points might be made with reference to figure 8. The Left-Hand domains refer loosely to "mind," and the Right-Hand domains to "body." These are ultimately nondual, but that nonduality can only be realized with causal-to-nondual development, at which point the mind-body problem is not solved, but dissolved: seen to be a product of nescience, ignorance, or nonawakening. Short of that, the mind-body problem cannot be satisfactorily solved (see *The Eye of Spirit,* chap. 3; and *A Brief History of Everything*). This nondual view is not a variety of philosophical monism, because the nonduality is realized only in the supramental, transphilosophical realms, and cannot be transposed downwardly into mental conceptions without generating antinomies and contradictions (see *Eye to Eye*, chaps. 1 and 2). There is an injunctive, but not descriptive, disclosure of nonduality (see chap. 3, *The Eye of Spirit*; and *Sex, Ecology, Spirituality*, 2nd ed.).

Short of nondual realization, what can be said, in a relative fashion, is that all four quadrants "tetra-interact"—they are mutually arising and mutually determining. It is not just that the individual mind and consciousness (UL) interacts with the individual body-brain-organism (UR), but that they both equally and mutually interact with the collective cultural mind (LL) and collective social body (LR).

Thus, this view is neither a monism nor a dualism. It is not a monism, because it does not maintain that mind and body are two aspects of an underlying reality, because that Reality, in its formlessness, does not have aspects (it is *shunya* of all conceptions). This is not psychophysical identity, for those aspects nonetheless have relatively real and irreducible differences. Neither is it traditional interactionism, because the quadrants, while relatively real, are still of the world of maya, and thus interactionism is not the ultimate word.

The dominant forms of "solving" the mind-body problem today involve mostly types of emergent materialism, functionalism, connectionism, and autopoietic theories, all of which are subtle reductionisms (reducing Left-Hand events to Right-Hand dynamical systems). The fact that many of these are holistic, hierarchical, connectionist, and emergent simply obscures the fact that they are still exterior holisms, not interior holisms (nor their integration). This is true even when they refer to themselves as "nonreductionist materialism"—they mean non-gross-reductionistic, not non-subtle-reductionistic. This tendency to subtle reductionism (a hangover from the project of flatland modernity) can best be countered by the simple reminder of "tetra-interactionism." See Wilber, "An Integral Theory of Consciousness," *Journal of Consciousness Studies*, vol. 4, no. 1, 1997 (CW7); *Sex, Ecology, Spirituality*, 2nd ed. (CW6), chap. 14, note 1; and chap. 14 of this book.

3. See *A Brief History of Everything* for a discussion of this topic.
4. See Wilber & Walsh in Velmans, *Investigating Phenomenal Consciousness*.
5. J. Broughton et al. (eds.), *The Cognitive Developmental Psychology of James Mark Baldwin*, p. 31.
6. Ibid., p. 32.
7. Ibid., p. 36.
8. Ibid., p. 40.
9. Ibid., pp. 280–1.
10. Ibid., p. 277.
11. Ibid., p. 296.
12. Kohlberg's stage six is an ideal limit, and not an actual stage. The evidence refers to his five stages, which to date have been found to be largely cross-cultural, universal, and nonrelativistic. See chap. 4 of this volume, the section "Objections."

13. Wallwork's summary of Baldwin's view, *The Cognitive Developmental Psychology of James Mark Baldwin*, p. 335.

14. Baldwin's "unity consciousness" is a gross-realm unity or nature mysticism (psychic level). It does not recognize archetypal mysticism, subtle consciousness, lucid dreaming, or savikalpa samadhi (all forms of deity or subtle-level mysticism); nor does it recognize formless consciousness (causal), and therefore it does not reach the pure nondual (which is a union of form and emptiness). Union with nature, when it does not recognize the formless state of cessation, is usually psychic-level, gross cosmic consciousness, or nature mysticism. Nonetheless, it is a genuine and profound transpersonal experience.

    One of the easiest ways to tell if a "unity experience" is gross realm (nature mysticism), subtle realm (deity mysticism), causal realm (formless mysticism), or genuine nondual consciousness (union of the form in all realms with the pure formless) is to note the nature of consciousness in dreaming and deep sleep. If the writer talks of a unity experience while awake, that is usually gross-realm nature mysticism. If that unity consciousness *continues into the dream state*—so that the writer talks of lucid dreaming, union with interior luminosities as well as gross exterior nature—that is usually subtle-realm deity mysticism. If that consciousness *continues into the deep sleep state*—so that the writer realizes a Self that is *fully present in all three states* of waking, dreaming, and deep sleep—that is usually causal-realm formless mysticism (turiya). If that formless Self is then discovered to be one with the form in all realms—gross to subtle to causal—that is pure nondual consciousness (turiyatita).

    Many nature mystics, ecopsychologists, and neopagans take the gross-realm, waking-state unity with nature to be the highest unity available, but that is basically the first of four major samadhis or mystical unions. The "deep self" of ecopsychology is thus not to be confused with the True Self of Zen, Ati of Dzogchen, Brahman-Atman of Vedanta, etc. These distinctions also help us situate philosophers like Heidegger and Foucault, both of whom talked of mystical-like unions with nature. Those were often profound and authentic experiences of gross-realm unity (Nirmanakaya), but again, those should not be confused with Zen or Vedanta, for the latter push through to causal formlessness (Dharmakaya, nirvikalpa samadhi, jnana samadhi, etc.), and then into pure nondual unity (Svabhavikakaya, turiyatita) with any and all realms, gross to subtle to causal. Many writers confuse Nirmanakaya with Svabhavikakaya, which ignores the major realms of interior development that lie between the two (e.g., Sambhogakaya and Dharmakaya).

15. This is Broughton and Freeman-Moir's felicitous summary of Baldwin's idea, *The Cognitive Developmental Psychology of James Mark Baldwin*, p. 331.

16. See Habermas, *The Theory of Communicative Action*; good overviews include Rehg, *Insight and Solidarity* and Outhwaite, *Habermas*. For Habermas's crucial corrections to the excesses of postmodernism, see *The Philosophical Discourse of Modernity*.

17. Aurobindo's yoga is referred to as "integral yoga"; thus his psychological system is properly referred to as "integral yoga psychology." See, for example,

Integral Yoga Psychology, by Dr. Reddy, and *The Concept of Personality in Sri Aurobindo's Integral Yoga Psychology and Maslow's Humanistic/Transpersonal Psychology*, by Dr. Vrinte.

CHAPTER 8. THE ARCHEOLOGY OF SPIRIT

1. As indicated in the text, states are very important, but for them to contribute to *development* they must become structures/traits. Planes or realms are important, but they cannot be conceived pre-critically as ontologically independent realities, but rather as coproductions of perceiving selves (see note 8.2). Thus, the simplest *generalization* is that individual development involves waves, streams, and self, without in any way denying the importance of all of those others factors, from states to planes to numerous heterarchical processes and patterns.

2. In my view, the basic structures in the Great Nest are simultaneously levels of both knowing and being, epistemology and ontology. For reasons discussed in the text (namely, modernity rejected most ontology and allowed only epistemology), I usually refer to the basic structures as "the basic structures of consciousness" (or "the basic levels of consciousness"); but their ontological status should not be overlooked. Generally, the perennial philosophy refers to the former as levels of consciousness (or *levels of selfhood*), and the latter as realms or planes of existence (or *levels of reality*), with the understanding that they are inextricably interwoven (see note 1.3). Thus, as Huston Smith pointed out (*Forgotten Truth*), the body level of consciousness corresponds with the terrestrial realm or plane of existence; the mind level of consciousness corresponds with the intermediate realm or plane of existence; the soul level of consciousness corresponds with the celestial plane of existence; and the spirit level of consciousness corresponds with the infinite plane of existence (see chart 2a). Since these are correlative structures (levels of consciousness and planes of existence), I include both of them in the idea of basic structures or basic levels of the Great Nest.

   However, on occasion it is useful to distinguish them, because *a given level of self can experience a different level or plane of reality*. I have often made this distinction when analyzing modes of knowing (see *Eye to Eye*, chapters 2 and 6; *A Sociable God*, chapter 8), and I will do the same in the text when we discuss modes of art. Moreover, in ontogeny, the structures develop but the planes do not (the self develops through the already-given planes or levels of reality); however, in both Kosmic involution and evolution/phylogeny, the planes/realms also develop, or unfold from Source and enfold to Source (so we cannot say that planes show no development at all: they involve and evolve from Spirit; see note 1.5 for the ways in which the planes themselves coevolve). But a given level of self, generally, can interact with different levels of reality, to various degrees, so that we need to keep these two (structures and realms) as independent variables.

   Thus, for example, as I pointed out in *Eye to Eye*, consciousness can turn its attention to the material plane (using its epistemological eye of flesh), the intermediate plane (using its epistemological eye of mind), or the celestial plane (using its epistemological eye of contemplation). The material, intermediate, and celestial *planes* are the *ontological* levels; in *Eye to Eye* I refer to them using the terms sensibilia, intelligibilia, and transcendelia (i.e., the objects in those planes or realms). The eyes of flesh, mind, and contemplation are the *epistemological* levels correlated with (and disclosing) those ontological planes of sensibilia, intelligibilia, and transcendelia. (Of course, this is just using a simple three-level version of the Great Nest; if we use five levels, there are then five planes of existence and five correlative levels of consciousness, and so on. In my scheme, since I often use seven to nine general levels of consciousness, there are likewise seven to nine general realms or planes of reality.)

But notice: you can make essentially the same points using only the levels of consciousness (since being and knowing are two sides of the same levels). You can say that the mind can investigate the intermediate realm, or you can simply say the mind can investigate other minds. You can say the mind can investigate the celestial realm, or you can simply say the mind can investigate the subtle level. They are essentially saying the same thing, as long as you realize that any given level of selfhood (or consciousness) can turn its attention to any level of existence (or plane of reality). These two independent scales, in other words, can be stated as "level of consciousness investigates planes of existence"; but they can also be stated as "level of consciousness investigates other levels of consciousness," as long as we understand the correlations involved.

I often use the latter formulation, simply because, as I said, it avoids the ontological speculations that modernity finds so questionable. Premodern philosophy was unabashedly *metaphysical* (i.e., it assumed the nonproblematic ontological existence of all the various planes, levels, and realms of transcendental reality); whereas modern philosophy was primarily *critical* (i.e., it investigated the structures of the subject of thinking, and called into question the ontological status of the objects of thought), and thus modernity brought a much needed critical attitude to bear on the topic (even if it went overboard in its critical zeal and sometimes erased all objects of knowledge except the sensorimotor).

A crippling problem with the perennial traditions (and the merely metaphysical approaches) is that they tend to discuss ontological levels (planes or axes) as if they were pregiven, independent of the perceiver of those domains, thus overlooking the substantial amount of modern and postmodern research showing that cultural backgrounds and social structures profoundly mold perceptions in all domains (i.e., the perennial philosophy did not sufficiently differentiate the four quadrants). For all these reasons, simply talking about "planes" as completely independent ontological realities is extremely problematic—yet another reason I have tended to emphasize the epistemological facets over the merely ontological ones.

This has led some critics to claim that I completely ignore planes of existence, but that is obviously incorrect. As we just saw, I often explicitly refer to the planes as "realms," "spheres," or "domains," and I have named the phenomena in the three major planes of terrestrial, intermediate, and celestial as sensibilia, intelligibilia, and transcendelia (I also refer to them as the physio/biosphere, noosphere, and theosphere; although, again, those realms can be subdivided into at least a dozen levels). It is true that I usually focus on the structures/levels of consciousness, but I *preserve these two independent scales* by saying that one level can interact with other levels. Thus, for example, in the charts in chapter 6 of *Eye to Eye* and chapter 8 of *A Sociable God* (which present five major modes of knowing: sensory, empiric-analytic, historic-hermeneutic, mandalic, and spiritual), the structures/levels of consciousness are on the left, and the structures/levels of existence (or planes/realms of reality) are on the right, so that these two scales are clearly differentiated. I will do the same thing in the text when we discuss modes of art.

Combined with an understanding of *states* of consciousness, the notions of *levels of consciousness* and *planes of reality* gives us a three-dimensional model (i.e., with three independent scales). I have been presenting this three-variable model since *A Sociable God* (1983). Recently, Allan Combs has offered a similar model, which has much to recommend it, but also has some fundamental problems, in my view. See note 12.12.

Most often, when it is not necessary to distinguish levels of consciousness and planes of existence, I try to use terms that can cover both (such as body, mind, soul, and spirit), and I implicitly use the basic structures or basic levels as referring to both, so as to avoid intricate discussions such as this. When it is important to distinguish them, I usually refer to the planes as "realms," "domains," or "spheres," although in each case the context will tell. See notes 1.3, 1.5, 1.9, 1.10, 8.1, 8.39, 12.12.

3. Alexander et al., *Higher Stages of Human Development*, p. 160, emphasis in original.

4. The question faced by any developmental model is, How much of a level in any line (moral, cognitive, affective, needs) do you have to satisfy before you can move on to the next higher level in that line? Research tends to suggest that a *general competence* needs to be established at each major wave in a stream in order for its successor to emerge. I have indicated this in figure 14. The nine basic waves are drawn as a cross-section of nine concentric circles. These are not "rungs in a ladder"—figure 14 is simply a cross-section of the concentric circles of the Great Nest (fig. 1), representing the holarchical waves through which the various developmental streams progress relatively independently (these holarchical waves or levels are the vertical axis on the psychograph, fig. 2). In other words, fig. 14 represents the basic levels in the various lines of development (morals, affects, cognition, needs, etc.), levels that span the entire spectrum from body to mind to soul to spirit. Since the various lines can develop relatively independently, overall development follows no linear sequence. But the question here is, *in any single developmental line*, how much of one stage/level in that line is necessary for the next stage/level in that line to stably emerge?

Using vision-logic as an example, I have drawn four subphases—*a, b, c,* and *d.* I am using the subphases *a* and *b* to represent a *basic competence* in vision-

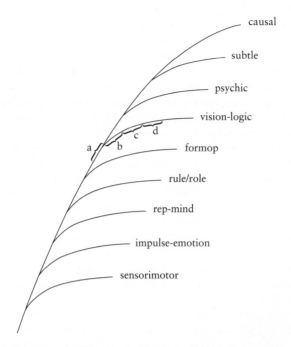

FIGURE 14. *The Basic Waves and Their Substages*

logic: a capacity to take multiple perspectives and to evidence some sort of postconventional, universal, panoramic awareness. This basic competence is necessary for higher, stable development. The subphases *c* and *d* are specialized, extreme developments of vision-logic, such as the capacity to think about systems of systems, and systems of systems of systems (what Commons and Richards call "paradigmatic" and "cross-paradigmatic" thinking; see chart 3a and notes 9.19, 9.27). These are *not* necessary for higher development. It is quite likely that Buddha and Christ would have passed tests for *a* and *b* (both the bodhisattva vow and the golden rule demand multiple perspectives), but they might have failed tests for *c* and *d* capacities; certainly many people have advanced into higher stages of development without mastering these intricate capacities for thinking about systems of systems of systems. In short, phases *a* and *b* represent postconventional awareness and multiple perspectives, which are necessary components (subholons) of higher development (transpersonal and spiritual) if the transpersonal is to become a stable adaptation and not merely a passing peak experience, but *c* and *d* are specialized, unnecessary developments.

The same conclusion would hold for each of the basic waves in any of the streams. The *a* and *b* subphases are the necessary prerequisites and/or ingredients of higher developments. A certain competence (*a* and *b*) is required in sensorimotor development, but one does not have to become an Olympic athlete (*c* and *d*), and so on. (Likewise, past saints and sages might not have mastered any of the extreme developments of vision-logic, but the people who gave the world the golden rule and the bodhisattva vow clearly mastered vision-logic to the degree necessary to transcend it.)

This diagram also indicates that, when figure 14 represents the basic structures themselves, which are mostly *enduring* structures, each wave remains in existence and can be exercised and developed on its own, indefinitely. One can extend and sharpen physical capacities, emotional intelligence, intellectual acuity, vision-logic capacities, and so on (i.e., one can even develop the *c* and *d* and even higher subphases in each of the basic waves).

Most of the *developmental lines*, on the other hand, are not enduring structures but transitional structures (see note 1.7). They still follow "transcend-and-include," in that each stage provides basic competences that are incorporated in the succeeding stages; but once a stage has served its purpose, it does not remain in existence as a *separate* function itself (e.g., a person at moral stage 5 does not simultaneously exercise moral stage 1, but a person at vision-logic can and does simultaneously exercise all of the lower basic structures, such as sensorimotor and emotional-sexual). But the same general developmental rule still applies: a general competence at each stage is required for the stable emergence of the next.

In many cases this competence is necessary but not sufficient for the emergence of the next stage; exactly why higher stages emerge, or conversely, why developmental arrest occurs in any line, is still not well understood, although theories abound. (The most likely candidate is a combination of numerous variables: individual constitutional factors, individual upbringing, individual interior dispositions, social institutions, life circumstances, possible past life history, cultural background, cultural values, and cultural encouragement/discouragement, to give a sampling from all four quadrants.) As for which aspects of a basic wave are *a, b, c*, etc., in most cases only empirical testing can tell.

5. See *Transformations of Consciousness*, chap. 1 (Jack Engler).

6. See M. Epstein, *Thoughts without a Thinker*.

7. In *The Atman Project*, I gave the following names and dates for the ego: early ego (ages 4–7), middle ego (7–12), and late ego (12–21). Those names and dates are still acceptable, but the problem is that the word "ego" is used in a thousand different ways by different theorists, which makes it very difficult to assign a definition. Psychological literature speaks of "early ego nuclei," "the bodyego," "the impulsive ego," "the mental ego," "the mature ego," "the synthesizing ego," "the analytic ego," and so on. I generally use the term "ego" in three different ways, reflecting common uses in the literature: (1) the ego is the sense of self or "I-ness" at any of the *personal* (or frontal) stages, from the material ego to the bodyego to the rational ego; (2) the ego is more narrowly the personal self that is based on formal-rational-reflexive capacities, which I also call "the mature ego"; (3) the ego is the separate-self sense or self-contraction in general, body to mind to soul. What *The Atman Project* called the early ego I now also call the self-concept (or the conceptual self; fulcrum-3); the middle ego (fulcrum-4) I often call the persona or the membership-self (in *The Atman Project*,

I used "membership self" to mean the *very beginning* of socialization, but since that socialization does not really become paramount until the rule/role mind, I now use "membership" and "mythic-membership" to refer to *the overall rule/role mind*, its worldview, and its fulcrum-4 self: a conformist role-self or persona); and the late ego (fulcrum-5) I generally call the mature ego. All of those terms as I now most often use them are indicated in chart 1a. Still, any of those terms are acceptable as long as we specify just what developmental period is meant, so in each case the context should tell.

8. One or two theorists have raised what they call a "devastating critique" of the centaur and vision-logic, namely: "We doubt the integrative capacity of the rational-egoic stage [fulcrum-5], at least as Wilber sees it. Either it does not fully integrate the mental with the physical, and then the developmental logic of transcend-and-include is violated, or it does fully integrate the mental with the physical, in which case the centaur [F-6] is redundant."

This criticism comes from using philosophical abstractions instead of concrete psychological research. There is not simply "the" physical body and "the" mind, such that you have only two choices: integrate them or not. What these critics call "the" physical body actually consists of about a half-dozen levels (e.g., sensation, perception, exocept, impulse, emotion), and what they call "the mind" is also about a half-dozen levels (image, symbol, concept, rule, formal, vision-logic). Beyond those are the transrational, transpersonal levels (psychic, subtle, causal).

If we use this more complete Great Nest, and not the simplistic "mind" and "body," the problem does not arise. Each of those levels accomplishes a great deal of integration at its own level—each follows "transcend-and-include." The formal-rational level (whose integrative power is questioned by these critics) transcends and includes (integrates) multiple concrete operations, numerous different perspectives, multiple roles, reversible operations, and mutual outlooks—it is an extraordinarily integrative structure! As integrative as the formal structure is, research shows that postformal cognition (i.e., vision-logic, whose existence is claimed to be redundant by these critics) is even more integrative. Postformal cognition transcends but includes (integrates) numerous formal operations, systems of thought, and meta-systemic perceptions (e.g., the work of Commons and Richards, Arlin, Fischer, Pascual-Leone, Sinnott, etc.). The evidence for both formal and postformal stages is quite substantial. But if your developmental stages include only body, mind, and their integration, you will miss all of that.

Likewise with the self at each of those stages. The self identified with the role mind is the persona; the self identified with the formal mind is the mature ego; the self identified with vision-logic is the centaur. As can be seen in charts 3a–b and 4a–c, there is an extraordinary amount of evidence for all of those cognitive stages and for all of those self-stages. Again, if your developmental sequence is nothing but body, mind, and their integration, all of that is missed.

Part of the difficulty these critics seem to be having is that, precisely because, barring pathology, each of those stages transcends and includes its predecessors, *each* of those stages shows a *relatively* greater capacity for integration. Thus "integration" is in fact a sliding scale whose potential capacity increases at every level. But researchers from Gebser to Neumann to Gilligan to Loevinger also call *specific stages* by the actual name "integrated"—usually, their very highest level is given that name, *not* because the lower levels lack all integration, but because this highest level has the greatest amount of it (and higher levels would have even more, since each is transcend-and-include, barring pathology).

Thus, I have often used Loevinger's summary of Broughton's highest stage (which correlates with the centaur): "Mind and body are both experiences of an integrated self." The critics have taken that to mean that the previous stage (the rational-egoic) has no integration of mind and body whatsoever—a strange notion—when all it actually means is that the ego has relatively less integrative capacity than the centaur, according to the research itself.

Each level, of course, has limits to its integrative power, which are the limits of that level itself. In the case of formal-rational, the limitations involve the inherently abstract nature of formal systems, which tend to close themselves off from other domains (even though those systems themselves have *already integrated* an enormous number of operations compared to the previous stage). These limitations, many researchers report, are themselves transcended with the development of vision-logic, which, because it begins to take a pluralistic, contextual, and relativistic stance (on the way to even higher integrations), can begin to include domains that formal rationality could not yet encompass. At each stage, once again, we see transcend-and-include. (The exception, of course, is pathology, which *is* pathology precisely because it does not transcend and include but denies and represses, fixates and arrests.)

Finally, a few critics have claimed that, according to the traditional Great Chain, there is nothing that would correspond with vision-logic and the centaur. On the contrary, as the charts show, almost every sophisticated Great Chain theorist had something that corresponded with vision-logic or higher reason (Plotinus's creative reason, Aurobindo's higher or integrative mind, Gebser's integral-aperspectival, and so on). Since the self can identify with any level in the Great Chain, I simply call the self at that level the centaur. If you use the complete Great Chain, and not simply a five-level or seven-level summary, once again this criticism does not arise.

9. For a discussion of the 1-2-3 process of each fulcrum (fusion/embeddedness, differentiation/disidentification/de-embedding/transcending, and integrating/including), see *Transformations of Consciousness*, *A Brief History of Everything*, and *The Eye of Spirit*.

10. See Mahler, Kernberg, Blanck and Blanck, Kohut, Gedo, Masterson, Stone, Neumann. See also notes 8.11 and 8.13.

11. As such, these three general levels of early self-development and self-pathology form only one part of a multifactorial etiology. It is an important part, but only a part, of a complex etiology that includes dispositions, constitutional factors, character types, predominant modes of functioning, independent defense mechanisms, interpersonal relations, environmental representations, among other

important factors (see, e.g., Stone's five-factor model in *Abnormalities of Personality*; Masterson and Klein, *Disorders of the Self*; Norcross and Goldfried, *Handbook of Psychotherapy Integration*). Moreover, not only are multifactorial approaches to the Upper-Left quadrant important, these need to be integrated with Upper-Right factors (neuromechanisms, neurotransmitters, brainwave states, psychopharmacology, etc.; e.g., Michel and Moore, *Developmental Neurobiology*; Harris, *Developmental Neuropsychiatry*; see note 14.17), as well as the Lower-Right and Lower-Left quadrants of social and cultural factors (e.g., Broughton, *Critical Theories of Psychological Development*, and the superb *Cultural Psychology* by Michael Cole).

As Lenzenweger and Haugaard put it in *Frontiers of Developmental Psychopathology* (1996), "Whereas many reports on developmental psychopathology focus on parent-child interactions, childrearing attitudes, dysfunctional parenting, and putatively related dysfunctional outcomes (e.g., maltreatment leading to impaired competence), few genuine attempts have been made to integrate genetic factors, neurotransmitter models, and neuroscientific processes, which as yet remain a relative rarity in the modal developmental psychopathology article or chapter. In the interest of not being misunderstood, we should like to emphasize that we are observing a relative imbalance in developmental psychopathology in favor of psychosocial models of pathological development over more biologically influenced models—quite frankly, however, we suggest that the best models will be those that *integrate across these levels* [my italics]. The importance of genetic factors in both normative and pathological development is indisputable (Rowe, 1994; Rutter, 1991) and the essential role of neurobiological factors in temperament (e.g., Kagan, 1994), emotion (Ekman & Davidson, 1994), personality development (e.g., Depue and Collins, in press), and the emergence of psychopathology (e.g., Breslin and Weinberger, 1990; Cocarro & Murphy, 1990; Grace, 1991) is axiomatic, some would even say confirmed. The meaningful integration of brain, emotion, behavior, and environmental influences currents represents an exceptionally active research area in various areas of psychological science, especially cognition and personality. In short, developmental psychopathology cannot afford not to heed these advances and emerging research strategies" (pp. vi-vii). Lenzenweger and Haugaard admirably stress at least some aspects in Upper Left, Upper Right, and Lower Right; but they are thin on Lower Left, and they ignore any of the higher levels in any of the quadrants. Still, this and other similar books show the steadily increasing interest in a more integral approach to psychology and therapy.

See also the superb *Handbook of Psychotherapy Integration*, edited by J. Norcross and M. Goldfried. Highly recommended, as working toward various types of psychology/therapy integrations over the past four decades, are the works of R. Woody, Jerome Frank, A. Ryle, Carl Rogers, S. Appelbaum, Aron Beck, L. Birk, A. Freeman, M. R. Goldfried, A. Lazarus, Deane Shapiro, J. Marmor, Stanley Messer (see his *Essential Psychotherapies*, coedited with A. Gurman), James Masterson, A. E. Bergin, J. Norcross, H. Arkowitz, John Gedo, V. Raimy, James Prochaska, J. Safran, H. H. Strupp, P. London, Paul Wachtel,

Abraham Maslow, and any of the brilliant works of Michael Mahoney (e.g., *Human Change Process*).

12. Daniel Stern, in such books as *The Interpersonal World of the Infant*, has argued that "undifferentiated" is an inappropriate term for early states, because even the earliest stages of an infant's awareness show certain discriminations and differentiations. Nonetheless, subsequent development shows even more of them; hence, the earliest stages, in comparison, are still properly referred to as relatively undifferentiated.

13. For a superb discussion of defenses in the first four fulcrums, see George Vaillant, *The Wisdom of the Ego* (1993).

In chart 1a, the earlier defenses (F-1 to F-3) are based largely on psychoanalytic ego psychology, object relations, and self psychology (e.g., Anna Freud, Margaret Mahler, Otto Kernberg, D. Winnicott, W. Fairbairn, S. Arieti, Heinz Kohut, Blanck and Blanck, George Vaillant, M. H. Stone, J. Gedo, James Masterson). The intermediate defenses (F-4 to F-6), on transactional analysis, cognitive therapy, attribution theory, construct theory, role theory, and symbolic interactionism (e.g., E. Berne, A. Beck, George Kelly, Selman, Mead). The higher defenses (F-7 to F-9) are culled from the existential and contemplative traditions (e.g., Jaspers, Boss, Binswanger, May, Bugental, Yalom; kundalini yoga, Kashmir Shaivism, Sufism, St. John of the Cross, the Victorine mystics, the Rhineland mystics, Dzogchen, Highest Yoga Tantra, etc.). See *Transformations of Consciousness*. See also note 8.20.

14. Gendlin's "felt meaning"—a zone between bodily feelings and mental concepts—is what Arieti (*The Intrapsychic Self*) calls "endocept," which I have listed as one of the basic waves in the charts. Endocepts, as the link between felt-body and thought-mind, are the gateway to the emotional shadow. Gendlin's "felt meaning" has often been confused with centauric awareness, whereas it is basically typhonic (i.e., it is pre-body/mind differentiation, not trans-body/mind differentiation). This confusion, in my opinion, is based on an underappreciation of the cognitive component of panoramic awareness offered by vision-logic. Endoceptual awareness is, by definition, part of centauric awareness (which transcends and includes all previous structures), but does not define it. For the place of endoceptual feeling in psychotherapy and meditation, see *One Taste*, Aug. 12 and Sept. 10 entries. See also notes 8.34, 8.35.

15. See *The Eye of Spirit* (especially chapter 6) for a full discussion of this theme and a critique of Washburn's retro-Romantic interpretation of this curative spiral. See also *One Taste*, Aug. 12 and Sept. 10 entries. See also notes 8.34, 8.35.

16. See notes 8.13, 8.17, 8.20.

17. See *Transformations of Consciousness*, *A Brief History of Everything*, and *The Eye of Spirit*. John Rowan's *The Transpersonal* is a good discussion of the pathologies and treatments at each of the nine fulcrums, marred only by an occasional confusion of mythic and subtle. This confusion is based on the pre/trans fallacy (which confuses prerational and transrational because both are nonrational—or any similar confusing of preformal and postformal, preconventional and postconventional, prepersonal and transpersonal, etc.; see *Eye to Eye*). This

confusion Rowan himself has spotted and redressed in subsequent publications, as well as a new afterword to the book, which Rowan sent me and from which I quote:

> When I finished writing this book in 1991 it was very much a pioneering effort. I was trying to put together a coherent story out of widely separated materials. And in doing so I did oversimplify one point.
>
> This is on the question of my definition of the transpersonal. In this book I consistently identified the transpersonal with the Subtle stage, the stage of the soul. The reason for this was that I wanted to make it very clear that this was the stage beyond the Centaur which was most relevant to therapy, and most used by therapists. . . .
>
> Well, this is perfectly OK and quite defensible. What is not defensible is to suggest that the Causal and Nondual stages are somehow not the transpersonal. Of course they are. They are just as much part of the transpersonal as the Subtle is, and much more studied and mentioned in the literature of transpersonal psychology. . . .
>
> On the other hand, I think I was right in emphasizing the importance of the Subtle. It is very much underrated and under-represented in the transpersonal literature. . . .
>
> One important reservation has to be made here, however. It is that people working in the subtle are typically rather careless about the Pre/Trans Fallacy. Because the prepersonal and the transpersonal are both rich in imagery, it is all too easy to slip from one to the other without awareness of the changeover.
>
> Joseph Campbell, one of the greatest proponents of the Subtle level and its importance, is also one of the great confusing people in the field, because he mixes up this [postformal Subtle] level with the [preformal] Mythic level quite habitually and as if thinking that they are the same thing. . . .
>
> What we can learn from all this is that if someone as well-read and capable as Joseph Campbell can make this sort of [pre/post] mistake, it must be even easier for those who are less experienced. In my own work I have done this, lumping together practitioners who are operating at the mythic level with those who are genuinely operating much of the time at the subtle level. This is something I intend to put right for the future, and what I have been trying to warn about here.

For further discussion, see notes 8.25, 8.27, 9.16.

18. See in particular the works of George Kelly, Aron Beck, and Albert Ellis. Transactional Analysis is still a fine approach to many of these scripts (see E. Berne, T. Harris).
19. See especially the pioneering works of Ludwig Binswanger, Medard Boss, Rollo May, Fritz Perls, Irvin Yalom, and Carl Rogers.
20. Good introductions to transpersonal psychology and therapy include Donald Moss (ed.), *Humanistic and Transpersonal Psychology*; Scotton et al., *Textbook of Transpersonal Psychiatry and Psychology*; Frances Vaughan, *The Inward*

Arc and *Shadows of the Sacred* (which are particularly recommended); Seymour Boorstein, *Clinical Studies in Transpersonal Psychotherapy* and *Transpersonal Psychotherapy*; Assagioli, *Psychosynthesis*; Grof, *Adventures in Self Discovery*; Tart, *Transpersonal Psychologies* and *States of Consciousness*; Washburn, *The Ego and the Dynamic Ground* and *Transpersonal Psychology in Psychoanalytic Perspective*; Zimmerman, *Eclipse of the Self*; Walsh and Shapiro, *Beyond Health and Normality*; Neumann, *The Origins and History of Consciousness* (see chart 4b); Chaudhuri, *Integral Yoga*; Epstein, *Thoughts without a Thinker*; Deikman, *The Observing Self*; Kathleen Singh, *The Grace in Dying*; Duane Elgin, *Awakening Earth*; Ferucci, *What We May Be*; anthologies/books of John Welwood; Adi Da, *The Dawn Horse Testament*; Wade, *Changes of Mind*; Grof and Grof, *The Stormy Search for the Self*; Jean Houston, *The Possible Human*; N. Schwartz-Salant and M. Stein (eds.), *Archetypal Processes in Psychotherapy*; Aurobindo, *The Life Divine*; Maslow, *The Farther Reaches of Human Nature*; John Rowan, *The Transpersonal* (as Rowan himself has made clear in his subsequent writings, this book tends to confuse mythic and subtle domains—see note 8.17—but it is otherwise a fine overview); Tony Schwartz, *What Really Matters*; Walsh and Vaughan, *Paths beyond Ego*; Wilber et al., *Transformations of Consciousness*; Almaas, *Pearl beyond Price*; J. Firman and A. Gila, *The Primal Wound*; Murphy, *The Future of the Body*; Murphy and Leonard, *The Life We Are Given*; Cornett, *The Soul of Psychotherapy*; Doherty, *Soul Searching*; Browning, *Religious Thought and the Modern Psychologies*; Sovatsky, *Words from the Soul*; Shapiro and Astin, *Control Therapy*; Frager and Fadiman, *Personality and Personal Growth*.

21. Even behavior therapy reinforces responses that help people experience what they have avoided. Incidentally, as Arieti (*The Intrapsychic Self*) demonstrates, classical behaviorism deals predominantly with the exoceptual level of cognition. Modern cognitive behaviorism deals predominantly with F-4 and F-5 verbal behavior. In other words, there is ample room in an integral theory for the enduring insights of behaviorism, though not for its reductionism. Finally, when I say awareness is curative, this includes the working through; awareness needs to be stable and pervasive; it needs to permeate the problem.

22. See John Rowan's superb book *Subpersonalities*; see also *Ego States*, Watkins and Watkins. In my view, each subpersonality exists as a subconscious or unconscious "I," an aspect of the proximate self that was defensively split off, but with which consciousness remains fused, embedded, or identified (as a hidden "I"), with its own wants, desires, impulses, and so on. The nature of the subpersonality is largely determined by the level at which it was dissociated (archaic, imagic, mythic, etc.). These "little subjects" are all those hidden facets of self that have not been turned into objects, let go of, disidentified with, de-embedded, and transcended, and so they hold consciousness circling in their orbit.

Each time the proximate self identifies with a basic wave, the self exists *embedded* as that wave: it is a material self, then a libidinal/emotional self, then a conceptual self, then a role self, then a reflexive self, then an integrated/authentic self, then a soul self, then a spirit self, each of which holarchically transcends and includes. As each "I" self is transcended, it becomes part of the "me" self (e.g., the feeling body, which was the proximate or "I" self of F-2, becomes simply "my body"—or part of the distal self or "me"—when the proximate self moves on).

A dissociated subpersonality results when facets of the "I" self are split off while consciousness *is still identified with them.* They thus become, not unconscious objects, but unconscious subjects, with their own morals, worldviews, needs, and so on (all determined by the level at which the subpersonality was split off). This is the key, in my opinion, *to distinguishing between repression and transcendence.* That is, dissociation (or repression) occurs when a proximate I is turned into a distal I; whereas transcendence occurs when a proximate I is turned into a distal me. In the former, the subjective identification/attachment (or I-ness) remains but is submerged (as an unconscious subject); in the later, the subjective identification is dissolved, turning the unconscious subject into a conscious object, which can then be integrated (transcend and include, not dissociate and repress). Therapy involves converting hidden subjects to conscious objects.

23. The lower-level subpersonalities are largely *preverbal* (archaic, uroboric, magical [UL]; reptilian/brain stem, paleomammalian/limbic system [UR]); the intermediate-level subpersonalities are *verbal* (mythic, roles, formal, postformal [UL]; neocortex [UR]); the higher subpersonalities are *transverbal* (mostly subtle [UL], theta states [UR]). Each of those impinge on consciousness in a different manner: the preverbal, often as impulses and inarticulated urges; the verbal, as vocal or subvocal narratives; the transverbal, as luminosities, higher cognitions, and transcendental affects (from bliss to cosmic agony).

    A dissociated component of any level of consciousness proceeds from a facet to a complex to a full-blown subpersonality, each layered with more complexity. This is similar to Grof's notion of COEX systems (systems of condensed experience). Any subpersonality includes one or more complexes, which themselves can be layered, going from the present level (say, F-5 or rational) back to earlier levels (mythic, magic, archaic), even back to perinatal matrices (F-0)—and further yet, some would claim, to past life experiences (however you wish to conceive that, from literally to phylogenetic residues; see *A Sociable God* for a further description of this layering of complexes). Likewise, some subpersonalities contain emergent qualities attempting to "come down" (from psychic, subtle, causal, or nondual domains).

24. For the highly controversial, possible role of F-0 in subsequent pathologies, see Grof, *The Adventure of Self-Discovery.*

25. "Archetype" has several different, very confusing meanings in the literature. I use it for both mythic forms and, occasionally, for subtle-realm forms. The original meaning, as with Plato and Plotinus, is of subtle-realm forms (the earliest forms in involution); but Jungians began using it to mean mythic forms (some of the earliest forms in evolution), a confusion that is impossible to uproot. See *Eye to Eye* and *The Eye of Spirit* for a full discussion.

    In any event, most of the mythic archetypes—as identified, say, by Jean Bolen in *Goddesses in Everywoman* and *Gods in Everyman*—are simply *concrete operational role personae*; they are preformal, not postformal. There is nothing inherently transpersonal about them, which is why, despite the many claims to the contrary, working with these mythic roles is usually a fulcrum-4 therapy. I happen to believe it is a powerful form of F-4 therapy, and I often recommend it, but it does not directly or necessarily issue in transpersonal states or structures of consciousness, although, by clearing out pathologies at this level, it can (as can any good therapy) make higher, transpersonal development more likely. See notes 8.27, 9.16.

Jungian therapy of this sort can occasionally issue in transpersonal awareness, simply because the process of *objectifying* these mythic roles often engages the Witness, and the postformal Witness—not the preformal mythic roles—is indeed transpersonal. I personally believe that Assagioli's Psychosynthesis and Hameed Ali's Diamond Approach are more effective in this particular regard, as is awareness meditation in general (vipassana, Zen, etc.).

26. See *Eye to Eye; Sex, Ecology, Spirituality,* 2nd ed.; and *The Eye of Spirit* for extensive discussions of the meaning of archetypes, from Plato to Jung. See especially *The Eye of Spirit,* chap. 11, section "Points of Light," no. 4.

27. Joseph Campbell (*The Portable Jung,* p. xxii) has given a wonderful summary of the general Jungian approach: "Briefly summarized, the essential realizations of this pivotal work of Jung's career were, first, that since the archetypes or norms of myth are common to the human species, they are inherently expressive neither of local social circumstance nor of any individual's singular experience, but of common human needs, instincts, and potentials [again, "common" or "collective" does not necessarily mean transpersonal, any more than the fact that human beings collectively have ten toes means that if I experience my toes I am having a transpersonal experience; the mythic archetypes are simply some of the deep features of the late preop and early conop mind, and thus they are basic forms at those levels, which are devoid of content but fleshed out by particular cultures and individuals; in other words:]; second, that in the traditions of any specific folk, local circumstance will have provided the imagery through which the archetypal themes are displayed in the supporting myths of the culture; third, that if the manner of life and thought of an individual so departs from the norms of the species that a pathological state of imbalance ensues, of neurosis or psychosis, dreams and fantasies analogous to fragmented myths will appear; and fourth, that such dreams are best interpreted, not by reference backward to repressed infantile memories (reduction to autobiography), but by comparison outward with the analogous mythic forms (amplification by mythology), so that the person may see himself depersonalized in the mirror" of the collective human condition. In other words, the aim is to differentiate from (and integrate) these mythic forms and roles. Many Jungians directly equate these preformal mythic roles with postformal subtle structures, which is an unfortunate pre/post confusion, in my opinion (for a discussion of the meaning of "archetype" and its pre/trans confusions, see *Eye to Eye* and *The Eye of Spirit*). But the effects of mythic differentiation-and-integration remain essentially the

same however it is interpreted: consciousness befriends and transcends the grip of mythic archetypes and is thus allowed to continue its journey free of their unconscious spell, a differentiation-and-integration that Jung called individuation.

28. The psychoanalytic, object relations, and self psychologists are increasingly recognizing a spectrum of treatment modalities up to and including F-5. As one example, on the charts I have included J. Gedo (e.g., *Beyond Interpretation, Advances in Clinical Psychoanalysis, Spleen and Nostalgia*), who admirably includes all of the first five fulcrums and their different pathologies and different treatments.

Various horizontal typologies—such as the Enneagram—can also be used to elucidate the types of defenses used by individuals. Each type proceeds through the various fulcrums with its own typical defense mechanisms and coping strategies. These horizontal typologies can be fruitfully combined with the vertical fulcrums, as suggested in chap. 4.

29. See *The Atman Project* and *Transformations of Consciousness*.

30. Grof and Grof, *Spiritual Emergency*.

31. Maslow, *The Farther Reaches of Human Nature*.

32. See *Transformations of Consciousness*; also notes 8.13 and 8.20.

33. For approaches to "soul therapy," see note 8.20.

34. Again, there are many overlaps and numerous exceptions, but in very general terms, the path of shamans/yogis deals with the energy currents in the gross realm and gross bodymind (exemplified in *nature mysticism*), leading up to the sahasrara (i.e., the energy currents or shakti from the first to the seventh chakra, at the crown of the head). The path of saints plumbs the interior depths of the psychic and subtle realm, often beginning at the fourth or fifth chakra, moving into the sahasrara, and then into numerous, more "within-and-beyond" spheres of audible illuminations and haloes of light and sound (exemplified in *deity mysticism*), occasionally culminating in pure formless absorption. The path of sages plumbs the pure emptiness of the causal domain (exemplified in *formless mysticism*), and often pushes through it to completely dissolve the subject-object dualism in any form (including that between self and God), to resurrect the nondual. The path of siddhas plays with *nondual mysticism*, which is always already accomplished in each and every gesture of this ever-present moment. See *Up from Eden*; *Sex, Ecology, Spirituality*, 2nd ed.; and *One Taste*.

35. A word on body therapy. In the sixties and early seventies, it seemed that body therapies, such as Rolfing, were aimed at the centaur, or a personal, postformal, bodymind integration; it has since become apparent that most of them, in themselves, deal with the preformal physical and emotional bodies. This does not mean that somatic therapy is useless; just the opposite, although it is less significant, it is more fundamental (see *Sex, Ecology, Spirituality*, 2nd ed.). Physical therapies of various sorts—from weight lifting to nutritional therapy to Rolfing, somatic therapy, and bodywork, insofar as they directly address the physical and feeling body (F-1 and F-2)—are all of great importance as the foundation, or first floor, of an integral therapy. But for postformal centauric

integration (e.g., achieving Loevinger's autonomous and integrated stages), vision-logic also has to be engaged and strengthened, and few body therapies actually do that.

Likewise, most of the therapies that call themselves "bodymind" therapies—such as bioenergetics and focusing—deal mostly with the predifferentiated aspects of the body/mind interface, not with the transdifferentiated or truly integrated aspects. That is, these "bodymind" therapies deal with the pranic dimension of vital emotional energy, endoceptual felt meanings, and visceral psychology, as they move from the bodily dimensions to the mental dimensions (from prana-maya-kosha to mano-maya-kosha), the F-2 to F-3 range. The emphasis remains on what I am feeling, and how I can articulate these vague somatic gestalts. These therapies do not usually address the specific issues of worldcentric moral consciousness and/or transpersonal revelations (centauric and higher), although of course if these issues arise on their own most bodymind therapists will accommodate them. But the main focal point of somatic therapy remains endoceptual, not vision-logic (see chart 1a). Nonetheless, bodywork of various sorts, as a *foundation*, remains fundamental to all subsequent phases of integral therapy (mind to soul to spirit), in my opinion. See note 8.14.

36. In the stream of evolution, we can trace cosmogenetic, phylogenetic, ontogenetic, and microgenetic development. Cosmogenesis refers to the developments in the physiosphere, leading, via systems far from equilibrium, to the brink of life forms, whereupon phylogenetic evolution begins, within which ontogenetic evolution unfolds. It is not that any of these strictly recapitulates the others, only that the basic holons out of which each is built can only, after they have creatively emerged, be arranged in so many ways, and thus subsequent developments follow the grooves of previous selections—and hence, in broad outline, ontogeny recaps phylogeny recaps cosmogeny—each holon in each of the lines transcends and includes its predecessors.

Microgeny is the moment-to-moment unfolding of a developmental line. Generally speaking, microgeny recaps ontogeny. Thus, for example, a person at formop, who sees a tree and tells me about it, has this general microgenetic sequence: there is the sensation of the tree, which leads to perception, and an image of the tree forms; affective factors color this image (pleasant/unpleasant), and the person searches for a series of words (symbols and concepts) with which to label the tree; these concepts arise within the cognitive space of conop and formop, and the preconscious high-speed memory scan for appropriate words occurs within the given cultural background (the language is English, say, and not Italian), driven in part by a desire for intersubjective communication and mutual understanding. All of this summates the person saying to me, "I see a tree."

That microgenetic sequence recaps a person's own ontogenetic sequence (sensation to perception to impulse to image to symbol . . .). If I have only developed to conop, my microgenetic processes will stop at conop; if I have developed to the subtle, my microgenetic processes will continue into the subtle: the tree will be seen, *directly perceived*, not as a object out there in perspectival space, but as a radiant manifestation of spirit. Overall: microgeny recaps ontogeny recaps phylogeny recaps cosmogeny: matter to sensation to perception to impulse to image to symbol to concept to rule to formop to . . . whatever level in the Great Nest that I am presently adapted to. When the person turns to me and says, "I see a tree," the entire history of the Kosmos, up to that point, is enfolded in that simple utterance.

Not all processes in consciousness are "bottom up"; many are "top down"— that is, many start at my present level (or higher) and move down the great holarchy. When I have a creative vision (e.g., psychic level), I might translate that vision downward into vision-logic, or perhaps artistic expression, or even into simple images and symbols; I might execute my vision by beginning to convert it into overt behavior and thus materialize the vision: perhaps a new invention, a new piece of architecture, a new way to interact with others, writing a novel, and so on (e.g., will is a microgenetic involutionary imposing of the higher on the lower). In microgenetic evolution, processes move up to the highest that you are; in microgenetic involution, the highest you are moves down into lower processes. Both of these are very important; and they represent a sliding scale: the more you develop, the fuller the range through which both can move, until, with nondual awakening, they can literally move throughout the Kosmos.

37. Unfortunately, what many New Age new-paradigm thinkers mean by "depth" is actually something lower on the evolution line, not something deeper on that line.

38. See note 7.2.

39. Thus, to the standard three-variable (or "three-dimensional") model of individual subjective *structures*, *states*, and *realms*, we need to add different brain states (UR), types and levels of cultural values (LL), and modes of social institutions (LR). This gives us six independent variables, any one of which can be distorted or pathological, with concomitant reverberations throughout the others. The three-variable model marked phase-2 and phase-3; the six-variable model marked phase-4 (the four quadrants). See notes 1.3, 1.5, 1.9, 1.10, 8.1, 8.2, 12.12. For phases 2, 3, and 4, see note 9.15.

40. See also note 8.11.

41. The most prevalent and accessible forms of relationship therapy include family therapy and group therapy; classic approaches to each include those of Virginia Satir and Irvin Yalom, respectively. See also S. Gladding, *Family Therapy*, and Mikesell et al. (eds.), *Integrating Family Therapy*. "Relational therapy" in the broad sense also includes higher, spiritual relationships, for which the work of Robert Forman and the Forge Institute might be mentioned. See R. Forman in Crittenden et al., *Kindred Visions*.

CHAPTER 9. SOME IMPORTANT DEVELOPMENTAL STREAMS

1. As we have seen, the proximate self is both a constant function and a developmental stream. It is a system of various functional invariants (the locus of identity, will, metabolism, navigation, defenses, tension regulation, integration,

etc.), which also undergoes its own development through the basic waves in the Great Nest (generally summarized as the nine fulcrums). As the locus of integration, the self is also responsible for balancing and integrating all of the levels, lines, and states in the individual. In this chapter, we are looking specifically at some of the more important developmental lines.

2. But the number of individuals reaching the greater depth becomes less and less (evolution produces greater depth, less span). The higher stages contain within themselves all of the lower stages, and thus the higher holons *themselves* become more and more significant and encompassing (cells embrace molecules which embrace atoms); but fewer individuals reach the higher stages (the span becomes less: there are fewer cells than molecules, fewer molecules than atoms). For human beings and the stages of consciousness development, this does *not* mean that only a few people can reach the higher stages; it only means they have to pass through the lower stages first (so that the total number of lower stages will always be greater than the higher, simply because growth starts at the lower; but growth can continue, and thus everybody at the lower can theoretically reach the higher). An atom cannot become a cell; but a precon individual *can* become con and then postcon.

Although I sometimes use "theocentric" and "theosphere" for the general transpersonal realms, I prefer terms like "pneumocentric" and "pneumosphere," in order to avoid confusion with mythic theism, which is almost always, as we saw, ethnocentric. The mythic God/dess is said to be universal, and all can be saved—but *only* if you embrace that particular God/dess.

3. Technically, I distinguish between the basic-structure needs and the self-needs. *Basic-structure needs* (or simply basic needs) are those that involve the constant functioning of the basic structures (insofar as they have emerged in a person's development). Basic needs include physical exchange (food, water, warmth); biological exchange (especially breath, sex, élan vital); mental exchange (communication, exchange of symbols and units of meaning), and so forth. As explained in *Up from Eden* and *A Sociable God*, every basic structure (or basic wave in the Great Nest) is a *system of relational exchanges* with other holons in the world at a similar level of structural development, and its very life depends upon those exchanges (all agency is agency-in-communion): hence, that *dependence* is inwardly *felt as a need*.

Likewise with the *self-needs*, except that, where the basic needs *remain in existence* (due to the enduring nature of the basic structures and their functional relationships), the self-needs are mostly transitional, phase-specific, and temporary, lasting only as long as the self is at a particular level of consciousness. Maslow's needs hierarchy (except for the physiological level) is a classic self-needs hierarchy, as are the motivational aspects of Loevinger's ego development. Thus, the self moves from impulsive needs to safety needs to conformist needs to autonomous needs, and each time it does so *the needs of the previous stage tend to be replaced by those of the higher stage*. At the autonomous stage, for example, one does not *simultaneously* have a huge set of impulsive needs— those have been transcended (barring fixation, dissociated subpersonalities, etc.); and yet the corresponding basic structures of those lower levels (images, symbols, and concepts) *remain perfectly present and fully functioning*, because they are basic rungs in the ladder of existence, and not a temporary by-product of the self's climb up those rungs. Thus those basic needs are still present and functioning (the need for food, breath, symbol exchange, and so on).

Overall, then, a person's *total motivations* include all of the basic-structure needs that have emerged to date (e.g., food, sex, symbolic communication, God communion), *plus* the major present self-need (e.g., safety, belongingness, self-esteem, self-transcendence), which is generated by the proximate self's exclusive identification with a particular basic structure or level of consciousness. I have included both of these two major types of needs in the "levels of food" chart; they are both the products of the demands of relational exchange at all levels.

In standard motivation theory, it is common to represent a "tendency to behavior" (T_B) as being the product of drive, expectation, and value $(T_B = D \times E \times V)$. For example, my tendency to go to the refrigerator to get something to eat is a product of how hungry (D) I am (the more hungry, the more likely I will go); the expectation (E) that I can find something in the frig (perhaps I realize there isn't much food in the frig; the more I expect something to be there, the more likely I will go); and the value (V) of what's there (what if I know there are only sardines, and I hate sardines; the more I value what is there, the more likely I will go).

Thus, overall behavior, in my opinion, is a summation of all of the basic and self drives, the expectations of satisfying them, and the values placed on them at any given moment. The result is a fairly sophisticated calculus of motivations spanning the entire spectrum of consciousness.

The aim of a complete course of development is to divest the basic structures of any sense of exclusive self, and thus free the basic needs from their contamination by the needs of the separate-self sense. When the basic structures are freed from the immortality projects of the separate self, they are free to return to their natural functional relationships: one eats without making food a religion, one communicates without desire to dominate, one exchanges mutual recognition without angling for self-gain. The separate self, by climbing up and off the ladder of the Great Chain, disappears as an alienated and alienating entity, ends its self-needs altogether, and thus is left with the simple and spontaneous play of the basic needs and their relationships as they easily unfold: when hungry, we eat; when tired, we sleep. The self has been returned to the Self, all self-needs have been met and thus discarded, and the basic needs alone remain, not so much as needs, but as the networks of communions that are Spirit's relationships with and as this world.

4. I sometimes use "worldview" and "worldspace" synonymously, although technically the former refers more to the cognitive component of a worldspace; worldspace itself includes all manner of cultural contexts, backgrounds, and practices, some of which are nondiscursive and precognitive.

5. See *Sex, Ecology, Spirituality*, 2nd ed., chap. 14, note 17, for an extensive discussion of the fact that subjective intentionality arises within an intersubjective worldspace, and a critique of theories ignoring this.

6. See notes 8.14 and 8.35.

7. See note 4.15. For the gender-neutral status of the basic developmental stages, see, e.g., two widely respected textbooks, Shaffer, *Social and Personality Development,* and Sroufe et al., *Child Development.* See also *The Eye of Spirit.*

8. Joyce Nielsen gives an excellent overview of a feminism using all four quadrants ("Fusion or Fission?," in J. Crittenden et al., *Kindred Visions,* forthcoming). See also Kaisa Puhakka, "The Spiritual Liberation of Gender," and Elizabeth Debold, "Beyond Gender," both in *Kindred Visions.*

9. See notes 1.3, 1.5, 1.9, 1.10, 8.1, 8.2, 8.39, 12.12.

10. I have not differentiated the examples in chart 8 into level of the subject (producing the art) and level of the object (being depicted); both are simply included on the chart, though the reader is invited to make the appropriate distinctions. For example, the sensorimotor realm depicted by magic is Paleolithic art, by perspectival reason is empirical Realism and Naturalism; the subtle depicted by mythic is literal religious iconic art, by the mental-ego is Fantastic Realist, and so on.

11. See notes 1.3, 1.5, 1.9, 1.10, 8.1, 8.2., 8.39, 12.12.

12. See *The Marriage of Sense and Soul* and *A Brief History of Everything* for a full discussion of this theme.

13. "Aesthetics," as I use the term in the very broadest sense, means the direct apprehension of form, in any domain. In this broad sense, it is quite similar to empiricism in the broad sense: sensory empiricism, mental empiricism, spiritual empiricism. With the differentiations of modernity, Western philosophy, following Kant, decided for the most part to make *spirituality* a matter of intersubjective *morals* (Lower Left), instead of seeing that authentic spirituality is also a matter of direct personal experience, radical empiricism, immediate phenomenology, and—in all those senses—aesthetic apprehension (Upper Left). For the great contemplative traditions, spiritual experience is a direct "inner" apprehension of immediate forms in consciousness, unfolding from gross forms to subtle forms, which are finally released into causal formlessness, and forms that therefore become more and more sublime (aesthetic). Spirituality also involves the intersubjective sharing of these forms in morals, ethics, sangha, and discourse, but it cannot (contra Kant) be reduced to mere moral injunctions.

More narrowly (and more traditionally), I also use "aesthetics" to mean the apprehension of forms judged to be pleasing, beautiful, sublime; the subjective judgments that are involved in judging forms to be beautiful; and the entire sphere of art, artistic production, and art criticism. Beauty is the depth of a holon, or its transparency to Spirit. Art is anything with a frame around it.

See *Sex, Ecology, Spirituality,* 2nd ed. and *The Eye of Spirit* (especially chaps. 4 and 5) for extensive discussion of art, art theory, and aesthetics. For an interesting view of aesthetic apprehension as spiritual discipline in Aurobindo and Tagore, see W. Cenkner, "Art as Spiritual Discipline in the Lives and Thought of Rabindranath Tagore and Sri Aurobindo Ghose," in *Ultimate Reality and Spiritual Discipline,* edited by J. Duerlinger.

14. For an extended discussion of development in the Big Three, see note 14.20.

15. That is, from a phase-2 to a phase-3 model.

I have, for convenience, divided my overall work into four general phases. Phase-1 was Romantic (a "recaptured-goodness" model), which posited a spectrum of consciousness ranging from subconscious to self-conscious to superconscious (or id to ego to God), with the higher stages viewed as a return to, and recapture of, original but lost potentials. Phase-2 was more specifically evolutionary or developmental (a "growth-to-goodness" model), with the spectrum of consciousness unfolding in developmental stages or levels. Phase-3 added developmental lines to those developmental levels—that is, numerous different developmental lines (such as cognitive, conative, affective, moral, psychological, spiritual, etc.) proceeding in a relatively independent manner through the basic levels of the overall spectrum of consciousness. Phase-4 added the idea of the four quadrants—the subjective (intentional), objective (behavioral), intersubjective (cultural), and interobjective (social) dimensions—of each of those levels and lines, with the result being—or at least attempting to be—a comprehensive or integral philosophy. The present book is, of course, a phase-4 work. For a discussion of these phases, see *The Eye of Spirit* and *One Taste*, Nov. 16 entry.

16. In fact, as it develops, even the gross-cognitive line becomes more and more subtle: whereas sensorimotor cognition is the perception of the material environment, and concrete operational cognition is "thought operating on environment," formop is "thought operating on thought," and thus formop is already, to a significant degree, involved with subtle perception. However, this perception is still organized such that its ultimate referents are objects and operations in the gross realm, and thus I include formop in the gross-cognitive line. Vision-logic can partake of both gross and subtle realms, and can be included as an important component in both of those lines. In the gross line, vision-logic is generally the very highest and concluding stage; in the subtle, it is an intermediate stage, preceded by etheric, astral, fantasy, and imagination, and superceded by psychic vision, subtle archetype, and intermediate-to-advanced meditative states.

Many psychological theorists who are investigating the subtle line of development—e.g., the Jungians, Jean Bolen, James Hillman—often confuse the lower, prepersonal levels in the subtle line with the higher, transpersonal levels in that line, with unfortunate results. James Hillman, for example, has carefully explored the preformal, imaginal levels of the subtle line, but constantly confuses them with the postformal levels of the subtle line. Just because theorists are working with dreams/images/visions does not mean they are necessarily working with the higher levels of that line (such as savikalpa samadhi or transcendental illumination); they are often working with the lower, prepersonal-to-personal levels in the subtle line (which they often mistakenly call the "soul," when what they are working with is more often the typhon, etheric/astral sheath, prana-maya-kosha, images/symbols, preformal mythic fantasies, and so on). All of the levels in the subtle line are important, but should not be confused or equated on that account. To do so is another type of "collapsing fallacy" (see note 9.18), where the various waves of a given stream of consciousness are collapsed and fused, simply because they are all in the same stream.

17. The causal sheath is viewed, by both Vedanta and Vajrayana, as the root source, and thus the "cause," of all the other levels of consciousness and reality. At the same time, it is itself one level among other levels (albeit the highest), and thus it is not ultimate. The ultimate or nondual state is not one level among others, but the ground, suchness, or emptiness of all levels and all states. That which obscures the realization of the nondual domain is precisely the subject/object dualism, and this dualism first arises in the causal domain as a constriction or contraction in consciousness (namely, as the dualism between subject and object, in this case, the unmanifest world of empty consciousness and the manifest world of objects). This dualistic contraction is the capacity for focused *attention*, which attends to this by *ignoring* that, and this *ignorance* (or attention forgetful of its nondual ground) is said to be the root cause of all suffering. The root of this attention is the causal realm, which is a constriction around the Heart, and appears in the form of the Witness, or the pure Subject split from the world of objects. This pure Witness or pure Subject then loses itself in the world of objects, which further fragments and splits consciousness, as it identifies with a soul, then an ego, then a body—all of which are actually objects, not the real Subject or Witness. In order to reverse this "fall," an individual has *first* to reestablish the capacity for Witnessing (by strengthening the capacity for attention, equanimity, and detachment—or disidentification from the objects of awareness, including the body, the ego, and the soul); and *second*, to then dissolve the causal Witness—and the root of attention—into pure nondual One Taste. In any event, the causal, as the root of attention, can be followed as a separate line of development in any of its forms of focused awareness, body to mind to soul to source.

18. To the gross, subtle, and causal lines, I have also added a "nondual line," for tracing the development of *states of subject-object union*, from prenatal to perinatal (e.g., cosmic fusion) to childhood (e.g., emotional bonding states) to adulthood (e.g., flow states) to states/traits of postformal samadhi to pure nondual One Taste. We are justified in including this nondual cognitive line because, just as with other cognitive lines, which were based on the existence of the *natural states* of waking, dreaming, and deep sleep (and thus available to all), so this nondual line is based on a *natural given*, namely, the natural mind or the primordial mind, the nondual mind that is ever-present in all sentient beings.

Unfortunately, most Romantic writers confuse low levels of the nondual line with high levels in that line, and then assume that contacting the higher levels in that line is actually a recontacting (or recapturing) of the lower levels in that line. This confusion is based, not so much on a pre/trans fallacy (which the Romantics deny anyway; this present critique does not rely on it), but rather on a type of "collapsing fallacy." That is, simply because subject-object fusion states can give a sense of wholeness, *any and all unity states are equated*, and thus, higher and lower fusion states are all collapsed into a single "Ground." Then *anytime* a unity state occurs, it is assumed that it must be due to contacting or recontacting this *single* Ground, whereas, in fact, the nondual line itself unfolds across numerous quite different waves. But if these are collapsed, then anytime any subject and any object are fused, it is assumed to be the action of this "single" Ground, so that this abstraction called "Ground" is reified and made the source of all nondual states. (Washburn typically exemplifies this collapsing fallacy, as do most of the Romantic theorists. I believe they also commit variations on the pre/trans fallacy, but that is an entirely separate issue and is not a part of this particular critique.) See note 9.16.

As with the other cognitive lines and states, the nondual itself only becomes a *permanent trait* with sustained postformal, post-postconventional development. Nonetheless, all four realms (psychic, subtle, causal, and nondual) can be traced as relatively independent cognitive lines all the way back to the earliest of stages.

19. Another benefit of this way of conceiving the relation between the cognitive lines is that it allows, for example, subtle cognition to begin *alongside* gross cognition, not simply *after* it. In the gross-reflecting cognitive line, the very highest stages involve, as I suggested (see note 9.16), various types of vision-logic. To use Commons and Richards's version, the highest levels of the gross-cognitive line involve meta-systematic, paradigmatic, and cross-paradigmatic thinking (which work with systems, systems of systems, and systems of systems of systems). I believe that is true; but that does *not* mean that being able to think about systems of systems of systems is a necessary prerequisite for developing into the psychic, subtle, and causal realms (which it would be if these were all sequential stages in a monolithic line). A *basic competence* in vision-logic is certainly required in order for overall consciousness development to move permanently into the higher realms (see notes 8.4, 9.27), but cross-paradigmatic thinking is simply an extreme accomplishment in the gross-cognitive line, which may or may *not* be mastered by various individuals in their overall growth into the transpersonal realms. Seeing gross, subtle, and causal cognitive lines as in some ways parallel allows us to further accommodate that fact.

But that doesn't mean gross, subtle, or causal cognition can be bypassed in general development, or that sequential development loses its significance. First of all, there is no evidence that gross, subtle, or causal realms can be significantly bypassed, only that the extreme versions of some of their stages are not necessary for further development (see notes 8.4, 9.27, 9.28). Second, imbalances in, or between, any lines contribute to pathology. Schizophrenia is in some ways the classic example of what happens when people get lost in subtle-cognition without a grounding in gross-cognition. Third, the strongest drive of the self is to *integrate* all of the various developmental levels and lines in its own makeup, and an unbalanced growth—too much subtle, not enough gross—is felt as a major self-dissonance. Fourth, the highest developmental insight is nondual, or an integration of all three major realms in one embrace, which includes a *competent* gross, subtle, and causal consciousness—a major defect in one will obviously preclude balanced integration.

Thus, even though various streams can progress relatively independently through the waves in the Great Nest, a fully *integral development* still involves the holarchical unfolding of all of the major levels in a conscious fashion, with the self fully adapting to each. See notes 8.4, 9.27, 9.28.

20. *One Taste*, Nov. 16 and 17. The self and therefore *all of the self-related lines* can be modeled in this fashion, with gross, subtle, causal, and nondual streams (of morals, perspectives, drives, etc.) developing relatively independently. It must be strongly emphasized, however, that the number of these streams—if any—that actually develop independently *can only be determined by careful research guided by models of this type.* The lines (cognitive, self-related, etc.) are prevented from total independence by both the self's overriding drive for integration and the necessities of holarchical development in general. Many of these lines are necessary but not sufficient for others, and all of them are bound to some degree by the self-system (see *The Eye of Spirit*). Although a few of these relationships can be logically deduced, most of them can only be determined by careful research. Recently, several transpersonal theorists have proposed models of this type (i.e., phase-3 models), but they do so by simply proclaiming them to be true. I believe they are true to some degree; but to what degree, only research can tell.

21. See note 2.2 for some of the extensive research on developmental stages.

22. In this general scheme of three major self lines (ego, soul, and Self), what I am calling "frontal" or "ego" includes all of the self-stages in the gross and gross-reflecting realm (i.e., bodyself, persona, ego, and centaur); "soul" includes psychic and subtle; and "Self" includes causal and nondual. Since I am postulating that these particular independent lines are based on the *natural states* of consciousness of gross, subtle, causal, and nondual, those are the four independent lines of cognition and self-stages that I am proposing. (In the text I am treating causal and nondual as one.)

    Within the gross domain the various self-stages, although they overlap once they emerge, nonetheless still emerge in a generally holarchical fashion (bodyself to persona to ego to centaur), as research overwhelmingly continues to confirm. Alongside those developments, the soul and Self can unfold in often independent fashions, in ways that I will suggest in the text, and, to the extent they show *development* (and not just states), they also follow the holarchical contours of their own unfolding streams, with all of them nestled in the Great Holarchy of Being.

23. These are all of those items that are not measured by most developmental psychologists, which is why they tend only to see frontal self-development.

24. The pure transcendental Self or Witness does not itself develop, since it is sheer formlessness. However, access to this Self does develop, and that is what I mean by development in this line. For all three self lines, see *One Taste*, Nov. 17 entry.

25. See Vaughan, *The Inward Arc* and *Shadows of the Sacred*. See also note 8.20.

26. See notes 8.14 and 8.35.

27. Because vision-logic is listed as a general wave in the Great Nest, does that mean, *in overall consciousness evolution*, that a general (not extreme) competence in vision-logic is required for stable growth into higher levels? Yes, I very much believe so. Why? Because everything from the golden rule to the bodhisattva vow is impossible to comprehend without vision-logic. You cannot sincerely vow to liberate all beings if you cannot take the perspective of all beings

in the first place, and, researchers agree, that is a vision-logic capacity. We are not talking about an extreme development in vision-logic (such as cross-paradigmatic thinking; see notes 8.4, 9.19), but simply its general capacity for postconventional, worldcentric, multiple perspective taking. Without general vision-logic as a foundation, the higher levels (psychic, subtle, causal, and nondual) are experienced only as passing, altered states, without becoming permanent realizations, and for the simple reason that it is the nature of those higher states to be universal and global, and without a frontal development *capable of carrying that global perspective* (namely, vision-logic), those states cannot "fit" permanently, and without distortion, into the self. Only as vision-logic becomes a permanent capacity can the even-higher levels themselves become permanent.

Notice that, in the traditions, it is said that although all sentient beings contain Spirit, only human beings can *fully awaken* to that Spirit. In Buddhism, for example, not even the Gods and Goddesses (*devas*)—or any of the beings in the subtle realm—can become fully enlightened. Nor can those who are absorbed in the causal unmanifest (since they are seeking their own nirvanic salvation, neglecting others, and thus they are not bodhisattvas). In other words, even if we achieve extraordinary development in the subtle line (as do the Gods and Goddesses), and even if we achieve extraordinary development in the causal line (as do Pratyeka-buddhas or solitary causal realizers), we still cannot achieve full Enlightenment. Why? Because our development is not *integral*—it does not include gross and subtle and causal in an equal embrace. Only as consciousness awakens in all three realms—gross, subtle, and causal—can we hope to be of service to all sentient beings and thus fulfill the primordial bodhisattva vow ("no matter how limitless beings, I vow to liberate them all"). And only vision-logic in the gross realm can grasp all sentient beings in the gross realm. Thus, without vision-logic, there is no final Enlightenment. Of course individuals can achieve extraordinary development in the subtle and causal lines (as do the Gods and Pratyeka-buddhas), but without an integral embrace, including vision-logic, one cannot become samyak-sambuddha: a fully Realized One.

A few words about vision-logic itself. As a basic structure, it includes, as subholons in its own being, all of the previous basic structures, sensorimotor to emotive to fantasy to formal to its own postformal being, and, ideally, it integrates all of these components. It is not that vision-logic is without fantasy or emotion or rules, but that it simply holds all of them in its own wider space, so that all of them can flourish to an even greater degree. Commons and Richards, Fischer, and Sinnott tend to emphasize the cognitive component of vision-logic (and often its extreme developments), while Basseches, Pascual-Leone, Labouvie-Vief, and Deirdre Kramer highlight more of its dialectical, visionary, integrative capacities. Arieti stresses that vision-logic is an integration of primary and secondary processes—fantasy and logic—and thus it can be very creative (the "magic synthesis"), and Jean Gebser stresses the transparency, integrative capacity, and multiple perspectives of the "integral-aperspectival" structure. All of those, in my opinion, are important snapshots of vision-logic taken from different angles.

Vision-logic, like any cognitive capacity, can take as its *object* any of the *levels* in any of the *quadrants*, resulting in drastically different perceptions. To focus first on the quadrants. When vision-logic looks at the Lower-Right quadrant, the result is dynamical systems theory in any of many forms, from cybernetics to chaos to social autopoiesis to complexity theories. What they all focus on are the networks of *interobjective* processes and the dynamical patterns of existence and development. When applied to the human aspects of the Lower-Right quadrant, the result is a social systems science (e.g., Parsons, Merton) that highlights the importance and influence of the material modes of social interaction, forces of production, and relations of production (exemplars include Comte, Marx, Lenski, Luhmann).

When vision-logic looks at the Upper-Right quadrant, the result is a systems view of the individual organism, which depicts consciousness as an emergent of hierarchically integrated organic and neuronal networks. This emergent/connectionist view is perhaps the dominant model of cognitive science at this point, and is nicely summarized in Alwyn Scott's *Stairway to the Mind*, the "stairway" being the hierarchy of emergents said to result in consciousness. All of these emergents and networks—including all of the very influential models of autopoiesis—involve *objective systems* described in *third-person* it-language; a similar objectivistic view of consciousness can be found in Tart's systems approach to states of consciousness. I am not saying these accounts are wrong; I am saying they cover, at best, only one-fourth of the story. I myself use these approaches, as well as structuralism, which are all Right-Hand approaches to the phenomenon of consciousness; but I emphasize that consciousness itself must *also* be studied in first-person, Left-Hand, phenomenal approaches—direct experiential investigations of consciousness via introspection and meditation (see chap. 14). For convenience' sake, I sometimes label a few of the levels in the Left-Hand quadrants with structural terms (e.g., conop, formop), but those are only markers for phenomenal events accurately seen and described only in first- and second-person terms. See *Sex, Ecology, Spirituality*, 2nd ed., CW 6 (especially chaps. 4 and 14) and "An Integral Theory of Consciousness," *Journal of Consciousness Studies* 4, no. 1 (1997), pp. 71–93 (CW 7).

When vision-logic looks at the Lower-Left quadrant, the result is an appreciation of the vast role of cultural contexts and backgrounds, a grasp of the role of mutual understanding, an intense focus on discourse, and a general understanding of hermeneutics. Exemplars in this approach include Heidegger, Hans-Georg Gadamer, Charles Taylor, Dilthey, and Kuhn, among others.

Incidentally, when these cultural or intersubjective *signifieds*, in their intersubjective semantic fields (LL), are viewed in terms of the exterior structure of their *material signifiers*—written word, spoken word, grammar and syntax (LR)—and especially when these signifiers are cut loose from any referents—the result is various forms of postmodern poststructuralism, from Foucault's archaeology (the grammar of discourse/archives) to Foucault's genealogy (the interobjective structures of power/knowledge) to Derrida's grammatology (the study of the chains of written signifiers)—all of which are LR approaches to LL phenomena, approaches that, used *exclusively*, destroy any genuinely intersubjective realms and, via performative contradiction, deny any existent referents. Again, I am not saying these approaches are wrong, but that they favor only one quadrant (in this case, they use LR techniques in an attempt to elucidate LL phenomena, and to the extent that these approaches go too far and deny the existence of the LL on its own terms, they end up committing subtle reductionism), and when they thus claim to have the final word, wind up in various untenable positions. (See *The Eye of Spirit*, chap. 5, note 12, for a discussion of an integral semiotics of signifier, signified, semantics, and syntax.)

When vision-logic is applied to the Upper-Left quadrant—when vision-logic looks within at its own domain—one of several things can result. First of all, as with any basic structure, the fact that a person has access to vision-logic does not mean that the person is *living from* vision-logic. Just as a person can have cognitive access to formop, and yet the self can still be at moral stage 1, so a person can have access to vision-logic and still remain at any of the lower levels of self and self-line development—moral stage 1, an impulsive self, safety needs, and so on (as we saw, basic structures are necessary, but not sufficient, for other developments). Thus, a person can be at a very low level of self, moral, and spiritual development, and yet still be a great systems theorist (they are applying vision-logic to the exterior world, but not to themselves). This is why simply learning the "new paradigm" does not necessarily transform a person, and why many "holistic" approaches often leave interior transformations untouched. (See *One Taste* and *Boomeritis*.)

It is only as the person's self—the center of gravity of the proximate self—moves from conop (where it is a conformist self or persona) to formop (where it is a postconventional self or mature ego) to postformal vision-logic (where it is a centaur, or relatively integrated, postconventional, global, autonomous, existential self)—only with that interior vertical transformation does vision-logic come to be directly applied to the person himself. His moral sense is thus postconventional and worldcentric; his needs are for self-actualization; his worldview is universal integral; and he stands on the brink of more permanent transformation into the transpersonal realms.

Likewise, vision-logic can be applied (as can most cognition) to any of the major *levels* (or realms) in any of the quadrants. As indicated in the text, I usually simplify these realms to body, mind, and spirit (or prepersonal, personal, and transpersonal). In its own quadrant (UL), vision-logic can look down to matter, across at mind, or up to spirit. Looking down to matter is the same as looking at any of the Right-Hand quadrants, since they are all material, and the result, we saw, is systems theory. Looking across at other minds is the same as looking at its own level in the Lower-Left quadrant, and the result, we saw, is hermeneutics. Looking up to spirit—or, alternatively, having a spiritual peak experience—results in the higher realms being interpreted according to the structures of vision-logic itself, and the result is what I have called mandalic reason (see *Eye to Eye*).

28. Can the subtle realm itself be completely bypassed in overall consciousness de-

velopment? Not in my opinion. Some theorists have suggested that various traditions—such as Zen—do not explore the subtle realm in their meditation practices and yet they achieve causal/nondual Enlightenment, so the subtle as a stage is not needed (or it can be completely skipped). Actually, all it means is that an extensive exploration of the subtle realm can to some degree be bypassed. But the subtle realm itself cannot.

The general subtle realm includes, for example, the dream state, and even fully enlightened beings continue to dream, but they do so *while remaining conscious* (e.g., lucid and pellucid dreaming; see *One Taste*). In other words, the subtle realm has become a *permanent conscious adaptation* in their own case. Intentionally and extensively exploring that realm as a means of awakening can to some degree be skipped, but not the realm itself, nor the fact that it becomes a *permanent basic structure* in the consciousness of the awakened one.

What can happen, particularly in the schools that emphasize causal and nondual techniques, is that extensive exploration of the subtle realm is largely set aside, and cognition in the causal and nondual lines is emphasized. Of course, the subtle realm is still present, since these individuals continue to dream. However, as causal witnessing becomes stronger and stronger, it tends to persist through the waking and into the dreaming state (pellucid dreaming—see *One Taste*); and thus, although the person is not *intentionally* investigating the subtle/dream realm, they are in fact *objectifying it* (thus transcending it, and thus including it in consciousness). The subtle as a *path* has to some degree been bypassed; but the subtle realm *itself* is transcended and included, as always, in permanent higher development. This *inclusion of the subtle* is also part of the self's inherent drive to integration. Thus, in overall consciousness development, the subtle realm is a permanent stage and structure in one's full development. See also *Sex, Ecology, Spirituality*, 2nd ed. (especially chap. 7) for a discussion of this theme. To say that somebody has "skipped" the subtle, even if it were possible (which it isn't), would only to be say that they had not completed integral development. See note 9.27.

Chapter 10. Spirituality

1. There is an important difference between the terms "postformal" and "postconventional," since the former usually refers to cognitive structures, the latter to the self-related stages (such as morals). Thus, in the cognitive line, development moves from preoperational to concrete operational to formal operational, and higher stages in that line are called *postformal*. The term *postformal* can technically apply to *all* cognitive developments higher than formal operational, and that would include both higher personal levels, such as vision-logic, and the more purely transpersonal cognitions (psychic, subtle, etc.). However, in the literature, postformal usually means just vision-logic (so that the more purely transpersonal cognitions we ought to call *post-postformal*; nonetheless, context will tell which I mean).

These cognitive developments (preop to conop to formop to postformal) are said to be necessary, but not sufficient, for the corresponding self-related stages (such as self-identity, morals, role-taking, and so on), which are generally said to develop from preconventional to conventional to postconventional, which covers development into the highest of the personal domains (the centauric). Several researchers (e.g., Kohlberg, Cook-Greuter, Wade, Alexander) have proposed that the self-related stages can also continue into genuinely *transpersonal* stages, in which case, to be consistent, we should refer to them as *post-postconventional* (which is what I do).

Nonetheless, you can see the semantic difficulties involved. There is no consistent agreement in the literature about how to use these "post" terms. I have tried to be consistent in my own usage, but the context in each case must be used for an accurate appraisal.

2. The difficulty with this definition is: how do you define a separate spiritual line in terms that do *not* use the other developmental lines, such as affect, cognition, or morals? In other words, if you say spirituality is one's capacity for love, love (or affect) is already itself a separate line, so you cannot use it to define spirituality if you want spirituality to be something different, to be its own separate line. Likewise, you cannot say spirituality involves awareness, cognition, morals, compassion, altruism, sense of self, or drives, for those are already separate lines themselves. In other words, coming up with a developmental line that is distinctively and purely "spiritual" is fairly difficult.

James Fowler, for example, has proposed that "faith" develops in five or six stages, but his test results are virtually indistinguishable from Kohlberg's, leading many theorists to suspect they are simply the same thing and Fowler has added nothing new. However, I think Fowler's stages of faith are a legitimate, distinct line of development (because they are actually a useful amalgam, as I will discuss below), but it does point up the difficulty involved with this definition. I have also suggested (in *The Eye of Spirit*) that *concern* (Tillich's definition of spirituality as "ultimate concern") might also be considered a separate spiritual line of development, and there are others that seem to fit the bill (e.g., Baldwin). In any event, they would, by definition, show stage-like development.

However, what most people mean when they speak of spirituality as a separate line of development is actually *an amalgam of other developmental lines*, which is probably how people often experience "spirituality" in any event, and accordingly this is a very legitimate and important approach. Fowler's stages of faith, for example, are a mixture of morals, capacity for role taking, and worldviews. As I said, I believe that is a completely legitimate approach. Moreover, it is extremely common. Almost all of the theorists presented in charts 6a–c use this amalgam approach, even when they focus on more specific items (such as meditative experiences, contact with the numinous, and so on). These amalgams are important because in all of the cases presented in these charts, the amalgams have been shown to unfold in a developmental stage sequence as a functional grouping. The aspects of spirituality presented in charts 6a–c, in other words, definitely show holarchical stages.

3. The important research of Engler and Brown is presented in *Transformations of Consciousness*, chaps. 1, 6, 7, 8; my italics.

4. Blanck and Blanck, in a series of books (e.g., *Ego Psychology, Ego Psychology II, Beyond Ego Psychology*) have summarized a century of psychoanalytic theory and research on the development of the self by saying that the *self metabolizes experience to build structure.* This is also consonant with Piaget's work on constructivism (and thought as internalized action). The idea, as I would reconstruct it, is that the inchoate flux of experience—beginning with the early stages, dominated by impulsiveness, immediate gratification, and overwhelming emotional flooding—is slowly "metabolized" or processed by the self into more stable patterns (or holistic structures) of experience and awareness. These holistic structures allow the self to transcend its immersion and embeddedness in a lower wave by constructing more encompassing and holistic waves. Thus, temporary experiences are metabolized to produce enduring holistic adaptations. I believe the same process is at work in converting temporary peak experiences and altered states into enduring traits and structures of consciousness—which is why I have always included "metabolism" as one of the main characteristics of the self.

CHAPTER 11. IS THERE A CHILDHOOD SPIRITUALITY?

1. Roger Walsh, who is familiar with research on human happiness, denies even this version of a childhood Eden, and points out how little research supports it. "This is the childhood-is-bliss myth." As parents will attest, infants spend much of their time crying.

2. For an overview of childhood peak experiences, see E. Hoffman, "Peak experiences in childhood," *Journal of Humanistic Psychology* 1, 38 (1998), pp. 109–20.

   This does point up the difficulty of calling childhood peak experiences "spiritual" in an unalloyed sense. For example, as I started to say in the text, if a child at the early preconventional moral stage—which cannot take the role of other—has a peak experience, it will be captured in an egocentric, narcissistic orbit. *Unable to take the role of other* means unable to genuinely care for the other or possess authentic love for the other (as anything but a narcissistic extension of self). And just how authentically spiritual can a lack of care and lack of love be? No matter how authentic the spiritual realm might be that is "peaked," it is instantly snapped up and necessarily clothed in the psychological structures that are present at that time (cognitive, moral, ego, and so on), and the bulk of those, research confirms, are preconventional. This does not preclude other types of spiritual access (see the next paragraph in the text), but it does show how very careful we must be in these interpretations of childhood spirituality.

   It should also be noted that almost all of the evidence for infant and child spiritual experiences (including perinatal recollections) comes from *adults* who are "remembering" these early experiences. The grave (though I do not think fatal) difficulty with this evidence is that, except for massive regression to preverbal states (which cannot even be verbally communicated at the time), most of these "recollections" occur *through* the psychological structures that are irreversibly in place in the adult doing the recollecting, and thus the capacities and competences of these structures (such as the capacity to take the role of other) are *retrojected* (as Roger Walsh puts it) back into the childhood states, whereupon childhood incorrectly appears to be a time of wonderful fluidity *plus* the higher adult capacities, when it is no such thing at all. As Becker and Geer put it, "Changes in the social environment and in the self inevitably produce transformations of perspective, and it is characteristic of such transformations that the person finds it difficult or impossible to remember his former actions, outlook or feelings. Reinterpreting things from his new perspective, he cannot give an accurate account of the past, for the concepts in which he thinks about it have changed and with them his perceptions and memories."

Moreover, just as in the example of videotaping children who go through a profound developmental milestone—when they have no experience of doing so at all—these "retrojections" do not give the slightest warning that they are operative. The person "recalling" an early childhood peak experience will often describe it in terms of perspectivism, being sensitive to the role of others, taking their viewpoints, and so on—when a massive amount of research on actual children at that age *shows no evidence of any of those capacities at all*. Furthermore, on the occasions when an early childhood or even infantile recollection is shown to be veridical (e.g., when I was 8 months old, mother got very ill), those are often merely sensorimotor imprints that can be resurrected and then retrofitted with adult perspectives.

My point is simply that, no matter how authentic might be some of the realms "peeked" into with a childhood peak experience, the *interpretation* and *expression* of those realms can only occur through whatever structures (linguistic, cognitive, moral, etc.) *are actually present*, and this does not deny, but does considerably complicate, the existence of "childhood spirituality."

3. See *The Eye of Spirit*. For one version of this view, see T. Armstrong, "Transpersonal experience in childhood," *Journal of Transpersonal Psychology* 16, 2 (1984), pp. 207–31. Note that most of his examples are monological experiences (preconventional), pointing out again the difficulty in calling them "spiritual."

4. Notice that these "glory" potentials are not something that are part of the infantile stage itself—they are lingering impressions from other, *higher* spheres. And therefore, what is *recaptured* in enlightenment is *not* the infantile structure itself, but the actual higher spheres. The Romantic notion that the infantile self *is itself* a primordial paradise remains therefore deeply mistaken. See also the "collapsing fallacy" on which the Romantic agenda rests; note 9.18.

5. See *The Eye of Spirit*, chap. 6, for a full discussion of this topic and a critique of Washburn's Romantic view, which depends on the collapsing fallacy (see note 9.18).

6. For a summary of this data, see Jenny Wade's *Changes of Mind*.

It should be emphasized that this deeper psychic self (or the subtle soul), which might be present in infancy, is *not* a causal or nondual self; it is not any sort of enlightened self or primal ground, but simply an intermediate level of the separate-self sense which migrates until Enlightenment. Romantic eulogizing of this separate-self sense is unwarranted.

7. None of this "watching from afar," however, is generally expressed by children at that time, possibly for the reasons I outlined in note 11.2 (they have not yet developed the frontal structures that could do the expressing). For this reason, none of this "deeper psychic" shows up on any of the tests developmentalists use. Nonetheless, a small amount of controversial evidence, summarized by Wade, suggest that this deeper psychic awareness undergoes a U-development, essentially the same U-development that tends to mark some of the subtle lines (as indicated, e.g., on chart 4b). As suggested in the text, however, this is not an unalloyed experience of the deeper psychic, because the structures that house it are still preconventional and egocentric. Only with the direct and permanent realization of the deeper psychic—which occurs at the psychic stage (or fulcrum-7)—does the soul itself begin to shine forth in its undiminished, unfiltered radiance.

Chapter 12. Sociocultural Evolution

1. For my numerous criticisms of the perennial philosophy, the classical Great Chain, and the traditionalists, see *One Taste*, June 5 entry; the Introductions to CW 2, 3, and 4; *The Eye of Spirit*, chaps. 1 and 2; and numerous entries in *Sex, Ecology, Spirituality,* 2nd ed. (CW 6).

2. See chap. 1 text ("The Great Nest Is a Potential, Not a Given") and notes 1.5, 8.2, and 12.1; see also the Introduction to CW 2, and *Sex, Ecology, Spirituality,* 2nd ed. (CW 6).

3. See *Sex, Ecology, Spirituality,* 2nd ed. (CW 6).

4. For an extensive discussion of this theme, see *The Marriage of Sense and Soul*.

5. See *Up from Eden*; and *Sex, Ecology, Spirituality,* 2nd ed. (CW 6); and *A Brief History of Everything* for a full discussion of this theme. I am talking here about collective evolution; individuals can advance on their own heroic efforts (usually in micro-communities).

6. Alternatively, the shaman might simply be at the magic level and have a temporary peak experience of the subtle realm. Should the shaman progress beyond random peak experiences, and begin to develop a competence in these temporary subtle journeys, even though his typical self remains at the magical structure, this indicates that, as per the discussion in Different Types of Cognitive Lines, the shaman is showing development in the subtle line, even while the gross line remains preformal and magical. In both of these cases, the subtle realm is distorted into preconventional and egocentric/power interpretations (as discussed in the text). But I also hold open the possibility, introduced in the text, that at least some shamans demonstrated frontal development into postconventional realms, which certainly seems possible, at least beginning with the late Paleolithic and Mesolithic (if there is evidence, as Habermas, Dobert, Nunner-Winkler et al. believe, that some individuals in foraging societies developed formop, I see no reason that a few could not have developed into postformal modes).

7. See R. Walsh, *The Spirit of Shamanism*.

8. Social systems theory remains indispensable for understanding the Lower-Right quadrant. The work of Talcott Parsons (and Robert Merton) is well-known, and still quite impressive. I would like especially to recommend the brilliant works of Jeffrey Alexander (*Theoretical Logic in Sociology*, four volumes; and *Twenty Lectures*) and Niklas Luhmann (especially *Social Systems*).

9. See, e.g., Thomas Sowell, *Marxism*; Leszek Kolakowski, *Main Currents of Marxism*, 3 vols.; A. Callari et al., *Marxism in the Postmodern Age*.

10. During the past several decades, it has been common for liberal scholars to assume that any sort of evolutionary theory of necessity marginalizes various peoples, and thus prevents their gaining the natural freedom that is every being's birthright. It has increasingly become obvious, however, that freedom is perhaps best defined as the freedom to have access to every level in the extraordinary spectrum of consciousness. The only way those levels become available is through growth and development and unfolding, and thus those liberal scholars who have shunned evolution have shunned an access to freedom for all of those whom they wished to protect. (See Afro-Caribbean specialist Maureen Silos's brilliant exposure of the standard liberal stance as being, in fact, highly reactionary, and evolutionary thinking as being the truly liberal stance, "The Politics of Consciousness," in J. Crittenden, *Kindred Visions*.)

11. G. Feuerstein, "Jean Gebser's Structures of Consciousness and Ken Wilber's Spectrum Model," *Kindred Visions*, edited by Crittenden et al. (forthcoming). For my critique of Gebser's archaic structure, see *Sex, Ecology, Spirituality*, 2nd ed. (CW6), note 17 for chap. 14.

12. Combs maintains that, in *Up from Eden*, I allow stages to be skipped, overlooking the fact that I presented each epoch as an average, not an absolute; and overlooking the fact that numerous altered states (or peak experiences) are available at all stages (both of those points are explained in the text and in note 12.14; see also the introduction to CW 2).

Combs then presents a three-dimensional model of consciousness that is in many ways indistinguishable from my three-variable model of structures, states, and realms, which Combs calls "structures, states, and planes." He claims that his model takes these three variables into account, and that my model does not, and thus he offers his model to "correct the liabilities" in mine, whereas in many ways he has simply restated my model. I am not accusing Combs of borrowing my model; I believe he arrived at it in a largely independent fashion. What I find lamentable is that Combs strongly claims that I do not deal with structures, states, and realms; this is an egregious misrepresentation of my work.

As for the particular version of this three-variable model that Combs presents, I believe it has some drawbacks, although I appreciate the care he has obviously given it; and I find it, on balance, to be a welcome addition to the field.

To start with the liabilities, Combs presents his version of states and structures by, in my opinion, getting the definitions of states and structures backwards. Instead of seeing that a given state (such as drug, waking, dreaming) can contain many different structures (e.g., the waking state can contain magic, mythic, and rational structures), Combs says that a given structure supports many different states (which is rarely true: the rational structure, for example, does not usually support the drunken state, the dream state, the meditative state, etc.).

This confusion of states and structures leads him to likewise misrepresent both the Vedanta and Mahayana systems because it forces him to confuse sheaths/levels with body/states. For example, in his Table 1 in chapter 6, he presents the Vedanta as giving five levels and a corresponding five bodies, but the Vedanta actually gives five levels and only three bodies, because the subtle body (corresponding with the dream state) actually supports three of the levels (or structures), as I explained in the text (see chap. 1). In other words, because Combs believes that one structure can house many states (when it is mostly the other way around), he does not see that in Vedanta one state supports several levels/structures/sheaths, so he is forced to misread the Vedanta as giving five bodies instead of three. For instance, he says "Next is the subtle body, termed the *vijnanamaya kosha*. . . ." But in fact the subtle body is termed *sukshma-sharira*, and it *supports* the vijnana-maya-kosha, the mano-maya-kosha, and the prana-maya-kosha—in other words, *three* levels/structures supported by *one* state/body. The sukshma-sharira is the vehicle of, for example, the dream state and the bardo state. Thus the correct view is that one state can support several levels or structures or sheaths, and not the other way around, as Combs has it.

This confusion is confirmed when Combs compares the Vedanta with the Mahayana Buddhist system of the Trikaya (Dharmakaya, Sambhogakaya, and Nirmanakaya). He says, "The highest is the dharmakaya or the 'body of the great order.' This 'body' is identical with transcendental reality and seems to correspond to the level of the Self in Vedanta. The second is the sambhogakaya or 'body of delight' which seems analogous to the causal level, the sheath of bliss of Vedanta. The third body is the nirmanakaya or 'body of transformation,' which corresponds to the physical body itself. Comparing this three-part system to Vedanta discloses several of the levels or sheaths to be missing" (p. 125). Actually, nothing is missing. Combs has again confused body/states with levels/structures. As the discussion on Highest Yoga Tantra makes clear (see chap. 10), the Mahayana/Vajrayana system has nine levels/structures of consciousness (the five senses, the manovijnana, the manas, the alayavijnana, and the pure alaya); treating the five senses as one level gives us five *levels*, just like the Vedanta. Further, the Three Bodies of Buddha are similar to the three bodies of Vedanta—gross, subtle, and causal, and they are all explicitly correlated with waking, dreaming, and deep sleep *states*, respectively. Again, by confusing levels/structures and states/bodies, Combs compares the three bodies of Mahayana with the five levels of Vedanta, and finds the Mahayana is "missing" levels; instead of comparing the five levels with the five levels, and the three bodies with the three bodies, and actually finding them in general agreement with each other as to *both* levels/structures and bodies/states.

Of course, one is free to define "state" and "structure" any way one wishes, as long as one is consistent, and Combs has given considerable care in doing so; and he is grappling with some very important issues in what I found a refreshing way. But I believe this general confusion haunts his model, and thus in my opinion his treatment, within his model, of my work, Gebser's, and Aurobindo's suffers. With my model, he ends up *equating* the basic structures with the separate developmental lines running through them (including worldviews). He thus collapses Gebser's structures (and their worldviews) with my basic structures, and he fails to differentiate the separate developmental lines involved with each. Combs thus talks as if by "structure" I mean only the narrow Gebserian structure, whereas for me "structure" is a term for any stable pattern in any level or line. When I then use the *worldviews* of the lower levels (such as archaic, magic, and mythic, which are not based merely on Gebser but on Piaget, Werner, Kernberg, Neumann, etc.), and I point out that development can *continue into higher levels* (such as psychic and subtle), Combs draws the erroneous conclusion that I am equating Gebserian structures with Vedanta planes, whereas there is simply a spectrum of consciousness (levels/structures of selfhood and levels/structures of reality)—and Gebser is addressing only some lines of a few of the lower-to-middle levels.

Tying "structures" to the narrow Gebserian version of structures (which Combs tends to do in his own model) means that, for Combs, his "structures" stop at Gebser's integral level, so that, as far as I can tell, *there are no genuinely transpersonal structures in Combs's model* (he only has *states* for the higher realms), making it impossible to account for permanent structural development into any of the transpersonal levels or sheaths.

Combs says he needs to do this, in part, because my "linear" model doesn't account for cross experiences (such as mythic-level experience of subtle states), overlooking the extensive discussion I gave of just that phenomenon in *A Sociable God* (1983), where I outlined a grid (which is discussed in the text as: psychic, subtle, causal, or nondual *states* interpreted by archaic, magic, mythic, or mental *structures*) that is quite similar to the grid Combs presents in Table 4 of chapter 9. Those two dimensions or variables (structures and states), when combined with the fact that the subject of one level can take an object from another level (realm or plane)—as happens with different modes of knowing, art, etc. (see notes 1.3, 1.5, 1.9, 1.10, 8.1, 8.2, 8.39)—gives us *three largely independent variables* (structures, states, and realms) that have been part of my model starting with phase-2 in 1983 (those three variables have remained intrinsic in phase-3 and phase-4). I do not in least mind the fact that Combs is using a similar model with these three variables to account for the many facets of consciousness and its evolution; I regret the fact that he has to portray my model as lacking them.

In short, I believe that working with the basic structures, streams, states, self, and the realms/planes of the Great Nest of Being gives us a multidimensional model that already accounts for all of the items that drove Combs to postulate his model, and it does so without his occasional misrepresentation of the Eastern systems and what seems to be confusion about states and structures. Moreover, my full model sets all of these variables in the context of the four quadrants (see note 8.39), which Combs seems to disregard completely, although he references *Sex, Ecology, Spirituality.*

Let me repeat, however, that Combs is grappling with some very important issues in his approach, and I believe we share much common ground. He does not, however, treat my work in a very comprehensive fashion, so his pronouncements on my material should be taken with caution. See notes 1.3, 1.5, 1.9, 1.10, 8.1, 8.2, 8.39.

13. For a fuller discussion of these themes, see *The Eye of Spirit*, chapter 2; *Sex, Ecology, Spirituality*, 2nd ed. (CW 6); and *A Brief History of Everything*. For various theories of macrohistory, see Galtung and Inayatullah, *Macrohistory and Macrohistorians*.

14. A few critics have claimed that this distinction (average and advanced) means stages are being skipped (i.e., if the overall general stages are archaic, magic, mythic, rational, psychic, subtle, causal, and nondual, how could somebody in a magic culture have a psychic experience without skipping stages?). Let me repeat the many reasons this is not a problem: (1) The average mode means just that, an *average*—any number of individuals can be above or below that average. We saw that Habermas believes that even in foraging societies, a few individuals had access to formal operational cognition; I have suggested that it is therefore completely plausible that a few individuals went even further and had access to postformal cognition, especially in its earliest transpersonal stages as psychic, and these individuals were, of course, the shamans (thus, stages are not being skipped). (2) Even if that type of higher structural development turns out not to be the case, there are two other intrinsic mechanisms that allowed the most advanced modes to reach considerably beyond the average, without violating stages where they apply. One is the existence of *peak experiences*. We have seen that virtually anybody, at virtually any stage of development, has access to various types of transpersonal peak experiences (psychic, subtle, causal, nondual). The contours of the shamanic voyage strongly suggest the presence of psychic/subtle level peak experiences, and these do not violate any stages. (3) If these peak experiences began to be mastered at will by a shaman—and there is evidence that this occasionally happened—this is evidence for, not just random or spontaneous peak experiences, but *development in the subtle line*, which can, we have hypothesized (see chap. 9), proceed *alongside* developments in the gross (even if the gross remains at the magical structure); and thus, again, no stages are being skipped.

Any or all of those three items explain why stages are not being skipped; they are either being followed (as in #1), or they are being followed while other, parallel events are also occurring (#2 and #3). Even a shaman (or an individual today) who is, say, at moral stage 3 in the frontal line, and who has repeated shamanic/psychic peak experiences (in the subtle line), will still, if he or she develops further morally, have to move to moral stage 4, then 5, and so on. There is no evidence whatsoever that any sorts of peak experiences, no matter how profound, allow those frontal stages to be skipped or bypassed (altered states might accelerate the rate at which the frontal stages unfold, but there is no evidence that those stages can be altered; see *The Eye of Spirit* for substantial research on this topic).

None of the three explanations given above violates any of those facts; and in no case are genuine stages *in any line* being skipped. There are either higher developments in one line, or parallel lines, and/or states occurring.

15. See note 12.14. The shamans were the earliest masters of bodily ecstatic energies—as with Mircea Eliade's classic definition of shamanism as "technique of ecstasy"—the earliest yogis, in that sense—and rode these energies and altered states to realms of the upper and underworlds (gross-to-psychic).

Joseph Campbell, in the *Historical Atlas of World Mythology*, gives what is probably one of the earliest, proto-kundalini experiences very likely common in even some of the earliest shamanic voyages. "The supreme occasion for the activation of the ntum is the trance dance. The exertion of the ceaselessly circling dancers heats their medicine power, which . . . they experience as a physical substance in the pit of the stomach. The women's singing, the men say, 'awakens their hearts,' and eventually their portion of ntum becomes so hot that it boils. 'The men say it boils up their spinal columns into their heads, and is so strong when it does this . . . , that it overcomes them and they lose their senses.' "

Those early yogic trances would be more extensively explored in subsequent yogic development and evolution. What we see with these "ntum experiences" is, I believe, an example of the early stages of the subtle line of development (especially psychic). This subtle line—the entire Sambhogakaya realm—would be explored in greater depth and detail by subsequent yogic paths; but these shamanic voyages are clearly in that lineage of early kundalini psychic-realm voyages. Eliade, *Shamanism*; Walsh, *The Spirit of Shamanism*; Harner, *The Way of the Shaman*.

16. See *Up from Eden*. Elements of shamanic trance mastery were taken up in subsequent yogic disciplines, refined, transcended, and included (see note 12.15). Shamanic techniques, in themselves, are still powerful tools for accessing psychic domains, and a few modern explorers of consciousness have found them useful in that regard. See especially the works of Michael Harner.

CHAPTER 13. FROM MODERNITY TO POSTMODERNITY

1. To differentiate art, morals, and science is to differentiate I, we, and it. Differentiating I and we meant that individuals had rights and freedoms that could not be violated by the collective, the state, the monarchy—which was a strong contributor to the rise of democracy, abolition, and feminism. See *The Marriage of Sense and Soul* and *A Brief History of Everything* for a full discussion of this theme.

2. See chap. 9 of *The Marriage of Sense and Soul* for a fuller presentation. See also *Sex, Ecology, Spirituality*, 2nd ed. (CW 6), for critical discussions of postmodernists such as Heidegger, Foucault, and Derrida (consult index).

3. See also *Sex, Ecology, Spirituality,* 2nd ed. (CW 6), chaps. 4, 12, 13, 14.

4. See *The Marriage of Sense and Soul* for Kuhn's embrace of scientific progress. No wonder John Searle had to beat back this extreme constructivist approach in his wonderful *The Construction of Social Reality*—as opposed to "the social construction of reality"—the idea being that cultural realities are constructed on a base of correspondence truth which grounds the construction itself, without which no construction at all could get under way in the first place. Once again, we can accept the partial truths of postmodernism—interpretation and constructivism are crucial ingredients of the Kosmos, all the way down—without going overboard and attempting to reduce all other quadrants and all other truths to that partial glimpse.

5. Why is modern philosophy largely the philosophy of language? Because phylogenetic consciousness is starting to go transverbal in many important ways, and thus consciousness can look at the verbal realm, which it could not do when it was embedded in it. There is also an irony here: most postmodern philosophy therefore came out of literature and language departments in universities, not philosophy departments, which accounts for both its freshness and its naiveté.

6. The standard Enlightenment (and flatland) notion was that a word gains meaning simply because it *points to* or *represents* an object. It is a purely monological and empirical affair. The isolated subject looks at an equally isolated object (such as a tree), and then simply chooses a word to represent the sensory object. This, it was thought, is the basis of all genuine knowledge. Even with complex scientific theories, each theory is simply a *map* that *represents* the objective territory. If the correspondence is accurate, the map is true; if the correspondence is inaccurate, the map is false. Science—and all true knowledge, it was believed—was a straightforward case of *accurate representation*, accurate mapmaking. "We make pictures of the empirical world," as Wittgenstein would soon put it, and if the pictures match, we have the truth.

This is the so-called *representation paradigm*, which is also known as *the fundamental Enlightenment paradigm*, because it was the general theory of knowledge shared by most of the influential philosophers of the Enlightenment, and thus modernity in general. Modern philosophy is usually "representational," which means trying to form a correct representation of the world. This representational view is also called "the mirror of nature," because it was commonly believed that the ultimate reality was sensory nature and philosophy's job was to picture or mirror this reality correctly.

It was not the existence or the usefulness of representation that was the problem; representational knowledge is a perfectly appropriate form of knowing for many purposes. Rather, it was the aggressive and violent attempt to reduce all knowledge to empirical representation that constituted the disaster of modernity—the reduction of translogical spirit and dialogical mind to monological sensory knowing: the collapse of the Kosmos to nothing but representations of Right-Hand events.

Saussure, with his early structuralism, gives one of the first, and still one of the most accurate and devastating, critiques of empirical theories of knowing, which, he points out, can't even account for the simple case of "the bark of a tree." The meaning doesn't come merely from *objective* pointing but from *intersubjective* structures that *cannot themselves be totally objectively pointed to.* And yet without them, there would be, and could be, no objective representation at all. All postmodern theories of knowledge are thus *post-representational.* Since they also draw more on vision-logic than on formop, they are also largely postformal. Thus: postmodern, post-representational, postformal.

7. Here, for convenience, is an edited version of the summary offered in *The Marriage of Sense and Soul* (chap. 9):

The postmodern poststructuralists took many of these profound and indispensable notions and, in carrying them to extremes, rendered them virtually useless. They didn't just *situate* individual intentionality in background cultural contexts, they tried to *erase* the individual subject altogether: "the death of man," "the death of the author," "the death of the subject"—all were naked attempts to reduce the subject (Upper Left) to nothing but intersubjective structures (Lower Left). "Language" replaced "man" as the *agent* of history. It is not I, the subject, who is now is speaking, it is nothing but impersonal language and linguistic structures speaking through me.

Thus, as only one of innumerable examples, Foucault would proclaim that "Lacan's importance comes from the fact that he showed how it is the structures, the very system of language, that speak through the patient's discourse and the symptoms of his neurosis—not the subject." In other words, Upper Left reduced to Lower Left, to what Foucault famously called "this anonymous system without a subject." And thus I, Michel Foucault, am not writing these words nor am I in any way primarily responsible for them; language is actually doing all the work (although this did not prevent I, Michel Foucault, from accepting the royalty checks written to the author that supposedly did not exist).

Put simply, the fact that each "I" is always situated in a background "We" was perverted into the notion that there is no "I" at all, only an all-pervading "We"—no individual subjects, only vast networks of intersubjective and linguistic structures. (Buddhists take note: this was in no way the notion of *anatta* or no-self, because the "I" was replaced, not with Emptiness, but with finite linguistic structures of the "We," thus multiplying, not transcending, the actual problem.)

Foucault eventually rejected the extremism of his early stance, a fact studiously ignored by extreme postmodernists. Among other spectacles, postmodernist biographers began trying to write biographies of subjects that supposedly did not exist in the first place, thus producing books that were about as interesting as having dinner without food.

For Saussure, the signifier and signified were an integrated unit (a holon); but the postmodern poststructuralists—and this was one of their most defining moves—shattered this unity by attempting to place almost exclusive emphasis on sliding chains of *signifiers* alone. The signifiers—the actual material or written marks—were given virtually exclusive priority. They were thus severed from both their signifieds and their referents, and these chains of sliding or "free-floating" signifiers were therefore said to be anchored in nothing but power, prejudice, or ideology. (We see again the extreme constructivism so characteristic of postmodernism: signifiers are not anchored in any truth or reality outside of themselves, but simply create or construct all realities, a fact that, if true, could not be true.)

Sliding chains of signifiers: this is the essential postmodern poststructuralist move. This is postSTRUCTURAL, because it starts with Saussure's insights into the network-like structure of linguistic signs, which partially construct as well as partially represent; but POSTstructural, because the signifiers are cut loose from any sort of anchoring at all. There is no objective truth (only interpretations), and thus, according to extreme postmodernists, signifiers are grounded in nothing but power, prejudice, ideology, gender, race, colonialism, speciesism, and so on (a performative contradiction that would mean that this theory itself must also be anchored in nothing but power, prejudice, etc., in which case it is just as vile as the theories it despises). Once again, important truths, taken to extremes, became self-deconstructing. We wish to include the truths of both the Upper-Left and Lower-Left quadrants, without attempting to reduce one to the other, which violates the rich fabric of those domains. We wish to stress the endlessly holonic nature of consciousness, and not only one version of it.

8. *On Deconstruction*, p. 215; my italics.
9. See Taylor, *Sources of the Self* and *Hegel*.
10. This is why one of the ways we can date the beginning of the general postmodern mood is with the great Idealists (note that Derrida does exactly that; Hegel, he says, is the last of the old or the first of the new).
11. To follow the genealogy of postmodernism is to follow an attempt to reintroduce the interiors and interpretation, through a series of reversals that ended up denying all of its original aims. We saw that postmodernism began as a way to reintroduce interpretation, depth, and interiors to the Kosmos—the world is not merely reflected by consciousness, it is co-created by consciousness; the world is not merely a perception but an interpretation. This emphasis on interpretation was eventually taken to extremes—there is nothing outside the text—and this removed objective truth from the postmodern script. Once truth was suspect, there was no way to finally judge anything, and the interior domains completely collapsed into nothing but subjective preferences. Depth collapsed entirely into equivalent surfaces and aperspectival madness—no within, no deep—and extreme postmodernism fell into the intense gravitational field of flatland. The genealogy of deconstructive postmodernism is a genealogy of despair, nihilism, and narcissism. The bright promise of a constructive postmodernism was largely derailed, for reasons explored in *Boomeritis* and the Introduction to CW 7. For examples of constructive postmodernism, see the excellent series of postmodern anthologies edited by David Ray Griffin (SUNY Press). The integral psychology that I am presenting is offered in the spirit of a constructive postmodernism.
12. See *Sex, Ecology, Spirituality*, 2nd ed. (CW 6), for a full discussion of this theme.

CHAPTER 14. THE 1-2-3 OF CONSCIOUSNESS STUDIES

1. See N. Humphrey, *Consciousness Regained*; K. Jaegwon, *Supervenience and the Mind*; M. Levin, *Metaphysics and the Mind-Body Problem*; G. Madell, *Mind and Materialism*; C. McGinn, *The Problem of Consciousness*; T. Nagel, *Mortal Questions* and *The View from Nowhere*; G. Strawson, *Mental Reality*; R. Swinburne, *The Evolution of the Soul*; A. Whitehead, *Process and Reality*; S. Braude, *First Person Plural*; C. Birch, *Feelings*; K. Campbell, *Body and Mind*; Paul Churchland, *Matter and Consciousness*; D. Dennett, *Consciousness Explained*; R. Penrose, *The Emperor's New Mind*; Popper and Eccles, *The Self and Its Brain*; D. Griffin, *Unsnarling the World-Knot*; W. Robinson, *Brains and People*; W. Seager, *Metaphysics of Consciousness*; R. Sperry, *Science and Moral Priority*; J. Searle, *The Rediscovery of the Mind* and *Mind, Language, and Society*; W. Hart, *The Engines of the Soul*; C. Hartshorne, *Whitehead's Philosophy*; O. Flannagan, *Consciousness Reconsidered*; R. Forman, *The Problem of Pure Consciousness*; G. Edelman, *Bright Air, Brilliant Fire* and *The Remembered Present*; J. Eccles, *How the Self Controls Its Brain*; Gazzaniga (ed.), *The Cognitive Neurosciences*; Patricia Churchland, *Neurophilosophy*; S. Pinker, *How the Mind Works*; Baars, *In the Theater of Consciousness*; Hunt, *On the Nature of Consciousness*; Scott, *Stairway to the Mind*; Deacon, *The Symbolic Species*; Finger, *Origins of Neuroscience*; Cytowic, *The Neurological Side of Neuropsychology*; Stillings et al., *Cognitive Science*; Carpenter, *Neurophysiology*; Varela et al., *The Embodied Mind*; D. Chalmers, *The Conscious Mind*; Hameroff et al., *Toward a Science of Consciousness*; Wade, *Changes of Mind*; Block et al., *The Nature of Consciousness*; Laughlin et al., *Brain, Symbol, and Experience*; Wilber, "An Integral Theory of Consciousness," *Journal of Consciousness Studies* 4, 1 (1997), pp. 71–93 (also in CW7).

2. *Body and Mind*, p. 131.

3. See Griffin, *Unsnarling the World-Knot*, for an excellent summary of the present state of this argument. See *Sex, Ecology, Spirituality*, 2nd ed. (CW 6), for a discussion of the "major dilemma of the modern era," namely, the relation of the subjective self (consciousness) and the objective world (nature), especially chaps. 4, 12, and 13.

4. *Mental Reality*, p. 81.

5. *The Rediscovery of the Mind*, p. 30.

6. *Supervenience and Mind*, quoted in Griffin, *Unsnarling the World-Knot*, p. 4.

7. *Mortal Questions*, p. 176.

8. *The Problem of Consciousness*, pp. 1–7.

9. *Mind and Materialism*, quoted in Griffin, *Unsnarling the World-Knot*, p. 3.

10. *Of Clocks and Clouds*, quoted in Griffin, *Unsnarling the World-Knot*, p. 3.

11. *The Self and Its Brain*, p. 105.

12. See note 15.

13. To say that subject and object are two aspects of an underlying reality begs the question as to what this underlying reality is, since it cannot be stated in terms that are not merely combinations of "subjective" and "objective." Either this

third entity, the underlying reality, has subjective and objective properties, or it does not. If it does, it is not really underlying; if it does not, it is not really unifying. Nagarjuna and other nondual philosopher-sages are adamant that the mind-body problem cannot be solved on a rational level. See *The Eye of Spirit*, chap. 3, for a full discussion of this topic.

14. See *The Eye of Spirit*, chap. 3.

15. More specifically, the mind-body problem involves three dilemmas: (1) how to relate Mind (interiors) and Body (exteriors, including brain); (2) how to relate mind (interior conceptual consciousness) and body (interior feelings); and (3) how to see the final relation of Mind and Body (subject and object).

In my opinion, those three items can be approached in this fashion, respectively: (1) acknowledge that every exterior has an interior (as shown in fig. 5), which binds Mind and Body; (2) acknowledge that there are interior stages of consciousness development (also shown in fig. 5), which binds mind and body; and (3) acknowledge that there are higher levels of consciousness development, which finally unites Mind and Body (thus preventing any form of dualism). To take them in order:

1. The problem of the relation of interiors (consciousness) and exteriors (matter) is usually stated as: the fundamental units of the universe (quarks, atoms, strings, etc.) consist of entities that possess no interiors; the mind possesses an interior; since the latter evolved from the former, how can you get interiors from exteriors? Since this seems to be impossible, we must either deny the causal reality of the interiors altogether (physicalism), or we must posit a miracle of existence (dualism), wherein an entirely new type of substance (interiors) jumps into being at some point. In the early part of the modern era, when God was still around, dualism was a popular solution, because God could be called on for this miracle. In today's world, this miracle—and its seeming impossibility—is one of the major reasons most philosophers flee to physicalism.

In my view, although the exact relation of interiors and exteriors is disclosed only in the postrational stages of development (the nondual wave), we can nonetheless understand rationally that every interior has an exterior, and vice versa, as indicated in figure 5. If interior and exterior really do arise correlatively, there is no miracle required; I will argue for this in a moment. (As for the nondual stage, when it is disclosed it does indeed involve spirit, but in the most ordinary and down-to-earth way: "How miraculous this! I draw water, I carry fuel." In no case is a supernatural miracle called for.)

This part of the solution (every exterior has an interior) would appear to involve some sort of panpsychism, except that, as explained in *Sex, Ecology, Spirituality,* 2nd ed. (notes 13 and 25 for chap. 4), every major form of panpsychism equates "interiors" with a *particular type of interior* (such as feelings, awareness, soul, etc.), and then attempts to push *that* type all the way down to the fundamental units of the universe (quarks, atoms, strings, or some such), which I believe is unworkable. For me, consciousness in the broad sense is ultimately unqualifiable (Emptiness), and thus, although interiors go all the way down, no *type* of interior does. I am a pan-interiorist, not a pan-experientialist, pan-mentalist, pan-feelingist, or pan-soulist. The *forms* of the interior show developmental unfolding: from a fuzzy something-or-other (see below) to prehension to sensation to perception to impulse to image to concept to rules to rationality and so forth, but none of those go all the way down in one specific form. Most schools of panpsychism take *one* of those interiors—such as feeling or soul—and maintain that *all* entities possess it (atoms have feelings, cells have a soul) and this I categorically reject. Cells have an interior, whose form is protoplasmic irritability (fig. 5), and electrons, according to quantum mechanics, possess a "propensity to existence," but none of those are "minds" or "feelings" or "souls," but rather are merely some very early forms of interiors.

I accept, in a very general sense, the notion of Whitehead (Hartshorne, Griffin) that we can picture "prehension" as perhaps the earliest form of interiors (every interior touches—prehends—an exterior at some point, since interior and exterior mutually arise), but when that prehension is explained in terms such as feeling or emotion, I believe that is overdoing it. This is also why, when I present the four quadrants, I usually say that readers are free to push interiors down as far—or as little—as they wish. Since interiors are *ultimately* unqualifiable (in my view, every interior is basically an opening or clearing in which correlative exteriors arise; see *Sex, Ecology, Spirituality,* 2nd ed. [notes 13 and 25 for chap. 4]), and since the relation between interiors and exteriors is finally disclosed only in postrational awareness (see item 3), I am not concerned to solve the mind-body problem by arguing that interiors go all the way down (although I believe they do); the final solution lies elsewhere (see item 3). Rather, for the average presentation, I am more interested in communicating to the reader why I believe that, at least by the time we reach human beings, there are four quadrants in existence, because it is the integration of the Big Three at the human level that is the most urgent requirement, in my opinion (and that integration will eventually help to solve the mind-body problem at all levels).

The major reservation I have about Whitehead's view of prehension is that it is largely monological. Each subject or I prehends its immediate ancestors as objects or its; each I then passes into the stream as an it for the new I: I becomes it as new I prehends old I. This stream of subjects/objects is partially true, I believe, and I think Whitehead's analysis of the phases of prehension is a brilliant addition to philosophy. But Whitehead, in *arguing from human experience to atoms of experience* (which I believe is justifiable), *has not started with the correct view of human experience,* and therefore he analogously injected the wrong types of actualities into the atoms of existence. Human experience is not a monological subject grasping monological objects, but is in fact a four-quadrant affair: every subject arises only in an intersubjective space (the essence of postmodernism). In other words, the atoms of experience are four-quadrant holons, not monological holons. Whitehead, as I argued in *The Eye of Spirit* (note 11 to chap. 10), has taken flatland and made it paradigmatic for all experience.

Most Whiteheadians strongly object to my characterization of their view as largely monological, pointing out that their real stance is *relational* and *ecologi-*

cal. But ecology is monological; and systems theory is a perfect example of a relational process view that is also monological. For it is not merely that a subject prehends its objects. Rather, *intersubjectivity* is the space in which the subject prehends its objects. The We is intrinsically part of the I, not as objective prehensions, but as subjective constitutive elements. The We space in which the I arises is not simply an object for the I, but rather is the background space *in which* the I arises to prehend its objects, and which therefore partly enters the I *for the first time* as subject component, not object prehension (this part of intersubjectivity is therefore not "an object that once was subject," which is the standard Whiteheadian reworking of causality as perception, and which is indeed relational, process, ecological, and monological, in my opinion. Partially true, it is not sensitive enough to the nonreducible realities in all four quadrants, all the way down).

David Ray Griffin's *Unsnarling the World-Knot* is a superb exposition of Whitehead's view, along with Griffin's proposed solution of panexperientialistic physicalism (based on Whitehead/Hartshorne). I am in a fair amount of agreement with his presentation, except for items 1 and 3 in this endnote (I do not identify interiors with feelings; and I believe the relation of interior to exterior is only finally disclosed in transrational nondual awareness; it cannot be "thought through" as Griffin and Whitehead propose). I believe I know what Griffin means by "feeling" (prehension in the most rudimentary sense), but the word "feeling" or "experience" is just "too much" to push all the way down. Also, as I just said, I do not believe the fundamental units of human experience or the universe are monological (Griffin tells me that he does not, either; see Introduction to CW8 for our exchange on this issue).

A minor point: Griffin's line of compound individuality does not quite seem complete, in my opinion. Griffin/Whitehead's view is, of course, "a hierarchy of emergent compound individuals" (a holarchy of holons). But Griffin seems to have an evolutionary lineage that moves from atoms to macromolecules to organelles to cells to neurons to mind. Neurons are the "highest-level enduring individuals" next to mind, and mind is the prehensive experience of billions of individual neurons. This is too great a jump, in my opinion, and a more accurate view is represented in figure 5. That is, the corresponding interior of neurons is sensation; the organism with a reptilian brain stem is a true compound individual (holon), whose interior is impulse; the organism with a limbic system is a true compound individual, whose interior is emotion; the organism with a complex neocortex is a true compound individual, whose interior is conceptual mind. At each of those levels, not only do interiors prehend their corresponding exteriors, they prehend their own past (Griffin would agree with that, I believe). This appears to account not only for Mind-Body (interior-exterior) interaction, but for interior causation, interior inheritance, and mind-body interaction.

Thus, Griffin jumps from neurons to mind too quickly, in my opinion. I believe he would say that neurons are the highest-level enduring individuals prior to mind because the reptilian stem and limbic system are simply organizational aggregates, not compound individuals, which is the point I would dispute. For example, the limbic system of a horse is a highly organized system that is converted from an aggregate to an individual by the skin boundary of the horse (which is analogous to the cell membrane of a eukaryote; if the latter is a compound individual, so is the former). The limbic-system compound individual is compounded again in the neocortex compound individual—these are distinct levels of both exteriors and interiors (fig. 5). Thus the jump from neurons to mind is not as large as Griffin presents it. Many philosophers have found it very hard to go straight from neurons to rational consciousness; but instead of one huge (and puzzling) jump, we have a series of mini-jumps: from neurons to neural cord to reptilian brain stem to paleomammalian limbic system to neocortex, which seems easier to see (as is the corresponding interior development from sensation to perception to impulse to emotion to image to concept to rule to rationality)—and each of those is a holon, a true compound individual.

The worldview of physics is often used to support the notion that the fundamental units (quarks, strings, atoms) do not have interiors. I do not argue, with the panexperientialists, that atoms must have feelings, but rather that exteriors have no meaning without interiors, and that if atoms have exteriors, they certainly have interiors. Wherever there is a boundary between physical objects— for example, between one atom and another atom—then those atoms have exteriors, and wherever there is an exterior there is an interior: you cannot have one without the other. Interior and exterior arise together with the first boundary of a universe—they are mutually arising and mutually determining—and thus, both interiors and exteriors go all the way down (as long as down has any meaning). To say that the physical universe is a universe of all exteriors and no interiors is like saying the world has all ups and no downs—it makes no sense at all. Inside and outside arise together whenever they arise; and interiors go as far down as down has any meaning.

At the very lowest levels, insides don't have much meaning because outsides don't either: have you really looked at the reality described by quantum mechanics? At the lowest levels of existence, both inside and outside become meaningless; they dissolve in that primordial miasma in which there might not be any mind, but there isn't any matter either; and when the outside crystallizes, so does the inside: they arise together whenever they arise. Every Left has a Right, and vice versa.

I agree entirely with Leibniz/Whitehead/Hartshorne/Griffin that only the entities known as compound individuals (i.e., holons) possess a characteristic interior. Holons are different from mere heaps or aggregates, in that the former possess actual wholeness (identifiable pattern, agency, regime, etc.). Individual holons include quarks, electrons, atoms, cells, organisms, and so on (as shown in fig. 5), whose interiors include prehension, propensity, irritability, sensation, tropism, perception, impulse, image, and so on (fig. 5). Heaps, on the other hand, are holons that are accidentally thrown together (e.g., a pile of sand). Holons have agency and interiors (every whole is a part, and thus every holon has an interior and an exterior), whereas heaps do not. A *social holon* stands between the two: it is more than a heap, in that its individuals are united by patterns of relational exchange, but it is less than an individual holon in terms of the tightness of its regime: social holons do not possess a locus of self-aware-ness at any stage of their development (whereas higher-level individual holons have interiors that become increasingly conscious, so that at the level of human compound individuals, self-awareness is possible in individuals, but not in soci-eties. The upper two quadrants are individual holons, the lower two quadrants are social holons. For extensive discussions of compound individuals, see *Up from Eden* and *Sex, Ecology, Spirituality,* 2nd ed.).

This simple distinction (holons have interiors, heaps do not [except for any holons that might be in the heaps]), along with the understanding that "inte-rior" means only the correlative to any exterior (it does not mean feelings, soul, self-consciousness, etc.—which are all types of interiors), goes a long way to making pan-interiorism more palatable. The common panpsychism view (but not Whitehead/Griffin's) is that, for example, rocks have feelings or even souls, which is untenable (and is, in fact, a belief of the magical-animistic level of development, not the nondual). Rocks as heaps have no interiors (there is the inside of a rock, but that is just more exteriors); rocks, however, do contain atoms, which are holons, and those holons have one of the very lowest types of interiors (propensities and patterns that endure across time)—but in no case does a rock have "feelings," let alone a soul. (A rock is a manifestation of spirit, but does not itself contain a soul.)

Both interiors and exteriors develop or co-evolve; and in both lines, there is *emergence*, with the introduction of some degree of genuine *novelty* or *creativ-ity* at each stage (which a physicalist calls "inexplicable" and an integralist calls "Eros"). Many physicalists (from Dennett to Alwyn Scott) agree with *emergent evolution*, but they try to derive *interior* consciousness by having it pop out at the top level of *exterior* development (because they believe only exteriors are real, and the "consciousness pops out at the top" is a concession to the hard-core intuition that consciousness exists—which is then explained as "nothing but" the functional fluke of complex exteriors; or more rarely, as a dualism). That is, as Eccles put it, "Just as in biology there are new emergent properties of matter, so at the extreme level of organized complexity of the cerebral cortex, there arises still further emergence, namely the property of being associated with a conscious experience." But the Left is not a higher level of the Right, it is the interior of the Right at every level, and both go all the way down (see *Sex, Ecology, Spirituality,* 2nd ed., chap. 4, and "An Integral Theory of Consciousness"). Nagel is quite right that a subject that has a point of view simply cannot arise out of exterior objects that do not. (Griffin calls this the "emergence cate-gory mistake," which I avoid by seeing that interiors and exteriors arise correla-tively.)

On the other hand, says Nagel, "if one travels too far down the phylogenetic tree, people gradually shed their faith that there is experience there at all." Quite right, which is why I do not push experience (or feelings or souls or any specific *type* of interior) all the way down; I simply maintain that wherever there are exteriors, there are interiors, and when it comes to the interiors of the lower levels, I don't think we are really able to say what is "in" them with any sort of assurance. I cannot prove what is in them for the same reason a physicalist cannot disprove them.

Dennett, incidentally, sees a type of sentience emerging with amoebas. I am willing to settle for that, not because I am being wishy-washy about levels lower than that, but because when we get to the atomic and subatomic realm, the mathematical formalisms of quantum mechanics become much weirder than can be imagined, and most physicists disagree strongly on what it all means anyway. I myself believe atoms have interiors, but I'm not going to argue the point to the death, simply because the universe gets too fuzzy at that level, and because the actual relation of interiors to exteriors is determined in the transrational, not prerational, realms. Human beings *can* know the transrational realms directly and immediately, whereas the subatomic realms are understood, if at all, only by abstruse mathematical formalisms, which are still in process of being formulated.

2. By acknowledging that the interiors develop (as do their exteriors), we can see that mind (interior mental consciousness) and body (interior feelings) are related as transcend and include (as shown in the Upper-Left quadrant of fig. 5, in figures such as 1 and 8, and in all of the charts showing interior development). The mind dangling in midair, as in figure 13, is plugged back into its roots in the felt body. This is explored in more detail in *Sex, Ecology, Spirituality*, 2nd ed., chaps. 12 and 13.

Interior development, precisely because it is composed of holons (as is exterior development), is composed of a series of wholes that become parts of subsequent wholes, indefinitely (as we saw, for example: sensorimotor is a whole cognition that becomes part of concrete operational, which is a whole cognition that becomes part of formop, which is a whole cognition that becomes part of vision-logic, and so on).

Nagel implies that perhaps the major problem with any sort of pan-interiorism is that we lack a conception of "a mental whole-part relation" that could explain the hard-core intuition of *the unity of experience* (i.e., how "a single self can be composed of many selves"). But we have seen innumerable examples of the fact that interior experience is composed of streams of holons, of whole/ parts, of wholes that pass into parts of succeeding wholes in a cohesive and seamless fashion. This is true of the self-stream as well (the subject of one stage becomes an object of the next—the whole proximate self of one stage becomes part of the distal at the next, so that at *every* stage "a single self is composed of many selves"). In each case "the many become one, and are increased by one"—Whitehead's famous dictum. Whitehead is discussing micro prehension, but the dictum is true for macro stages as well, since the former is the basis of the latter, and both are simply yet another version of *transcend and include*. Nagel's major objection, in other words, seems to be handled by the consensus conclusions of developmental psychology.

3. By acknowledging higher levels of development, including the nondual stages, the final relation of Mind and Body (interior and exterior, subject and object) is disclosed in a clear and satisfactory fashion: Mind and Nature are

both movements of Spirit, which is why there is neither dualism nor reduction-ism. This is discussed in more detail in *Sex, Ecology, Spirituality,* 2nd ed., chaps. 12, 13, and 14.

The "hard problem"—the jump to qualia (i.e., how can exterior quantities give rise to interior qualities?)—is finally solved, not by seeing that every exterior has an interior (item 1), since that merely says they are correlative (and leaves the hard problem still pretty hard)—but by *developing* to the nondual realm, whereupon the problem is radically (dis)solved. The solution is what is seen in satori, not anything that can be stated in rational terms (unless one has had a satori, and then rational terms will work fine). The reason the hard prob-lem cannot be solved—and has not yet been solved—in rational and empirical terms is that the solution does not exist at those levels. Philosophical geniuses trying to solve the mind-body problem at that level have failed (by their own accounts) not because they are stupid, but because it can't be solved at that level, period. See *The Eye of Spirit,* rev. ed. (CW 7), chap. 11.

16. *Journal of Consciousness Studies* 4, 1 (1997), pp. 71–93.

17. See Gazzaniga (ed.), *The Cognitive Neurosciences;* P. Churchland, *Neurophilo-sophy;* Edelman, *Bright Air, Brilliant Fire* and *The Remembered Present;* Pinker, *How the Mind Works;* Baars, *In the Theater of Consciousness;* Hunt, *On the Nature of Consciousness;* Scott, *Stairway to the Mind;* Deacon, *The Symbolic Species;* Finger, *Origins of Neuroscience;* Cytowic, *The Neurological Side of Neuropsychology;* Stillings et al., *Cognitive Science;* Carpenter, *Neurophysi-ology.*

Not that all of those approaches are reductionistic; but for approaches to consciousness (mind and brain) that are avowedly nonreductionistic, see, e.g., Chalmers, *The Conscious Mind;* Hameroff et al., *Toward a Science of Con-sciousness;* Griffin, *Unsnarling the World-Knot;* Wade, *Changes of Mind;* Block et al., *The Nature of Consciousness;* Laughlin et al., *Brain, Symbol, and Experi-ence;* Wilber, "An Integral Theory of Consciousness," *Journal of Consciousness Studies* 4, 1 (1997), pp. 71–93 (also in CW7). See especially Varela et al., *The Embodied Mind,* and my constructive criticism of it in *Sex, Ecology, Spiritual-ity,* 2nd ed., chap. 14, note 1.

18. *The View from Within,* p. 2.

19. See Robert Forman's excellent, "What Does Mysticism Have to Teach Us About Consciousness?" in *Journal of Consciousness Studies* 5, 2 (1998), pp. 185–202. Forman is one of the theorists mentioned who is also alive to the importance of stages of development. See also his *The Problem of Pure Consciousness, The Innate Capacity, Meister Eckhart,* and *Mysticism, Mind, Consciousness.*

20. In present-day ontogeny, there are two different senses in which we can speak of third-person (or Right-Hand) development. In individuals, there is the growth of the Upper-Right quadrant itself: the growth of the biological organ-ism, neuronal pathways, brain structures, and so on. This growth and develop-ment is investigated by biology, neurophysiology, and organic systems theory, for example (see note 14.17). Holons in this quadrant grow, develop, and evolve (as do holons in all quadrants), and that development can be investigated

using empirical sciences. These objective holons and their behavior can be approached with the natural sciences, and hence are "third-person" in that sense—they are development *in* the Right-Hand domains.

But there is also the growth, in individual consciousness (Upper Left), of the capacity to cognitively grasp objective, Right-Hand domains, and this cognitive capacity (of the Upper Left to grasp Right-Hand objects) is the capacity studied by Piaget and by most cognitive psychologists. "Cognition," recall from the text, is defined by most Western researchers as the capacity to grasp objective phenomena, and this capacity (of the Upper Left to grasp Right-Hand objects) grows and evolves from sensorimotor to preop to conop to formop. This is the development, in the first-person individual subject, of the capacity to accurately grasp third-person objects, and thus this is the second sense in which we can speak of the growth of third-person consciousness.

When I say that in individuals, aesthetics, morals, and science all evolve (or that there is development in first-person, second-person, and third-person consciousness), "science" or "third-person" is meant in both senses—the growth of the objective organism (as disclosed by science, neurobiology, etc.), and the interior growth of the cognitive (scientific) capacity to grasp objects. (This is another example of the difference between levels of self and levels of reality, or structures and realms/planes—or again, growth in the epistemology of the subject, and growth in the objects that are known, ontology. Unless otherwise stated, I generally mean both, although context will tell.)

Of course, both first-person and third-person consciousness exist interrelated with networks of second-person, intersubjective structures, and these, too, grow and develop (i.e., the quadrants *themselves* develop, and the *subject's* capacity to grasp those quadrants develops). In other words, all of these quadrants are intimately interrelated (e.g., the growth in the other quadrants—such as biological neuronal pathways and intersubjective structures of discourse—are requisite for the subject to even be able grasp these other quadrants).

The integral psychology that I am presenting argues for an integrated approach to development in all of those quadrants—more precisely, an "all-level, all-quadrant" approach: following all of the levels and lines in all of the quadrants. This means following both the growth *in* each quadrant, and the growth in the capacity *of* the subject to grasp each quadrant (i.e., the growth in the subject's capacity to grasp its own subjective quadrant and the other quadrants as well). This means following the self's growth *in relation* to three environments or three worlds (the Big Three), namely, its relation to its own *subjective* world of inner drives, ideals, self-concepts, aesthetics, states of consciousness, etc.; its relation to the *intersubjective* world of symbolic interaction, dialectical discourse, mutual understanding, normative structures, etc.; and its relation to the *objective* world of material objects, states of affairs, scientific systems, cognitive objects, etc. Each of those evolves from prepersonal to personal to transpersonal waves (i.e., each of the quadrants evolves, or can evolve, through all of the levels in the Great Nest, body to mind to psychic to subtle to causal to nondual), and thus an all-level, all-quadrant approach follows the developments of all of the levels and lines in all of the quadrants.

(I am simplifying the lines of development to the three major ones: aesthetics/ subjective, morals/intersubjective, and science/objective, but the actual number of lines in each of the quadrants is quite numerous: in the subjective or UL domain we have seen upwards of two dozen developmental lines, for example. All of those are implied in the simple formula, "all of the levels and lines in all of the quadrants," or even simpler, "all-level, all-quadrant.")

Dobert, Habermas, and Nunner-Winkler ("The Development of the Self," in Broughton, *Critical Theories of Psychological Development*), have presented a model that, although it is not all-level, is admirably and impressively all-quadrant in many ways. That is, it traces the development of the self in relation to the Big Three realms (subjective, intersubjective, and objective). They attempt an integration of the Big Three domains in self identity formation, pointing out that in doing so they are also integrating three of the most influential schools of developmental psychology (Freudian, or subjective; symbolic interactionist, or intersubjective; and Piagetian cognitive psychology, or objective). This identity formation involves the development of the self (as it does in integral psychology: in my view, identification is one of the functions of the self), and thus their formulations in some ways are quite consonant with the views presented here.

"The developmental problems linked with the concept of identity formation have been dealt with in three different theoretical traditions: (1) the cognitivist psychology of development founded by Jean Piaget, (2) the social psychology of symbolic interactionism that goes back to G. H. Mead, and (3) the analytic ego psychology derived from Sigmund Freud. In all of these theoretical formulations, the developmental trend is characterized by increasing autonomy vis à vis at least one of three particular environments [the Big Three]. In other words, development is characterized by the independence the self acquires insofar as it enhances its problem-solving capacities in dealing with: (1) the reality of external nature of both manipulable objects [UR] and strategically objectified social relations [LR]; (2) the symbolic reality of behavioral expectations, cultural values, and identities . . . [LL]; and (3) the inner nature of intentional experiences and one's own body [UL], in particular, those drives that are not amenable to communication. Piaget's theory of cognitive development tackles the first aspect, Mead's theory of interactive development the second, and Freud's theory of psychosexual development the third. Certainly, we must not overestimate the convergence of the three approaches. But there is no denying the fact that the theoretical perspectives they stress complement each other" (pp. 278–79).

Indeed they do. And these Big Three domains, according to the authors, are all tied together by the *self* (as we have seen; the self is the navigator, and integrator, of all the waves and streams in the individual being). Note that the authors point out that for these three major schools, development involves *increasing autonomy* (which is one of the twenty tenets of evolution; see *Sex, Ecology, Spirituality,* 2nd ed., chap. 2). Increasing autonomy is one of twenty tenets shown by all evolving systems, including the self—and the final Autonomy is simply the pure Self, outside of which nothing exists, which is therefore a state of full autonomy: the pure Self is the entire Kosmos in all its radiant wonder, and is fully autonomous because there is nothing outside of it. The reason that development shows increasing autonomy is that development is headed toward the ultimate Autonomy of the pure and nondual Self.

In note 10.4, I hypothesized that the self metabolizes experience to build structure, and that this is the mechanism that converts temporary states into enduring traits. I noted the broad similarity of this concept to that proposed by psychoanalytic ego psychology and Piagetian constructivism. Dobert et al. also note these similarities. "For all three theories, the transposition of external structures [and nonstructured actions] into internal structures is an important learning mechanism. Piaget speaks of 'interiorization' when schemes of action—meaning rules for the manipulative mastery of objects—are internally trans-posed and transformed into schemes of comprehension and thinking. Psychoanalysis and symbolic interactionism propose a similar transposition of interaction patterns into intrapsychic patterns of relations, one which they call 'internalization.' This mechanism of internalization is connected with the fur-ther principle of achieving independence—whether from external objects, refer-ence persons, or one's own impulses—by actively repeating what one has first passively experienced" (p. 279). (Note that increasing "interiorization" is also one of the twenty tenets.)

Furthermore, the authors maintain that each of those domains, according to the preponderance of evidence, "reflects a hierarchy of increasingly complex structures" (p. 280). (Increasing complexity/structuration is one of the twenty tenets.)

Central to the model of Dobert et al. is the notion of *interactive competence*, which is the major integrating factor of the self and its development. Moreover, according to the authors, this interactive competence develops *in three major stages* (or waves), which are preconventional, conventional, and postconven-tional, with each growth representing an expansion of consciousness and an increase in interiorization and autonomy. "For the preschool age child, still situated cognitively at the preoperational level, the action-related sector of the symbolic universe consists primarily of individual concrete behavioral expecta-tions and actions as well as the consequences of actions that can be understood as gratifications or sanctions. As soon as the child has learned to play social roles, that is, to participate in interactions as a competent member [conven-tional, mythic-membership], its symbolic universe no longer consists of actions that express isolated intentions only, for instance, wishes or wish fulfillments. Rather, the child can now understand actions as fulfillments of generalized be-havioral expectations or as offenses against them. When, finally, adolescents have learned to question the validity of social roles and action norms, their symbolic universe expands once again. There now appear [postconventional] principles according to which controversial norms can be judged" (p. 298).

Unfortunately, their all-quadrant model of self-development is not all-level, and thus it falls short of a truly integral psychology. It deals only with the gross line of personal development. Nonetheless, as far as it goes, it is much more comprehensive than most available developmental models, and its insights are important contributions to any truly integral psychology.

21. See *Sex, Ecology, Spirituality,* 2nd ed. (esp. notes for chaps. 4 and 14) for a discussion of the importance—and limitations—of phenomenology.

Dobert et al. (see note 14.20) criticize phenomenology, as I have, for its incapacity to comprehend intersubjective structures not given in the immediacy of felt bodily meaning, and thus its incapacity to deal effectively with the *development* of consciousness and the social world. "Indeed, phenomenological research has a similar intention, in that it aims to capture general structures of possible social life worlds. However, from the beginning, the execution of this program was weighed down by the weakness of a method copied from the introspective approach of the philosophy of consciousness"—namely, an immediate introspection that, as useful as it is, does not spot any of the *intersubjective* structures in which subjective introspection occurs (e.g., somebody at moral stage 5 can introspect all they want, and they will never see the structure of moral stage 5). "Only the points of departure taken by competence theory in linguistics and developmental psychology have created a paradigm that combines the formal analysis of known structures with the causal analysis of observable processes" (p. 298). See also *Sex, Ecology, Spirituality,* 2nd ed., chap. 14, note 1. This is also the major problem with Whitehead's prehension: he made paradigmatic this same weakness of the philosophy of consciousness (see note 14.15; see also the Introduction to Volume Eight of the *Collected Works* for a dialogue with David Ray Griffin on Whitehead's "monological" stance).

States and Structures

A final word on states and structures. States—including normal or natural states (e.g., waking, dreaming, sleeping) and nonnormal, nonordinary, or altered states (e.g., meditation, peak experiences, religious experiences)—are all temporary, passing phenomena: they come, stay a bit, and go, even if in cycles. Structures, on the other hand, are more enduring; they are fairly permanent patterns of consciousness and behavior. Both developmental levels and developmental lines (waves and streams) are largely composed of structures of consciousness, or holistic, self-organizing patterns with a recognizable code, regime, or agency. (This is not to be confused with the school of structuralism, with which I have, at best, tangential relations. See the Introduction to Volume Two of the *Collected Works*.)

Structures, in other words, are quite similar to enduring holons; and these basic structures or basic levels are essentially the basic levels in the Great Nest of Being. When these levels refer to the subject, we speak of levels of consciousness, levels of selfhood, or levels of subjectivity; when these levels refer to objects, we speak of levels of reality, realms of reality, or spheres of reality (see notes 1.3, 8.2, 12.12).

States of consciousness, although they have structural features, tend to be more temporary and fluid. However, it is important to recognize two general categories of states, which might be called "broad" and "narrow" (not to be confused with normal and nonnormal). Allan Combs calls these *states of con-*

sciousness and *states of mind*, the former referring to broad patterns (such as sleeping and waking) and the latter referring to moment-to-moment "small" states (such as joy, doubt, determination, etc.). Allan believes that these are related in a multileveled fashion, with structures of consciousness forming the broad base, within which various states of consciousness occur, and within those, various states of mind. While that is one possible scheme, I believe Allan has the relationship between states of consciousness and structures of consciousness reversed (see note 12.12). A broad state of consciousness, such as waking, has numerous different structures of consciousness within it (e.g., the waking state includes mythic, rational, centauric, etc.), but not vice versa (e.g., you cannot be in the rational structure and then be in several different states, such as drunken or sleeping). Thus, within the broad *states* of consciousness, there exist various *structures* of consciousness.

But within those structures of consciousness, there exist various states of mind. Those structures do indeed constrain and implicitly mold all of the states of mind that occur within them (e.g., a person at concrete operational thinking will have most of his thoughts—and states of mind—arise *within* that structure). Thus, the overall relation of these three items, in my opinion, is: broad states of consciousness, within which there exist various structures of consciousness, within which there exist various states of mind.

At the same time, the relationships among these various states and structures are definitely holonic and intermeshing. They are not simply plunked down on top of each other like so many bricks, but are interwoven in mutually influential ways. The difficulty with many psychological theories and models is that they tend to focus only on broad states, or on structures, or on narrow states, and thus take as fundamental items that are quite relative and partial. Neither altered states, nor psychological structures, nor phenomenology alone can give us an integral understanding of mind and consciousness.

CHAPTER 15. THE INTEGRAL EMBRACE

1. It is formop, not preop or conop, that has the capacity to differentiate the value spheres. As Cook-Greuter pointed out, preop possesses first-person, conop second-person, and formop third-person, and thus only formop can differentiate all three spheres of I, we, and it (aesthetics, morals, science). Thus, to say that modernity collectively differentiated the spheres is also to say that modernity was an evolution from mythic-membership (conop-based) to perspectival-ego (formop-based). The early Greeks, who precociously developed aspects of formop and vision-logic, also famously differentiated the Good, the True, and the Beautiful, which is why they are considered, in this regard, forerunners of modernity. They did not press this rationality (with its postconventional morals) into culture on a truly widespread scale, however (or they would have ended slavery, among other things). At the same time, the most highly evolved philosopher-sages—from Plato to Plotinus to Asanga—always differentiated the Big Three (because they had access to vision-logic and beyond); but there was little support for this in the

average level of cultural consciousness: that awaited modernity and its dignities. We might say: a Christ could see the Golden Rule (and beyond), but it took modernity to make it a law and back it with full cultural sanction.

2. This is one of the many reasons that we cannot merely say that the ontological planes of reality are lying around waiting to be perceived. Those planes coevolve with the growing tip of consciousness, for all of them are open to evolution, which is simply Spirit-in-action in all domains. Those models that have recourse to independent ontological planes are metaphysical in the "bad" or pre-critical sense, and have not come to terms with the modern and postmodern refinements necessary to accommodate the ongoing differentiation-and-integration of all realms of being and knowing. See note 1.5.

3. For a description of the methodology of "simultracking" levels and quadrants, see "An Integral Theory of Consciousness" (CW 7). Psychology traditionally focuses on the levels and lines in the Upper-Left quadrant. Integral studies in general focus on the levels and lines in all of the quadrants. For example, lines in the Lower-Right quadrant include forces of production (from foraging to horti-cultural to agrarian to industrial to informational), geopolitical structures (towns, states, countries), ecosystems, written legal codes, architectural styles, modes of transportation, forms of communication technologies, etc. Lines in the Upper-Right quadrant include organic structures, neuronal systems, neurotrans-mitters, brainwave patterns, nutritional intake, skeletal-muscular development, etc. Lines in the Lower-Left quadrant include worldviews, intersubjective linguis-tic semantics, cultural values and mores, background cultural contexts, etc. The point is that, even though psychology focuses on the Upper-Left quadrant, all four quadrants are required for psychological understanding, since all four quad-rants determine the state of consciousness of the individual.

Index